D1562663

Insei: Abdicated Sovereigns in the
Politics of Late Heian Japan, 1086–1185

STUDIES OF THE EAST ASIAN INSTITUTE
COLUMBIA UNIVERSITY

INSEI

Abdicated Sovereigns in the Politics of
Late Heian Japan
1086–1185

G. Cameron Hurst III

1976
New York and London
Columbia University Press

Library of Congress Cataloging in Publication Data

Hurst, G. Cameron, 1941–
  Insei.

  (Studies of the East Asian Institute, Columbia University)
  Originally presented as the author's thesis, Columbia University.
  Bibliography
  Includes index.
  1. Japan—Politics and government—794–1185.
  2. Japan—Emperors. I. Title. II. Series: Columbia University. East Asian Institute. Studies.
  DS856.H83   1975   320.9'52'01   75-26574

To Carol

The East Asian Institute of Columbia University

The East Asian Institute of Columbia University was established in 1949 to prepare graduate students for careers dealing with East Asia, and to aid research and publication on East Asia during the modern period. The faculty of the Institute are grateful to the Ford Foundation and the Rockefeller Foundation for their financial assistance.

The Studies of the East Asian Institute were inaugurated in 1962 to bring to a wider public the results of significant new research on modern and contemporary East Asia.

Preface

I was early in 1968 that I first determined to study retired sovereigns in Heian Japan. That year, as a graduate student in the Department of East Asian Languages and Cultures at Columbia University, I submitted a dissertation proposal to work on the *insei*. This book is an outgrowth of that proposal, but it has undergone several changes since then. I originally planned to write a detailed political history of the so-called *insei* period (1086–1185), encompassing essentially chapters 4 through 7 of the present work. By mid-1968 I had read virtually all the Japanese secondary materials covering the period; accepting rather uncritically the approaches, generalizations, and categorizations of Japanese historians, I intended to handle the phenomenon of the insei, or "cloister government," in a manner similar to theirs.

It was only after I became more familiar with the primary materials for late Heian Japan that I began to question Japanese approaches to the study of Heian political history in general and the insei in particular. I discovered what appeared to me to be an over-reliance upon questionable materials. Moreover, I found numerous unanswered questions, as I point out in chapter 1, which forced me to go back to the earliest periods of Japanese history for explanations. An inquiry into these unanswered, indeed frequently not even posed, questions yielded a great amount of information that

Japanese scholars had ignored and forced me to alter the scope of my study.

The result of this inquiry is that I have attempted to deal with the insei on two different levels. On the basic level, I have been concerned with attempting to explain how and why abdicated sovereigns emerged as important political figures in the late Heian period. On another level, I have attempted to reevaluate the manner in which Japanese scholars have treated the abdicated sovereign in the politics of the period. Here I have been concerned largely with the concept of the insei in Japanese history: has this concept, created by later historians, been a useful one for explaining the admittedly confusing political events of late Heian Japan; or has it, on the other hand, oversimplified matters to the extent that it has confused rather than clarified the events?

For purposes of organization and analysis, the book is divided into two parts. Part one, chapters 1 through 7, is essentially a narrative discussion of the origins and development of abdication in Japan and the rise of abdicated sovereigns to political power. Having traced this development rather fully, I then turn in part two to an analysis of the structure and function of the *in no chō*, or ex-sovereign's office, which, according to Japanese scholars, functioned essentially as a separate government.

One note concerning terminology is necessary. I dislike the usual English translation of insei as "cloister government" for two reasons. First, the word "cloister" suggests a religious element which was sometimes, but not always, present. While most abdicated sovereigns eventually took the tonsure, their actions before and after taking Buddhist vows seem not to have differed significantly. Second, I do not feel that the abdicated sovereigns organized and conducted a "government," as many others state or imply. I avoid, then, the term "cloister government" and use the word insei in appropriate contexts or simply refer to the political activities of the retired sovereigns. Likewise, I do not refer to the abdicated sovereign as the "cloister"; throughout I employ interchangeably the terms abdicated sovereign, abdicated emperor, retired sovereign, retired emperor, ex-sovereign, and ex-emperor.

This study owes much to many different individuals and institutions. I am indebted to the Foreign Area Fellowship Program and the East Asian Institute of Columbia University for financial support for fifteen months of research in New York and Japan during 1968–69. H. Paul Varley of Columbia directed my dissertation from the outset, giving unstintingly of his time and energy through several drafts. Herschel Webb, also of Columbia, read the entire manuscript and made several valuable suggestions. Together, these two men have had the greatest influence on my interests in and approaches to early Japanese history, and my greatest debt is to them. At the Yale University Faculty Research Seminar on Medieval Japan in the spring of 1972, I received many helpful corrections and suggestions from John W. Hall, Cornelius J. Kiley, and Jeffrey P. Mass. In Japan I was fortunate to enjoy the assistance of a number of outstanding scholars: Akamatsu Toshihide of Kyoto University, who directed my research at that institution; Takeuchi Rizō, Fujiki Kunihiko, Kuwayama Kōnen, Suzuki Shigeo, and Hashimoto Yoshihiko in Tokyo; Hayashiya Tatsusaburō, Murai Yasuhiko, Kurokawa Naonori, and Inoue Mitsuo in Kyoto.*

I would also like to offer special thanks to two men who, while in no way involved with the direct writing of this book, have profoundly influenced my scholarly development: George Akita of the University of Hawaii, whose exceptional dedication in every aspect of his personal and professional life caused me to seek a career in Japanese studies in the first place; and Kamikawa Rikuzō of Tokyo, whose rigorous training in Japanese language has given me the most important tool I could have acquired.

While acknowledging my debt to these various scholars and teachers, I must, of course, absolve them from any responsibility for errors in fact or judgment. These remain my own special contribution.

Finally, I wish to thank Columbia University Press for its editorial diligence. In particular, I am indebted to Mrs. Beth Kodama for her excellent work on the manuscript.

* Personal names are given in the Japanese order, i.e., surname first.

Contents

List of Abbreviations

CYK	*Chūyūki*
FSRK	*Fusō ryakki*
GKS	*Gukanshō*
GNJ	*Gonijō Moromichiki*
HHK	*Heihanki*
HRS	*Hyakurenshō*
KGBN	*Kugyō bunin*
NHKK	*Nihon kōki*
NHKR	*Nihon kiryaku*
NHSK	*Nihon shoki*
SDJR	*Sandai jitsuroku*
SNHG	*Shoku Nihongi*
SNHKK	*Shoku Nihon kōki*
SPBM	*Sompi bummyaku*

ONE

Abdicated Sovereigns in Ancient Japan

⋞ ONE ⋟

The Concept of Insei *in Japanese History*

INSEI IS a term Japanese historians use to characterize the set of political circumstances that developed in the late Heian period, specifically during the one hundred years from 1086 to 1185. Commonly rendered in English as the system of "cloister government," the term is a very broad one encompassing many different aspects, but the standard definition can be summarized as follows.

Insei refers to the system of government in which decisions of state were made by the abdicated sovereign. He conducted politics from his retirement palace, which was guarded by his own body of warriors and in which was located the *in no chō*, or ex-sovereign's office. This office was the administrative agency through which he conducted his rule. Staffed with the ex-sovereign's own personal officials, the in no chō issued documents that possessed more authority than those of the imperial government. This system of rule was conceived by the emperor Go-Sanjō as a means to curtail the power of the Fujiwara regents and reassert the lost power of the imperial house. Go-Sanjō died before he was able to realize his plan, but his son Shirakawa established the system upon his abdication in 1086. He continued to rule as retired emperor until his death at the age of seventy-seven in 1129. Toba and Go-Shirakawa followed in his footsteps, ruling the country from abdication until the establishment of the Kamakura shogunate in 1185.[1] All three were absolute rulers who completely ignored the emperor and the established channels of imperial government.

By the term insei, then, Japanese historians mean a distinct political system established at a particular time in history by a certain individual with a specific motive. The period during which the system was in effect is called the insei period, and it marks one stage of political development in ancient Japan. During the Nara period (710–784) the *ritsuryō* state,[2] a centralized bureaucratic imperium modeled after T'ang Chinese institutions, functioned much as it was envisioned; but after the move of the capital to Heian, alternate forms of political control developed which undermined this imperial state system. There were three such new forms —*kurōdo-dokoro seiji, sekkan seiji,* and insei—all of which Japanese scholars regard as "abnormal political forms" (*hentai seiji*) as opposed to this ritsuryō state structure.

In the early ninth century Emperor Saga established the *kurōdo-dokoro* (sovereign's private office) as a temporary means to ensure personal control over information in official documents during a crucial factional split at court.[3] The office became a permanent one and for much of the rest of the century its influence was so great that some Japanese scholars see this as a period during which politics was conducted within the sovereign's private office (kurōdo-dokoro seiji).[4] Owing to skillful political maneuvering and a close marital relationship with the imperial house, the regent's house (*sekkanke*) of the Fujiwara clan subsequently attained political supremacy and controlled virtually all court affairs. At the height of their power, from the mid-tenth to mid-eleventh centuries,

---

[1] Some scholars also include Go-Toba within the scope of the insei period, dividing it into early insei (Go-Sanjō and Shirakawa) and late insei (Go-Shirakawa and Go-Toba).

[2] The term *ritsuryō* derives from the two codes that formed the legal basis of the state: the *ritsu*, or penal laws, and the *ryō*, or administrative laws.

[3] For a discussion of the split between Saga and his elder brother, ex-Emperor Heizei, see chapter 3.

[4] See, for example, Fujiki Kunihiko, *Heian jidai no kizoku no seikatsu,* pp. 76–78. (For publication information on this and other sources cited in the footnotes, see the Bibliography.)

Fujiwara regents made most of the important political decisions within their own household administrative office (*mandokoro*). Documents issued by this office, called *kudashibumi*, bore more weight than imperial edicts. Scholars refer to this system of political control as the politics of the regent's house (sekkan seiji).[5]

It was in reaction to the dominance of the Fujiwara regents that Go-Sanjō conceived and Shirakawa established the system of rule by abdicated emperors (insei, or sometimes *in no chō seiji*). This system was so similar to the rule of the Fujiwara regents, however, that one common way to explain the political change in late Heian Japan is to say that the "Fujiwara '*mandokoro*' was transferred to the office or council chamber of the retired sovereign." [6]

This then is what the concept of insei means to Japanese historians. Although the term itself is of relatively recent origin, the concept has a long history. Late Heian sources indicate quite clearly that the three successive ex-emperors Shirakawa, Toba, and Go-Shirakawa enjoyed considerable political power. There is no indication, however, that anyone noticed the establishment of a new political system, and to the best of my knowledge the term insei does not appear in any contemporary source. It was not until the thirteenth century that anyone discerned a common pattern characterizing this one-hundred-year period.

Shortly before the outbreak of the Shōkyū War in 1221, Jien, the chief abbot of the Tendai sect and younger brother of the regent Kanezane, wrote the *Gukanshō*, a work generally regarded as the first interpretive history of Japan. History for Jien was the unfolding of a predetermined historical principle (*dōri*) by which all change could be explained. From the age of the gods until his own time, Jien discerned seven changes in the Japanese body politic, each change producing a distinct period characterized by its own principle (dōri), or spirit of the times.[7]

Beyond his seven enumerated periods of history, Jien considered

---

[5] Ibid., pp. 78–90. See also Fujiki's comments on *sekkan seiji* in Fujiki and Inoue Mitsusada, ed., *Seiji I*, pp. 126–81. For a criticism of the concept of sekkan seiji, see Hashimoto Yoshihiko, "Sekkan seiji-ron," pp. 60–66.

[6] George B. Sansom, A *History of Japan to 1334*, p. 201.

[7] Jien discusses these seven changes in his final chapter. See GKS, pp. 124–26.

the one hundred years from 1086 to 1185 as a separate age characterized by the political dominance of the ex-sovereigns.[8] He condemned their influence because it compromised the authority of
the emperor and curtailed the power of the Fujiwara family. This
shift of political power was for Jien proof that Japan had entered a
degenerate age. It was Jien who first offered the interpretation that
Go-Sanjō conceived of and Shirakawa instituted rule by abdicated
sovereigns.[9] He had little to say, however, about the manner in
which the ex-sovereigns ruled. He pointed to the fact that the ex-
emperor was attended in his palace by his own officials, the *in no
kinshin*, who came between the emperor and his proper advisers,
that is, the Fujiwara courtiers.[10] He also mentioned the existence of
an armed body of warriors who guarded the ex-sovereign's palace.[11]
It was thus Jien who first established the concept that later came to
be called insei.

More than a hundred years later Kitabatake Chikafusa wrote the
Jinnō shōtōki in order to clarify the question of imperial succession, which had plunged the land into a divisive war. Throughout
the work Chikafusa was heavily influenced by Jien, but particularly
so in his discussion of the three ex-emperors in the latter part of the
Heian period. He added one important piece to the development
of the concept of the insei when he stated that documents issued
by the ex-sovereign's office were more authoritative than those of
the imperial government.[12]

In 1713 the great Confucian scholar and shogunal official Arai
Hakuseki wrote his *Tokushi yoron* in which he expressed his own
view of Japanese historical development and offered his own pe-
riodization. Arai enumerated nine changes of political control before Japan fell under complete military rule with the Ashikaga, and
five more from that time until his own. As one distinct period, he

---

[8] Jien refers to the age of the three retired emperors several times. GKS, pp. 104,
149–50, 158, 332.

[9] GKS, pp. 149–50, 188–89, 333.   [10] GKS, pp. 332–33.

[11] This body of guards was called the *in no hokumen*, or "ex-sovereign's warriors
of the northern quarter." See chapter 8, below.

[12] *Jinnō shōtōki*, p. 142. The extant documents of the *in no chō* are discussed in
chapter 8, below.

called the hundred years from 1086 to 1185 the "age of rule by abdicated sovereigns."[13] Much of his information was taken from the *Gukanshō*, but Arai was the first historian to treat the latter part of the Heian period as a completely separate age.

Near the end of the Tokugawa period, in 1837, Rai San'yō published the *Nihon gaishi*, a history of Japan relating the rise and fall of the families that held political power at one point or another. Much of Rai's account of Heian history was also based upon Jien's work, but he appears to have been the first person to use the term *insei* to describe the rule of the abdicated sovereigns.[14] Thus the concept of rule by the retired emperors, which had been noticed as early as the thirteenth century, was at last given a name. The concept of insei has been further expanded and systematized in more recent times by such noted scholars as Kuroita Katsumi, Wada Hidematsu, Takeuchi Rizō, and Yoshimura Shigeki, and today is a standard term in the jargon of both Japanese and Western students of Japanese history.

Modern historians appear to have developed a precise explanation of the development of the system of rule by former emperors and its place in Japanese political history. Yet I am not at all convinced that this concept captures the political realities of late Heian Japan. My main criticism is that the concept lacks a firm factual basis. The entire concept rests upon statements made by Jien and Chikafusa, both of whom were writing after the system had declined; both were highly prejudiced against any political influence by ex-sovereigns; and both were extremely general in their treatment, giving no substantial proof for their statements. Besides these two secondary and biased historical works, modern students of the late Heian period have relied heavily upon works of a literary and pseudo-historical nature. Little work has been done with primary materials for this period.

In the last ten or fifteen years a few scholars, predominately those of Marxist leanings, have begun to examine in greater detail certain aspects of the insei. Noticing the acquisition of extensive

---

[13] *Tokushi yoron*, pp. 37–73.   [14] *Nihon gaishi*, p. 42.

estate holdings (*shōen*) by the imperial house during the late Heian period, one such historian has claimed that the establishment of the insei was an economic necessity. Although it was contrary to the basic spirit of the codes that formed the legal basis of the imperial state, the acquisition of shōen was permissible so long as the proper legal procedures were followed. But, as head of this imperial state, the emperor could not effectively engage in the acquisition of shōen. The retired sovereign, unhampered by such institutional restraints, could and did seek to acquire estate holdings for the imperial house.[15]

Perhaps the most useful refinement of the concept of insei along these lines was added by Kuroda Toshio. He sees the emerging political structure of medieval Japan as one of competition between a number of powerful families, or kinship blocs (*kemmon*), of which the imperial house was one.[16] What is important in his concept of insei is the establishment of the ex-sovereign's office and the acquisition of shōen by the imperial house. In his commentary on the insei, John Hall, relying upon Kuroda's work, concludes that these two developments indicate that "the imperial house itself . . . was obliged to look to its own house organization and to assert itself as a separate kinship bloc in the contest for power at court." [17]

Kuroda's work is highly suggestive. Perhaps the developments of the late Heian period should be seen not as the rise of a new political system in Japan but rather as an organizational attempt on the part of the imperial house to reassert its control over the rest of society, within the existing system.

It is true that former kings can never revert to being ordinary members of a dynasty in any society. But the degree of power and influence exercised by ex-sovereigns in late Heian Japan was extraordinary, and in order to explain this phenomenon a number of questions must be answered. What was the structure of the im-

---

[15] This interpretation seems to have been suggested first by Ishimoda Shō. See Ishimoda, *Kodai makki seijishi josetsu*, pp. 366–67.

[16] Kuroda Toshio, "Chūsei no kokka to tennō," 261–302. Kuroda explained his views more fully in *Shōensei shakai*, pp. 103–36.

[17] John Whitney Hall, *Government and Local Power in Japan, 500–1700*, p. 118.

perial house before the late Heian period? Within that structure what were the respective roles of the emperor and the abdicated emperor? Furthermore, given the emergence of the abdicated emperor as a major figure in the politics of the late Heian period, how did the tradition of abdication originate? What was the position of the abdicated sovereign in society prior to the insei period? Under what circumstances was the ex-sovereign's office created? How was it structured and staffed? Were its documents in fact more authoritative than those of the imperial government? How did the ex-sovereign manage to acquire extensive estate holdings? Only after a thorough examination of such questions can we hope to understand the retired sovereigns in the late Heian period. And only after we gain such an understanding can we determine whether the concept of insei as presently used accurately describes the realities of late Heian politics.

✒ TWO ✑

Structural and Functional Aspects of
Heian Kinship Organization

THROUGHOUT JAPANESE history competition for political power has normally been a struggle among groups, usually kinship units, rather than individuals. Both Kuroda Toshio and John Hall have characterized the political situation in late Heian Japan as competition among a small number of powerful houses (*kemmon seika*) with strong house organizations and extensive *shōen* holdings. In their view, the political activities of the abdicated emperors beginning with Go-Sanjō in the late eleventh century were intended to organize the imperial house so that it might compete effectively with the other powerful houses. Unfortunately, neither Kuroda nor Hall gives us a complete picture of the manner in which these houses were organized and competed for power. A more detailed investigation of Heian political society may shed some light on this subject.

Several different levels of kinship groupings can be identified in Heian Japan, and their interrelationship requires clarification. The

This chapter first appeared in John W. Hall and Jeffrey P. Mass, eds., *Medieval Japan: Essays in Institutional History* (New Haven: Yale University Press, 1974). Reprinted here by permission of the publisher.

most inclusive unit was the *uji*, or clan.[1] Each uji was divided into a number of lineages and sublineages, usually called *-ke*. Within the Fujiwara clan, for example, there was the *hokke*, or northern branch, which included all the descendants of Fusasaki, one of the four sons of Fujiwara no Fubito. Further segmentation within the hokke had resulted in a number of sublineages, such as the sekkanke, or regent's house, Kan'in, Hamuro, and so forth. The lowest level kinship unit was the household (*ie*) which was at any one time the basic unit of social and political interaction (see figure 1).

Hall has suggested that, although it was a less cohesive unit, the Heian uji was probably not too different from its pre-Taika predecessor.[2] There were differences, however, since the uji underwent both structural and functional changes following the establishment of the imperial state.

Prior to the political reorganization of the seventh century the uji was the most important functional group in society. Japan was a loosely united federation of uji, which were heterogeneous units bound by both territorial and kinship ties.[3] An uji exercised hegemony over a specific territory in which it held rice lands worked by groups of producers (*be*) subject to uji control. The different

[1] The terminology for various kinship units is quite complex, even for anthropologists. I am here following the practice of Robin Fox, in *Kinship and Marriage* (Middlesex, Eng.: Penquin Books, 1967), pp. 45–50. A "clan" is a descent group in which common descent is assumed but not necessarily demonstrable. Where the actual relationship between members of the group can be demonstrated, the group is a "lineage." Thus "clan" and "lineage" refer to higher- and lower-order descent groups. Furthermore, I use the term "house" to refer to a larger kinship unit, usually a sublineage (-ke in *sekkanke*) and "household" to refer to a lower-order unit.

[2] John W. Hall, *Government and Local Power in Japan, 500–1700*, p. 117.

[3] The nature of early Japanese society is still the object of intense study by Japanese scholars. At present, however, the predominance of territorial ties over consanguineal ties in the uji is generally accepted, though no one is sure to what degree kinship relations—either real or putative—bound the various units of the uji together. See Takeuchi Rizō, "Uji no chōja," in Takeuchi, *Ritsuryōsei to kizoku seiken*, 2:344; Tsuda Sōkichi, *Nihon jōdaishi kenkyū*, pp. 590–91; Hirano Kunio, "Taika zendai no shakai kōzō," in *Iwanami kōza Nihon rekishi*, 2:83. See also Herbert Passin's discussion of Japanese society in *Encyclopedia of the Social Sciences*, 8:242. For a recent and perceptive English-language treatment of early Japanese society, see Cornelius J. Kiley, "State and Dynasty in Archaic Yamato."

FIGURE 1

Heian kinship organization: The Fujiwara clan in the time of Yorimichi

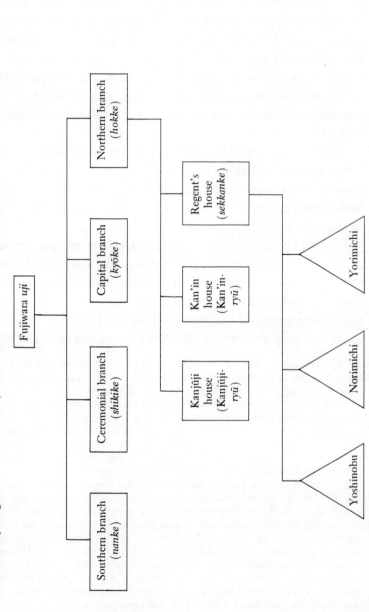

familial groups within the uji were under the leadership of the uji chieftain (*uji no kami*) who was the most important member of the main family. He had complete control over the uji: he led the uji members in the worship of the chief deity (*ujigami*), exercised judicial control over their activities, and was their political leader in their associations with the Yamato court.[4]

The Yamato court was a federation of the most powerful of those uji chieftains who recognized the authority of the chieftain of the Yamato uji. The Yamato court had become sufficiently sophisticated by the sixth century to be classified as an emergent state.[5] The Yamato chieftain was recognized as ruler for much of the period, but his duties appear to have been more religious than political.[6] The most powerful of the uji chieftains served as hereditary court officials, and lesser chieftains served in regional capacities. At this stage of development, however, particularistic uji interests predominated over the universalist interests of the emerging state.

It was in order to overcome this particularism and to secure the preeminence of the Yamato uji's authority that certain of its members, beginning with Prince Shōtoku (574–622), attempted to "reform" the Yamato state by the adoption of Chinese political ideology and institutions. From the Taika coup d'état of 645 until the second decade of the eighth century, the Yamato uji expended great energy in efforts to centralize the state. By 710 the process was largely complete. A new capital city had been established at Nara; an imposing governmental structure under the authority of a Chinese-style emperor (the chieftain of the Yamato uji) and

[4] Takeuchi, "Uji no chōja," pp. 343–48.

[5] Lawrence Krader suggests a minimum set of political conditions for an emergent state, including territorial integrity, concentration of religious and secular power in the hands of the ruler, and a degree of delegation of power by the central authority. By these criteria Japan would seem to qualify, although the degree of unity of religious and secular *power* is questionable at best. By stipulating a "concentration of religious and secular *authority*" and avoiding the question of the exercise of power, we shall have no trouble classifying Japan as an emergent state. See Lawrence Krader, *Formation of the State*, p. 48.

[6] Herschel Webb, *The Japanese Imperial Institution in the Tokugawa Period*, pp. 14–19.

based upon detailed administrative and penal codes had been created; well-defined administrative divisions had been set up; and standardized taxation procedures had been initiated.

Thus the state came to exercise a measure of control over the various uji. The Yamato uji, now the imperial house, succeeded in incorporating the old uji into the new state structure by eliminating their bases of power. The rice lands and groups of unfree persons under uji control were declared imperial property in order to establish the principle of public control over what had previously been private interests. Under this new imperial state the uji were transformed both structurally and functionally. An uji was no longer a territorial but solely a consanguineous unit. It also lost most of its functional importance.

As early as 664 the emperor Tenji had established a certain hierarchy among the uji when he granted the uji chieftains swords of differing size to designate relative rank.[7] A few years later it was stipulated that all uji were to select chieftains, who would then be recognized by imperial edict.[8] Uji and uji chieftains had previously existed only according to custom and unwritten private law, but now their existence was recognized by the imperial government. The position of uji chieftain underwent significant change after the establishment of imperial government. The person designated as uji chieftain was to be the highest-ranking uji member in the new state bureaucracy. From the early eighth century on, the term for uji chieftain was no longer uji no kami, but uji no *chōja*, a more explicit term meaning highest-ranking man within an uji. In pre-Taika times the chieftain had held a hereditary post at the Yamato court by virtue of the fact that he was leader of a powerful uji. Now the situation was reversed: a man became uji chieftain because he, of all the uji members, held the highest governmental position. Furthermore, his chieftainship was now confirmed by imperial edict. Thus the uji and its members were brought within the

---

[7] *NHSK*, 2: 360. Tenji 3/2/9. Here and throughout the book, Japanese-style dates consist of era name, year, month, and day. Thus Tenji 3/2/9 refers to the ninth day of the second month of the third year of the Tenji era.

[8] *NHSK*, 2: 456. Temmu 11/12/3.

structure of the state, and the uji chieftain served as the connecting link between the state and the uji.

Despite a Herculean effort to adopt Chinese political ideas and institutions, the traditional attitudes of the old uji society were not greatly altered in Japan. The new state assumed many of the functions of the uji but did not try to abolish them as social units. The social features of the uji were not compatible with the requirements of imperial government, however, and consequently the imperial state never functioned quite as intended. Over the four centuries of the Heian period private interests continued to expand at the expense of imperial government, a process Hall has aptly termed a "return to familial authority." [9]

Hence, although the uji continued to exist during the Heian period, it had undergone both structural and functional change. The chieftains of these uji (which can certainly be called clans, by the Nara period) no longer exercised total control over uji members as they had in pre-Taika times, but they continued to play an important role in the lives of uji members. First, the chieftain maintained some religious leadership over the uji members through his control of clan temples and shrines. Second, he controlled an educational institution established for the youth of the clan. Third, the chieftain had the power to secure an important appointment for one of his uji members in the appointments to rank (joi) held at the beginning of each year. He could recommend one clan member who had not yet reached the junior fifth rank for appointment to that rank. Since one's social, political, and economic status increased markedly from the fifth rank up,[10] this was an important power which the chieftain could exercise on behalf of his clan members.

The continued importance of the position of uji chieftain in Heian Japan is most easily demonstrated in the case of the Fujiwara. The transfer of the chieftainship in this clan was the occasion for a huge ceremonial banquet at which the old chieftain

[9] Hall, *Government and Local Power*, pp. 99–128 passim.
[10] The ranking system is explained more fully later in this chapter.

passed the symbols of the position to his successor. These included red lacquer utensils (*sugi*) and five red lacquer tables (*taiban*) which were used in important ceremonies. The new chieftain was also given the seal of the chieftain (*chōja-in*); and somewhat later, after the time of Tadazane in the twelfth century, a group of four estates called the *denka no watari-ryō* was also transferred to the control of the new chieftain.[11]

As imperial power waned during the course of the Heian period, the chieftainship of the Fujiwara clan once again came to be regarded as a purely private matter, not requiring an imperial edict when it was passed from one uji member to another. Thus when a dispute arose between the brothers Yorinaga and Tadamichi over the chieftainship, their father, Tadazane, was able to remark that, whereas the posts of regent and chancellor were granted by the emperor, the uji chieftainship was transferred from father to son and was thus a private affair.[12]

In somewhat changed form, then, the uji persisted as a social unit throughout the Heian period, but it had lost a great deal of its functional importance.[13] It was no longer the large uji but the lower-order kinship units—the lineage and the household—that became the focus of social and political interaction. Uji membership did not constitute the most important criterion of social and political association in the capital at Heian. The uji were no longer territorial units whose members lived in close proximity. Associations in the Heian period were increasingly with others of similar social status rather than mere kinsmen. Class was an important determinant of social and political relationships. Thus we must be extremely careful when we refer, for example, to the power of the Fujiwara during the Heian period. The Fujiwara clan was quite

[11] Takeuchi, "Uji no chōja," p. 399. See also Mitobe Masao, "Denka no watari-ryō no seikaku," pp. 238–47.

[12] *Taiki*, 2: 41. Kyūan 6/9/26.

[13] In discussing the function of the uji in Heian Japan, William McCullough points out that "its functions were primarily ceremonial and political, and it was related only tangentially to the family life of the individual" ("Japanese Marriage Institutions in the Heian Period," p. 141). As I have suggested here, however, the functions of the clan were predominantly ceremonial rather than political.

large, but it was only the members of a few select lineages within the clan who enjoyed power. In fact, certain courtiers from other clans who had formed close associations with the regent's house benefited more from "Fujiwara power" than did Fujiwara courtiers of other lineages.

The segmentation of large clans like the Fujiwara was quite common. In the early Nara period, for example, the Fujiwara clan had split into four lineages, the so-called northern, southern, ceremonial, and capital branches, each descended from a son of the courtier Fubito. Political misfortune befell all but the northern branch, with the result that the other three branches ceased to be politically important after the late Nara period. Due to clever political maneuvering and a close marital relationship with the imperial house, the northern branch of the Fujiwara came to dominate all other kinship groups in Heian political society. Through the maternal connection (*gaiseki*) with the emperor certain members of the northern branch came to hold the two extralegal posts of regent and chancellor, jointly referred to as *sekkan*. These posts were passed on hereditarily among one sublineage within the northern branch, which thus came to be called the *sekkanke*, or regent's house, of the Fujiwara.

The monopolization of major governmental positions by members of the sekkanke over an extended period of time meant that non-sekkanke members of the northern branch had increasing difficulty obtaining important posts. As such members became more and more removed from the sekkanke, in terms of both genealogical distance and relative political power, segmentation into several other sublineages resulted. Thus, within the northern branch of the Fujiwara there were several sublineages: the sekkanke, Kanjūji, Kan'in, Nakamikado, Kazan'in, and so on.[14] Often it was one of these houses rather than those of other clans that provided the major threat to the monopolization of power by the sekkanke. For

---

[14] Herbert Passin suggests that Japanese clans, lineages, and other such organizations tend to be functional in nature and rarely become very large. They tend toward segmentation, or fission, into smaller, more functional groups. This is in contrast to Chinese clans, for example, which seem to be able to expand infinitely.

example, when the sekkanke reached the peak of its power and
glory under Michinaga in the late tenth and early eleventh centuries, Michinaga's chief rival at court was another Fujiwara, the
Ononomiya minister of the right, Sanesuke. His descendants came
to be known as the Ononomiya house; but they were a sublineage
of the northern branch of the Fujiwara clan.

Like the Minamoto, Takashina, Ōe, and other major clans,[15] the
Fujiwara clan was a complex unit composed of a number of lineages and sublineages. These were in turn made up of the extended
families or households (ie) which at any one point in time formed
the lowest order of kinship organization. In the dynamics of political competition in Heian Japan, it was the household that constituted the basic and most important functional unit. Competition was conducted on the basis of households; several households
of a lineage might cooperate for mutual benefit, but there were
few instances in which one can speak of the entire clan as a functional unit in Heian politics. These complex relationships between
different levels of kinship groupings make up the "familial" basis
of authority to which Kuroda and Hall both refer.

The rivalry among these familial groups centered on appointments to court office and rank, or, more accurately, the acquisition
of the economic and social benefits such appointments brought.
The aristocratic governing class in Heian Japan was divided into
three distinct groups by a nine-rank system. The highest level of
society was composed of the kugyō, which included those courtiers
of the third rank and above, plus all those who held the office of
imperial adviser (sangi). Courtiers of the fourth and fifth rank

---

[15] In the Nara and Heian periods there were at least twelve uji that maintained
the tradition of having an uji no chōja and thus at least a measure of clan unity:
Ō, Minamoto, Fujiwara, Tomo, Takashina, Tachibana, Nakatomi, Imibe, Urabe,
Koshiji, Sugawara, and Wake. See Takeuchi, "Uji no chōja," pp. 249–352. Certainly there were more uji than this, but by the Heian period all important political
positions were dominated by members of about eight uji, and other uji names dis-
appear from the literature. A check of the Kugyō bunin from 645 to the end of
the Heian period reveals that courtiers from some fifty uji at one point held positions of the third rank and above. See Akagi Shizuko, "Kugyō bunin yori mita
ōchō no seisui" p. 51–52.

constituted a second level of court society; and the lowest level was composed of courtiers from the sixth through the ninth ranks, largely persons who possessed technical skills in law, medicine, and astronomy.

The kugyō households were quite large and consequently required considerable personnel to handle their economic, legal, and social affairs. In recognition of this fact, the Law of Household Administrative Appointment (*Keryō shokuin-ryō*) was included in the Yōrō Code of 718 to provide official administrative aid for these households.[16] Five different levels of household officials were created to serve the kugyō courtiers and imperial princes of the fourth rank and above. Four categories of household officials were appointed to both princely and kugyō households (see table 1). A

TABLE 1

The household official system of the Yōrō code

Household head		Number and kind of officials assigned to household				
Position	Rank	Bungaku	Keryō	Kafu	Kajū	Shori
Imperial prince	1	1	1	1	2	2
	2	1	1	1	1	2
	3	1	1	1	1	1
	4	1	1	1	1	1
Courtier	1		1	1	2	2
	2		1	1	1	2
	3		1	1	1	1

steward (*keryō*) was in charge of all household matters including the direction of the other household officials. Beneath the steward were an assistant (*kafu*) and an inspector (*kajū*), who was charged with investigation of household matters. Princely and kugyō house-

16 *Ryō no gige*, pp. 75–76. The Yōrō Code of 718 (actually not put into practice until 757) was the basic body of administrative and penal law of the *ritsuryō* state. Although most of the bodies it provided for were already outmoded by the tenth century, formally at least it remained in effect until the Meiji cabinet system of 1885.

holds of the first rank had two inspectors, and other households one. Finally, there were scribes (*shori*), who drafted household documents and kept records. Princes and officials of the top two ranks had two scribes; others had only one. Besides these officials, who served in all high-ranking households, princes' households also had a tutor (*bungaku*). These officials were known collectively as keryō.

While duly recognized as officials according to the law codes, the keryō were nevertheless quite different from other government officials, and these differences largely determined the pattern of their later development.[17] First, their court ranks were awarded at a lower level than others of equivalent positions. Second, their semiannual allotments for rank and office were paid at a lower rate than others of equivalent status. Third, while the performance of other officials was judged by the head of their office—in which case household officials ought to have been judged by the household steward—keryō were in fact evaluated by the head of the household they served. And last, keryō were not granted the one holiday every six days to which other officials were entitled by law.

The seemingly discriminatory distinctions between keryō and other officials stemmed from the fact that their appointment was considered more private than public. The relationship between the head of a household and his keryō was unlike the superior–subordinate relationship within a government bureau: it was based upon personal, reciprocal ties rather than bureaucratic hierarchy. While keryō were publicly appointed by the Ministry of Ceremonials (Shikibu-shō), selections were made at the request of the household head. Once appointed, a keryō could be dismissed or transferred only with the recommendation and approval of the head of his household. Moreover, the punishment of the keryō lay in the hands of the household head rather than with the government.

A further indication of the private nature of the relationship between household head and keryō is the existence of fictive familial ties binding them together. Keryō were allowed, for example, to

17 Ōae Akira, "Heian jidai no keishi seido," p. 26.

participate in important family ceremonies, along with actual family members.[18] Thus, despite their public appointment, keryō were actually private officials, under the control of the head of the household they served. It would appear that they were given lower salaries and fewer privileges in the expectation that these deficiencies would be more than compensated for by the household head through private means. Through the public appointment of officials serving private purposes, the new state had perpetuated the proclivity for the development of an extensive leader–follower, or patron–client, system based upon reciprocal private obligations.[19]

After the shift of the capital to Heian in 794, the keryō system underwent great expansion and modification in conjunction with the general growth of private, familial interests at the expense of public authority. What had originally been a very limited system of household officials established by the state for the purpose of helping households administer their affairs developed in the Heian period into an extensive clientage system [20] over which the state lost all control.

The term *keishi* replaced keryō as the generic term for household official. Alongside the old household administrative posts established in the Yōrō Code, a number of new positions were created, the most important of which was that of the directors (*bettō*), who headed most of the bureaus within the household office. Not only were

---

[18] Ibid., p. 27.

[19] The tendency to form patron–client relationships in all forms of social organization appears at every period of Japanese history, from early tribal days down to and including the postwar "new" Japan.

[20] I am using the term clientage here in a very general sense to characterize the private dependent relationship of a lower-ranking person upon one of higher status. The client's position was not a legal one, as was the case in Roman society, nor was there any sense of shame in becoming a client in Heian Japan, as there seems to have been in many other societies. See, for example, Jean Buxton, " 'Clientship' among the Mandari of the Southern Sudan," p. 229. Miss Buxton has coined the term "clientship" in her description of a servile institution among the Mandari. In this society neither the chiefs nor the clients wish to admit the existence of "clientship," but such was not at all the case in ancient Japan. Clientage was eagerly sought by both patron and client, and the latter, far from falling into disgrace, hoped to attain a measure of political and economic mobility through the sponsorship of his patron.

such new positions created, but the number of persons appointed to specific household positions was greatly expanded. This expansion was brought on by the development of extensive shōen holdings, the construction of granaries and storehouses, residences, family temples and shrines, all of which required increased administrative personnel. Furthermore, in imitation of the kugyō, courtiers of fourth and fifth rank also began to develop household administrative apparatus which they staffed with keishi-like officials.[21]

The most important development in the nature of the household official system during the Heian period was in the increasingly personal and private ties between household head and keishi.[22] During the Nara period the system had been instituted by the state and the keryō were considered only semiprivate officials. During the Heian period, however, the last vestiges of public control over household officials disappeared, and the relationship between household head and keishi became wholly a private leader–follower arrangement. This private relationship was, as in most Japanese cases, based on fictive kinship relations, and keishi appear to have been treated scarcely differently from family members by the household head.[23]

The duties the keishi performed for the head of the household were largely private in nature. They accompanied their patron on outings, visits to the family temples and shrines or the household of another courtier, and to household ceremonies. They frequently served as messengers, prepared documents pertaining to household business, and performed other miscellaneous services. A keishi could expect to be rewarded for his service by advancement in the court bureaucracy. The kugyō patron would in effect sponsor his keishi client at court. The basis of the patron–client relationship was thus mutual need: the need of the kugyō for administrative help within his household and the need of lower-ranking courtiers for a kugyō to sponsor their interests.

[21] Ōae, "Heian jidai no keishi seido," p. 29.
[22] Ibid., p. 39.
[23] Such treatment is not at all unique to clientage in Japan. See, e.g., Lucy Mair's discussion of patterns of clientage among certain African tribes for this and other similarities with Japanese practices (*Primitive Government,* rev. ed. [Middlesex, Eng.: Penguin Books, 1964], pp. 113–15).

The keishi all held positions within the imperial government; they not only served as private household officials but held public positions as well. They were normally courtiers of the fourth through the sixth ranks, perhaps themselves men of relatively important households. Most of the keishi of the sekkanke, for example, seem to have been fourth- and fifth-rank courtiers, and some even appear to have become kugyō through their associations with this most powerful of Fujiwara houses. The sekkanke seems actively to have recruited middle-ranking courtiers to serve as their keishi, particularly those who were or had been provincial governors.[24] Diaries of Fujiwara nobles make frequent mention of such officials (called *zuryō keishi*) serving sekkanke courtiers. The regent's house could utilize both the administrative talents and the personal wealth of such governors in the administration of its private affairs.[25] Provincial governors, on the other hand, might be able to guarantee their continued appointment to lucrative governorships if they had a powerful patron such as the regent. Other types of persons the kugyō sought to serve in their households were those with technical skills such as accounting and mathematics.

While the basis of this patron–client relationship would appear to have been solely materialistic, ethical considerations were important and a strong bond of loyalty united the two. There appear to have been three ways of entering into the clientage of a kugyō.[26] The kugyō himself could select a person, perhaps because of kinship or upon the recommendation of another courtier. The relationship could be established through the good offices of a third party, the traditional Japanese go-between. Or one could request appointment directly from a kugyō.

But service as a household official was just one form of clientage in the Heian period. While keishi formed the top level of persons tied to the head of a kugyō household by personal bonds, far more numerous were the housemen (*ke'nin*), the retainers (samurai), and the personal servants and attendants (*chōdai shijin*, or *toneri*).

24 Ōae, "Heian jidai no keishi seido," p. 40.
25 See chapter 9 for a more detailed examination of the post of provincial governor in the Heian period.
26 Ōae, "Heian jidai no keishi seido," pp. 43–44.

Although there is debate among scholars concerning the origin of the term ke'nin, it seems clear from Heian documents and literature that it referred to all those private followers of a household who were not keishi, that is, all those who did not hold titled administrative positions with relatively specific duties.[27] They were also followers or clients of the lord who entered his service for protection and advancement within the imperial state system. Their functions seem to have been quite diverse and unspecified, ranging from attendance in the capital to service as estate officials in the provinces. These housemen were bound to the lord by the same type of ties as were the keishi, although the keishi ranked higher within the household.

There was one group of housemen whose duties were specific, however. These were the samurai, or retainers, who performed military, police, and guard duties for the household. In the case of the highest-ranking households, such retainers were frequently descendants of aristocratic families or imperial lineages and leaders of large bands of retainers (rōdō) of their own. The Seiwa Genji, for example, served as samurai for the sekkanke and came to be known as the "teeth and claws" of the Fujiwara. In return for loyal service the Seiwa Genji became influential at court through the patronage of the sekkanke. The retainers attached to lower-ranking noble households were more frequently called rōdō and tended to be men of the local landholder (myōshu) class. In return for military duties in the capital or in the provinces—where they might serve as private troops for their master while he was provincial governor—they were often able to ensure the tax-free status of their lands. These samurai and rōdō provided military protection for their lord in both his public and private duties.

The lowest level of clients attached to a kugyō household included servants and attendants, or toneri. Those of princely households were called chōdai ("within the curtain") and those of noble houses shijin ("resource men"). These servants were somewhat like keishi in that they were originally allotted to noble and princely

27 Ōae Akira, "Heian jidai no rōdōsei to keninsei," p. 154.

households by the state according to certain legal stipulations. But they too soon lost their public character as large numbers of peasants absconded from their lands, fled to the capital, and entered into the private service of the great households. The motivation in the case of these peasants was to escape the harsh corvée labor service owed to the state. Toneri were exempt from such corvée labor, and the practice of entering into the service of an important household became increasingly popular during the Heian period.

Thus large numbers of clients of the great kugyō households enjoyed a similar relationship with their patron. While the nature of the relationship was private, the rewards they sought for their service were generally public. The higher-ranking keishi, housemen, and samurai sought better official government posts, while the toneri desired to escape harsh government corvée labors. Another similarity between these different levels of clientage was the tendency for all to become hereditary. The personal bonds that drew patron and client together continued over the generations so that one family might provide keishi for a particular kugyō household for four or five generations. The same was true for housemen, samurai, and toneri.

The accepted manner for prospective keishi, housemen, and samurai to formalize their clientage relationship with a kugyō patron was to call upon him at his residence, present one's name placard (*myōbu*),[28] and request an audience.[29] After the formalization of the relationship, the client was expected to render loyal service to the patron, whom he referred to as lord or master (*nushi* or *shujin*). For his part, the kugyō was obligated to look after the needs of his client, normally by sponsorship of his career at court. Both the prac-

[28] The *myōbu* seems to have been somewhat like the name card (*meishi*) in universal use in Japan today. On it was written one's office, court rank, and name. While it was used to announce one's service at the palace and for other such formal purposes, it was frequently presented to higher-ranking personages to enter into a patron–client relationship in the Heian period.

[29] *Kenzan* was a term frequently used for such an audience, but there does not appear to have been a standard word. Frequently, a prospective client simply "came before" (*mairu*) the kugyō. In other cases, reference was made to the "first audience" (*shozan*) of the client. See, for example, Gyokuyō, 3: 147. Bunji 2/1/27.

tices and the terminology involved in this system of clientage are quite similar to those of the vassalage relationship between Japanese feudal warriors. Indeed, these relations of clientage appear to be one source for the later development of feudal relationships in Japan, much as the Roman patrocinium can be seen as a remote root of European feudalism.[30] True, the Heian patron's benefice did not take the form of the grant of a fief (although, as implied above, he was often able to secure tax-free status for the estate holdings of a client), and the service of the clients, with the exception of the samurai, was not military. Yet the binding personal relationship between patron and client expressed in terms of fictive kinship is in many ways similar to later Japanese feudal practices.[31]

During the Nara period, when the imperial government had provided a small number of officials to handle their affairs, households of these high-ranking nobles had developed administrative councils (*mandokoro*) to deal with family business. When in the Heian period kugyō households came to control extensive estate holdings and attract numerous clients, their administrative organs expanded correspondingly. The mandokoro was still the administrative apparatus for all matters, but a number of lesser bureaus were added to it.

The mandokoro of the Fujiwara regent's house was somewhat larger than that of other courtier households, but its organization was characteristic of Heian kugyō households.[32] It included a documents bureau (*fudono*) for handling complaints and other types of correspondence. There was also a secretariat (*kurōdo-dokoro*) modeled on that established by Emperor Saga. A retainers' office (samurai-dokoro) was added to coordinate the activities of the

[30] As I have already indicated, patron–client relationships seem to have been important in Japanese social organization from earliest times, but the formalization and regularization of forms of clientage appear to date from the late Nara-early Heian period.

[31] For a further discussion of this point, see Ōae, "Heian jidai no keishi seido," pp. 50–51. Also see idem, "Heian jidai no shiteki hogo seido," esp. pp. 13–16.

[32] The *Shūgaishō*, p. 366, provides the outline for the organization of the sek-kanke house organization. See also Fujiki Kunihiko, "Nara-Heianchō ni okeru ken-seika no kasei ni tsuite," pp. 1–20.

warriors in the service of the household. There was a well-staffed stable (*mimaya*) which cared for the horses, oxen, and ox carts needed by Heian courtiers. An attendants' bureau (*zuishin-dokoro*) was established to control the attendants allotted by the court to high-ranking nobles. There was an office for court dress (*gofuku-dokoro*) to store and care for all the ceremonial robes belonging to the household. The *shimmotsu-dokoro*, or provisions bureau, handled the receipt and storage of rice and other grains, vegetables, fish, and other foods for the household's meals; and the *zen-bu*, or cooks' bureau, was in charge of the actual preparation of the food.

All these different bureaus within the mandokoro were headed by directors (*bettō*) under whose authority were a number of lesser household officials: keishi, *azukari, anju, shimogeishi,* and so on. During the Heian period court officials of the fourth and fifth rank —who were frequently keishi in the service of kugyō households— began to develop their own household administrative agencies, modeled after those of the kugyō. These were normally smaller, however, and the officials who staffed them had somewhat different titles.

In the Nara period household officials had been able to issue documents (*kachō*) of a strictly private nature to subordinates within the jurisdiction of the household. Communication with any public body, which was frequently necessary, required the personal document of the household head. By 804, however, household officials, acting on instructions from the kugyō, were able to use these documents to communicate with governmental bodies. To avoid confusion, it was required that the rank, office, and surname of the household head be clearly written at the top of the document and the seal of two stewards (keryō) be affixed at the end. In the Heian period a number of other documents came to be used by kugyō households in the conduct of their business, the most important of which was the *kudashibumi* (order). These various documents dealt with private affairs of the household, most frequently with its shōen holdings. This was true even of the sekkanke, although Japanese historians often make the unsubstantiated claim that orders of the regent's house actually took the place of imperial edicts.[33]

Heian court society was thus dominated by a small number of high-ranking court nobles who were heads of powerful familial interest groups.[34] Their households had complex administrative bodies staffed by numerous clients. It was these households that formed the basic unit of social and political interaction, not the more inclusive clan. The clan persisted in the Heian period, but as a functional unit it was replaced by the lower-order kinship group, the household. It was these powerful households and the larger lineages they composed, commonly referred to in the literature of the time as *kemmon seika* ("influential houses and powerful families"), that bore a certain resemblance to the pre-Taika uji.

The imperial state structure formed the arena of political competition for these various households. Despite the growth of extensive private interests and the increasing "familialization" of authority, the Chinese-style state structure did not wither away and die but continued to function as the source of ultimate legitimacy. Within the imperial bureaucracy created in the Nara period, decisions of state were made by the kugyō who met in the Grand Council of State. The decision reached by these courtiers was ratified, rejected, or returned for reconsideration by the emperor. Japanese emperors throughout history have normally been little more than legitimizers of decisions made by others, but during the Nara

---

[33] Kitayama Shigeo also points out that documents issued by the sekkanke mandokoro did not replace imperial edicts but dealt almost exclusively with private household matters. He further warns against the oversimplifications that have resulted from dependence upon the concept of sekkan seiji and mandokoro (politics of the regent's house). See Kitayama, "Sekkan seiji," pp. 3–20. All the extant kudashibumi issued by the regent's house can be checked for content. A number are collected in *Heian ibun*, ed. and comp. Takeuchi Rizō. A number of others are contained in section 7 of *Chōya gunsai*, in *Kokushi taikei*, pp. 173–94. Kitayama expands on his critique of "sekkan seiji" in *Ōchō seijishiron*, esp. pp. 257–60.

[34] The high-ranking courtiers, or kugyō, who composed the highest echelon of court society, usually numbered between fifteen and twenty from the early Heian period through the reign of Emperor Ichijō (r. 986–1011). Thereafter there were normally twenty-five to thirty. The increase in the number of kugyō corresponds to the beginning of the domination of the court by the Fujiwara regent's house.

period, under the still strong influence of Chinese political ideas, emperors and empresses exercised considerable influence in the actual decisions of state.

Certain changes in the imperial state system during the Heian period made it more responsive to the realities of Japanese society. The complex process of drafting edicts, for example, was simplified with the institution of the sovereign's private office. Originally established by Saga in 810 as a temporary measure, the office became permanent; and it functioned as an intermediary body between the emperor and the kugyō, exercising considerable influence in affairs of state. Moreover, the meeting place of the kugyō was moved from the Grand Council of State offices to the headquarters of the inner palace guards (*konoefu*). Here the kugyō, expanded in the Heian period with the creation of councillors and imperial advisers, met to discuss and decide matters of state. This process was referred to as *jin no sadame* or *jōgi*.[35] At such gatherings, the head of the controlling board (*benkan*) would review the precedents—often Chinese as well as Japanese—and then have a secretary (*geki*) prepare a recommendation. Then all the kugyō, beginning with the lowest-ranking imperial adviser, would express their views on the issue. The ranking member, the prime minister, or the minister of the left if the former post was unfilled,[36] would find the consensus and announce the final decision. One of the imperial advisers would write up the decision and forward it to the sovereign's secretary (*kurōdo*), who in turn would seek the emperor's approval and have it properly drafted in document form.

Modern-day Japanese patterns of decision-making exhibit a considerable degree of continuity with the past. Consensus, or the appearance of consensus, rather than simple majority appears to have

---

[35] See Fujiki Kunihiko's discussion of *jin no sadame* in *Nihon rekishi daijiten*, 10: 321.

[36] Prime minister (*dajō daijin*) was the highest post within the civil bureaucracy, and the person appointed prime minister was supposed to set an excellent example for the rest of society. Since moral qualities were a major determinant in appointment to the position, it was not to be filled unless a properly qualified individual was available.

been a major concern then as it is now. Each kugyō was essentially
the leader of a faction made up of kinsmen and clients whose interests he represented. Consultation and compromise, as well as
bribery and pressure, were utilized to achieve a workable balance
among these various interests. Before formal meetings of the whole
body, individual kugyō frequently visited others at their residences
to discern their views on the upcoming issue, whether it was a
decision over court appointments, rewards for special military service rendered to the court, or more ceremonial matters. Household
officials of these kugyō often acted as go-betweens to feel out positions on various issues. The courtiers met at poetry recitations, banquets, and other social events which often functioned as arenas of
political discussion, just as Japanese leaders today meet in small,
informal groups at geisha houses and cabarets to discuss politics.
Alliances were formed, promises extracted, and compromises made
so that general consensuses probably had already been arrived at before the more formal *jin no sadame*. The ultimate decision was
determined by the relative strengths of these courtier households,
although the formalization of these decisions through jin no sadame
and ultimate imperial approval was taken very seriously by Heian
courtiers.

In this discussion of the nature of Heian political society, I have
said little about the emperor and the imperial house, but this over-
sight has been intentional. Although the emperor was the ultimate
source of political authority, the emperor and the imperial house as
a whole exercised little real power between the early ninth century
and the latter part of the Heian period. In the Nara and very early
Heian period there had been emperors who exercised substantial
power, and certain members of the imperial house had occupied
major governmental posts; but throughout the period the number
of nonimperial kugyō, particularly Fujiwara uji members, increased.[37]
Thereafter, only on rare occasions did imperial princes reach the

[37] Akagi Shizuko, "*Kugyō bunin* yori mita ōchō no seisui," pp. 53–55. Based upon
her study of the *Kugyō bunin*, Akagi has discovered that during the Nara and early
Heian periods as many as thirty different uji produced kugyō; from the mid-tenth
century, however, all kugyō came from only eight of these uji. Ibid., p. 52.

upper echelon of court power, and consequently the imperial house was rarely represented in the kugyō meetings.[38]

Imperial attempts to curb the primacy of private interest had been unsuccessful. Ironically, however, by initiating and championing an imperial state system, the imperial house had eliminated its own private, familial base of power; and as a result it was unable to compete effectively for power for most of the Heian period. The emperor was the symbol of public authority, largely dependent upon public revenues for support. While other familial groups took ample advantage of the incompleteness of the nationalization of land and accumulated vast private estates, the emperor and his house suffered financially as a result of the development of these estates. As a personification of public authority it was neither seemly nor possible for the emperor to participate in the alienation of public land.[39] Furthermore, by providing household officials and servants for the great kugyō households, the state unwittingly facilitated the development of an extensive system of private clientage. Thus the kugyō households all developed private, familial bases of power which functioned as instruments for political competition. Only the imperial house, tied to the public structure by its own policy, was without a private base of power.

Moreover, the imperial house was somewhat different structurally from other kinship groups in Heian Japan. There was no imperial clan including all persons of real or putative common descent; neither was there a common surname uniting all imperial descendants. One lineage provided the emperor, and the members of this lineage were known as the imperial house. Since emperors usually had several consorts and were surrounded by concubines and various female attendants, imperial offspring tended to be quite numerous. An imperial clan including all such persons could have been enormous. To avoid a strain on the treasury and to limit the number

---

[38] There were some exceptions during the reign of Saga in the ninth century, when a number of kugyō from the imperial offshoot Minamoto uji did tend to cooperate, forming what some scholars have called an imperial faction. See Hayashiya Tatsusaburō, "Insei," in *Zusetsu Nihon bunkashi taikei*, 5: 63–64.

[39] Ishimoda Shō, *Kodai makki seijishi josetsu*, p. 361.

of persons eligible for dynastic succession, many princes outside the
direct line of succession were granted surnames and allowed to
function as other courtiers. The imperial house was thus a lineage,
like the sekkanke; but no clear picture of an imperial clan corresponding to the Fujiwara uji has thus far emerged.

Princes who were cut off from the imperial house could be
granted one of two surnames, Taira or Minamoto. These two off-
shoots of the imperial house were considered clans, just like the
Fujiwara, Ōe, Takashina, or any other uji; and they developed
similar traditions. For example, all those persons with the name
Minamoto formed a structural clan. There was a clan chieftain who
performed the same ceremonial functions as other chieftains. As
was the case in other clans, one lineage monopolized the chieftainship; in the Minamoto case, it was the Murakami branch. The clan
was composed of several different lineages, each one descended
from and named after the emperor who had originally granted the
surname. Thus there were lineages of the Minamoto clan (or
Genji, in the Sino-Japanese reading) called Uda Genji, Daigo
Genji, Seiwa Genji, Murakami Genji, and so on. As in the case of
other clans, the lineages or houses were more important as functional units than the entire clan, and the immediate household
was most important of all; as a consequence, the clan chieftain did
not enjoy extensive power.

The other imperial offshoot clan, the Taira or Heishi, were even
less organized as a clan. The individual lineages were similar to the
Minamoto in that they were named after the emperors who had
granted the surname, but there seems to have been no tradition of
chieftainship held by one of the lineages.[40] In the latter part of the
Heian period, when successive members of the Ise branch of the
Kammu Heishi—Masamori, Tadamori, and Kiyomori—rose to political power at court, there seems to have evolved some clan
solidarity under their general leadership. Even then, however, they
were little different from the Fujiwara sekkanke, working largely
for the advancement of the fortunes of immediate family members

[40] Takeuchi, "Uji no chōja," p. 353.

and clients, with little concern for the well-being of the entire clan.

The imperial house itself, lacking a private, or familial, base of power, did not function like other kinship blocs. The emperor was solely a public person, constantly surrounded by officials, servants, empresses, and concubines. After the Taika reforms, early empresses were chosen from among imperial house females, resulting in some degree of familial solidarity. In 729 this tradition was broken, however, and Fujiwara Fubito's daughter Kōmyō became Shōmu's empress. From that time on empresses and concubines were almost always selected from Fujiwara families, most frequently the regent's house. Because of the nature of Heian marriage institutions, maternal kinsmen, particularly maternal grandparents, had a dominant influence within the household.[41] Consequently emperors were surrounded by Fujiwara mothers and grandmothers, wet nurses and female attendants.[42] Most of the women in their lives were from some Fujiwara household, usually the sekkanke, and this was equally true of the men with whom they came into contact. Such a situation made it difficult for the imperial house to maintain much cohesion as a separate family; the emperor was as much a member of the Fujiwara regent's house as he was of the imperial house.

In the pre-Taika period, then, the Yamato ruler had been only the first among equals. Like other uji chieftains he had both private and public roles, acting on the one hand as chieftain of his own uji, and on the other as ruler of the Yamato court. After the attempted transformation to an imperial state system, great household heads maintained joint public and private functions, between which there appears to have been minimal distinction. A man might be minister of the right in his public position, but he was also the leader of a large private social unit, including his own family members and a number of clients. The emperor, however, was different. He no longer played a private role as head of a household. His dual

[41] McCullough, "Japanese Marriage Institutions," esp. pp. 141–47.

[42] The rearing and even education of young children of aristocratic houses in Heian Japan was frequently left in the hands of wet nurses. See Wada Hidematsu, "Rekishijō ni okeru menoto no seiryoku," in Wada, Kokushi kokubun no kenkyū, pp. 182–201.

role was eliminated and he functioned solely as a public figure, head of the state structure and symbol of legitimacy.

One would expect the emperor to have had a position analogous to that of the Fujiwara regent, who as highest-ranking public figure of the clan served as chieftain, head of his own extensive household unit, and patron of numerous subordinate followers. As the highest-ranking public figure among imperial descendants, the emperor ought to have been chieftain of the clan; he also should have been head of his immediate household, with many clients in his service. But he filled none of these roles. His only role was a public one, and that largely social and ceremonial. He possessed enormous prestige and ultimate political authority as descendant of the Sun Goddess and emperor, and he was the focus of Heian cultural life, but his influence in real political life was minimal.

For despite the heavy overlay of Chinese political institutions and ideas in premodern Japan, native traditions of kingship doggedly persisted. Long before the Chinese-inspired Taika reforms the duties of the ruler appear to have been frequently ritualistic and sacerdotal, "while the decision-making functions of government were exercised at a level where they were responsive to the competitive interests of the group of families that constituted a ruling oligarchy." [43] Indeed, even Pimiko, the first Japanese ruler mentioned in historical sources, held herself above the realm of actual politics, while her brother handled such responsibilities. With few exceptions this has been the pattern of rule for most of Japan's premodern history: the emperor has been the symbol of authority, the "legitimizer of group consensus," as Hall puts it, while someone else among the ruling group—prince-regent, regent, ex-emperor, or shogun—has exercised real power. Both privately within the imperial house and publicly in politics, the emperor has normally been above the realm of real power.

It was also part of the Japanese tradition of kingship that only a member of the imperial house—a descendant of the Sun Goddess—was eligible for the position of emperor. Thus in political

[43] John W. Hall, "A Monarch for Modern Japan," p. 20.

struggles the supreme goal was to control or dominate the imperial position rather than to usurp it, as in so many other societies. It was, in a sense, a human chess game where the object was to capture the king—but the king could not be removed from the board. Furthermore, the most powerful tool in the game was the queen, demonstrated most forcefully by the lengthy domination of the imperial family by the sekkanke.

Thus, although the Japanese emperor was not expected to rule, his position as the sanctifier of political decisions was of overriding importance: the emperorship was the major political asset of the imperial kin group. In ancient Japan the periods of greatest imperial house weakness were those times when the imperial position was controlled by some other family or faction—the Soga clan, the priest Dōkyō, and the sekkanke, for example. Conversely, control over this asset by the imperial house itself was the surest means of aggrandizing its own power. It was this latter phenomenon that occurred during the final century of Heian rule.

⤳ THREE ⤶

Abdication and Abdicated Sovereigns Prior
to the Insei *Period*

JAPANESE HISTORIANS most often preface their remarks on the *insei* with the observation that there were a few occasions prior to the late Heian period in which the abdicated sovereign exercised a measure of political power, but they are careful to point out that such instances were exceptional and unrelated. No one has conducted a comprehensive study of the practice of abdication and the political role of retired emperors in Japanese history before the insei period.[1] And yet it is impossible to arrive at any definitive conclusions about the political role of the ex-emperor in the late Heian period without a thorough understanding of his role prior to that time. This is particularly true if we accept the contention that the emperor Go-Sanjō intended to exercise political power as retired sovereign after abdicating in favor of his son; for this suggests that there was a precedent for such action, or at least that the role of the ex-emperor in Japanese society was such that Go-Sanjō could conceive of this course of action. We need, then, to investigate the history of abdication in Japan, with particular

---

[1] Ironically, the most extensive treatment of the subject is by a foreigner. See R.A.B. Ponsonby-Fane, "Abdication in Japan," in Ponsonby-Fane, *The Imperial House of Japan*, pp. 229–91.

emphasis upon the role of the ex-emperor within both the imperial house and the society at large.

In examining the cases of abdication in Japan prior to that of the emperor Go-Sanjō, I will be particularly concerned with the following five questions: (1) What were the reasons for the abdications? (2) What was the nature of the relationship between the abdicated and titular emperors? (3) What type of administrative offices were established to handle the affairs of the ex-sovereign and what type of men staffed them? (4) What was the political role—if any—of the retired sovereign? (5) What kind of economic support did the ex-sovereign enjoy? There are a great number of primary materials that can be utilized in an attempt to find the answers to these questions. They include official and unofficial histories,[2] diaries of court noblemen, and extant official documents.

My survey of imperial abdications will cover a period of more than four hundred years, which, for purposes of analysis, can be divided into three distinct periods: (1) from the abdication of the empress Kōgyoku in 645 to the end of the Nara period, (2) from the beginning of the Heian period through the death of En'yū in 991, and (3) from the reign of Ichijō through that of Go-Reizei (991–1068). Of the seventy sovereigns who reigned during the entire period prior to the accession of Go-Sanjō, twenty are recorded as having abdicated. (For a complete list of emperors through 1185, see appendix 3.)

Kōgyoku to Kammu, 645–806

The earliest Chinese accounts of Japanese history make no mention of abdication. As in the case of the female ruler Pimiko, it

[2] By "official history" I mean one compiled under the auspices of the imperial government. More specifically, this refers to the "six national histories," or *rikkokushi*: *Nihon shoki, Shoku Nihongi, Nihon kōki, Shoku Nihon kōki, Nihon Montoku jitsuroku,* and *Nihon sandai jitsuroku.* An "unofficial history" is one compiled in a form similar to an "official history" but not commissioned by the government. This includes work like *Nihon kiryaku, Fusō ryakki,* and *Hyakurenshō.* For a more extensive discussion of these and other sources, see the Bibliographic Note.

seems to have been the custom for the sovereign to reign until death. It is not until the time of Kōgyoku, recognized as the thirty-fifth sovereign in the official imperial line, that the first case of abdication [3] appears to have occurred. The *Nihon shoki*, Japan's first official history (completed in 720), records that Kōgyoku "yielded the succession" to Emperor Kōtoku and at the same time confirmed her son Naka no Ōe as crown prince.[4] There is no reason given for her abdication. She appears to have been in fine health and she lived for sixteen more years, even reascending the throne in 655 as Empress Saimei. The reasons for her abdication—and second accession—can only be deduced from an examination of the political situation at the time, and, more specifically, the politics of imperial succession.

Kōgyoku was the consort of Emperor Jomei, and she ascended the throne only in order to avert serious problems in the matter of succession after the death of the emperor.[5] The chief contenders for the throne were Prince Yamashiro, son of Prince Shōtoku, and Prince Furuhito, Jomei's eldest son by a daughter of Soga no Umako. The Soga family was strongly opposed to the accession of Yamashiro, and trouble appeared likely. Thus, in order to avoid a succession dispute, Kōgyoku became empress after her husband's death, following the example of Empress Suiko.[6] Kō-

---

[3] Some scholars recognize Keitai as the first sovereign to have abdicated, but I do not concur with this conclusion. The *Nihon shoki* records that Keitai "made his great elder brother emperor" and passed away the next day (*NHSK*, 2: 48). The term abdication (*jōi*) does not appear in the text, and Keitai is still referred to as emperor at the time of his death. It may well be that Keitai simply confirmed Ankan as his successor before passing away. There was a serious dispute over the matter of succession at this time, and it is clear that Keitai wished Ankan to succeed him. There are a number of perplexing problems, however, in the history and historiography of Keitai which cannot be dealt with adequately here. See Inoue Mitsusada, *Nihon no rekishi*, vol. 1: *Shinwa kara rekishi e*, pp. 468–519. See also Hayashiya Tatsusaburō, *Kodai kokka no kaitai*, pp. 1–39. Mizuno Yū, the controversial scholar who has been frequently criticized for his discussion of Japanese history as the story of "using the emperor," has an interesting discussion of Keitai's reign in his book *Nihon kokka no seiritsu*, pp. 118–39.

[4] *NHSK*, 2: 267. Kōgyoku 4/6/14.

[5] Inoue Mitsusada, *Nihon kodai kokka no kenkyū*, p. 226.

[6] Suiko had also ascended the throne only to avoid dynastic troubles and was apparently the first female ruler to ascend the throne for this reason. Inoue, *Kodai kokka*, pp. 225–26.

gyoku, then, like all other early Japanese female rulers in historic times, ascended the throne only as an expediency to avoid dynastic schism.[7] Still concerned that Yamashiro might someday become emperor, the Soga had him killed in 643 as part of a plot to secure the accession of Prince Furuhito. But there was widespread reaction to such high-handed action, resulting in the assassination of the Soga leaders Emishi and Iruka and the inauguration of the Taika reform in 645.

By 645 the Soga leaders had been eliminated, and the most important figure at court was Kōgyoku's son, Crown Prince Naka no Ōe. Kōgyoku's accession had prevented a succession dispute; and, now that the Soga leaders who were likely to have precipitated such a dispute were dead, there was no longer any reason for her to remain sovereign. Therefore, she resolved to abdicate in favor of Naka no Ōe.[8] There was considerable discussion of the matter between the prince and Nakatomi no Kamatari, his co-plotter in the overthrow of the Soga and a prime figure in the reform movement. Kamatari opposed Naka no Ōe's accession at this point because his elder brother Furuhito was still alive, and for him to ascend the throne would violate the Confucian principle that the younger brother ought to follow the elder brother.[9] This problem could be resolved, however, by making Naka no Ōe's uncle, Prince Karu, emperor.

Prince Karu was approached but declined to accept because he felt that Furuhito was the proper person. Accordingly, Prince Furuhito was asked to become emperor, but he too declined, saying that he would prefer to assist the emperor by becoming a priest and devoutly practicing the way of the Buddha.[10] Whether the succession was actually offered to Furuhito or whether this was an invention of later historians writing from the point of view of Naka no Ōe (Emperor Tenji) is difficult to determine. It is obvious that neither Naka no Ōe nor Kamatari was particularly desirous of Furuhito's accession, and the prince himself was aware how little support he would have enjoyed, with the Soga

[7] Ibid., p. 228.   [8] NHSK, 2: 269. Kōgyoku 4/6/14.   [9] Ibid. Same date.
[10] Ibid. Same date.

leaders now dead. At any rate, Kōgyoku abdicated in favor of Prince Karu, who reigned as Emperor Kōtoku.

The actual effect of Kōgyoku's abdication was to confirm Naka no Ōe as crown prince—a position of great political importance in ancient Japan [11]—and ensure his eventual accession. Her abdication appears to have been motivated by the desire to bring about the latter. That her role was to act as custodian of the imperial position until such time as Naka no Ōe was ready to assume it is further corroborated by the fact that she reascended the throne in 655 upon the death of Kōtoku, while Naka no Ōe remained crown prince. He exercised actual power at court for some thirty years and was the one designated to be emperor, but he seems to have felt that he could accomplish more as crown prince than as emperor.[12] The accession, abdication, and subsequent reaccession of Kōgyoku can only be interpreted as a series of moves designed to preserve the succession for her son Naka no Ōe and to prevent any dynastic schism during a time of great social and political upheaval in Japan.

The sources do not yield any information about the life of Kōgyoku during the period after her abdication. These were the years during which Naka no Ōe, Kamatari, and some of those who had earlier been sent to China for study were hard at work creating a centralized state on the Chinese model, and the records deal largely with their activities. The only real mention of the retired empress states that after abdication she was granted the honorific title "great imperial mother" (sumemioya no mikoto).[13]

The next Japanese sovereign to abdicate was Empress Jitō, the second daughter of Tenji (Naka no Ōe) and consort to his brother, Emperor Temmu. She is recorded as having helped Temmu rule

---

[11] For a discussion of the crown prince as the actual political leader at the Yamato court at this time see Inoue, Kodai kokka, pp. 192–222.

[12] In addition to Inoue, Ienaga Saburō has also argued persuasively that at this time in Japanese history it became customary for the emperor not to rule but to have the crown prince actually handle political matters. See his "Asukachō ni okeru sesshō seiji no honshitsu: Shōtoku taishi sesshō no shiteki chi'i."

[13] NHSK, 2: 271. Kōgyoku 4/6/14.

from the time she was first made consort,[14] and for some four years after his death she seems to have acted as a stand-in and ruled without actually ascending the throne.[15] During these four years her son, Crown Prince Kusakabe, seems to have been the major political figure at court; but after his untimely death at the age of twenty-eight in 689 she finally ascended the throne and reigned for seven years. In 697 she abdicated in favor of Kusakabe's son, Prince Karu (Emperor Mommu), and was granted the honor-ific title "great abdicated sovereign" (dajō tennō)[16] by which all future abdicated sovereigns came to be known.

While once again the sources fail to provide a reason for the abdication, the evidence suggests that it was related to the tense political situation at the time, both within the imperial house and at court. Upon the death of Temmu, the chief claimants to the throne were Crown Prince Kusakabe and Prince Ōtsu. The choice of a successor had not been an easy one for Temmu. Ōtsu was a very popular young man, accomplished in the military arts and yet of high intelligence; his sole fault seems to have been impetuosity, a dislike for conventional procedures.[17] In contrast, Kusakabe seems to have been a weaker man of lesser ability, but he had the advantage of the support of his mother, the future empress Jitō.[18] Temmu seems to have settled upon Kusakabe as crown prince only after long deliberation, since it was not until the tenth year of his reign that Kusakabe was appointed to the position. (The heir apparent was normally designated early in a reign.) Even after Kusakabe's appointment, however, Ōtsu was an important participant in court politics.[19] It is conceivable that Temmu even considered changing his mind. But shortly before

---

[14] NHSK, 2: 485. Jitō 2.

[15] NHSK, 2: 487. Shuchō 1/9/9. This situation whereby one ruled without actu-ally ascending the throne was called shōsei. Naka no Ōe had also ruled in this man-ner from 661 on but had not actually become emperor until 668. For the role of stand-ins, see Jack Goody, "Introduction," in Goody, ed., Succession to High Office.

[16] FSRK, p. 68. Jitō 11/8/1.   [17] Naoki Kōjirō, Jitō tennō, pp. 159–60.

[18] Ibid., pp. 159, 160–61.

[19] Nihon shoki, for example, says that Ōtsu "conducted politics" (chōsei o kiku). NHSK, 2: 457. Temmu 12/2/1. See also Naoki, Jitō tennō, p. 174.

his death Temmu issued an edict declaring that all matters should
be discussed with the empress and crown prince, and Kusakabe's
position appeared unshakable.[20]

Less than a month after Temmu's death, a plot by Prince Ōtsu
was uncovered. He and thirty followers were seized, and although
he himself was executed most of his co-plotters were treated
leniently. This has led to a good deal of speculation by historians
that Ōtsu did not really intend to revolt but was only the victim
of a plot by Empress Jitō to ensure the political future of her son
Kusakabe.[21] At any rate, after Ōtsu's death Jitō seems merely to
have acted ceremonially as empress while Kusakabe handled affairs
of state as crown prince.

When Kusakabe died prematurely in 690, his own son was
only eight years old and unable to deal with the difficult process
of centralization which was taking place at the time. It was only
as a temporary measure at this time that Jitō ascended the throne.
As soon as the young boy (Emperor Mommu) came of age, she
abdicated in his favor and dedicated herself to Buddhist devotions.
Her abdication was prompted by the desire to ensure the accession
of the designated heir of Kusakabe and strongly suggests a typical
role pattern for female sovereigns during the early period of Japanese history.

When Emperor Mommu died after only ten years on the throne,
he was succeeded by his mother, Gemmei, another daughter of
the emperor Tenji. It is clear from the sources that she too became
sovereign only as a temporary measure; the crown prince (the
future emperor Shōmu) was only seven years old and too young
to act as emperor.[22] Since she was the mother of the deceased
emperor rather than his empress, Gemmei's case is somewhat
different from that of previous female rulers. She tried to dispel
any objections to her enthronement by claiming that her accession
was at the urging of Emperor Mommu, who had even tried to

[20] *NHSK*, 2: 479. Shuchō 1/7/15.
[21] Naoki suggests this in *Jitō tennō*, p. 184.   [22] *SNHG*, p. 31. Keiun 4/7/17.

abdicate in her favor; she also said it was in accord with an "immutable law" (*kawarumajiki tsune no nori*) of succession in the senior male line, as established by Tenji.[23] Yet, insofar as she ascended the throne only in order to guarantee the eventual succession of the designated heir, Gemmei's accession is consistent with the general pattern followed by female sovereigns in early Japan. In 715, after eight years as empress, Gemmei indicated a desire to abdicate in favor of Shōmu because of the pressures that the duties of sovereign had brought to bear on her physical and mental state. But since she still felt that Shōmu was too young to rule effectively, she abdicated instead in favor of his sister Genshō.[24]

Although there is no record of her having received the title, Gemmei is referred to as dajō tennō several times in the *Shoku Nihongi*, the second of the official histories, compiled in 797. Like the previous empresses who had abdicated, Gemmei showed no particular inclination toward politics and seems to have devoted herself largely to Buddhism. In 721, due to illness, she shaved her head and took Buddhist vows,[25] becoming the first retired sovereign to do so.

The empress Genshō, then, became sovereign because it was felt that Shōmu was still too young, although he was fifteen at the time. Perhaps because this was a time when much of the foundation of the centralized Japanese state was being laid and there were a number of intense political rivalries at court, Shōmu's accession was postponed. At any rate, like earlier Japanese female sovereigns, Genshō was made empress simply in order to effect a

[23] This "immutable law" is still a matter of great controversy. The prevalent view has been that it was a separate succession law of lineal transfer of the kingship to the eldest son of the sovereign's chief consort. In accord with Gemmei's accession edict, the law has been attributed to Tenji, but it seems strange that Tenji should be responsible for a law he could not himself uphold. (His chief consort, Yamato-hime, was childless.) In a recent, thorough study, Takeda Sachiko has suggested that it was a fictive "law" invented in Gemmei's time to justify the accession of Shōmu. See Takeda Sachiko, " 'Fukai jōten' ni tsuite," pp. 54–66.

[24] *SNHG*, p. 61. Reiki 1/8/2.   [25] *SNHG*, p. 86. Yōrō 5/5/6.

smooth transmission to the recognized male heir. At length, in 724, she abdicated in favor of Shōmu, who reigned for the next twenty-five years.

We have somewhat more information about the activities of Genshō after her abdication than for previous retired sovereigns. After receiving the title of dajō tennō, Genshō appears to have changed her residence frequently. She also made several visits to temples and palaces in the capital region. It is recorded that upon one occasion she issued an edict (*mikotonori*) in which she lamented the fact that, whereas in earlier times everyone had worn hair decorations made of iris flowers to a particular ceremony in the fifth month, the practice had fallen into disuse. Henceforth, she declared, no one would be admitted to the palace for the ceremony without such flowers.[26] Both Jitō and Gemmei are said to have issued mikotonori after abdicating, but these were instructions for their own burial and thus were private matters. Genshō seems to have been the first abdicated sovereign to issue an edict dealing with court affairs.

Few emperors in Japanese history were as devout in the pursuit of Buddhahood as Emperor Shōmu, and it was during his reign that Buddhism became institutionally established in Japan. Shortly after his abdication and receipt of the dajō tennō title in 749, Shōmu took Buddhist vows.[27] Thereafter he devoted himself wholly to Buddhist matters, the most noteworthy of which was the completion of the Tōdai-ji, a temple in the capital at Nara. Since he abdicated in favor of his daughter Kōken, Shōmu broke the "immutable law" of father to son succession; but there was a certain rationale behind this decision. His only son had died, and he seems to have felt that it was better to keep the succession in his own line rather than revert to the earlier principle of brotherly succession.[28] Shōmu's abdication, too, can be seen as intimately related to the transfer of imperial succession to a specific person

---

[26] SNHG, p. 192. Tempyō 19/5/5.
[27] SNHG, pp. 202-3. Tempyō shōhō 1/7/2.   [28] Inoue, *Kodai kokka*, p. 235.

in the hope of avoiding conflict. It was probably not due simply to a desire to throw off worldly cares and concentrate on Buddhist devotions, as is sometimes claimed.

Empress Kōken was one of the strongest female sovereigns in Japanese history and certainly the most controversial. After ten years as sovereign, she abdicated in favor of Emperor Junnin, due largely to the urgings of his supporter, Fujiwara no Nakamaro. Yet, despite her retirement Kōken does not appear to have abandoned politics. Furious at the manner in which Nakamaro used his connection with Junnin to monopolize power at court, Kōken issued an edict in the year 762 declaring that she was "leaving the world to become a disciple of the Buddha." [29] She continued: "In regard to matters of government, the emperor shall carry out regular ceremonies and minor affairs. I will deal with important affairs of state and rewards and punishments." [30] Thereafter she and Dōkyō, a Buddhist priest and chief minister of state as well as her reputed paramour, seem to have conducted politics as they saw fit. When it became obvious that Nakamaro was plotting with the emperor against them, he was forced into revolt and killed. Kōken then deposed the emperor and had him banished to the island of Awaji, thus causing him to be known to history as the deposed emperor of Awaji (Awaji haitei). Kōken then reascended the throne as the empress Shōtoku and entrusted all affairs of state to Dōkyō.

When Shōtoku died in 770 and Dōkyō was discredited, the chief ministers of state selected the major councillor, Prince Shirakabe, to be crown prince and handle all affairs at court.[31] Shōtoku had also left a decree saying that Shirakabe should be made crown prince by virtue of his position as senior imperial prince.[32] Thus, at the age of sixty-two Shirakabe was made first crown prince and then emperor (Kōnin) by the ministers of state,

[29] SNHG, p. 288. Tempyō hōji 6/6/3.
[30] SNHG, pp. 287–88. Tempyō hōji 6/6/3.
[31] FSRK, p. 107. Jingo keiun 4/8/4.   [32] Ibid.

chief among whom were the Fujiwara leaders Nagate, Yoshitsugu, and Momokawa. The son of another imperial prince, Kōnin was the great grandson of Tenji; and his accession represented an important political change since it involved a shift in the line of succession from the descendants of Temmu to those of Tenji.

Kōnin was then an old man, completely dominated by the Fujiwara ministers who were responsible for his accession. In 781, after twelve years as emperor, he abdicated in favor of Prince Yamabe (Emperor Kammu). Originally Kōnin's crown prince had been Osabe, whose mother was a daughter of Shōmu. In 772, however, this lady had been accused of plotting against Kōnin's life. Consequently, she and her son Osabe were thrown into prison, where they died three years later. To replace Osabe as crown prince, Fujiwara Momokawa and his followers had supported Prince Yamabe. Although Yamabe was Kōnin's eldest son and thus the chief candidate, the fact that his mother was of Paekche lineage caused considerable opposition to him. It was only due to the strong support of the Fujiwara that he eventually became crown prince and emperor. Kōnin was in his seventies at the time of his abdication, and perhaps it was his advancing age that prompted his decision. Yet the fact that both Emperor Kōnin and Prince Yamabe had the strong support of the Fujiwara leaders and, further, that it was these men rather than the emperor who made decisions of state suggests that Kōnin was quite possibly coaxed into abdication to guarantee the succession of Yamabe. At any rate, he abdicated, became dajō tennō, and died within eight months.

During Kammu's reign the capital was moved from Nara north to the city of Heian and a new era ushered in. Documentation on abdicated sovereigns becomes much fuller in the Heian period. But before proceeding to the second period of examination, let me summarize the information on the nature of abdication and abdicated sovereigns in this early period of Japanese history.

The Japanese officially recognize the reign of fifty rulers through the Nara period. Of these only seven appear to have abdicated.

The first case of abdication came in the thirty-fifth reign, however, so from that time onward seven of sixteen sovereigns abdicated. More importantly, seven of the eight sovereigns immediately prior to Kammu abdicated; only Mommu, who died while on the throne, did not. Thus the practice was already well established by the end of the Nara period, and in the Heian period it became customary procedure for the succession to be transmitted by abdication.

Japanese scholars consider the frequency of abdication in the history of their country a result of the fact that the emperor was required to participate in a great number of court ceremonies and rituals which were extremely onerous. Particularly after the increasing monopolization of actual power by the Fujiwara regents in the Heian period, the "job" of emperor became a matter of performing tedious rituals, with little actual power, and thus emperors longed to retire to a more pleasant style of life. While this is considered the major motivation behind the frequent abdications, there were, it is recognized, more immediate personal reasons such as illness, a desire to devote oneself to Buddhist devotions, impending death, and so on.

The focus of such an analysis by Japanese scholars is solely upon personal factors which caused individual emperors to abdicate in favor of something more desirable. It sees abdication as a negative act taken for purely private reasons. Such an analysis tends to obscure the political import of abdication, which was, after all, a highly political act. The transmission of imperial succession was extremely important, involving the continuation of the dynastic line. And the Japanese have for some time been extremely proud of the long duration of their dynasty. Thus, as a means of ensuring continuity in imperial succession, abdication could have been, and I believe was, a crucial political act.

It is in connection with the problem of imperial succession that the practice of abdication first developed in Japan. The earliest examples occurred when the imperial kin group was attempting to consolidate its hegemony over the other great uji. One reason this was difficult was the frequency of succession disputes, which eroded its internal solidarity and invited the formation of factions around the opposing claimants for the throne. It has been customary to view early Japanese imperial succession as having been from father to son, with the later examples of brother to brother as exceptions; but the situation seems actually to have been the reverse.[33] By around the fifth century, when our records become relatively reliable, one can detect the existence of two separate elements in imperial succession. In imitation of the Chinese practice, the eldest son of the emperor possessed from birth the qualification for becoming emperor. But at the same time father to son succession was limited by the concept of the great elder brother (ōe). Succession passed to the eldest son of the emperor, who was designated ōe, but then it passed to the ōe's brothers until the fraternal line was exhausted. Then it reverted to the eldest son of the ōe. It was a rather complex blending of lineal and fraternal, or lateral, succession. This appears to have been similar to the practice in other uji during this period and indicates a process of change from fraternal succession to a father-son pattern.

The result of this complex situation was that on the death of an emperor there were often two persons having claims to succession: his brother and his eldest son. There were a number of occasions in early Japanese history when disputes broke out between two such claimants. The classic example, of course, is the Jinshin War of 672, in which the brother of the deceased emperor Tenji defeated the latter's eldest son and became Emperor Temmu. Tenji, a strong advocate of the adoption of Chinese practices, had tried to bypass his brother in favor of his son according to Chinese principles but the attempt ended in failure.

Because of the distinct possibility of such succession disputes, there must have been considerable apprehension at the impend-

---

[33] The following ideas on imperial succession in early Japan are largely those of Inoue Mitsusada, with the exception of the discussion of practice of abdication, about which he has nothing to say. Inoue, *Kodai kokka*, pp. 179–218 passim.

ing death of an emperor. Again the classic example of this is the case of Tenji. He went to great lengths, including at least twice having his chief ministers swear to support his son after his death, to ensure a smooth succession. The practice of having the main consort of an emperor succeed him as sovereign had developed as a safety device to avoid conflict between two or more claimants for the throne. An examination of all the female rulers in Japan in the period after historical records become reliable shows that the reason for their accession was in every case to avoid a possible schism in the royal group over the issue of succession.[34]

It seems clear to me that abdication, which developed in Japan at the same time as this practice of female rulers serving as stop-gaps to prevent succession disputes, arose as a corollary to female accession. An empress came to the throne simply to avoid succession troubles and ensure transmission of the succession to the proper person. Once the troubles had been settled—one of the claimants had died, for example, or a younger crown prince had come of age—then there was no longer any need for the empress to remain on the throne. Thus abdication was a convenient, and actually the only, means for realizing the accession of the properly designated person without waiting for the empress to die. This I believe was the reason for the development of the practice of abdication by Japanese sovereigns in the seventh century.

A look at the first sovereigns to abdicate shows that five of seven were women. More importantly, the first four were female. They all reigned during the post-Taika period when the imperial kin group was attempting to reaffirm its authority over the other uji, and they all abdicated in order to effect a smooth transmission of the imperial position to the designated male heir. Only thereafter did the practice of abdication come to be utilized by male sovereigns as well. Abdication was another means of ensuring a successful transfer of the title without conflict between different claimants. After the reign of the Empress Kōken/Shōtoku, female rule was discontinued because it had proved unsuccessful, but

[34] Ibid., p. 224.

abdication was retained and heavily relied upon as the surest means of guaranteeing a peaceful transfer of the imperial succession. This was the reason that the practice of abdication developed in Japan, and we must not overlook the important political aspect of this act.

Thus by an examination of the reasons for these early instances of abdication in Japan we have discovered something about the origins and nature of the practice. The other questions to which we were seeking answers cannot be answered for these early sovereigns on the basis of the material available today. The relationship between the retired and titular sovereigns is unclear. Ex-sovereigns were mothers, grandmothers, or fathers of titular rulers, but that is all we know. As such exalted personages—with the title of dajō tennō—and as senior members of the imperial kin group, ex-sovereigns must have enjoyed a considerable degree of authority within the dynastic nobility. In society at large, however, it is difficult to ascribe any role to abdicated emperors and empresses at this time. It appears that many of the abdicated sovereigns in the early period, especially the women, devoted much of their time to religious activities. The ex-empress Genshō showed some concern for court affairs, but only Kōken displayed a great determination to participate in politics after her abdication. Furthermore, the records at this time do not yield a clear picture of the nature of the household organization and financial support that these ex-sovereigns had. We can only assume that they probably had some sort of administrative machinery and that they received some form of stipend, much like the ex-sovereigns in the Heian period.

Heizei to En'yū, 806–991

Abdication became more frequent in the Heian period, reaching a point where it was the practice for almost all sovereigns. But despite its frequency abdication never lost the very important political function it had been developed to perform. Succession within the Japanese imperial line continued to be complex, and no one pattern became clearly established. Both fraternal and lineal patterns were followed, although the Chinese practice of passing succession from father to son was the ideal. Some emperors wished the succession to be passed among their sons, while a number of emperors showed great hesitation to abdicate in favor of a younger brother. The trend was definitely toward transferring the succession within one's own direct line.

Situations frequently arose in which an emperor was faced with a choice between naming his brother as successor according to his father's wishes or passing the succession to his own son. Claimants to the throne were usually brothers or sons of the emperor, but succession disputes were generally avoided, largely due to the increased reliance upon abdication, coupled with early preemption of the succession. Quite often the focus of abdication was the position of crown prince. Abdication settled the immediate issue of the next emperor, but the simultaneous designation of the crown prince was crucial in determining the direction of the succession. Thus on many occasions abdication was a technique not simply for passing the imperial title to the next emperor but for keeping the succession in a particular line by guaranteeing the appointment of the crown prince and future successor. Examples of this are numerous.

The emperor Kammu had forty-two offspring by various women, and he wished to pass the throne among his sons. But at the beginning of his reign his younger brother, Prince Sawara, was made crown prince. Subsequently Sawara was implicated in the murder of Fujiwara no Tanetsugu during an abortive attempt to move the capital to Nagaoka. He was exiled and killed, and Kammu made his own son, Prince Ate, crown prince in 785. After Kammu's death this son became the emperor Heizei in 806. He reigned for three years, during which time he continued his father's attempts to reinvigorate the declining *ritsuryō* system by the adoption of such measures as the appointment of provincial inspectors.

In 809 Heizei abdicated in favor of his brother, Crown Prince Kamino (Emperor Saga), not because of his own desire, but because his father had wished it.[35] The conditions surrounding his abdication and the subsequent events are recorded in the third of

[35] Kitayama Shigeo, *Nihon no rekishi*, vol. 4: *Heian-kyō*, p. 104.

the six national histories, the *Nihon kōki,* and deserve examination in some detail.[36] Heizei abdicated after a prolonged illness and on the same day had his own son, Prince Takaoka, named crown prince. Shortly thereafter, the ex-emperor sought a cure for his illness by moving to several different locations within the capital. After five such moves, he at length established his palace at the old capital of Nara, where he spent the remaining years of his life. The *Nihon kōki* attributes the decision to move to Nara not to the ex-emperor but to his favorite palace attendant, Fujiwara no Kusuko.

Kusuko first came to know Heizei when he was crown prince and her daughter was made his consort. She subsequently became so intimate with him that the emperor Kammu was appalled at their conduct and had her dismissed from court. But when Heizei succeeded his father, he recalled her and she came to exercise great power within the women's quarters as a palace attendant (*naishi*). In fact, the *Nihon kōki* records that Kusuko even went so far as to issue edicts without Heizei's authorization. Because of Kusuko's close connection with the emperor, her brother Nakanari also came to be a power at court, and after Heizei's abdication they both continued to serve him.

Even in retirement, Heizei continued to issue orders as though he were still emperor.[37] Six months after abdication, for example, he ordered a new palace built in Nara and appointed commissioners to supervise the building, Sakanoue no Tamuramaro, Fujiwara no Fuyutsugu, and Ki no Taue among them. The province of Yamato was ordered to allot its rice tax to the construction of this new palace. When Heizei moved into the palace even before its completion, he took the entire staff of the women's quarters and half of the courtiers with him. Those who accompanied him were Fujiwara no Manatsu, Akishino no Yasundo, Fujiwara no Ōtomo, Funya no Watamaro, Ta no Iruka, and Ōnakatomi no Kiyomaro. This brought about a situation of great confusion, and in one of

---

[36] The information concerning the abdication of Heizei and the revolt of Kusuko and Nakanari comes from *NHKK,* pp. 84–91 passim.

[37] See, for example, *NHKK,* p. 85. Kōnin 1/9/6.

his edicts the emperor Saga accused Heizei of having created two separate courts.[38]

There was considerable grumbling about this movement of men and material to Nara, and finally Saga determined to take action against the ex-emperor and those around him. He had Nakanari seized and imprisoned in the headquarters of the right division of the palace guards and then appointed governor of Sado in preparation for his banishment to that distant island. He further ordered Kusuko stripped of her ranks and offices. Then he issued an edict blaming Kusuko and Nakanari for the split in the court. This angered Heizei, and he and Kusuko set out for the capital leading a body of troops. When Saga heard this, he ordered Tamuramaro and Watamaro to guard the approaches to the city.[39] He further ordered Nakanari put to death. Finding the city militarily prepared, the ex-emperor's troops fled, and the revolt came to an end. Kusuko poisoned herself, and Heizei returned to Nara, where he shaved his head and became a monk.

As a result of the revolt, those courtiers who had followed Heizei to the old capital were demoted and exiled. Furthermore, Heizei's son, Prince Takaoka, was replaced as crown prince by another son of the emperor Kammu in accordance with Kammu's wishes. Heizei had hoped to be succeeded by his offspring, but after the accession of Junna—the third son of Kammu—imperial succession remained in Saga's line. The Fujiwara clan also underwent a major disaster. The *shikike* (ceremonial) branch of the Fujiwara, which had attained great power at court during Tanetsugu's time, came to an end when both Nakanari and Kusuko were killed. In its stead, the northern branch (*hokke*) flourished under Fuyutsugu, a trusted courtier of the emperor Saga. Eventually this branch of the family came to dominate the Fujiwara clan and the entire court.

[38] Ibid. Kōnin 1/9/10.
[39] As we have seen, Funya no Watamaro was one of those who joined the ex-emperor at the old capital, but he was ordered to return to Kyoto by Saga. Saga intended to imprison Watamaro, but on the advice of Tamuramaro, who had a high respect for his military capabilities, he was made a commander of the force that defended the capital against the troops of the ex-sovereign.

The politics of Heizei's abdication were thus quite complex. He appears to have been ill and to have abdicated in favor of Saga in order to install his own son as crown prince and heir to the throne. This would have shifted imperial succession from his brothers to his own direct descendants. His attempt ended in failure, however, when Saga replaced Crown Prince Takaoka with another brother of the late emperor Kammu. Traditional accounts have placed the entire blame for the revolt upon Kusuko and, to a lesser extent, Nakanari: the ill (perhaps even mentally unstable) Heizei was urged to reascend the throne by these two when they saw their power at court diminish after Heizei's abdication. Indeed the political scheming of Kusuko and Nakanari was an important factor in the eventual outbreak of hostilities between Heizei and Saga, but Heizei must shoulder a good deal of the responsibility. It is quite obvious that he was gravely concerned with ensuring the succession of his own direct descendants. Perhaps the fact that Saga also became ill shortly after his accession gave Heizei cause to fear that Saga's death or prolonged illness might lead to an attempt to divert succession to the brotherly line, in accord with Kammu's wishes. At any rate, there was a serious disagreement between the ex-emperor and the emperor over the matter of imperial succession.

This was the first time in Japanese history that there had ever been an elder brother–younger brother relationship between the abdicated and titular emperors. Previously all abdicated sovereigns had been parents or grandparents of the emperor, senior members of the imperial group who had generally displayed an attitude of loving guidance toward the sovereign. Emperors, in turn, seem to have shown great filial respect for such retired sovereigns. In this case, however, the dominant feeling between the two was definitely animosity. Neither one could lay claim to a superior position within the imperial house; indeed it appears that both were fighting to establish their own claim to imperial leadership.

We have seen that a number of courtiers chose to follow Heizei to the old capital, but it is unclear in what capacity they served him. We do know that he had some form of administrative organization as there is mention in the sources of *shoeifu kanjin* (guards and officials) and *shoshi* (officials) for Heizei's palace.[40] This would appear to be the first reference in Japanese history to a body of officials who served the various needs of the abdicated sovereign, and it hints at the development of the extensive system of *inshi* (officials of the ex-emperor) that appears in later records. Furthermore, we saw that the retired emperor had the use of some of the tax revenues from Yamato province for the construction of his palace, so it appears that he received official allotments for the conduct of his affairs.

Saga was ill when he became emperor through the abdication of his brother Heizei, so ill in fact that he even had Fujiwara no Sonohito return the sacred mirror.[41] Immediately afterward he was faced with the revolt of Kusuko and Nakanari and the machinations of the retired emperor. It was in order to deal with this situation that Saga instituted the *kurōdo-dokoro* (sovereign's private office). He appointed Fujiwara no Fuyutsugu and Kose no Notari as the first *kurōdo no tō*,[42] or chief secretaries, to coordinate the administration of this new office, the purpose of which was to handle secret documents to prevent their falling into the hands of the rival faction of Kusuko and ex-Emperor Heizei. This kurododokoro, an extracodal office which ultimately developed into an official imperial organ, was chiefly responsible for the issuance of edicts based upon the orders of the sovereign. Prior to its establishment, however, edicts, called *naishisen*, were most frequently issued by the *naishi no tsukasa* (office of palace attendants). The naishi no tsukasa was provided for in the codes and was the highest office within the women's quarters. It was this office that Fujiwara no Kusuko had headed when she exercised so much power during the reign of Heizei; she had issued naishisen that covered matters not actually sanctioned by the emperor. In Saga's time, however, edicts were issued through the sovereign's private office by his secretaries,

[40] *NHKK*, p. 103. Kōnin 2/7/13.
[41] *NHKR*, 1: 314. Kōnin 14/4/16.
[42] Only the *Kugyō bunin* mentions the establishment of this office, in 810. *KGBN*, 1: 84.

all of whom were men. This fact has led a number of scholars to the conclusion that at least some of the functions that were once handled by women in the office of palace attendants were shifted to the men who served in the kurōdo-dokoro.[43]

When Heizei abdicated, all the women from the women's quarters and half of the court officials accompanied him to the old capital, which made the conduct of politics difficult for the new emperor Saga. As we have seen above, because the emperor's subsequent illness caused him even more difficulty in dealing with governmental matters, he set up the sovereign's private office to replace the office of palace attendants; and, aware of the power that Kusuko was able to exercise because of the hold she had on Heizei, he decided to appoint male secretaries.[44] This office came to work very closely with the emperor and the imperial house, and it was very important in the development by the imperial house of an administrative apparatus of its own.

In the fourth month of 823, Saga moved to a palace called the Reizei-in,[45] and on the same day he informed Fujiwara no Fuyutsugu that he intended to abdicate in favor of his brother (Junna). Fuyutsugu was against such a plan, because he felt the poor crop conditions in the past few years might make it difficult to support two ex-emperors as well as the emperor.[46] Given the fidelity of the Fujiwara leaders to the ritsuryō governmental system

[43] Watanabe Naohiko, "Saga inshi no kenkyū," p. 58.
[44] Ibid., p. 58.
[45] *NHKR*, 1: 314. Kōnin 14/4/10.
[46] Heizei was still alive so both he and Saga would be ex-sovereigns at the same time, requiring substantial allotments to provide for their livelihood. Fuyutsugu's argument was certainly a valid one. Finance had been a major divisive issue at court since Kammu's time. It was apparent to all that the financial base of the court was shrinking with the increasing impracticability of the allotment field system (*kubunden*) and the growth of large tax-free tracts of land. This financial problem—decreasing resources and increasing expenditures—had been the basis of the earlier dispute between Fujiwara no Otsugu and Sugano no Mamichi: whether to cut back expenditures or continue with great building projects. During Heizei's reign there were a number of emergency measures to curtail economic decline, and the leaders of the main branch of the Fujiwara family—Uchimaro, Sonohito, Otsugu, and Fuyutsugu—had supported economy measures by returning to the throne special land grants alloted to the clan for service they had rendered to the state.

and their commitment to public land control in this early period, Fuyutsugu's concern appears to have been a genuine one. His worry over economy was so great that at one point he pleaded successfully with the emperor Junna to cut the expenses involved in the *Dajō'e* ("Great Thanksgiving") ceremony.

Saga informed Fuyutsugu that he was determined to abdicate and could not be dissuaded. In later years Saga claimed that he abdicated in order to escape the bonds of office and enjoy the beauty of nature, but he also seems to have had a political motive. Just like the emperor Heizei, Saga abdicated in favor of a younger brother and at the same time made his own son crown prince, demonstrating a clear intention to keep the succession in his own line and away from that of Heizei. Although the records say that another son of Kammu was offered the position and "refused," Saga's desire to guarantee his son's eventual succession seems quite clear. Heizei and his offspring were not completely impotent at this time. Prince Takaoka had been allowed to return from exile and was even promoted, and another son, Prince Abo, had also been promoted. Heizei himself enjoyed eminent stature as dajō tennō.

Furthermore, Saga's actions immediately after his abdication indicate that he did not wish to cut himself off completely from court politics to enjoy the beauties of nature. As we have seen, he resided first at the Reizei-in, a palace that seems to have been built sometime during his reign. It was a substantial edifice located just to the southeast corner of the imperial palace, right in the path of courtiers on their way to and from the palace, an ominous reminder of the fact that the ex-emperor was still very much at the center of court affairs. Perhaps the very location of the residence was ample indication that Saga was taking great pains to see that the course of politics—and imperial succession—did not run counter to his desires. If he was not concerned with such matters, he could have moved to the outskirts of the city. Instead, he remained right in the midst of the bustle of court activities.

And yet during the reign of Junna there is a little indication of Saga's involvement in politics at court. The most conspicuous ex-

ample came in 824—one month and two days after thc death of
Heizei—when Saga issued an edict pardoning the courtiers who
had been involved in Kusuko's revolt and allowing them to return
to the capital.[47] Although this had been a major affair of state, involving an attempt to dethrone an emperor, it was concluded not
by imperial edict but an edict of the retired emperor. Perhaps it
was thought that, because Saga had been emperor at the time of
the revolt, it was more appropriate for him to bring the matter to
conclusion. Still, nothing in the legal statutes of the times gave the
ex-emperor the right to issue edicts or in any way to participate in
politics: the only reference to dajō tennō in the codes mentioned
that it was an honorific title given to a sovereign upon his abdication.

Saga's activities during the rest of Junna's reign were limited, it
would appear from the sources, to nonpolitical matters such as
poetry banquets, hunting parties, and imperial house affairs. Among
the latter were such things as formal visits as well as other meetings
with female members of the imperial house and visits by Saga's
own princes and those who had been given the surname of
Minamoto.[48] He also held a celebration for the young prince who
was born to the emperor Junna in 826.[49] And in 831 Saga held the
coming-of-age ceremony for one of his grandsons, Minamoto no
Sadamu.[50] Thus most of the activities of the ex-emperor Saga during the reign of Junna seem to have been confined to overseeing
affairs within the imperial house. After the death of Heizei, Saga
was the senior member of the imperial house, and he seems to have
functioned as the head of the house, a role that becomes clearer
during the reign of the next emperor, Nimmyō.

Early in the year 833 the emperor Junna moved his residence to
the Sai-in in order to prepare for abdication.[51] This palace, later re-

---

[47] NHKR, 1: 319. Tenchō 1/8/9.
   [48] These were the sons of Prince Katsuwara. Earlier in the same year the prince
had requested permission to grant them the surname but had been refused. NHKR,
1: 320. Tenchō 2/3/24.
   [49] NHKR, 1: 324. Tenchō 5/5/20.   [50] NHKR, 1: 331. Tenchō 8/2/7.
   [51] NHKR, 1: 334–35. Tenchō 10/2/24–28.

named the Junna-in, was selected to be the retirement palace for Junna, and officials were appointed to staff it prior to his abdication. Four days later he abdicated in favor of Nimmyō, Saga's eldest son, while at the same time his own son Prince Tsunesada was made crown prince. For the second time in Japanese history there were two retired sovereigns at the same time. This time, however, the relationship between the two men was quite cordial and no trouble arose. Saga, father of the emperor, was the senior of the two retired sovereigns, and in all respects he acted as the head of the imperial house. Junna was also given the title of dajō tennō; he was known as *nochi no dajō tennō*, or junior retired sovereign, while Saga was called *saki no dajō tennō*, senior retired sovereign. Saga and his favorite, the great empress dowager Tachibana no Kachiko, moved from the Reizei-in to a new palace, the Saga-in.

Traditional records give no reason at all for Junna's abdication, but in this case too the politics of succession seem to have been intimately involved. Saga apparently wished to have his own son on the throne while he was retired sovereign, perhaps because it would enable him to exert a good deal of political influence and also to establish imperial succession in his own line. It would appear that he named one of Junna's sons as crown prince and successor in return for Junna's abdication. Junna was not ill, did not devote himself exclusively to Buddhism, and continued to be on good terms with Saga after abdication. Saga's increased power as head of the imperial house and father of the emperor Nimmyō suggests that it was at Saga's urging that Junna abdicated.

During Nimmyō's reign Saga exerted a very strong influence in court politics, and on at least four occasions he made important political decisions. In 834 Saga went hunting on an estate belonging to the minister of the right, Kiyowara no Natsuno, after which he made appointments of rank to three of Natsuno's sons.[52] The appointments were made in an edict (*choku*) but it is not precisely clear who issued the edict. Most likely it was issued by the

[52] *SNHKK*, p. 26. Jōwa 1/4/21.

proper offices within the Grand Council of State (Dajōkan) at
Saga's suggestion. Also in 837 the ex-sovereign awarded ranks to
those who had accompanied him on a hunting trip.[53] Here it is
clear that the edict for the appointment was issued at Saga's "suggestion" (*fushi*), which strongly suggests that the earlier case was
handled similarly.

In 838 Ono no Takamura was exiled to the Oki Islands because
of the wrath of the abdicated sovereign.[54] Takamura had been appointed deputy envoy to T'ang China to accompany the envoy
Fujiwara no Tsunetsugu. Their first attempt to reach China had
ended in failure, and on the occasion of their second effort a
quarrel broke out between the two men, and Takamura refused to
go. Instead he wrote a poem lampooning the post of envoy to
China and thus incurred the ex-emperor's wrath. Saga and the entire court at this time were greatly enamored of Chinese culture,
and such an insult quite understandably brought on his great anger.

Shortly before his death in 840, the junior retired sovereign Junna
discussed the matter of his burial with the crown prince.[55] He requested that his bones be crushed and scattered over the earth.
Deeply concerned over the impoverishment of the country, he
cautioned simplicity and frugality to avoid great expense by the
country. The middle councillor Fujiwara no Yoshino felt that this
would be an extremely undignified act: all previous emperors had
been buried in proper tombs and so should Junna. Unable to reach
a decision, the courtiers referred the matter to the senior retired
emperor Saga, who decided in favor of Junna's request. Six days
after his death, Junna's bones were pulverized and, as requested,
scattered on the top of Nishiyama, a mountain in Ōharano.[56]

On a number of occasions, then, during the reigns of Junna and
Nimmyō—the latter's in particular—the retired emperor Saga
either made political decisions or significantly influenced them. On
at least one occasion he issued an edict just as though he were still
emperor, although there was no legal basis for him to do so. The

[53] Ibid., p. 69. Jōwa 4/10/28.   [54] Ibid., p. 81. Jōwa 5/12/15.
[55] Ibid., p. 102. Jōwa 7/5/6.   [56] Ibid., p. 103. Jōwa 7/5/13.

authority that Saga was able to exercise came not from any institutional position but derived rather from the fact that he functioned as head of the imperial house. As elder brother, and then father, of the emperor, he was able to exert a good deal of familial authority over the emperor. That he held such a position in the imperial house is obvious from the fact that he made a number of decisions that involved familial matters—Junna's burial, succession, and so on. Further proof can be found by examining the relationship between Saga and the emperors Junna and Nimmyō.

As mentioned above, with the abdication of Junna relations within the imperial house became quite complex: there were two retired sovereigns, a great empress dowager, and an emperor. At the beginning of the new year (834) the emperor made a number of formal visits, variously styled as *chōkin* and *ekkin*, to both retired sovereigns and the great empress dowager. By the next year the procedure for these visits had become somewhat regularized. On the third day of the new year, the emperor paid a formal familial visit (chōkin) to his parents Saga and Kachiko. Thereafter this ceremony was repeated yearly; after the death of Saga, the emperor continued to pay such formal visits to the great empress dowager. This practice later became a standard court ceremony, where the emperor every new year paid this formal visit to the retired sovereign.

These early-ninth-century developments seem to indicate a complete reversal of the Chinese principles of imperial government that had been imported into Japan. Under the Chinese pattern, the emperor was to be the Son of Heaven, exalted and powerful above all, having no father and mother, the human embodiment of the state structure. Yet here we find the emperor formally visiting his father, the retired sovereign, as a dutiful son and treating him with honor and respect beyond that which should have been due the emperor himself. Beneath the facade of Chinese institutions of government, the traditional Japanese familial society continued to exert a strong influence on the conduct of affairs. Here quite clearly the private, familial relationship between imperial house members took precedence over the public relationship which should have placed the emperor in the position of highest respect and authority.

Prior to this time, however, the emperor does seem to have retained the highest measure of respect and authority within the imperial family in accord with his public position. For example, even though the retired sovereign Genshō was his mother, Emperor Shōmu appears never to have directly petitioned her in any form but rather contacted her through the good offices of Tachibana no Moroe, emphasizing exclusively the public nature of the office. Another instance of this position can be seen when the empress Kōken abdicated. In her edict of abdication she expressed sorrow over the fact that as empress she had not been able to fulfill the filial duties that she owed to her mother, the empress dowager Kōmyō.

Yet in the Heian period the situation changed. After his abdication, Saga corresponded with the emperor by "offering up a letter" (*jōsho*), but in reply the emperor referred to himself by the term *shin*, or subject. In a communication from Saga to his elder brother the retired emperor Heizei, Saga too referred to himself as shin. From the time that Saga became retired sovereign, all communications from the emperor to the retired emperor came in the form of "offering up an epistle" (*jōhyō*), and the emperor always referred to himself as shin. This was exactly the form in which a courtier petitioned the emperor. Thus from Saga's time on the private relationships between members of the imperial house came to be of greater import than the public relationships stemming from the theoretical position of the emperor.

It is also during Saga's years as retired sovereign that we see considerable development of the administrative apparatus supporting the person of the abdicated emperor. Although some form of organization had existed previously, it appears that not until Saga's time was a coherent system of officials for the ex-emperor developed. As noted earlier, these officials who served the needs of the retired sovereign were called *inshi*, or officials of the retired emperor's palace. Saga lived in the Reizei-in and then the Saga-in; officials who were appointed to serve at these palaces were called inshi. At this time the term *in* referred only to the palace of the ex-emperor, but sometime later the man himself came to be referred to as *in*, and from that time on inshi may be regarded as ex-emperor's officials. At this early point, however, they seem to have been considered officials who served at the palace of the retired emperor.

There is no record of Saga having appointed inshi at any specific time, but the *Montoku jitsuroku*, an official history completed in 879 which covers the reign of Emperor Montoku, mentions a number of persons as having been inshi for the ex-sovereign Saga.[57] Among these were: Minabuchi no Nagakawa, Fujiwara no Mitsumori, Abe no Yasundo, Nagamine no Takana, Takahashi no Bunyamaro, and Prince Masayuki. Beyond these there were certainly a number of women and servants who attended to Saga's personal wants. The backgrounds and official careers of these inshi indicate certain patterns. Many of them were persons close to Saga all his life who had served as secretary (kurōdo) or chief secretary (kurōdo no tō) during his reign; after his abdication they were appointed *bettō*, or director, the highest rank among the inshi. The others were men with specific technical skills, such as document drafters and Confucian teachers. After Saga's time, there developed a fairly definite pattern of appointments as inshi, a ladder whose rungs included secretary to the crown prince, kurōdo, and at the top inshi, or rather bettō. The system of inshi clearly had its beginnings during Saga's years.

These inshi served at the Reizei-in and the Saga-in, two palaces that seem to have been built during Saga's reign, although no exact dates are known. The first reference to the Reizei-in is in 816, when Saga held a poetry recitation there; a number of the participating courtiers were rewarded with grants.[58] A later encyclopedia of ancient court practices, the *Shūgaishō*, gives the name of the

---

[57] These names are easily found in the *Montoku jitsuroku*. N. Watanabe's "Saga inshi" has a very useful analysis of their background which I have summarized here.

[58] *Ruijū kokushi*, 1: 174.

Reizei-in as the Kōnin-tei (Kōnin palace) which has led scholars to conclude that it was built sometime during the Kōnin era (810–823).[59] And since Saga visited it in 816 the date of construction must have been between 810 and 816. It was thus used as a detached, temporary palace by the emperor for entertainment and diversion during his reign, and it can be assumed that some means of support and a number of attendants were necessary for the upkeep of the Reizei-in. Only after his abdication do we know positively that Saga appointed officials (inshi) to handle affairs at the Reizei-in.

The Saga-in is first mentioned in the unofficial history *Nihon kiryaku*, two years before the first record of the Reizei-in, in 814,[60] when the emperor Saga held a poetry recitation there after hunting in Kitano. While the Reizei-in was located next to the imperial palace, the Saga-in was to the northwest of the city in Kadono district. During his reign Saga visited this palace—also referred to as "Saga no bekkan" (Saga detached residence) and "Saga-shō" (Saga manor)—a number of times for such hunting parties and banquets. As was the case with the Reizei-in, monies and a staff of attendants for the management of the palace were necessary, and we can assume that they were provided. Later these two palaces were frequently used as residences by abdicated sovereigns, and the common term that was applied to them was *goin*, or retirement palaces.

On a number of occasions while the ex-emperors Saga and Junna were using these palaces after their abdication waste fields were allotted for their support.[61] Besides this type of economic support, the ex-emperors also received sustenance households (*fuko*) from the government. Saga received at least two thousand, while the great empress dowager Kachiko, who resided with him, received

---

[59] Yashiro Kuniji, "Goin no kō," p. 39.

[60] *NHKR*, 1: 300. Kōnin 5/7*/27. (An asterisk after the month indicates that it was an intercalary month.)

[61] According to the *Shoku Nihongi*, there were at least three such allotments totaling 184 *chō* for the Reizei-in and 507 chō for the Saga-in (one chō equaled 2.94 acres). Mezaki Tokue, "Seijishijō no Saga jōkō," p. 22.

another fifteen hundred.[62] Together the two of them had a considerable amount of financial support, but it was certainly not excessive in comparison with what some of the courtiers of the time enjoyed.[63] At a time when the court was having financial difficulties, this might, perhaps, seem to have been unwise, especially when Fujiwara leaders like Otsugu and Fuyutsugu had returned many of their sustenance households to the public coffers to alleviate the situation. It must be remembered, however, that these courtiers received a number of regular emoluments according to their official position and rank: sustenance households provided additional income beyond these. The ex-sovereign was not an official and consequently did not receive payments for performing an official job. He had to depend largely upon such sustenance households for his economic support. At a later point in history it was precisely this matter of continued economic support for their livelihood—and that of the entire imperial house—that was to be of such concern to retired sovereigns.

That such economic problems were of great concern to the imperial house during Saga's time is reflected in the appearance of the goin, or retirement palace, sometime during the reigns of Junna and Nimmyō. In the Heian period the goin fulfilled three functions: [64] (1) it served as a temporary palace to which the em-

---

[62] *NHKR*, 1: 316 (Kōnin 14/6/2), lists 1,500 fuko for Saga, and p. 319 (Tenchō 1/8/8) lists 500 more. The 1,500 for Kachiko were granted on the same day as the 1,500 for Saga. Sustenance households were granted to both imperial house members and high-ranking courtiers in Nara and early Heian times. The individual received as income half (later all) the rice tax as well as the taxes in kind from a fixed number of households.

[63] In the case of courtiers, sustenance households consisted of a number of different types: *ifu*, which were awarded on the basis of rank (*i*); *shikifu*, which were granted in terms of office (*shiki*); and *kōfu*, which were awarded for meritorious service (*kō*). At one point in his career, for example, Fujiwara no Kamatari received 15,000 sustenance households for life. At another point he returned 5,000 to imperial control, and later he received another 3,000. Other Fujiwara leaders during the Nara and early Heian period returned these privately controlled sustenance households to the public realm to ease the growing economic problem.

[64] Hashimoto Yoshihiko, "Goin ni tsuite," p. 15. This is an extremely well conceived and documented article which tries to clarify some of the generalizations and oversights in the works of Yashiro Kuniji and Nakamura Naokatsu.

peror could move for some special reason, such as after the destruction of the main palace by fire; (2) it functioned as a retirement palace for the emperor after abdication; and (3) it acted as an office for administering the private landholdings and wealth of the emperor. It appears that the first two functions developed sometime in the mid-Heian period; in the beginning the goin seems to have functioned entirely as an administrative office for imperial house lands and revenue.[65] Scholars have not yet agreed upon an identification of the goin—whether the Reizei-in was what the sources were referring to when the term goin was used, or whether there was a separate palace called the goin. By mid-Heian times one of the emperor's detached villas was designated as a goin while he was emperor and officials were appointed to operate it; after abdication he moved there, and it was no longer called goin but rather the palace of the ex-emperor. There seems to be no proof that this was the case in the early Heian period. What seems certain is that the imperial family was attempting to establish its own bloc of privately controlled lands in order to compete with the great courtier families and Buddhist institutions who were acquiring shōen; thus there are numerous textual references to goin fields, goin edict fields, goin pastures, and the like. Judging from Saga's activities as emperor and ex-emperor, it is understandable that an attempt to bolster the economic foundations of the imperial kin group began while he was retired sovereign and head of the imperial house.

In retrospect, it is clear that Saga expended a great deal of energy in strengthening the imperial house. As emperor, he sought to revamp the institutions directly connected with the personal life of the sovereign and his conduct of governmental affairs through the creation of the sovereign's private office. He abdicated in order to ensure the succession of his own line and to prevent its passing to the descendants of his brother Heizei. He was abdicated sovereign during the reigns of his younger brother and his son, and during this time he asserted himself as the functioning head of the imperial

---

[65] Mezaki, "Seijishijō no Saga jōkō", pp. 20–26 passim. Mezaki has added a few refinements to Hashimoto's conclusions, stressing the fact that initially the function of the goin was purely an economic one.

house and enjoyed great political influence. He dealt with all the strictly private matters of the imperial house and played an advisory role in court politics, even making a number of important political decisions. He was responsible for the construction of at least two palaces which continued to be used by later emperors and other royal personages. It was during his years as abdicated sovereign that a system of officials to handle the ex-emperor's affairs took shape and an attempt was made to secure a private economic base for the imperial house outside the ritsuryō governmental structure.

While the two ex-emperors Saga and Junna were alive, they seem to have worked out an arrangement for succession: Saga's son Nimmyō was made emperor and Junna's son, Prince Tsunesada, became his crown prince. But Nimmyō subsequently had a son, Michiyasu, by a daughter of Fujiwara no Fuyutsugu, and there was considerable pressure brought to bear by influential Fujiwara courtiers to have Michiyasu made crown prince. The emperor himself seemed agreeable to such an arrangement, and at one point Tsunesada did try to yield in favor of Michiyasu. But while they were alive the two ex-emperors would not allow such a move. Junna died in 840, but Saga lived for another two years. Shortly before his death a plot was uncovered which brought about a change in the succession arrangement. This was the "revolt" in 842 of Tomo no Kowamine, an attendant of the crown prince, and Tachibana no Hayanari, the provisional governor of Tajima.

According to the sources,[66] these two had planned to take Tsunesada eastward and raise a revolt. They had enlisted the support of Prince Abo, but he leaked the information to Kachiko, the great empress dowager, only five days before Saga's death. Subsequent investigation proved Tsunesada blameless, but he was nevertheless dismissed as crown prince, and Kowamine and Hayanari were both exiled. Actually, the entire affair appears to have been a plot concocted by Yoshifusa, the leading Fujiwara courtier and the grand-

---

[66] The events of this affair, known from the era name as the Jōwa incident, are recorded in NHKR, 1: 364–65, Jōwa 9/7/17–8/4.

father of Michiyasu. With the aid of Prince Abo, Yoshifusa succeeded in getting his own grandson named crown prince in place of
Tsunesada and at the same time eliminated a number of rivals at
court.

The order of succession was thus altered and, upon the death of
Nimmyō, Prince Michiyasu ascended the throne as Emperor Montoku. During this reign Yoshifusa was prime minister (*dajō daijin*),
and a perusal of the *Montoku jitsuroku* leaves no doubt that he was
responsible for most political decisions. Yoshifusa was especially
concerned with succession, and he was strongly opposed to Montoku's favorite son, Koretaka, as crown prince because his mother
was the daughter of a powerful court rival, Ki no Natora. Yoshifusa's influence was too great for the emperor to overcome, so
another son, Prince Korehito, was named crown prince instead.
Korehito's mother was Akirakeiko, also a daughter of Yoshifusa.
When he became Emperor Seiwa upon the death of Montoku in
858, he was only nine years old and completely under the control of
his mother and maternal grandfather.[67] In 866 an edict was issued
ordering Yoshifusa to "carry out the governing of the realm." [68] And
thus, in 866, Yoshifusa became the first nonimperial house member
to hold the title of regent (*sesshō*), although he had actually acted
in that capacity since the beginning of Seiwa's reign; the edict
simply legitimized his actions.

Seiwa abdicated in 876 at the early age of twenty-seven. In the
edict of abdication he said that frequent fevers and bodily fatigue
had kept him from performing the required duties of emperor, with
the result that politics had come to a standstill, and thus he had
determined to abdicate.[69] Actually, the account of his reign in the
last of the six national histories, *Sandai jitsuroku*, does not indicate
an illness of serious magnitude, and he did live for four more years
after abdicating. While he may indeed have been a sick man, I
suspect that Seiwa's abdication was due more to the urging of

[67] Seiwa was born in Yoshifusa's residence in the eastern part of the city, Ichijō-
tei; three months later he was named crown prince.
[68] "Tenka no matsurigoto o sekkō su." *SDJR*, p. 193. Jōgan 8/8/19.
[69] *SDJR*, p. 384. Jōgan 18/11/19.

Fujiwara no Mototsune—Yoshifusa's son—than to illness. Mototsune may well have taken advantage of Seiwa's illness to convince the emperor to abdicate; his abdication certainly served to enhance Mototsune's political position at court.

Yoshifusa had been authorized to act as regent during Seiwa's minority, but he seems to have held the post until his death in 872, by which time Seiwa was twenty-three. Because Yoshifusa was prime minister and the most powerful of all the courtiers, it probably mattered very little that the position of regent was not in theory supposed to extend to the emperor's majority. His other governmental positions and the maternal relation to the emperor (*gaiseki*) enabled Yoshifusa to control court politics until his death. He was succeeded as head of the Fujiwara clan by his adopted son Mototsune, who was only minister of the right and who did not have the same relationship to the emperor as Yoshifusa. Furthermore, at court Mototsune was junior to the minister of the left, Minamoto no Tōru. In order to continue the political domination of the Fujiwara that Yoshifusa had solidified, it was in Mototsune's favor to have as emperor someone other than Seiwa, preferably a young boy related to him in the maternal line.

Seiwa abdicated in favor of his son Yōzei, whose mother was Fujiwara no Takaiko, Mototsune's sister. Since Yōzei was only nine when he became emperor, Mototsune was made regent in accordance with the precedent of Yoshifusa.[70] One can only speculate from these results that Mototsune had much to do with Seiwa's decision to abdicate. It would not be the only time that a Fujiwara minister had urged an emperor to abdicate in order to continue the Fujiwara family's political hegemony.

After abdication Seiwa seems to have resided for most of the time in the Somedono no miya, one of Yoshifusa's mansions, which was later renamed the Seiwa-in. After that, he moved to a palace called the Awata-in, owned by Mototsune. Shortly after the move to this palace, Seiwa took the tonsure and became a lay priest. Although he was the father of the reigning emperor, Seiwa did not

70 *SDJR*, p. 387. Jōgan 18/12/1.

exercise the patriarchal authority within the imperial house that Saga had. Yōzei was kept largely under the watchful eyes of his mother, Takaiko, and his uncle Mototsune. Seiwa does not appear to have functioned as the head of the imperial house: indeed, both he and Yōzei seem to have been more like adjunct members of the regent's house. There is no record, for example, of the continuance of the formal filial visits initiated while Saga was abdicated sovereign.

From the types of communication adopted between the two men, however, there is a strong indication that private familial relationships continued to take precedence over public positions. On the ninth day after his abdication Seiwa was given the title of dajō tennō; at the same time various allotments were made for the upkeep of his palace and two thousand sustenance households were set aside for his personal use.[71] Some two months later a director (bettō) of Seiwa's palace, Fujiwara no Yamakage, requested that the emperor take back these sustenance households because they were an economic drain on the court.[72] The emperor objected in an epistle (kōhyō) to the abdicated sovereign, saying that according to precedent Seiwa should accept the sustenance households.[73] Yōzei mentioned that even when there were two abdicated sovereigns—Saga and Junna—these sustenance households were halved and tax rice was given to both with no economic ill effects. However, Seiwa again refused to accept.

What is important here is not the content of the correspondence, for it was customary procedure in Heian times to decline offices and honors several times, but rather the form. Yōzei, like Nimmyō and Junna before him, assumed the form that a courtier would use to send an epistle to the emperor. He further referred to himself as "your subject" (shin) and to the retired emperor as "Your Majesty" (heika). This is quite clearly in line with the practices established in Saga's time: despite the theoretical public superiority of the imperial position, he was still the son of the abdicated sovereign and

[71] SDJR, p. 388. Jōgan 18/12/8.   [72] SDJR, p. 396. Gangyō 1/2*/15.
[73] Ibid. Gangyō 1/2*/25.

this private familial relationship had by at least the mid-ninth century come to be more important than the public relationship based on borrowed Chinese concepts. The abdicated sovereign seems to have made his desires known by issuing edicts (choku). For example, he ordered that certain rice allotments for eleven of his ladies in waiting be terminated.[74] So Seiwa seems to have been able to exercise some degree of familial and court authority through his position as father of the emperor.

Little information is available on the administrative apparatus that handled affairs at Seiwa's palaces, but we know that there were inshi, since Fujiwara no Yamakage was a director. At Seiwa's death there is mention of "upper and lower officials" (jōge no shojin) that had served at the Seiwa-in. A study of Yamakage's career reveals that he followed the same course as the inshi during Saga's time. He first served Seiwa when the latter was crown prince; he was kurōdo, then kurōdo no tō, and finally was made bettō after Seiwa's abdication.[75]

The Sandai jitsuroku mentions several times the matter of economic support for the palaces of the abdicated emperor Seiwa, and we have already seen that revenue and sustenance households were granted. Although there were several attempts to return these households, the matter never seems to have been settled, and we can assume that the ex-emperor continued to enjoy the income from them. In addition, more than sixty chō of land in Tsuzuki and Shigaraki districts of Yamato province were allotted for the support of the Somedono no miya (Seiwa-in) in 877.[76] Public fields from the district of Atago, also in Yamato, were given for the support of a Buddhist structure that Seiwa had constructed within the Zen-rin-ji.[77] In 878 the Seiwa-in received an allotment of destroyed fields in the province of Tango totaling more than 325 chō.[78] In 879 Yamato province was ordered to send one hundred to of rice to the

---

[74] SDJR, p. 449. Gangyō 3/3/17. [75] KGBN, 1: 139. Gangyō 3.
[76] SDJR, p. 402. Gangyō 1/4/13. [77] SDJR, p. 417. Gangyō 1/12/27.
[78] SDJR, p. 424. Gangyō 2/3/23.

Seiwa-in,[79] and later money and supplies were given to Seiwa when he made a religious trip to visit famous temples in Yamato.[80]

Seiwa died in 880. At this point Yōzei was fifteen and was completely under the control of his uncle, Mototsune. As we have seen, Mototsune had served as regent during Yōzei's minority, but when the emperor underwent the coming-of-age ceremony his uncle was given the new position of *kampaku* (chancellor), which allowed him to maintain his control over the emperor even though Yōzei was now an adult. Less than a month after becoming chancellor Mototsune was named prime minister. In these capacities he was able to control Yōzei, but this was not by any means an easy task. The emperor was frequently ill, and the state of his mental health has been questioned by many historians. Contemporary sources yield several instances of erratic behavior on Yōzei's part. There was even a rumor that he had beaten a courtier to death in the waiting room of the imperial audience chamber.[81] Faced with such a wild and uncontrollable emperor, Mototsune resolved to replace him with someone more manageable.

Mototsune at length persuaded Yōzei to abdicate. In the edict of abdication, Yōzei mentioned illness as the reason for his action, but it appears that, like his father, Yōzei was coaxed off the throne by the leading Fujiwara courtier, who desired a sovereign more amenable to his own suggestions. Yōzei abdicated in favor of Prince Tokiyasu (Emperor Kōkō), a fifty-five-year-old son of the late emperor Nimmyō who had held a number of governmental positions at both the central and provincial levels. To say the least,

[79] SDJR, p. 459. Gangyō 3/10/20. One *to* equals 4.8 gallons.

[80] SDJR, p. 460. Gangyō 3/10/22. See also p. 473. Gangyō 4/3/19.

[81] SDJR, p. 544. Gangyō 7/11/10. The incident was kept secret and outsiders were not permitted to learn of the affair. Yōzei's actions—and those of his retainers—continued to be wild after his abdication. Minamoto no Tōru once said that he was an "evil lord of no value to the country (*akushu wa kuni ni oite eki naki nari*)." Once he is recorded as having ridden his horse right into someone's residence, followed by a number of companions, terrifying the women and children (*FSRK*, p. 158, Gangyō 1/10/25). A number of other instances of such behavior are recorded on the same page. Seiwa was ill, as we have seen, with repeated fevers, and it could easily be that Yōzei inherited the illness, which caused his mental unbalance. As we shall see, others in the imperial line suffered from it later.

Tokiyasu was greatly surprised to be named emperor at this point in his life and was extremely grateful to Mototsune, who was responsible for his succession. Immediately upon becoming emperor, Kōkō had Mototsune confirmed as chancellor and prime minister, and the Fujiwara leader continued to be the most influential man at court.

Little is known of Yōzei after Mototsune succeeded in getting him to abdicate. He lived on until 949, and was eighty-two at his death. We know that he resided first in the Nijō-in within the capital and later in the Yōzei-in, where he died. He was allotted at least two thousand sustenance households for the maintenance of his palaces,[82] and he had a number of attendants and other menials to serve him.[83] He seems, however, to have been left pretty much alone by the other members of the imperial house and the Fujiwara, and he had no close relationship with the emperor at all.

Kōkō was grateful to Mototsune both for his own succession and for the prospect that at least one of his sons would succeed him on the throne. Indeed, upon Kōkō's death, his son Prince Sadami (Emperor Uda) succeeded him under very strange circumstances. Prince Sadami had already been cut off from the imperial house; he had been given the surname of Minamoto and had held a number of official positions before being chosen—by Mototsune—to be emperor. This was completely without precedent, which seems not to have bothered Mototsune in the least. Earlier, at the time of Seiwa's abdication, Minamoto no Tōru had asserted a claim to the throne because he was a son of the late emperor Saga, but Mototsune had opposed this because there was no precedent. Yet, when he desired to make Prince Sadami emperor, precedents mattered little to Mototsune. He must have thought that the prince would be so grateful to him that, like his father, he would allow Mototsune a free hand in running court politics.

---

[82] SDJR, p. 554. Gangyō 8/3/19.   [83] SDJR, p. 602. Ninna 1/12/29.

Things did not go the way Mototsune had planned, however. Soon after his accession, Uda became involved in a dispute over Mototsune's position. Expecting to be reconfirmed as kampaku (chancellor), Mototsune was outraged when, in an edict drafted by Tachibana no Hiromi, he was given the title *akō*.[84] Mototsune claimed that this Chinese title was purely honorific and not an office through which he could govern; he said it was a plot to oust him from his position. Unable to resist Mototsune, Uda rescinded the edict and reconfirmed Mototsune as chancellor. Mototsune lived for only four years after Uda became emperor, and the two men do not seem to have been on good terms during this period.

Mototsune died in 891, and Uda had his eldest son, Prince Atsuhito, made crown prince in 893. This prince, the future emperor Daigo, was a boy of nine at the time. Although his mother, Taneko, was a Fujiwara clan member, she was the daughter of Takafuji, a sixty-year-old man who was far removed from the main line of Yoshifusa and Mototsune. Mototsune's son Tokihira was a powerful man at court, but he lacked the maternal relationship with either the emperor or the crown prince that would have allowed him to exercise the degree of power his father and grandfather had enjoyed. Tokihira's power at court was further checked by Sugawara no Michizane, the brilliant scholar whom Uda promoted to guard against Tokihira's ascendancy. When the prince reached the age of thirteen, Uda abdicated in his favor with the warning that he seek the advice of both Tokihira and Michizane, the ministers of the left and right, in ruling the country. Both men were given the right to inspect civil documents (*nairan*), something the chancellor was always appointed to do.

Uda abdicated in 897 at the young age of thirty-one in order to guarantee that his son would succeed him. As abdicated sovereign he could protect him from any attempt at deposition by Fujiwara courtiers. He knew that both Seiwa and Yōzei had been

---

[84] *Akō* was an alternate name of Yi In, a famous minister of the Shang dynasty in ancient China.

pressured off the throne by self-seeking Fujiwara leaders, and he did not wish to have his son, Emperor Daigo, meet the same fate. As soon as Emperor Daigo fathered a son, Prince Yutaakira, Uda had this grandchild named crown prince in order to guarantee the succession of his own line, and further because this prince, like Daigo, had no close relationship with Tokihira.

Uda's role as abdicated sovereign was reminiscent of that of Saga, although Uda was even more influential politically. The reign of the emperor Daigo has always been looked upon nostalgically as a time when the real spirit of the ritsuryō government was honored, but it is obvious from Miyoshi no Kiyotsura's memorial how far governmental practices had deteriorated.[85] Culturally, it is true that a number of laudable accomplishments were made during this time, such as the compilation of the poetic anthology *Kokinshū*, the legal compendium *Engi-shiki*, and so on. Some have suggested that perhaps the real reason later Japanese looked back to this period as ideal is that it was a time when there was no Fujiwara regent or chancellor, and the emperor headed the government in conformity with the Chinese theory borrowed to buttress the imperial institution. There was indeed an imperial upsurge as the Fujiwara lost their hold over the imperial house temporarily, but it was ex-Emperor Uda who was responsible for this and not Daigo.

Shortly after Uda's abdication, the formal familial visits initiated during Saga's time were revived, and Daigo made them almost yearly. As had been the case previously, the communications between the ex-emperor and the titular sovereign reflected the fact that their private relationship took precedence over the public. Uda was in all respects head of the imperial house as father of the emperor and as abdicated sovereign of the Suzaku-in (Suzaku-in dajō tennō). Later he took the tonsure and lived for the most part in the Ninna-ji, a temple to the northwest of the capital in Kadono district. Throughout his tenure as retired emperor Uda

---

[85] This was the famous *iken fuji* to the emperor urging that steps be taken to halt the economic and political decline that had set in in Japan.

was very active physically, making numerous visits to a wide variety of places.

Like Saga before him, Uda used his relationship with the emperor to make his will known in court politics. For example, in the year 900 there were more than fifty persons in provincial positions who had not yet received their documents of dismissal, which would permit them to return to the capital. Uda selected the eleven most needy among these individuals and gave each a hundred *to* of rice.[86] Upon one occasion an envoy from the Manchurian–Northern Korean country of Parhae visited Japan with a number of attendants. It is not recorded that they ever had an audience with Uda, but the retired emperor did present them with a document of some sort.[87]

One striking example of Uda's involvement in politics was his attempt to promote the interests of Michizane over Tokihira. In 900 Emperor Daigo went to the Suzaku-in to discuss matters with his father. Subsequently, an edict was issued making Michizane chancellor, but Michizane refused to accept the appointment.[88] Nowhere is there any further mention of the matter, and it would appear that Tokihira's power as head of the Fujiwara clan and minister of the left was too great for Michizane to oppose so blatantly. The office had been held only by Fujiwara courtiers, a precedent that must have bothered Michizane. Tokihira was worried lest Michizane, with Uda's help, acquire too much power. The next year Tokihira accused Michizane of trying to have his own son-in-law made emperor and had his rival banished to Kyūshū. On the day this was decided and announced at court Uda was greatly angered at the high-handedness of Tokihira. He immediately rushed to the imperial palace but was unable to get inside because the various entrances were guarded. So he laid out a grass mat in the garden by the west gate of the chamberlain's palace, and, facing north, he sat there for the whole day waiting in

[86] *NHKR*, 2: 5. Shōtai 2/7/1.   [87] *NHKR*, 2: 23. Engi 20/5/17.
[88] *FSRK*, p. 170. Shōtai 3/1/3.

vain to be received. Uda was attended by his close associate, Ki no Haseo. As night began to fall, the abdicated sovereign finally left the palace and returned to his own residence.[89]

A number of other political decisions seem to have been made by Uda, either overtly or by prior discussion and arrangement with Tokihira and other high-ranking courtiers. In 920 an edict was issued ordering the construction of a pagoda for the Tōdai-ji.[90] This was an official edict (*senji*), but it was issued at the request of the ex-emperor. Uda was very close to the monks of the Tōdai-ji since it was there that he had been baptized and initiated into the Shingon priesthood as well as because it was in a sense an imperial temple. On another occasion he attempted to get certain lands belonging to Tōdai-ji recognized as a legal estate holding by the court. He issued a document known as an *in no senji*, or *inzen*, an edict of the retired sovereign.[91] Later this came to be the form of edict by which ex-emperors made their desires known. This particular inzen appears to have been the first one of its kind, and it is the only one extant until the late Heian period. While Japanese scholars view this as the only such document prior to Shirakawa's time, there is at least one other such reference—to an inzen of the ex-emperor Kazan—and I believe that such documents were probably issued more frequently than the records indicate.

Earlier, ex-sovereigns had issued edicts (both *choku* and *shō*) in the same manner as the emperor, seemingly through the regular governmental bodies that handled such documents. In this case, however, the inzen was drafted and signed by Ki no Haseo, a learned Confucian scholar well versed in the art of document composition. It woud appear that the retired sovereign was beginning to develop his own machinery for the issuance of documents, perhaps in imitation of other nonpublic bodies such as the Fujiwara regent's house. The inzen may also have been developed to clarify the confusing situation in which both the ab-

---

[89] Ibid. Engi 1/1/25. [90] Ibid. Shōtai 2/10/15.
[91] *Todai-ji yōroku*, 11: 160–61. Enchō 6/8/28.

dicated and titular sovereigns issued similar edicts. This practice seems to stop with Uda, however. In this particular document Uda lamented the fact that the sustenance households and lands nominally under the control of the Tōdai-ji had not been paying regularly the taxes owed the temple, with the result that the buildings were in disrepair and the livelihood of the priests difficult to sustain. He declared that all such unpaid taxes must be paid within the year (Enchō 6), authorized the surveying of shōen holdings to determine the capacities of the various fields, and advocated the opening of new lands. There is no evidence that this inzen was particularly effective in accomplishing its purpose, but it serves as one indication of the extent of political participation and power enjoyed by the retired emperor Uda.

There is no dated record of Uda's appointment of inshi, but we know that there were such officials serving at his palaces; furthermore, there seem to have been both secular and ecclesiastical officials. Ki no Haseo was one of those who served him, although in what capacity is not clear. We do know that there existed at this time the position of scribe (hōgandai). In later days, documents of the retired emperor were always drafted by hōgandai, who were most often scholars, frequently ones with experience in such positions as the controlling board. Therefore, it is likely that Haseo held the position of hōgandai. Further, Minamoto no Sadatsune, one of Uda's younger brothers, served as a bettō.

Some information on the type of offices ministering to the needs of the ex-emperor during Uda and Suzaku's time is contained in the Saikyūki, an encyclopedia of court ceremony and practice compiled sometime in the mid-tenth century by Minamoto no Takaakira.[92] He mentions that there were a clerk's office (sakan-dokoro), a medicinal bureau (kusuri-den), and a janitorial bureau (haki-be), each headed by a bettō. When the emperor abdicated, secretaries (kurōdo) of the fifth rank became attendants (jisha) and secretaries of the sixth rank became scribes and clerks (sakan-dai). Warriors who had guarded the palace as special forces of

92 Saikyūki, pp. 380–81.

the sovereign's private office (*takiguchi*) became guards for the ex-sovereign (*musha-dokoro*).[93] Further, five guards each from the right and left divisions of the inner palace guards (*konoefu*) accompanied the abdicated emperor when he went out of his palace. Thus, the offices that served the ex-sovereign had undergone a good deal of regularization since Saga's time.

Since Uda's political influence was extensive, Tokihira appears to have made every attempt to get along with him. One of his sisters was made an imperial concubine to Uda, and he must have had high hopes of her producing an heir. On the occasion of the celebration of Uda's fortieth birthday, Tokihira held a banquet in the ex-emperor's honor at which he himself played music; later he played *go* with Prince Atsuzane and was awarded a horse for defeating his younger opponent. When Tokihira died in 909, his brother Tadahira became head of the Fujiwara clan, but he was only a middle councillor at the time and there were three others superior to him in rank and position, all Minamoto clan members who were close associates of the ex-emperor.[94] Two of these he passed the next year. Since the previous year there were thirteen men ahead of him (including Tokihira), Tadahira had made a meteoric rise in only three years. The main reason for his rise was that he was named head of the Fujiwara clan.

Uda's influence at court is quite clear from a reading of Tadahira's diary. After he became minister of the right, and later minister of the left, Tadahira made frequent visits to one or another of Uda's palaces, either at the request of the ex-emperor or on his own initiative. A number of times Tadahira attended banquets or outings with Uda. At least six or seven times Tadahira records that a messenger of the retired sovereign came to his residence bearing directives.[95] In most instances the contents of the directives are unknown, but on one occasion Uda noted that there was a vacancy in the right division of the inner palace guards and

[93] The *takiguchi* was established in the *kurōdo-dokoro* in Uda's reign.
[94] *KGBN*, 1: 102.
[95] *Teishinkōki*, pp. 114, 121, 135, etc. These directives are called *goshōsoku* in Japanese.

ordered Tadahira to fill it.[96] Another directive from Uda had to do with the disposition of government rice at Dazaifu.[97] It would appear that in running the government as the highest-ranking public official, Tadahira worked quite closely with the abdicated sovereign Uda, who seems to have been a real force behind much of the politics of Daigo's and Suzaku's reigns.[98]

Uda's son, the emperor Daigo, abdicated because of a severe illness. He took the tonsure immediately thereafter and died within a matter of days. He was succeeded by the emperor Suzaku, his eleventh son, who reigned for sixteen years. Only during the first year of his reign was the retired sovereign Uda still alive. Suzaku's accession was an important opportunity for Tadahira, since his sister Onshi was Suzaku's mother; now the maternal relationship between the head of the Fujiwara clan and the emperor was restored. Prime Minister Tadahira was regent while Suzaku was a minor and became chancellor when the emperor came of age in 941. In 946 Suzaku abdicated in favor of his younger brother, Emperor Murakami. Murakami was also a son of Onshi, and Suzaku's abdication appears to have been at the urging of Tadahira and Onshi, who wanted to bring another of her sons to the throne. This brought her and her family even more honor, and soon after Murakami became emperor she was made great empress dowager (taikō taigo).

Immediately after his abdication Suzaku moved to the Suzaku-in, where he resided with his mother, Onshi. Although he was the elder brother of the emperor—as Saga had been to Junna—Suzaku does not seem to have exercised any degree of familial authority over Murakami. The main reason, of course, was that both men were Onshi's sons and were largely under the domination of the Fujiwara regent's house. Formal visits were made by Murakami to the ex-sovereign, though in this case they were called haietsu (audiences) rather than chōkin. More importantly, the emperor

---

[96] Ibid., p. 141. Shōhei 1/4/13.   [97] Ibid., p. 142. Shōhei 1/4/23.
[98] For a somewhat similar evaluation of Uda's position, see Ryō Susumu, "Engi no ji," in Heian jidai pp. 61–75 passim.

always visited his mother first and then went to see Suzaku. Even though he was not the father of the emperor, the abdicated emperor Suzaku was treated with great respect, and the emperor continued to address him as a subject would. It would appear that, at least by this time, despite the emperor's public position, it was the retired sovereign who held the greatest respect and honor within the imperial house.

But because of the power of Onshi and Tadahira, Suzaku was unable to use his position as ex-emperor to exercise any political influence. He was, however, quite active after his abdication, making frequent visits to religious institutions and taking pleasure trips. One of his great loves seems to have been horses, and he held frequent horse races and mounted archery contests and often went to inspect horses. On such occasions he was always accompanied by a large number of the high-ranking courtiers as well as his own personal attendants.

Quite a bit of information is available concerning the nature of the inshi during Suzaku's time. Shortly after his abdication, there is mention of *in no denjō*, or courtiers in attendance at the ex-emperor's palace.[99] These were quite obviously similar to the *denjōbito* at court—those persons who were allowed to wait in attendance upon the emperor—but this appears to be the first reference to courtiers in attendance on the ex-emperor. The actual term inshi does not appear in the sources dealing with Suzaku; instead, the term *jishin*, or "attendant officials," is used. Inshi was only a general term for all officials serving the retired emperor, and on a specific level we find a number of appointments of officials. In 947 Suzaku appointed sakandai (clerks), *tsukae-dokoro* (servants), and *gyosho bettō* (a director in charge of documents).[100] On another occasion he appointed a number of scribes and later several miscellaneous officials (*tokoro-dokoro no shiki*). He even appointed a number of specially selected priests to recite Buddhist sutras. There is also mention of a special stable for the horses

99 NHKR, 2: 49. Tenryaku 1/3/18.   100 NHKR, 2: 50. Tenryaku 1/5/3.

of the ex-emperor and officials to staff it (*mimaya-shi*). While there is no record of how many persons were appointed to these positions, at one hunting expedition there were twenty officials present, which suggests that Suzaku's staff must have been fairly sizable.

Suzaku was obviously on very good terms with many of the high-ranking officials of the time and commanded a great deal of respect from them. On one hunting trip he was accompanied by Fujiwara no Morosuke, Minamoto no Takaakira, and Fujiwara no Morouji. Morosuke records in his diary frequent visits to the palace of the ex-sovereign (*san'in*) like Tadahira before him. On another occasion a number of kugyō paid a visit of respect to him, and Suzaku once called the right and left inner palace guards to the Suzaku-in and had them engage in mounted archery and horse races.[101] Some of the persons in Suzaku's service, however, seem to have considered their position in society above reproach. In 949 a number of menials (*genin*) of the Suzaku-in attacked and destroyed some barracks belonging to the palace guards. Two days later several hundred of the servants (*toneri*) from these barracks massed and avenged themselves by destroying the house of one Suketada, the head of the retired emperor's stables (*mimaya no azukari*).[102]

In many of the primary sources of this time the Suzaku-in was referred to simply as *in*, particularly in the diaries of court nobles when they mentioned visiting the ex-emperor's palace (san'in). It would appear that the ex-emperor had become such a customary figure in society that there was no need to refer to his palace as anything other than in. At this time, however, the term was not used to apply to the person of the retired sovereign. He was called dajō tennō, or jōkō (an abbreviated form of the term), and Suzaku was even referred to posthumously as the emperor of the Suzaku-in. Somewhat later, emperors' posthumous names came to include the word in; posthumously an emperor—provided he had abdicated—was called the retired emperor rather than the emperor

---

101 *NHKR*, 2: 50. Tenryaku 1/5/9.

102 *NHKR*, 2: 63. Tenryaku 3/6/4–6. Suketada is clearly Fujiwara no Suketada, a descendant of Matsushige. He had a good deal of administrative experience in provincial posts. *SPBM*, 1: 359.

(for example, Go-Sanjō-in, not Go-Sanjō tennō). Soon thereafter, abdicated sovereigns were frequently called simply in. In Suzaku's time the evolution of such terminology is clear.

Murakami ruled for fifteen years after the death of Suzaku. Along with that of the emperor Daigo, his reign is considered to be a high point in imperial rule, again because there was no Fujiwara regent or chancellor. After Tadahira resigned the post and died in 949, no chancellor was appointed since none of the Fujiwara courtiers had a close maternal relationship with Murakami. The composition of the kugyō council at this time shows that the Fujiwara did not monopolize all the important positions, and thus some sort of compromise was unavoidable. In 950, of the sixteen courtiers in the position of imperial adviser and above, seven were Fujiwara and eight non-Fujiwara (five Minamoto, one each of Taira, Ōe, Ōtomo, and Ono).[103] This was far different from the situation in 915, for example, when the Fujiwara held nine of thirteen such posts, or in 943 when they still held nine of fourteen.

For the next few years the balance was in favor of the non-Fujiwara courtiers, and the major figure at court was Minamoto no Takaakira, a son of the late emperor Daigo. He was the minister of the left, the second-highest-ranking courtier after Fujiwara no Saneyori. In 968, however, Saneyori concocted a plot which successfully got rid of Takaakira. Murakami's empress, Fujiwara no Anshi, had borne him a number of sons, the favorite among whom was Prince Tamehira. The Fujiwara strongly opposed his accession, however, because his consort was a daughter of Takaakira. Therefore another son of Anshi, Norihira, was made emperor (Reizei) instead. Shortly after Reizei's accession, Takaakira was accused of complicity in a plot to put Prince Tamehira on the throne and was exiled to Kyūshū along with a number of others. By 969 there were thirteen Fujiwara ministers, five Minamoto, and one Tachibana; the weight of the political balance had shifted in favor of the Fujiwara once again.

Reizei ruled for only three years before abdicating in favor of

103 KGBN, 1: 191–92.

Emperor En'yū, another son of Murakami and Anshi. While no reason is given for Reizei's abdication, and Japanese historians see it simply as being in accord with established custom, it seems much more logical to assume that the abdication was the work of Anshi and Saneyori. With the accession of Reizei, Saneyori had been appointed chancellor, and, after twenty years during which it had suffered a slight decline, the northern branch of the Fujiwara clan had regained the position of dominance it had enjoyed from 858 to 949. Saneyori was chancellor—by virtue of the fact that he was the uncle of Anshi, mother of both Reizei and En'yū—prime minister, and head of the Fujiwara clan. There seems to be little doubt that he and Anshi pressured the twenty-year-old Reizei into abdicating in favor of his brother, for En'yū was only eleven at the time and Saneyori became his regent, an office somewhat more secure than that of chancellor since it involved acting in place of a child.

Reizei lived for another thirty years, until 1011, when he died at the age of sixty-two. He was not the father of the emperor, and thus, although he received the respect due an abdicated sovereign, he was not close to En'yū and did not exercise any degree of familial—or governmental—authority. Furthermore, Anshi was the mother of both the retired and titular sovereigns. In actuality, both of these emperors were as much a part of the Fujiwara regent's house as the imperial house, brought up essentially by Fujiwara women, living often in Fujiwara residences, surrounded by Fujiwara serving maids, concubines, and courtiers. While this was true to an extent for most of the Heian period, the pattern was particularly marked from 967 to 1068, with the exception of the period during which En'yū was the abdicated sovereign, 984 to 991.

En'yū abdicated in 984 at the age of twenty-six, apparently at the urging of the Fujiwara chancellor, this time Yoritada. Reizei's son ascended the throne as Emperor Kazan, and Yoritada was reconfirmed in his position. Thus En'yū became retired emperor and immediately began to organize the administrative machinery for his palace. Less than two months after his abdication En'yū set up his palace administration, or in no chō, and appointed one scribe, Fujiwara no Nobutaka.[104] As far as can be ascertained, this is the first mention of the establishment of an in no chō by a retired sovereign in Japanese history. All the previous abdicated sovereigns had appointed officials to serve them at their retirement palaces, and those officials—bettō, hōgandai, sakandai, and so on —were analogous to the ones that En'yū appointed to oversee his affairs. In his case, however, we find that for the first time all these offices together were referred to as the in no chō.

What importance should we attach to this? Japanese historians view this as the first "opening" of an in no chō by an abdicated sovereign, a precedent followed by future ex-emperors. Yet in his diary one of En'yū's associates, Fujiwara (Ononomiya) Sanesuke, mentions the appointment of officials to the in no chō very casually, not as though it was something new and unprecedented.[105] Indeed, all previous abdicated sovereigns had done substantially the same thing. This would strongly indicate that the entity, if not the name, had existed for a long time. We know that an administrative organ for the conduct of ex-emperor's affairs had been in existence at least since Saga's time and that it had been staffed by officials generically referred to as inshi. By En'yū's time there was a name for that organ, in no chō, and thenceforth, upon abdication, ex-emperors held a ceremony for the appointment of officials and the commencement of its operations (in no chō koto-hajime). The nature of the primary source materials is such that we cannot determine whether this administrative agency for the retired emperor was previously called in no chō, or whether indeed it had any name. We are extremely fortunate that for the period during which En'yū was retired sovereign one of his close associates kept a very detailed diary which supplements the official histories and documents. Consequently, we have perhaps more

---

104 *Shōyūki*, 1: 49–50. Eikan 2/10/7.

105 Sanesuke's diary, *Shōyūki*, is one of the most important of the mid-Heian period. He was a frequent opponent of Michinaga at court, and he commented on a number of aspects of society that other sources do not mention.

information on the personal activities of En'yū than any previous retired emperor, but this body of information presents us with the problem of determining whether or not these activities were significantly different from those of earlier abdicated emperors. As indicated above, I do not attach too much importance to the appearance of the term in no chō at this time.

En'yū, following the precedent of previous emperors who had abdicated, set up a number of offices to deal with his affairs and appointed officials to staff them; the entire apparatus was called the in no chō. Four days after opening the office, En'yū carried out the appointment of officials to staff the office (*tokoro-ate*).[106] Sanesuke's diary does not give the names of those appointed nor offices; thus, since the names of those appointed to major positions such as bettō and hōgandai were usually listed, this must have been an appointment of lesser officials, perhaps like the miscellaneous officials (tokoro-dokoro no shiki) appointed in Suzaku's time.[107] In 985 there is a reference to guards of the retired emperor's palace (in no musha-dokoro) as well as to his secretariat (kurōdo-dokoro).[108]

As a director in En'yū's in no chō, Sanesuke was in charge of the household administrative affairs of the retired sovereign. On one occasion—when a pavilion was to be constructed in one of En'yū's palaces, the Horikawa-in—Sanesuke sent an order (kudashibumi) to Fujiwara no Korechika, who was a chief secretary of the sovereign's private office at the time, to have the matter recorded.[109] As far as I am aware, this is the first historical mention of the issuance of a kudashibumi by the office of the retired sovereign. Officials who had served previous ex-emperors had obviously corresponded with both public and private bodies, but we have no record of the form such communication took. It would appear that by En'yū's time such communication was conducted in the form of kudashibumi.[110] The document was issued by the office of the

[106] Ibid., p. 51. Eikan 2/10/21.   [107] See n. 98, this chapter.
[108] *Shōyūki*, 1: 87. Kanna 1/3/14.   [109] Ibid., p. 138. Shōreki 1/11/8.
[110] This type of document came into use in the Heian period, first by offices outside the governmental structure, such as the kurōdo-dokoro. The ex-emperor's office

ex-emperor to the sovereign's private office, so that the matter was essentially an internal affair of the imperial house. That the document was "sent down" (*kudasu*) from the retired emperor to the emperor—through the medium of their respective offices—is a further indication that their private relationship within the imperial house superseded their public relationship; En'yū was father of the emperor and functioned as head of the imperial house.

One incident involving both Sanesuke and En'yū serves to demonstrate the degree of political influence of the ex-sovereign as well as his close relationship with his directors. It occurred in 989, before Sanesuke had become a kugyō. In the second month of that year, the newly appointed middle councillor Fujiwara no Michinaga went as a messenger from the regent Kane'ie to En'yū's palace to announce the appointment of imperial advisers.[111] En'yū requested that Sanesuke be appointed, but Kane'ie remarked that it would be difficult. This angered En'yū, who said it was his affair and not a matter for others to criticize. The next day he even sent one of the other middle councillors to the palace to discuss the appointment. Later this middle councillor went to Kane'ie's mansion, where the two of them discussed it deep into the night, deciding in favor of Sanesuke's appointment. The next day Sanesuke visited Kane'ie. Kane'ie lamented that the "requests" of the retired emperor were "weighty and hard to refuse." Sanesuke's appointment was credited solely to En'yū's pressure on his behalf. On quite a number of occasions the ex-emperor appears to have applied such pressure.

En'yū had abdicated in favor of Reizei's son Kazan, but the latter reigned only between 984 and 986, during which time, despite the comments immediately above, En'yū seem to have had little familial authority or governmental influence. But Kazan in turn abdicated in favor of Emperor Ichijō, En'yū's son, and while this emperor was on the throne the retired sovereign was one of

_____

and the offices of imperial ladies (*nyoin no chō*) as well as courtier's private offices (*mandokoro*) also used them.

111 *Shōyūki*, 1: 162. Eiso 1/2/19.

the most influential men at court. In 985 he had fallen ill and
taken Buddist vows, and he was given the honorific title *dajō hōō*
after the example of Uda. Despite his priestly position, however,
En'yū's court influence and honored position in society only increased. About a month after taking his vows, he moved to the
En'yū-in, and a grand precession was held, attended by all the
high-ranking nobles and important priestly dignitaries, including
his close associates Minamoto no Masanobu and the priest
Shōkan.[112] On almost all the trips and pleasure excursions he made,
En'yū was accompanied by many of the kugyō, including the regent on some occasions. He appears to have received more respect
and deferential treatment than the emperor himself; he was certainly more influential politically.

As noted, En'yū abdicated owing to pressure by Kane'ie. Much
of En'yū's reign had been the story of conflict among the Fujiwara
courtiers for headship of the clan and the highest position at court.
In 970 Koretada, Kanemichi, and Kane'ie were all in their prime
and were about the same age: forty-seven, forty-six, and forty-two
respectively. When Koretada died in 972, competition between
Kanemichi and Kane'ie became intense, and Kanemichi even
went so far as to pass the position of chancellor to Yoritada
rather than let Kane'ie have it. Later, however, Kane'ie's chances
took a turn for the better when his daughter Senshi gave birth to a
son by En'yū, Prince Kanehito. In order to ensure this grandson's
succession, Kane'ie pressured En'yū into abdicating in favor of
Reizei's son Kazan and naming Kanehito crown prince. Although
En'yū at length yielded, he did attempt to check the main line of
the Fujiwara clan. It was Yoritada's daughter Junshi, and not
Senshi, whom he favored above all, and he had hoped for the
accession of a son by her. Sanesuke was Yoritada's nephew and
adopted heir and was consequently quite close to Junshi, serving in
her household office after she became empress. En'yū, Sanesuke,
and Junshi represented a strong bloc to Kane'ie's monopolization

[112] *NHKR*, 2: 155. Kanna 1/9/19.

of power. En'yū even went so far as to ask Sanesuke to act as guardian for his son Prince Kanehito (Emperor Ichijō), but Sanesuke declined on the grounds that Kan'ie would be incensed.

Although his grandson was in line for succession, Kane'ie gained little with Kazan's accession. His cousin remained chancellor, but neither had a close maternal relationship with the emperor. Kazan's mother was Kaishi, daughter of the late Fujiwara no Koremasa. Her brother Yoshichika, as eldest maternal relative of the emperor, came to exercise a good deal of power during Kazan's reign, even challenging that of Kane'ie and Yoritada. But Kane'ie had one bit of good fortune: Kazan's health. Reizei had been mentally ill—one factor that made it prudent to have him abdicate—and Kazan inherited the illness in a more extreme form. In 985 Kazan's favorite consort died, and he fell into a very serious state of depression. Kane'ie seized the opportunity and, through his son Michikane, urged the emperor to abdicate in order to devote his time to praying for this lady's soul. Kazan did abdicate and immediately took Buddhist vows, followed the next day by Yoshichika and another relative, Koreshige.[113]

After his abdication, Kazan seems to have devoted himself almost entirely to Buddhist matters, making numerous pilgrimages and constructing a number of temples. We can assume that he was surrounded by inshi who looked after his affairs. In the sources, however, there is only one reference to anyone attending Kazan, and that only a vague mention of "attendants" (*kojū no mono*) who accompanied him on a trip to Harima in 986.[114] There is a document concerning Kazan's visit to Harima, however, which gives some information about this ex-emperor—and abdicated sovereigns in general, perhaps—that has been overlooked by previous historians.

Kazan made the visit to Harima in the seventh month of the

---

[113] Ibid., pp. 157–58. Kanna 2/6/23–24.
[114] *Dai Nihon shiryō*, ser. 2, 1: 28. This document is from the *Shoshazan Enkyō-ji kyuji.*

year, and he went specifically to a temple called the Enkyō-ji. In the eleventh month of the same year Joku, a priest of that temple, wrote to the retired sovereign requesting that the Enkyō-ji be made an imperial temple (*goganji*).[115] He asked that Kazan issue an ex-emperor's edict (*inzen*) to confirm this action. In the fifth month of the next year an inzen was in fact received from the office of the retired sovereign, making the Enkyō-ji an imperial temple.[116] Thus, although Japanese historians mention Uda's inzen of 928 as the only one prior to Shirakawa, Kazan quite clearly issued one in 986. Unfortunately we only have a record of the receipt of the document; the inzen itself is not extant. But we now know of two specific instances of the issuance of an inzen prior to the insei period, and there may well have been more. The fact that the priest Joku asked Kazan specifically to issue an inzen strongly suggests that such documents must have been more common than the materials extant today would indicate.

Ichijō to Go-Reizei, 991–1068

Emperor Ichijō reigned from 986 to 1011, and during the first five years of his reign his father, En'yū, exercised a good deal of political influence as father of the emperor and head of the imperial house. In the years after En'yū's death, there was a struggle within the Fujiwara regent's house involving Kane'ie's sons Michikane and Michitaka. Ichijō remained on the throne until the very end of his life, when he became seriously ill and abdicated in favor of Prince Iyasada (Emperor Sanjō), the second son of Reizei and Kane'ie's daughter Chōshi. Six days after abdication he took Buddhist vows and three days thereafter he passed away.[117] Even during that short time, however, it appears that inshi were appointed because a certain Kinnobu is mentioned as being one.[118]

Sanjō ruled from 1011 to 1016, during which time he exercised a fair amount of political power for a Japanese sovereign. More im-

---

[115] Ibid., p. 141.   [116] Ibid., p. 145.
[117] *NHKR*, 2: 225. Kankō 8/6/13–22.   [118] Ibid., Kankō 8/7/8.

portantly, he managed to keep Fujiwara no Michinaga, head of the Fujiwara clan and minister of the left, from completely monopolizing power at court. Unfortunately, however, Sanjō was ill throughout his life, complaining of failing eyesight, loss of hearing, and numerous other ailments. Some have concluded that he probably suffered from a disease of the central and peripheral nervous system which brought on his many illnesses.[119] The seed of his disease appears directly traceable to his father Reizei,[120] but, unlike his father and his brother Kazan, Sanjō was more than competent mentally. As emperor he was fortunate that Michinaga was not a close maternal relative; as a consequence, Sanjō enjoyed a degree of freedom from Fujiwara domination that his predecessors had not. Since the main branch of the Fujiwara clan had lost this maternal relationship, no regent or chancellor was appointed from 995 to 1016. Michinaga was appointed civil examiner (*nairan*), however, which gave him some of the same authority. But the essence of the power of the regent and the chancellor was the maternal relation, and without it Michinaga could not completely dominate the emperor.

As Sanjō's health grew steadily worse, Michinaga urged him to abdicate, but Sanjō held out as long as possible. At length his eyesight grew so poor that he agreed in 1016 to abdicate in favor of Michinaga's grandson, Prince Atsunari (Emperor Go-Ichijō).[121] About two weeks later he appointed inshi to serve him at his palace, the Sanjō-in.[122] From then until his death the next year, there are only scattered references to Sanjō, and these most often are about his visits to Mount Hiei and other holy places to seek a cure for his eyes. His health continued to deteriorate, and in 1017, ten days after taking the tonsure, he died.[123]

After the death of Sanjō, the Fujiwara regent's house gained

[119] Akagi Shizuko, "Sekkan jidai no tennō," p. 18.

[120] For a discussion of the history and nature of the illness that afflicted the three emperors Reizei, Kazan, and Sanjō, see Murai Yasuhiko, *Heian kizoku no sekai*, pp. 86–87.

[121] *NHKR*, 2: 237. Chōwa 5/1/13.   [122] Ibid. Chōwa 5/1/29.

[123] Ibid., p. 244. Kannin 1/4/29, 1/5/9.

completc mastery over the imperial house, the next three emperors —Go-Ichijō, Go-Suzaku, and Go-Reizei—all being grandsons of Michinaga. As we have seen, Go-Ichijō became crown prince and subsequently emperor only because of the pressure Michinaga applied on Sanjō. Michinaga attempted to placate Sanjō by making his son, Prince Atsuakira, crown prince to Go-Ichijō. After Sanjō's death, however, Atsuakira had little support at court and became increasingly estranged from others in society. People were so afraid of offending Michinaga that few would accept appointment to serve the prince in any capacity. In deep despair, the prince was "allowed" to resign as crown prince, but his resignation was quite obviously due to pressure applied by Michinaga. So that the move would not appear any more disgraceful than it was, the prince— supposedly at his own request—was granted the palace name (*ingō*) of an abdicated sovereign and was from then on known as Koichijō-in.[124] He was also allotted the annual offices (*nenkan*) and annual ranks (*nenshaku*) [125] customarily given to abdicated sovereigns and other high-ranking members of the imperial house. In Atsuakira's place Michinaga had Prince Atsuyoshi named crown prince; this prince, the future emperor Go-Suzaku, was the son of Ichijō and Michinaga's daughter Shōshi. For the first time in Japanese history, both the emperor and the crown prince were grandsons of the head of the Fujiwara clan, and the imperial house was completely dominated by the Fujiwara.

[124] The story of the fate of Koichijō-in is movingly told in the *Ōkagami*, pp. 101– 14.

[125] Together nenkan and nenshaku were called *nenkyū*, annual allotments, and were given to ex-emperors, empresses, high-ranking nobles, and so on. Such persons were allotted the right to propose (and their proposals were always accepted) a number of persons to a certain office—generally a provincial post—or a certain rank—junior fifth rank. The person who made the proposal was then rewarded by the appointee with a fee for appointment. Such a system amounted to the selling of offices and ranks in the government, working to the advantage of both the one who proposed an appointment and the appointee. The system arose sometime during the ninth century, when the economic foundations of the *ritsuryō* government had begun to collapse and the imperial house in particular was in a grave financial situation.

Go-Ichijō died without abdicating and was succeeded by Go-Suzaku. Go-Suzaku did abdicate, in 1045, but this was only a very few days before he became a priest and passed away, so he really did nothing as abdicated sovereign. Both he and his successor, Go-Reizei, yet another grandson of Michinaga, were completely controlled by Michinaga's son Yorimichi, who became head of the Fujiwara clan after his father and served as chancellor from 1017 to 1067. While Yorimichi's power over these emperors was complete, it was exercised through the maternal relationship of his sisters—Michinaga's daughters—with the emperor. His own daughter Kanshi was an empress of Go-Reizei, but unfortunately no sons were born of the union. Thus Yorimichi's daughter was unable to produce an imperial prince, and the possibility of imperial succession passing to someone with close maternal relations with the Fujiwara main house was slim. This resulted in a very serious disagreement over the selection of Go-Reizei's crown prince. It was only over a strong protest by Yorimichi that Prince Takahito was named crown prince. This prince, who became Emperor Go-Sanjō, was the son of the late emperor Go-Suzaku and Princess Teishi, daughter of Sanjō. Takahito was thus not born of a Fujiwara mother, and consequently he was not under the complete domination of the family. Quite obviously Yorimichi was not desirous of having such a man as emperor, so he discouraged any attempt on the emperor's part to abdicate in favor of Takahito. As long as Go-Reizei was emperor and Kanshi his empress, there was always a chance for a grandson as a possible heir. This dream was not realized, however, and the loss of the maternal relationship with the imperial house during the reign of Go-Sanjō proved disastrous for the political fortunes of the Fujiwara *sekkanke*.

We have now considered all cases of abdication in Japan prior to that of Go-Sanjō and have examined thoroughly the position of these abdicated sovereigns in society. In the first period considered, 645 to 806, abdication apparently developed in conjunction with female rule during a time of great political change in Japan. Along with female rule, abdication functioned as a means of guaranteeing the successful transfer of imperial succession to the desired heir and of avoiding succession disputes. Most of the sovereigns who abdicated during this period were females. After abdication they were given the title "great abdicated sovereign" (dajō tennō) and treated with great respect. With the exception of ex-Empress Kōken, however, they appear to have had little familial or governmental influence. In the second period, 806 to 991, pre-mortem succession became the rule: eleven out of fifteen emperors during this period abdicated. More importantly, ex-emperors became the most venerated figures in the land, and they frequently exercised a considerable degree of influence both within the imperial house and in the central government. In the third period, 991 to 1068, the Fujiwara regents gained a complete stranglehold over the imperial house. They maintained a close watch over the matter of succession and seemed quite hesitant to allow abdication except in the face of imminent death of the emperor. This was probably due to the decline they suffered during the second period, when retired sovereigns exercised a good deal more influence in political affairs than was desirable from the standpoint of the sekkanke. An emperor could be more easily controlled than an abdicated sovereign, particularly if the retired emperor was the father of the titular sovereign.

Returning now to the five specific questions I posed at the beginning of this chapter, let me outline the patterns that have emerged from this very detailed examination of the historical record. First, what were the reasons for abdication? Abdication developed as a means of assuring a smooth and safe imperial succession by avoiding disputes among rival claimants for the throne; such succession disputes had been frequent in early Japanese history. Subsequently, abdication became the standard method of passing on the imperial title. A ceremony was held involving both the abdication of the imperial title (jōi) by the retiring sovereign and the acceptance of his abdication (juzen) by the crown prince. That this ceremony became the accepted means of changing emperors is demonstrated by the fact that it was held even after the deaths of Emperors Go-Ichijō and Go-Reizei, although neither one had technically abdicated.[126]

The "job" of emperor was a difficult and taxing one. His presence was required at a myriad of official ceremonies; his prescribed duties were innumerable. Yet in terms of actual decision making the emperor, at least for most of the Heian period, was powerless. Historians have usually stressed the point that the nature of the imperial position thus made it quite desirable to abdicate, since abdication amounted to a surrender not of power but of responsibility for time-consuming, often bothersome duties. It created, in other words, a natural inclination toward abdication. In addition, personal reasons, such as illness, impending death, or a desire for a religious life, and pressure applied by others are often cited as specific reasons for abdication. But by stressing such personal and social reasons, historians have overlooked the political motive behind abdication which, as I have contended here, was always a factor, if not the major one.

Two kinds of abdication were possible: voluntary and forced. It was in the beginning a voluntary practice of a ruler, taken in order to ensure that a succession dispute would not follow his or her death: by abdicating and enthroning a new emperor while he was still alive, an emperor could be quite certain of avoiding trouble and possibly bloodshed. Further, he could ensure the accession of his particular choice among a number of possible claimants. Since abdication was a relatively simple way to guarantee the enthronement of a favored prince, when the regent's house achieved its domination of the imperial house in the late ninth century, they "urged" the abdication of a number of emperors in order to bring about the accession of princes of Fujiwara mothers. Personal reasons such as illness were often used as pretexts for pressuring em-

126 Koji Ruien Kankōkai, ed., *Koji ruien*, 12: 455–526 passim, deals with the matter of abdication in Japanese history. This particular reference is from p. 455.

perors into abdicating, as in the cases of Reizei, Kazan, Yōzei, and others. In any event, whether the crucial factor was an emperor's desire to see his own son become emperor or to keep imperial succession in a certain line, or whether it was a Fujiwara scheme to keep emperors born of Fujiwara mothers on the throne, the political reasons behind abdication were the most important. Illness and other personal reasons often determined the timing of abdication, but usually not the act.

Our second concern was the nature of the relationship between the abdicated sovereign and the emperor, and here we have seen a great change in the four hundred years of history covered thus far. According to the Chinese concepts the Japanese borrowed to buttress the imperial institution from about the seventh century, the emperor was a transcendent political and religious figure, "without mother and father," [127] the embodiment of the public state structure. In the first period we studied, this held true; despite the fact that the retired sovereign was the mother or father of the emperor, the emperor was superior in all aspects. Yet in the second period we find that private relationships within the imperial house came to supersede public positions. Emperors paid formal visits of filial respect to retired sovereigns if the relationship was father–son; even if the retired emperor was his elder brother, an emperor paid him great respect. In terms of official communication, emperors sent epistles and requests to ex-emperors in the same manner as courtiers addressed the emperor: the abdicated sovereign was called "Your Majesty," while the emperor referred to himself as "your subject." Whereas in the earliest period of Japanese history the emperor had acted as both head of the imperial house and sovereign, by the early Heian period, whenever an abdicated sovereign's son came to the throne, the abdicated sovereign functioned as senior ranking member, or head, of the imperial house.

During the second period we discovered that retired emperors developed an extensive administrative apparatus to handle their

---

[127] Having neither father nor mother meant, of course, that the emperor was not even subject to parental authority, as were others in society.

affairs. This came to be referred to as the *in no chō*, or ex-sovereign's office. Within this office there were a number of bureaus staffed by officials, called inshi. This was an official name, and the men who served ex-emperors most closely were more commonly referred to as "close associates" (*in no kinshin*, or *kinjū*, or *jishin*). Not much is known about who these men were, but usually two types of persons seem to have been appointed: (1) men who had always been close to the emperor, serving him while crown prince, then in his private office while emperor, and finally becoming inshi after his abdication; and (2) men of technical knowledge, particularly those skilled in the Chinese language, Confucian teaching, and the handling of documents. Another observation that can be made is that such men, almost without exception, were not members of the regent's house of the Fujiwara clan. While this suggests a definite effort on the part of emperors to surround themselves with non-Fujiwara officials, it is due as much to the fact that such positions were not high level but only of middle rank. Many Fujiwara courtiers did serve in the sovereign's private office, but only while young men, later moving on to more important governmental posts. Still, the political and familial background of such inshi is significant. Furthermore, it should be pointed out that these officials of the retired sovereign normally did not serve him exclusively but usually performed some official job in the government simultaneously.

Abdicated emperors often had a number of palaces in which they resided, and these were guarded by warriors in the service of the ex-emperor as well as being staffed by inshi. Retired emperor's palaces—Reizei-in, Saga-in, and so on—came to be referred to simply as *in*, as ex-emperors became a common feature of society. Sometime later, the person of the ex-emperor himself came to be known as *in*. Officially, he was given the title of "great abdicated sovereign," and official documents referred to him that way. Yet in diaries courtiers came to talk of the ex-emperor as *in*, and later, during the insei period, official materials used this appellation at times. Even posthumous names for emperors came to be taken from the

palace in which they lived subsequent to abdication: Saga, Junna,
Uda, Suzaku, En'yū, and so on. Furthermore, although they did
not actually abdicate, the emperors Go-Ichijō and Go-Reizei are
referred to as *in* in later works.[128]

The fourth question concerned the matter of political participation by retired sovereigns. This is a difficult question, and it has
always given Japanese historians a good deal of trouble. Institutionally, the abdicated sovereign had no power, no authority, no position; it was an honorific title given to an emperor or empress who
had yielded the throne. Yet from the beginning the retired emperor
continued to enjoy some of the powers of the emperor. Specifically,
early retired sovereigns issued edicts (choku and shō) in the same
manner as the emperor, and it appears that these were processed
in the same governmental offices as those of the emperor. By the
mid-Heian period, however, this practice seems to have stopped as
ex-emperors developed their own mechanism for issuing documents.

These documents were issued and drafted by the inshi who
staffed the ex-sovereign's office. As we have seen, prior to the time
of Go-Sanjō edicts of the ex-emperor (inzen) and orders of the ex-
emperor's office (kudashibumi) had been employed to communicate the desires of the abdicated sovereign. In only one case, however, that of Uda's inzen calling for the payment of taxes and
securing of legal estate rights in certain lands owned by the Tōdai-ji,
can these documents be considered to have dealt with matters of
public government. The other cases involved private matters of the
ex-sovereign or the imperial house. Since the retired emperor had
no official status in the state structure, his political participation
was not formal.

It was through his position as father of the emperor and head of
the royal kin group that an ex-emperor could exercise a good deal of
political influence outside the formal governmental structure. This

---

[128] See for example, *GKS*, pp. 185–86, for a discussion of the reigns of Go-
Ichijō-*in* and Go-Reizei-*in*.

was most marked in the cases of Saga, Uda, and En'yū; all these retired sovereigns saw their sons become emperor and exercised a
great deal of familial authority over them, and political influence
at court through them. The situation was not unlike the hold that
Fujiwara leaders were able to exert over emperors born of Fujiwara
mothers. Thus, contrary to what is usually said of retired emperors
prior to the insei period, they often enjoyed a good deal of political
power. This power stemmed not from any institutional position
but from their position within the imperial house and their relationship with the emperor.

Economically, we have seen that ex-sovereigns were supported
by the allotment of sustenance households from the court; later
they also received annual allotments. Waste fields and other lands
were granted for the upkeep of their palaces, and it appears that
these grants to the palaces were continued after the death of the
emperor. They became permanent income for retirement palaces.
Sometime in the Saga-Junna era, the *goin*, or retirement palace,
seems to have been established as an agency for the handling of
economic assets of the imperial house. With the decline of tax
revenue–producing public lands in Heian times, it became necessary for the imperial house to develop a source of private economic
support to keep up with the other court families, who were acquiring large estate holdings. During his reign, an emperor would select
one of the many palaces belonging to the imperial family and
designate it as his retirement palace. Officials were then appointed
and lands allotted for its upkeep. After abdication, the emperor
moved to this palace, and it ceased to be called a goin, becoming
the ex-emperor's palace. From the references in the sources to
lands and other holdings of the goin, it would appear that the imperial family had begun to develop a fairly substantial economic
base of its own. Such lands seem to have been controlled by the
emperor while he was on the throne and by the retired sovereign
once he abdicated.

We have examined here a great deal of material related to the practice of abdication and the position of abdicated sovereigns in Japanese history prior to the insei period. We are now better prepared to attempt to evaluate the developments during the latter part of the Heian period, beginning with the accession of Go-Sanjō in 1068.

ᴥᢖ FOUR ᢖᴥ

The Reign of Go-Sanjō and the Revival of Imperial Power

THE REIGN of Emperor Go-Sanjō was an important watershed in Japanese political history, marking the end of the supremacy of the Fujiwara regent's house and heralding the revival of the fortunes of the imperial house. After a reign of only four years, during which he exercised considerable personal power for a Japanese sovereign, Go-Sanjō abdicated in favor of his son Shirakawa. Japanese historians have long felt that by his abdication Go-Sanjō attempted to institute a new political system, the *insei*, whereby the abdicated sovereign controlled the decision-making apparatus at court. However, a careful consideration of the events leading to his accession, his activities as emperor, and the circumstances surrounding his abdication suggests the need to reevaluate the assumption that Go-Sanjō attempted to "institute the insei."

The Accession of Go-Sanjō

Fujiwara no Yorimichi, the eldest son of Michinaga, served as regent and chancellor for over fifty years during the reigns of Go-

This chapter first appeared in *Monumenta Nipponica* 27 (1972): 65–83. Reprinted here by permission of the publisher.

Ichijō, Go-Suzaku, and Go-Reizei, longer than any of the other famous Fujiwara leaders. His total career as a member of the *kugyō* spanned some seventy years. During this period he added considerably to the estate holdings of the *sekkanke*, and it may even be that the house enjoyed greater power and glory under Yorimichi than it had under Michinaga. Yet Yorimichi was all too aware of the vulnerability of sekkanke power.

The power of the Fujiwara regent's house depended upon its domination of the imperial house through maternal ties. Yorimichi's position as chancellor was based upon the maternal relationships of his sisters Shōshi, mother of both Go-Ichijō and Go-Suzaku, and Kishi, the mother of Go-Reizei. This was not so desirable a situation as one in which one's grandson was on the throne; but it was sufficient to allow Yorimichi extensive power. Of far more serious consequence was that there was no prince of sekkanke blood to succeed Go-Reizei. Thus, the continuity of the political power of Yorimichi and his descendants was in serious jeopardy. Yorimichi's daughter Kanshi was made empress to Go-Reizei, along with an adopted daughter, but neither woman gave birth to a boy. The same was true of the daughter of Norimichi, Yorimichi's younger brother. Go-Reizei was able to produce only girls.

The only prince available as a possible successor to Go-Reizei was Takahito, the future emperor Go-Sanjō. The second son of Go-Suzaku, Takahito was born in 1034 while his father was still crown prince. His mother was Princess Teishi, known as the lady Yōmeimon'in, the third daughter of the late emperor Sanjō. The possibility of the future accession of this prince who had no direct sekkanke relationship was a grave threat to Yorimichi.

In the last few months of 1044 Go-Suzaku became seriously ill and expressed the desire to abdicate in favor of his eldest son. In the first month of the new year Yorimichi visited the dying emperor, and the matter was decided: the crown prince became Emperor Go-Reizei. On the same day, however, Go-Suzaku also issued instructions that Takahito be named crown prince, since Go-Reizei had no male children, and it was Go-Suzaku's wish that Takahito

become emperor after his elder brother. Traditional accounts credit
Fujiwara no Yoshinobu with convincing Go-Suzaku to make Takahito crown prince.[1] Indeed, the emperor Shirakawa is said to have
remarked once that had it not been for Yoshinobu neither he nor
his father, Go-Sanjō, would ever have come to the throne.[2]

It was not for reasons of national consideration that Yoshinobu
supported the candidacy of Takahito, but rather because of personal ambition. Yoshinobu was also a member of the sekkanke, the
fifth son of Michinaga, and thus Yorimichi's younger brother. Although he was a major councillor, as Michinaga's last son he could
not look forward to a future nearly so prosperous as Yorimichi and
his descendants. Yoshinobu appears to have been very antagonistic
toward, and jealous of, Yorimichi.[3] His adopted daughter, however,
was the consort of the young prince Takahito. If the prince should
be designated successor and actually come to the throne, and if
his daughter should bear Takahito a male heir, the future of
Yoshinobu's household would be greatly enhanced.

Yorimichi, for his part, was clearly unhappy with the decision to
appoint Takahito crown prince.[4] In the end, however, he yielded to
Yoshinobu's arguments about the urgency of the matter, and
Takahito was duly appointed. However, Yoshinobu's pressure in itself hardly seems likely to have been sufficient to force a man as
powerful as Yorimichi to agree to such a distasteful political decision. Apparently he was also influenced by two other considerations. One was the tradition that a crown prince should always be
designated at the accession of a new emperor, except in unusual

[1] GKS, p. 187.

[2] GKS, p. 188.

[3] The Kojidan, an early thirteenth-century collection of stories and anecdotes, contains the story of the happenings at the banquet held to celebrate Yorimichi's appointment as prime minister. To honor him for this exalted appointment, Norimichi
knelt down before Yorimichi; but this action was criticized by Yoshinobu, who
said that he had never heard of a court minister humbling himself so (Kojidan,
p. 29). There are other examples of Yoshinobu's feelings toward Yorimichi. See the
notes to GKS, p. 413.

[4] The Kojidan records that, when Yorimichi was told of the decision to make
Takahito crown prince, "he said nothing, but there was a look of great displeasure
on his face." Kojidan, p. 15.

circumstances. Second, it was the dying wish of Emperor Go-Suzaku that Takahito be appointed, and even the most powerful of regents during the Heian period was wary of disregarding such a desire. Thus, Yorimichi agreed to the confirmation of Takahito as crown prince because, lacking a candidate of his own, he had no other course of action.

And yet Yorimichi was not reconciled to having Takahito as the future emperor of Japan. During the entire period that Takahito was crown prince, Yorimichi's attitude appears to have remained antagonistic. One story alleges that Yorimichi went so far as to refuse Takahito the "bowl-cutting sword" (*tsubokiri no tsurugi*), which was the insignia of the office of crown prince.[5] Yorimichi claimed that the sword was only for crown princes of sekkanke blood, and thus there was no necessity to hand it over to Takahito. After Takahito's enthronement as Emperor Go-Sanjō, Yorimichi finally offered him the sword, but the emperor said that, since it would be of no use to him, he did not want it.[6] Whether or not this story is true, it illustrates the antagonism between the two men.

Takahito remained crown prince for an unprecedented twenty-four years. Despite the fact that Go-Suzaku had expressed his desire to see him become emperor, Yorimichi was in no hurry to bring this about. As I indicated in chapter 3, I believe that Yorimichi purposely, in contradiction to custom, prevented Go-Reizei from abdicating in favor of Takahito. Yorimichi was certainly aware of the possibility that an abdicated sovereign might exercise considerable political influence through an emperor who had no ties with the Fujiwara regent's house. Go-Reizei, as head of the imperial house, might work through the new emperor (Takahito) for the advancement of imperial interests at the expense of those of the regent's house. Yorimichi wished to avoid such a situation, and thus he stalled the abdication of Go-Reizei and the accession of Takahito as long as possible.

[5] Kawaguchi Hisao, Ōe no Masafusa, p. 62. The quote is taken from Gōdanshō, a collection of conversations of Masafusa written down by Fujiwara no Sanekane.
[6] Ibid., p. 62.

Given this animosity of Yorimichi toward Takahito, there was no small danger that the prince might fall victim to a plot. At the end of the eighth century, during an abortive attempt to move the capital to Nagaoka, Crown Prince Sawara had been neatly disposed of. In more recent times—during Yorimichi's lifetime in fact—Prince Atsuakira (Koichijō-in) had been "allowed" to resign as crown prince, thus opening the way for one of Michinaga's grandsons to be appointed to the post. And in fact one incident that occurred while Takahito was crown prince looks suspiciously like an attempt to eliminate him as a threat to the continued power by the regent's house. The imperial police appeared one day in full military dress and surrounded the prince's palace, claiming that they were protecting him from a dangerous criminal who was loose in the neighborhood.[7] This incident is mentioned only in the literary historical work *Ima kagami* and there is no other evidence to support it. Nevertheless, Japanese historians feel that it was indeed an attempt upon Takahito's life. At any rate, it can be assumed that the prince had many an apprehensive moment during his many years as crown prince.

Takahito spent most of his time in preparation for his reign. He read the Confucian classics and investigated the mysteries of esoteric Buddhism; he studied the ancient Japanese chronicles and engaged in the composition of poetry. He received instruction largely from the two men designated as "tutors of the crown prince," Fujiwara no Sanemasa and Ōe no Masafusa. Neither of these men had any connection with the Fujiwara regent's house. Although a Fujiwara, Sanemasa was far removed from the main lineage, and Masafusa was a member of the Ōe clan, which produced many famous Confucian scholars and ranked with the Sugawara as a leading source of court scholars. Under their tutelage, Takahito became a skilled poet, and his gift for learning and wisdom impressed all who came in contact with him.

At the death of Go-Reizei in 1068, Takahito finally, at the age of thirty-five, ascended the throne. He was the first emperor in one

---

[7] Ibid. This story first appeared in the *Ima kagami*.

hundred years not born of a Fujiwara mother. His long-time adversary Yorimichi seemed reconciled to the inevitable. Extracting a promise from his younger brother Norimichi that he would in turn yield the position of chancellor to Yorimichi's son Morozane, Yorimichi abdicated his position in favor of Norimichi and retired to his villa at Uji. Norimichi, however, broke the promise and Yorimichi took the tonsure in 1072 and died two years later at the age of eighty-five.

Factional Alignments during Go-Sanjō's Reign

Although he reigned for only four years, Go-Sanjō has been glorified by later historians as one of the greatest of Japanese emperors, along with Daigo and Murakami. We have already seen that the latter two emperors were praised less for their actual deeds than for the fact that they ruled in the manner Confucian historians thought a Japanese emperor ought to rule, that is, without the "assistance" of a regent or chancellor. Go-Sanjō also ruled directly,[8] without any such assistance.

Although there had been neither regent nor chancellor during the reigns of Daigo and Murakami, Fujiwara no Norimichi continued to serve as chancellor during Go-Sanjō's reign. Yet, since he lacked the firm control over the emperor that his predecessors had enjoyed, Norimichi exercised little political power through this office. Go-Sanjō ruled directly, or at least as directly as was possible for a Japanese emperor. He depended heavily upon the close confidants who staffed the sovereign's private office, men of scholarly inclination who did not represent the highest echelon of court society. Furthermore, he supported and was supported by certain factions within the kugyō who were antagonistic to the Fujiwara regent's house. With such support and cooperation Go-Sanjō was effectively able to curtail much of the power of the sekkanke and to

[8] The nature of the Japanese imperial institution is clearly illustrated by the fact that there is a specific term meaning "to rule directly (alone)" (shinsei).

breathe new life into the rapidly declining imperial state and imperial house.

Among the persons close to Go-Sanjō three stand out in particular: Ōe no Masafusa, Fujiwara no Tamefusa, and Fujiwara no Korefusa. These three men are known to later Japanese historians as the "former three fusas" (saki no sambō).[9] None of the men was of high rank, and only Korefusa became a kugyō during Go-Sanjō's lifetime. More importantly, none of them was closely connected with the sekkanke. Tamefusa was a member of the Kanjūji branch of the Fujiwara, descended from Takafuji. Korefusa was the grandson of Yukinari (Kōzei); while he too was of the northern branch, he was not a member of the regent's house. Masafusa was, of course, a member of a lesser uji which produced scholars and provincial governors, and he had no connection at all with the sekkanke.

Both Masafusa and Tamefusa served as secretaries in Go-Sanjō's private office. Korefusa was made the chief secretary of that body at the accession of Go-Sanjō in 1068, and thus all three men worked very closely with the emperor in the day-to-day administration of the government. Masafusa is thought to have been the author of the major legislation during this reign, the shōen (private estates) regulation ordinances. Besides these three men Go-Sanjō's old tutor Sanemasa continued to serve the emperor as Confucian adviser. Along with Masafusa, Sanemasa was made tutor to the emperor's eldest son, Crown Prince Sadahito.

And yet Go-Sanjō could not rely solely on these men. The council meetings of the kugyō still constituted the major arena for decision making, and he needed support among its members. During the reign of Go-Reizei, as it became increasingly clear that Takahito would eventually ascend the throne, a change had taken place in the composition of this kugyō group, and in the alliances among its

[9] These courtiers are referred to as the "former three fusas" in contrast to Kitabatake Chikafusa, Yoshida Nobufusa, and Madenokoji Fujifusa, courtiers in the service of Go-Daigo in the fourteenth century who were known as the "later three fusas."

members, which threatened the supremacy of the sekkanke. Faced with the distinct possibility that it might lose its domination of the imperial institution, the sekkanke apparently was unable to command the authority it once had. This, of course, worked to Go-Sanjō's advantage.

During the heyday of Yorimichi's tenure as chancellor in the reigns of Go-Ichijō and Go-Suzaku, the sekkanke had dominated the top positions among the kugyō, and Fujiwara uji members never constituted less than 80 percent of the total number of kugyō (see table 2). A few Minamoto clan members did become kugyō, but they were completely shut off from the higher positions. Be-

TABLE 2

The composition of the Kugyō: *Go-Ichijō through Go-Sanjō*

		Number of Kugyō			Number of high-ranking Kugyō *		
Emperor	Year	Total	Fujiwara	Minamoto	Total	Fujiwara	Minamo
Go-Ichijō	1017	28	22	5	9	8	1
	1023	26	22	4	9	8	1
	1030	25	20	5	9	9	0
	1036	26	21	4	7	6	1
Go-Suzaku	1037	27	22	4	7	6	1
	1040	27	24	3	7	6	1
	1043	32	28	4	8	7	1
	1045	29	25	4	7	6	1
Go-Reizei	1046	28	23	5	7	6	1
	1055	26	19	7	7	6	1
	1062	28	19	9	9	8	1
	1067	32	22	10	9	7	2
Go-Sanjō	1068	29	20	9	9	6	3
	1069	27	18	9	8	5	3
	1070	26	17	9	8	5	3
	1071	33	24	9	9	6	3

* Major councillor (*dainagon*) and above.
Source: *Kugyō Bunin*, vol. 1.

cause of his great power and consequent ability to reward con-
federates, Yorimichi was able to command the loyalties of nearly
all the Fujiwara kugyō. As clan chieftain he was able to achieve a
fair amount of intraclan cooperation in political matters.

During the reign of Go-Reizei, however, certain changes began
to appear in the composition of the ranks of the kugyō as well as in
the nature of the alliances among the different members. The gap
between the number of Fujiwara and Minamoto courtiers decreased. In the two previous reigns there had never been more than
four or five Minamoto; now there were always seven or eight. In
1067, the last year of Go-Reizei's reign, there were ten Minamoto
kugyō, almost one-third of the total. More importantly, Yorimichi's
ability to maintain cohesion among the different Fujiwara lineages
declined. Dissension reached into the sekkanke itself as Yorimichi
and his brother Yoshinobu clashed over the issue of succession.

Both the tendency toward increased infiltration of kugyō ranks
by Minamoto courtiers and the dissension within the regent's house
continued after the accession of Go-Sanjō. During the four years of
his reign, Minamoto uji members composed one-third of the total
kugyō membership, but, more importantly, at least three Minamoto
courtiers held positions of major councillor and above. These
Minamoto kugyō tended to cooperate with Go-Sanjō and his confidants in what one scholar has described as a "revival of the imperial faction." [10] Furthermore, the cleavage between the relatives
of Yoshinobu and Yorimichi within the sekkanke grew wider, re-
ducing the potential threat of a major bloc allied against Go-Sanjō.
Through his adopted daughter Moshi, Go-Sanjō's empress and
mother of Prince Sadahito, Yoshinobu's relatives established a close
relationship with the emperor, but this relationship never threatened to take on the binding nature of the maternal relationships
once exercised by the sekkanke. Go-Sanjō appears to have exercised
extreme caution to avoid such a situation.

[10] Hayashiya Tatsusaburō, *Zusetsu Nihon bunkashi taikei*, vol. 5: *Heian jidai II*,
pp. 63–64.

The Economic Policies of Go-Sanjō

Amidst these various court factions—none of which was strong enough to dominate the imperial institution—Emperor Go-Sanjō was able to operate with relative freedom for a Japanese emperor. Numerous stories in later historical accounts praise Go-Sanjō's wisdom, virtue, and piety, but little in the way of concrete information on the man and his specific actions remains today. What evidence we do have suggests that he was indeed one of the most forceful and effective rulers in Japanese history; along with perhaps Temmu, Kammu, and Go-Daigo, Go-Sanjō best fits the image of the ideal emperor conceived by Japanese historians. His major concern was with the economic rehabilitation of the decaying imperial state structure, and at least four steps were taken during his reign to halt the process of decline.

The most important and ambitious scheme of Go-Sanjō and his associates was an attack on the widespread development of private estates (shōen) by the Buddhist institutions, Shinto shrines, and the high-ranking courtiers. By decreasing the amount of public land available for taxation, the growth of shōen brought about a serious decline in public revenue upon which the imperial state and thus the imperial house depended. In 1069 two separate ordinances for the regulation of shōen were issued.[11] These provided that all shōen established after 1045 (the year of Go-Reizei's accession) were illegal; through a process known as shukō, they were to be "confiscated and returned to the public domain." They further stipulated that even shōen established prior to that date would be subject to confiscation if their documents were not in order or if they were a "hindrance" to the conduct of provincial affairs.

The regulation of estates was by no means an innovation of Em-

---

[11] The *Fusō ryakki* and the *Hyakurenshō* both give the twenty-third day of the second month as the date of the ordinance, while a document issued by the provincial governor of Iga (contained in the *Tonam-in monjo*) gives the same day in the third month. Takeuchi Rizō has argued convincingly that two separate ordinances were issued on these two days. See Takeuchi Rizō, *Ritsuryōsei to kizoku seiken*, 2: 393–94.

peror Go-Sanjō. There had been attempts to halt the continued transfer of public lands into private hands ever since the early tenth century. Throughout the Heian period both emperors and courtiers lamented the growth of private estates at the expense of public lands. Ononomiya Sanesuke, during the regency of Michinaga, bemoaned the fact that "all the land in the country belongs to the regent's house. There is not even enough public land left to stand upon. What a lamentable world!" [12] Yet despite the feeling that the possession of private estates was somehow unethical as well as illegal, the courtiers felt rather helpless to stop the growth of such estates. With the decline of imperial authority and the rise of private, or familial, authority there was a decrease in tax revenues; consequently there was a corresponding decrease in the amount of courtiers' official stipends. Faced with decreased public income, courtiers felt that, "without shōen, they could not fulfill their public and private obligations." [13] Thus it was exceedingly difficult to curtail the growth of estates. Those courtiers with the power to do so were unable, or afraid, to try, since an increasingly large proportion of their own income depended upon the ownership of such estates.

From the beginning of the growth of estates certain persons or institutions simply claimed de facto ownership of land taken by force; others attempted to have their control over the lands recognized legally to avoid future complications. There were two kinds of legal estates, one more secure than the other. The safest guarantee of continued ownership of one's lands was to have the central government confirm it. This required two charters, one from the Grand Council of State (Dajōkampu) and one from the Ministry of Popular Affairs (Minbushōfu). Such estates were called chartered estates (kanshōbu shōen). In the charter the exact borders of the estate were minutely spelled out, and central government, provincial government, and estate holder representatives visited the

---

[12] Quoted in Murai Yasuhiko, Kodai kokka kaitai katei no kenkyū, p. 213.
[13] Ibid., p. 375. The quote is from Fujiwara no Koremichi's Taikai hishō, a series of political opinions he presented to Emperor Nijō in the twelfth century.

estate to mark these borders clearly. Much less secure was an estate that existed at the pleasure of the local provincial governor. Estates that were guaranteed only by documents from the provincial authorities were called provincially exempted estates (*kokumen shōen*). Such shōen were usually secure during the term of office of the governor who granted the exemption, but they ran the risk of being confiscated by his successor. Thus it was desirable to have one's lands declared chartered estates if such status could possibly be secured.

During the Heian period a number of regulations regarding private estates were issued, but the result was to control the development of these shōen rather than to prevent it. The first legal attack on the growth of private lands was a series of six ordinances issued in 902.[14] The main target of the ordinances appears to have been the *chokushiden*, or edict fields, developed by the imperial house during the ninth century. Private estates accumulated by high-ranking court officials and religious institutions were also singled out for regulation. All edict fields and estates established after 897 (the date of the accession of the reigning emperor, Daigo) were declared illegal, and the further development of such private holdings was prohibited. More important than the indictments and prohibitions contained in the ordinances, however, was the fact that all estates and edict fields predating Daigo's reign and possessing proper documentation were exempt from the prohibitions, that is to say, were legalized. Although the possession of private estates was contrary to the spirit of the imperial law codes, by the early tenth century it was recognized as legal so long as certain procedures were followed.

On the same day in 902 that these estate regulation ordinances were issued, there was also promulgated an edict calling for the improvement of the allotment field system practiced on public lands. Taken together, the regulation of shōen and the encouragement of reallotment indicate a sincere effort on the part of the central government, under the guidance of the minister of the

[14] *Ruijū sandaikyaku*, pp. 604, 607–8.

left, Fujiwara no Tokihira, to carry out economic reform.[15] It did succeed in eliminating the chokushiden, and it seriously hindered the imperial family from developing a private economic base outside the *ritsuryō* governmental structure. On the other hand, the later passage of regulation ordinances of a similar nature indicates that the growth of private estates belonging to courtiers and religious institutions continued unabated. Yet the regulation ordinances of 902 do appear to have been quite effective for a time. It was not only because these were the first regulation ordinances that they became the model for later ordinances; it was also because they had been effective.[16]

At least three other shōen regulation ordinances were issued between those of 902 and Go-Sanjō's: in 984, 1045, and 1055. There may have been others as yet undiscovered by historians, and there was certainly frequent discussion of the desirability of issuing regulation ordinances. For example, Yorimichi clashed with the emperor Go-Suzaku over the matter of shōen regulation in 1040. Yorimichi expressed a determination to impose strict controls and Go-Suzaku adopted a more lenient attitude. The matter was dropped, but the rather restrictive ordinance issued shortly after Go-Reizei's accession in 1045 appears to have resulted from Yorimichi's desire for such legislation.[17]

There were, then, several attempts to control the growth of estates in Heian Japan, but the increasing frequency with which regulations were issued attests to the general ineffectiveness of these attempts. While the ordinances appear to have been issued in good faith, no machinery was ever instituted to handle the regulation procedure. The matter appears to have been left completely in the hands of the provincial officials. Some scholars feel that provincial governors did a relatively efficient job of controlling shōen development because it was in their own interests to do so. They had no desire to see high-ranking courtiers gain power and

---

[15] Kawakami Tasuke, *Nihon kodai shakaishi no kenkyū*, pp. 340–42.

[16] Ibid., p. 342.

[17] The discussion between Yorimichi and the emperor is recorded in *Shunki*, pp. 163–68. Chōkyū 1/6/3–8.

influence in their provinces, nor did they wish to see public revenue decline since that affected their own incomes. Other scholars emphasize the greed of the provincial officials, who would collaborate with court nobles to set up estates in their province in return for a share of the yield of the shōen. These scholars feel that there was little hope for sincere shōen regulation by such provincial officials.

The truth is, of course, that provincial attitudes toward estates differed widely according to the personality of the governor. Some governors were sincerely disturbed by the growth of such estates and sought to control the process. Others more interested in personal profit, eagerly participated in the scramble for estate holdings. The result was that many provincially exempt estates—like the famous Ōyama-shō owned by the Tō-ji—were established under one governor, confiscated by the next, and then reconfirmed by his successor. With such an inconsistent policy toward the implementation of estate regulation, it is hardly surprising that regulation ordinances had little effect.

Go-Sanjō made a sincere effort to remedy this situation by establishing the Office for the Investigation of Estate Documents (Kiroku Shōen Kenkeisho), better known in English as the Records Office from the abbreviated Japanese title Kirokujo. This Records Office was set up in the dining hall of the Grand Council of State in the intercalary tenth month of 1069.[18] As mentioned earlier, the regulation ordinances issued in the second and third months of that year had declared all estates established after 1045 illegal and had further stipulated that even older estates that did not have sufficient legal documentation or were a "hindrance" to provincial affairs (in other words, were not provincially exempt estates) would also be confiscated. The Records Office was charged with the complex and tedious task of examining all the documents submitted by estate holders and of determining their legality.

The Records Office was in existence from 1069 to 1071, and seven different men served as the officials in charge. There were two

18 GKS, p. 194.

different types of officials in the Records Office: directors (*jōkei*) and scribes (*yoriudo*). An analysis of the type of men appointed to these positions is revealing. The four directors were Minamoto no Tsunenaga, Minamoto no Takatoshi, Minamoto no Suketsuna, and Fujiwara no Yoshinaga. The first three were Minamoto uji members—Tsunenaga was an Uda Genji and the other two were of the Daigo lineage—and thus part of the "imperial faction." Yoshinaga was the son of Yoshinobu, and his sister Moshi was Go-Sanjō's empress. The three scribes were Ōe no Masafusa and Fujiwara no Korefusa, two of the secretaries close to Go-Sanjō, and Otsuki no Takanobu, a courtier of the fifth rank who was a doctor of arithmetic (*sanhakase*) and thus skilled at the calculations required for such an undertaking. In this office, then, we see a small group of officials with specific skills who were closely associated with the emperor and who, more importantly, had no attachment to the regent's house.

Two related questions concerning the shōen regulation carried out by the Records Office have plagued scholars: Who was the major target of the ordinances? How effective were they? Some feel that Go-Sanjō directed his major effort against the estates of the sekkanke, while others feel that it was religious institutions that were his main concern. According to the *Gukanshō*, Go-Sanjō seems to have intended to include all shōen, but since Yorimichi refused to comply with him the emperor had no choice but to exempt the estates of the sekkanke from the jurisdiction of the ordinance.[19]

For years this claim was generally accepted by scholars, but it appears to have been an error on the part of Jien, author of the *Gukanshō*. At least two later, reliable Fujiwara sources confirm that sekkanke courtiers complied with the law and submitted the requested documents to the Record Office.[20] The sekkanke as a house

---

[19] *GKS*, p. 195.

[20] *GNJ*, 3: 188. The writer, Moromichi, mentions that the Doi-shō was confiscated, thus confirming the fact that sekkanke estates fell under the jurisdiction of the regulation ordinances (*GNJ*, 2: 197, Kanji 5/12/12). There is also a document in the *Konoe-ke monjo* which proves that Yorimichi did submit the estate documents to the Records Office. See Takeuchi, *Ritsuryōsei*, 2: 394.

was by no means exempt from the regulation ordinances, and in actuality it appears that its holdings were dealt a serious blow by the estate regulation of Go-Sanjō's reign.[21] There was most likely, however, an edict exempting those shōen owned personally by Yorimichi, which suggests the origin of Jien's error.[22]

We do have a number of documents which testify that this shōen regulation was carried out with unusual vigor and that a number of holdings were indeed confiscated. For example, in 1071 the Grand Council of State sent a document to the Gokoku-ji of the Iwashimizu Hachiman-gū concerning the holdings of that temple.[23] Based upon a detailed examination of the relevant documents by the Records Office, twenty-four estates claimed by the temple were declared to be legal, tax-exempt holdings, whereas thirteen others were deemed illegal and confiscated. Thus, this one temple lost more than one-third of the estates over which it claimed legal ownership. A number of other documents exist that similarly attest to the effectiveness of the Records Office.[24]

Like their predecessors, Go-Sanjō and his associates were not opposed to shōen ownership per se. Indeed, in the case of the Iwashimizu Hachiman-gū, more estates were confirmed as legal holdings than were confiscated. The goal was to limit rather than eliminate shōen. His efforts were directed toward the prevention of illegal estates, that is, those without proper charters or provincial exemption. The basis for legality was the validity of the documents possessed by the estate holder.

This stress upon the possession of proper documentation suggests that the primary target of Go-Sanjō's estate regulation was Yorimichi, and the holdings of the sekkanke. Yorimichi's attitude toward estate ownership was ambivalent. On the one hand he

---

[21] Murai Yasuhiko, "Fujiwara no Yorimichi," entry in *Nihon rekishi daijiten* 16: 118.

[22] Yorimichi had nine shōen connected to his Byōdō-in temple and an unspecified number attached to his Uji villa that we can identify today. See Fujimoto Kō'ichi, "Enkyū shōen seiriryō ni kansuru gakusetsu hihan," pp. 34–47, for the most recent study of Go-Sanjō's shōen regulation ordinance.

[23] *Heian ibun*, 3: 1092–1107, doc. 1083.

[24] See ibid., docs. 1043, 1046, 1058, 1061, and 1719.

actively supported the regulation of estate ownership, while on the other he received the commendation of estates from numerous persons in the provinces. Sekkanke estates in fact increased greatly during his regency.

He seems to have been very careless in his handling of these estates, however. Often he appears to have accepted the commendation of estates simply by verbal contract rather than concluding the matter with careful legal documentation. This was consistent with his approach to the management of lands owned by the Fujiwara clan. He was once severely criticized by Ononomiya Sanesuke for failing to exercise his responsibility as clan chieftain to protect certain lands owned by the clan temple, the Kōfuku-ji, when they were confiscated by a provincial governor.[25]

The long-standing animosity between Go-Sanjō and Yorimichi, the traditional domination of the imperial house by the sekkanke, the sekkanke's position as largest estate holder in the realm, and Yorimichi's rather casual and unforceful attitude toward the legal status of the family's holdings lead me to believe that Go-Sanjō's major effort was directed against the estates of the regent's house.

Besides this negative policy of curtailing sekkanke estates, Go-Sanjō followed the more positive one of increasing the private holdings of the imperial house, which at the time were almost negligible. With the decline of edict fields due to the regulation ordinances of the early tenth century, the imperial house had developed only the *goin* holdings, a few fields which provided specific support for certain palaces owned by the house. Now, however, Go-Sanjō added to these a number of new edict fields which were substantially different from earlier ones. Instead of being cultivated by the public labor of the peasants on the lands, these new chokushi-den were indistinguishable from the estates owned by other courtiers. It appears that most of these were created from estates that had been declared illegal and confiscated by the Records Office.[26] Thus Go-Sanjō had a dual policy in shōen regulation: the curtailment of

25 Kawakami, *Kodai shakaishi*, pp. 345–46. The quote is from the *Shōyūki*.
26 Okuno Takahiro, "Go-Sanjō tennō goryō," in *Nihon rekishi daijiten*, 8: 93.

illegal landholdings by religious institutions and other court families, the sekkanke in particular, and the acquisition of similar private lands by the imperial family. It was from this time on that the imperial house entered the competition for private estates, and within a hundred years it was to become the largest holder of shōen in Japan.

The regulation of other shōen and the expansion of imperial family private holdings was only one of Go-Sanjō's policies for economic rehabilitation of the state and the imperial house. As one essential step in the policy of shōen regulation, Go-Sanjō issued a law standardizing the measuring box (*masu*) used for taxation purposes.[27] This was the famous "imperial edict measuring box" (*senji masu*) of 1072. With the legal codes of the eighth century there had been established a standard-size measuring box to ensure uniform taxation payment. There were a large box and a small one, the former three times the size of the latter. Brass models were kept in the Ministry of the Treasury (*Ōkurashō*), and the wooden ones in actual use were all supposed to conform to these brass models. During the Heian period, however, with the growth of private landholdings on a large scale, this official measuring box lost its effectiveness and a number of private ones came into use. A shōen holder, for example, might even use two different boxes, one for the receipt of rents due him and another, slightly smaller, for measuring amounts he had to pay out. There was understandably a great deal of confusion.

The necessity of standardizing measures was recognized during Go-Sanjō's reign. Both the *Gukanshō* and the *Kojidan* contain the story of Go-Sanjō personally handling the matter.[28] He ordered someone to bring a measuring box and some rice from the granary. After carefully measuring the size of the box, he had it filled with pebbles from the small garden in the imperial palace. This amount was taken to be the officially recognized capacity for the masu, and it was proclaimed throughout the land by edict, thus giving rise to the name "imperial edict measuring box."

[27] *FSRK*, p. 311. Enkyū 4/9/29.   [28] *GKS*, p. 194. *Kojidan*, p. 17.

Two other economic policies mentioned in the sources appear to have been measures adopted by the emperor and his advisers to bring some order to the chaotic financial situation of the time. In 1072 a law was issued concerning price control and other market matters (*kokahō*).[29] Laws dealing with commerce had been passed in the early eighth century, but, with the increase of commercial activity and the influx of merchants in the capital during the Heian period, control over the market had become increasingly difficult. Go-Sanjō's efforts seem to have been directed at standardizing and controlling commercial prices in the capital. In 1070, for example, there was an ordinance providing for the control of silk and cotton.[30] Since both kinds of cloth were often used as means of payment, it is probable that this was an attempt to fix by law the official equivalence between these kinds of cloth and rice, the official medium of exchange.

The Abdication of Go-Sanjō

In 1072, after only four years on the throne, the emperor Go-Sanjō abdicated in favor of his eldest son, Sadahito (Emperor Shirakawa), and on the same day he made his second son, Sanehito, crown prince.[31] This abdication has been of great interest to later Japanese historians. In fact, it has been the subject of more study than any other abdication in Japanese history, and virtually every student of ancient Japan, from Jien down to the present, has felt compelled to set forth his views on it.

Why did one of the most powerful emperors in all Japanese history abdicate after only four years on the throne, at the relatively young age of forty? Three reasons, separately or in combination, have been advanced to explain the abdication of Go-Sanjō. The reason most frequently suggested is the one first postulated by Jien in the *Gukanshō*: Go-Sanjō abdicated with the intention of continuing to rule from his retirement palace as abdicated sovereign.

---

[29] *HRS*, p. 33. Enkyū 4/8/10.   [30] *FSRK*, p. 307. Enkyū 2/2/7.
[31] *HRS*, pp. 33–34. Enkyū 4/12/8.

This statement by Jien is the basis for the commonly held belief that Go-Sanjō wanted to institute the system of rule by abdicated sovereigns. A second reason frequently advanced to explain the emperor's early abdication is poor health: Go-Sanjō died only five months after his abdication. Still a third reason concerns imperial succession: Go-Sanjō abdicated in order to make Prince Sadahito emperor and to protect him from domination by the sekkanke.

Unfortunately, no reliable primary source gives valid substantiation for the factors involved in Go-Sanjō's abdication. The *Gukanshō*, written a century and a half later in 1220, seems to have been the first historical work to attempt an explanation. There is no concrete evidence, however, to support its thesis that Go-Sanjō abdicated in order to institute the insei. This seems to have been an invention of Jien's own historical bias. Living as he did in a time when the retired sovereign commanded the greatest amount of respect and power at court, Jien perhaps sought a reason to explain such a development. Since it was during the reign of Go-Sanjō that the power of the Fujiwara regent's house declined and that of the imperial house increased, he concluded that Go-Sanjō had some sort of blueprint for the future which made possible the power of the retired emperors in the latter part of the Heian period.

Likewise, there is insufficient evidence to support the claim that Go-Sanjō's abdication was motivated by reason of poor health. There is no record of his having been ill prior to abdication; the two unofficial histories *Fusō ryakki* and *Hyakurenshō* both mention illness for the first time in the third month of 1073, more than three months after the abdication.[32] Since the illness became quite serious in the next month and Go-Sanjō died in the fifth month of the same year, it is certainly possible that he was ill before he relinquished the throne and that, indeed, illness may have influenced his decision to abdicate. But the sources indicate that it was a sudden illness, which casts serious doubts on the credibility of this theory. In short, we simply do not have sufficient evidence to support the claim that Go-Sanjō's abdication was motivated by illness.

[32] FSRK, p. 315, Enkyū 5/3/18. HRS, p. 34, Enkyū 5/4/7.

I have already noted that abdication was an important political act in Japan, the safest means of transferring the imperial succession to the desired person. Abdication had been used both by emperors and by Fujiwara regents to achieve the accession of specific emperors. In my opinion, Go-Sanjo's abdication can also best be explained by a study of the possibilities of succession to the throne after his death.

It was customary to name a crown prince upon the accession of a new emperor. Yet despite his age (sixteen) and obvious qualifications as eldest son, Sadahito was not made crown prince at the time of his father Go-Sanjō's accession. Perhaps even the remote possibility that the sekkanke might reestablish its hold over the imperial house through this prince cautioned prudence; for Sadahito's mother was Fujiwara no Moshi, a daughter of Yoshinobu. We have noted that, although Yoshinobu was a member of the sekkanke, there was great animosity between him and Yorimichi. And thus, while the danger of the sekkanke gaining control over Sadahito does not appear to have been too serious, it must have been the fear of just such a possibility that motivated Go-Sanjō to postpone Sadahito's confirmation as crown prince. Go-Sanjō had worked too hard for the revitalization of the imperial house, after more than a century of manipulation by the sekkanke, to risk it all in one rash act. Since one of his empresses was a daughter of the late emperor Go-Ichijō and another a daughter of Minamoto no Motohira, it is likely that he hoped one of these women might give birth to a prince with no direct sekkanke connection who could be made crown prince.

But Go-Sanjō, like Yorimichi before him, could not long challenge custom, so in 1069 Sadahito was made crown prince.[33] In 1071 Motohira's daughter Motoko gave birth to Go-Sanjō's second son.[34] Six months later this son was made an imperial prince (*shinnō*) and was given the name Sanehito. Go-Sanjō's future actions leave no doubt that he desired the eventual accession of this younger

[33] HRS, p. 33, and FSRK, p. 307. Enkyū 1/4/28.
[34] FSRK, p. 310. Enkyū 3/2/10.

prince more than anything else. The accession of such a prince would guarantee the independence of the imperial house from the domination of the sekkanke. Therefore, in the twelfth month of the next year Go-Sanjō abdicated in favor of Sadahito and made Sanehito crown prince although he was only three years old (by Japanese reckoning) at the time. Go-Sanjō's treatment of Sanehito is in marked contrast to the way he handled the problem of crown prince at his own accession, and it demonstrates quite clearly his concern for the eventual transmission of imperial succession to Sanehito.

As for Go-Sanjō's political role, his postabdication activities do not seem to have been any different from those of previous retired sovereigns, and they certainly do not indicate any strong political desires of the kind suggested by Jien. Two weeks after abdicating he held the ceremony for the opening of his private office (*in no chō no kotohajime*), at which time he appointed a number of officials.[35] A month later he made further appointments of *inshi* to the in no chō. None of the positions to which he appointed officials was a new one; they were all posts that had long been in existence in the private offices of retired emperors.

The people Go-Sanjō appointed to serve as inshi were similar to those whom previous ex-emperors had appointed: close associates who had long served the emperor, and men not of the highest echelon of court society who owed no allegiance to the sekkanke. The six directors (*bettō*) included his confidants Korefusa and Sanemasa, the Minamoto middle councillor Suketsuna, Yoshinobu's son Yoshinaga, Fujiwara no Sukenaka (an associate since Go-Sanjō's days as crown prince), and Fujiwara no Sanesue, whose sister Moshi was Yoshinobu's adopted daughter and the mother of Shirakawa.[36]

Go-Sanjō's other recorded actions after abdication tell us little. Besides a visit to the residence of the chancellor with the emperor

---

[35] "Tamefusakyōki." Enkyū 4/12/21.

[36] Ibid. Tamefusa has a relatively detailed account of the activities of Go-Sanjō in this month and the first month of the next year.

and trips to a few temples, there are no other items of information recorded. In the middle of the third month he became ill, and the illness grew worse in the next month. On the twenty-first day of the fourth month he took the tonsure and became a monk because of his illness.[37] Two weeks later he died. He had been abdicated sovereign for only six months, and during this time he certainly did not engage in any activities that could be interpreted as political. Hence I cannot accept the thesis that he was attempting to institute a new form of government.

Go-Sanjō was, I believe, motivated to abdicate for precisely the same reason as previous emperors who had done so: to ensure the eventual accession of a particular person. Since he had restored a degree of actual power to the imperial house, Go-Sanjō was extremely concerned over the issue of succession. He appears to have been hesitant to name Sadahito crown prince since even his slight connection with the sekkanke was a potential threat. As soon as his Minamoto consort gave birth to a son, however, Go-Sanjō abdicated in favor of Sadahito and named this new son Sanehito crown prince. A final piece of evidence to prove that it was his fervent desire to ensure the succession of non-sekkanke princes to the imperial position was his instruction to Shirakawa that Sukehito, another prince born of Motoko shortly after Go-Sanjō's abdication, be next in the line of succession after Sanehito.[38]

By his abdication, Go-Sanjō sought to look after the interests of his son Shirakawa while he was emperor, to be certain that the sekkanke did not gain control over him. As retired sovereign he was the acting head of the imperial house with the responsibility for its private affairs. While he showed no indication of desiring to rule from his abdication palace, Go-Sanjō no doubt expected to exert a good deal of influence over his son, the emperor. He was the guardian of succession to the throne, and he tried to ensure successful transfer to his non-Fujiwara sons. Abdication was the safest

---

[37] HRS, p. 34, and FSRK, p. 315. Enkyū 5/4/21.

[38] Takeuchi Rizō, Nihon no rekishi, vol. 6: Bushi no tōjō, p. 161. The Gempei seisuiki first made this assertion. See chapter 5 for further discussion.

method for ensuring that transfer. Go-Sanjō's abdication was thus consistent with all the policies he followed during his lifetime: it was an attempt to curtail the power of the sekkanke and to reestablish the imperial house as the central authority in the imperial state.

FIVE

The Insei *Period I: Shirakawa*

UPON THE abdication of his father, Go-Sanjō, in 1072, Prince
Sadahito became the seventy-second emperor in Japanese history.
As Emperor Shirakawa he reigned for fourteen years before abdicating in 1086, and even after abdication he remained the most
powerful figure at the Heian court until his death in 1129. For fifty-
seven years, as emperor and retired emperor, Shirakawa dominated
the political scene as have few other members of the imperial
house in the whole of Japanese history. Far from falling under the
domination of the Fujiwara regent's house, as his father had feared,
Shirakawa continued the imperial revival initiated by Go-Sanjō;
and during his lifetime the imperial house enjoyed greater prestige
and political influence than it had during his father's.

Shirakawa's abdication is usually interpreted as an attempt to
institute a new political system, conceived by his father Go-Sanjō,
in which politics was controlled by the abdicated sovereign. But
Go-Sanjō seems to have had no such plan. His abdiction, as we
have seen, had been prompted by a desire to guarantee the eventual
accession of those of his sons without *sekkanke* mothers, as well as
to prevent the sekkanke from dominating Shirakawa. As abdicated
sovereign Go-Sanjō could wield considerable influence in court
politics; and as head of the imperial house, now freed from the
restrictive duties required of emperors, he could act effectively as a

guardian for Shirakawa. His actions after abdication do not indicate any intentions of a broader political nature.

Neither was Shirakawa's abdication motivated by a desire to institute a new political system of rule by ex-emperors. His abdication was, like his father's, prompted by the more personal and less grandiose desire to transmit imperial succession to his own offspring. Specifically, Shirakawa abdicated in order to divert imperial succession from the other sons of Go-Sanjō to his own sons. An examination of the events that took place during Shirakawa's reign and long tenure as retired sovereign makes this clear.

The Reign of Emperor Shirakawa

For fourteen years, in much the same manner as Go-Sanjō, Shirakawa practiced "direct imperial rule"—that is to say, he participated actively in the decision-making processes of government. Most of those courtiers who had served his father continued to hold important positions during the reign of Shirakawa. Two of the most notable of these were the scholars Ōe no Masafusa and Fujiwara no Sanemasa, both of whom had served as tutors to Shirakawa when he was still crown prince.

Throughout Shirakawa's reign, however, members of the sekkanke continued to serve as chancellors: Norimichi held the position until his death in 1075, when he was succeeded by Yorimichi's son, Morozane. Morozane and the members of his immediate household continued to hold many of the highest positions at court, but since Morozane lacked a strong maternal connection with Shirakawa he was prevented from exercising the kind of power that many of his predecessors had enjoyed. Indeed, once Go-Sanjō had broken its hold over the imperial house, the sekkanke was never able to regain its former power.

This is not to suggest that the main lineage of the Fujiwara clan fell into political obscurity. It continued to be the most powerful and wealthy of the court families, far surpassing its nearest competitors. Morozane's daughters were married into the imperial house, and Emperor Horikawa was the son of one of his adopted daughters.[1] But once the long-standing domination of emperors by Fujiwara regents was broken, it was not easily reestablished. Shirakawa, in order to guard against a revival of Fujiwara control, appears to have devoted a good deal of effort in his postabdication days to the protection of his son Horikawa from possible manipulation by Morozane. From Go-Sanjō's time on, the sekkanke was replaced as the most influential familial group at the Heian court by the imperial house, usually under the active headship of the abdicated emperor.

The freedom of action that this new independence from the sekkanke allowed the successive emperors Shirakawa, Toba, and Go-Shirakawa created a marked increase in imperial power. An independent imperial house, headed by a strong emperor, or abdicated emperor, coupled with its traditional prestige, was able to attract the support of numerous clients who had previously depended upon the sekkanke for advancement within the imperial government. Clients began to seek the patronage of the imperial house, mainly by the commendation of landholdings, but also by the construction of palaces and temples. As a result, the imperial house became the largest landholder in Japan and came to command the loyalties of numerous clients who served in various household offices. Thus, it was able to compete successfully for power against other familial blocs.

During Shirakawa's reign the major decision-making body, the *kugyō* council, continued to reflect the pattern established during Go-Sanjō's time: while the sekkanke controlled most of the important positions and Fujiwara clan members enjoyed a majority, there continued to be a strong representation of Minamoto courtiers, particularly of the Murakami branch. The "imperial faction" that had reappeared during Go-Sanjō's reign remained a powerful force in court politics, giving Shirakawa more influence within the kugyō ranks than any emperor had enjoyed since the early Heian

---

[1] Horikawa's mother, Kenshi, was adopted by Morozane but was actually the daughter of Minamoto no Akifusa.

period. Furthermore, although chieftain of the Fujiwara clan, Morozane was unable to unite the various clan lineages into a single cooperative political force. Many Fujiwara courtiers, especially those of middle rank but even kugyō of non-sekkanke lineages,[2] found it more expedient to seek alliance with the imperial house.

Among the courtiers in the ranks of the kugyō who gave support to Shirakawa, both during his reign and after his abdication, were several who had previously served Go-Sanjō: the "former three fusas," Ōe no Masafusa, Fujiwara no Tamefusa, and Fujiwara no Korefusa, as well as Fujiwara no Sanemasa. All these men advanced into the kugyō council during Shirakawa's time, and they appear to have served the emperor in important advisory capacities.

In order to revitalize the imperial governmental system and to re-establish imperial power, Go-Sanjō had concentrated his efforts on curtailing the illegal expansion of private landholdings throughout the country. This policy appears to have been carried out with equal vigor and sincerity by Shirakawa. Only three years after his accession, in 1075, a new ordinance (shinsei)[3] was promulgated calling for the same type of shōen regulation Go-Sanjō had instituted.[4] The issuance of such a regulation ordinance only a few short years after the one in 1069 suggests that Go-Sanjō's efforts were incomplete, but it also demonstrates a similar commitment to shōen regulation on Shirakawa's part.

Although Shirakawa's effort was somewhat less successful than his father's, at least one extant document attests to the effect of the new law.[5] The governor of Mino, in accord with the stipulation that shōen which hindered the conduct of provincial affairs be confiscated, seized two holdings of the powerful Tōdai-ji. Continued

[2] This includes members of such branches as the Kan'in, Kinsue, and Kanjūji. See chapter 9.

[3] Shinsei were additions—by imperial edict—to the existing body of law in ancient and medieval Japan. Shōen regulation ordinances, for example, fall into the category of shinsei. The best study of shinsei is Mitobe Masao, Kuge shinsei no kenkyū. See esp. pp. 65–70 for shinsei during Shirakawa's years as abdicated emperor.

[4] Heian ibun, 3: 1128, doc. 1118.

[5] Ibid.

mention in courtiers' diaries of Shirakawa's concern with shōen, both as emperor and abdicated emperor, further indicates his concern over the increasing acquisition of illegal landholdings.

If some success was achieved in the area of shōen regulation during Shirakawa's reign, there was at the same time a marked increase in social unrest. The inability of the central government to control the provinces, particularly those far from the capital, became increasingly apparent as powerful provincial warriors continued to struggle among themselves for local control. More importantly, unrest came to the immediate region of the capital as the so-called warrior monks (sōhei or akusō) [6] attached to the various temples and shrines in the area began to demand imperial consideration of their grievances, which were motivated by dissatisfaction with ecclesiastical appointments or disputes over shōen holdings.

Violent outbursts by armed monks of the major Buddhist centers were not a new phenomenon. These monks had been a source of irritation before, but there had been no significant trouble from them for nearly forty years. [7] In 1079, however, more than a thousand monks from Mount Hiei, clad in fighting gear and carrying Buddhist sutras, entered Kyoto and gathered at the Kanshin-in. They were disturbed over the resignation of Kaijo, chief priest of the Gion Shrine. [8] The court dispatched warriors to quell the monks, but they were not defeated without a fierce fight.

Again, in 1081, ecclesiastical matters proved disruptive when a long-standing, though temporarily quiescent, dispute between the Enryaku-ji on Mount Hiei and the Onjō-ji (Mii-dera) on the

[6] *Sōhei* is the term normally applied to these monks, but it came into general usage only in Tokugawa times. In ancient and medieval Japan the armed monks were usually referred to as *akusō* ("unruly monks"). See Hirata Toshiharu, *Heian jidai no kenkyū*, pp. 72–226. Also, see the same author's *Sōhei to bushi* for an updated treatment.

[7] In 1039 some three thousand monks from Mount Hiei rushed into the capital and gathered at Yorimichi's Takakura mansion. They had come to protest the appointment of the chief abbot of the Tendai sect. Yorimichi was forced to call out armed guards to control them. *HRS*, p. 20. Chōryaku 3/2/17.

[8] *HRS*, p. 36. Jōryaku 3/6/2.

shores of Lake Biwa broke out anew.[9] In the sixth month of that year, Enryaku-ji monks attacked and burned the buildings of the Onjō-ji. Three months later the Onjō-ji monks retaliated, but they were immediately subjected to a counterattack by the Mount Hiei group. The fighting between the two temples was so severe and the quarrel so bitter that widespread conflict was feared in the capital region. Order had deteriorated to the point where, in the tenth month, when Shirakawa made a visit to the Iwashimizu Hachiman-gū, it was necessary for him to be accompanied by an armed escort of Minamoto warriors led by Yoshiie.[10]

Shirakawa and the Politics of Succession

Yet from a reading of the diaries and histories of the era one comes away with the feeling that it was neither shōen regulation nor the disturbances of the armed monks that weighed most heavily on Shirakawa's mind during his reign. His major concern seems to have been the future of the imperial house as a political force; his greatest worry was the question of imperial succession. Shirakawa was concerned not only with preventing the reestablishment of Fujiwara control over the emperor but also with controlling the direction imperial succession would take after his own rule came to an end.

Go-Sanjō had established a succession pattern for Shirakawa to follow. Minamoto no Motoko's two sons Sanehito and Sukehito were to succeed Shirakawa. As we have seen in chapter 4, this was an attempt on Go-Sanjō's part to assure that princes without sekkanke ties would come to the throne. Although Shirakawa appears to have been equally determined to prevent the regent's house from dominating the emperor, this pattern was unsatisfactory to him since it effectively cut his own descendants off from imperial succession.

It was Go-Sanjō's third son, Sukehito, later termed the "third palace" (*san no miya*) by Shirakawa, who became the focus of

---

[9] FSRK, pp. 322–24. HRS, p. 37. Eihō 1.   [10] HRS, p. 37. Eihō 1/10/14.

the emperor's succession worries. His mother, Motoko, was the daughter of Minamoto no Motohira, who had been connected with an earlier succession issue. (Motohira was the son of the unfortunate crown prince Atsuakira [Koichijō-in] whom Michinaga had "allowed" to resign in 1017. Motohira had been given the name Minamoto and made a subject, but his loyalties and those of his daughter were still with the imperial house.) Motoko had first served in the household of Go-Sanjō's daughter, Princess Shōshi, but she attracted the attention of the emperor and was eventually taken into the women's quarters. In 1071 she gave birth to Sanehito and two years later to Sukehito. As was discussed earlier, Go-Sanjō's desire to see these two Minamoto princes succeed stemmed from a legitimate fear that the sekkanke might reestablish its hold on the imperial house through Shirakawa. His own mother, Moshi, was the adopted daughter of Yorimichi's brother Yoshinobu. Furthermore, his consort during his days as crown prince had been the lady Kenshi, daughter of Minamoto no Akifusa but adopted by Yorimichi's son and heir, Morozane. Thus there was the distinct possibility that the regent's house might once again establish a strong maternal relationship over a future emperor.

By enjoining Shirakawa to transmit the succession to the sons of Motoko, Go-Sanjō sought to undercut the potential revival of sekkanke power. The succession issue, however, was not a matter of importance for the regent's house and the imperial family alone. It was the Murakami branch of the Minamoto (Murakami Genji) that stood to gain most from the accession of Motoko's sons. Even though the sekkanke continued to be the most prestigious family at court, by the reign of Shirakawa the Murakami Genji, whose ranking member Morofusa held the chieftainship of the Minamoto clan, had come to occupy an important place in the court hierarchy. In 1074 Morofusa was minister of the right. In the following year he moved up to the post of minister of the left and became the second-highest-ranking courtier, next to Morozane.[11]

Morofusa's sons Toshifusa and Akifusa rose rapidly in the

[11] KGBN, 1: 333. Jōhō 2.

bureaucracy. In 1082 Toshifusa was minister of the left and his brother minister of the right,[12] this being one of the rare occasions in Japanese history when any house other than the sekkanke held both posts simultaneously. Eleven years later the family reached its zenith within the imperial bureaucracy. Fujiwara (Nakamikado) no Munetada noted with some concern that ministers of both the left and the right and both major captains (taishō) were Genji.[13] Beyond that, Minamoto courtiers held three of five major councillor posts, five of six captains of the guard, and four of seven controllers. Since this would have been unusual for any other house, Munetada warned that this was reason for the Fujiwara to be apprehensive.

The political advancement of the Murakami Genji in the late Heian period did not stem solely from the fact that they were an offshoot of the imperial house. Of even greater importance was the close bond of alliance, forged largely by marriage ties, with the regent's house. Morofusa's two sisters had been married to Yorimichi and Norimichi, and his own daughter was the wife of Morozane. Marriage ties were thus forged with three successive Fujiwara regents. Beyond that, Morofusa himself was married to one of Yorimichi's sisters. Thus, the Murakami Genji were as intricately intermarried with the sekkanke as the latter were with the imperial house. They were also intimately involved in the politics of imperial succession.

In 1075 Shirakawa acquired an heir of his own when Empress Kenshi gave birth to Prince Atsufumi. Unfortunately, the prince died soon after in a severe smallpox epidemic which swept the country, taking the lives of a great many courtiers and commoners alike.[14] In 1179 Kenshi bore Shirakawa another son, Prince Taruhito, the future emperor Horikawa. Shirakawa now faced a dilemma. He was committed—through the instructions of his deceased father—to the succession of his brothers Sanehito and Sukehito, but he was anxious to transfer the succession to his own

---

[12] KGBN, 1: 341, Eihō 2. Also, FSRK, p. 325, Eihō 3/1/19.
[13] CYK, 1: 108. Kanji 7/12/27.   [14] HRS, p. 35. Jōryaku 1.

son. The course of subsequent events indicates the intensity of Shirakawa's desire to divert imperial succession to his son.

In 1084 Shirakawa suffered a severe personal tragedy when lady Kenshi died.[15] Shirakawa's grief and depression over the loss of his beloved consort have led scholars to speculate that Kenshi's death was a major factor in his eventual decision to abdicate. However, although Shirakawa was no doubt exceedingly fond of Kenshi, it is more reasonable to assume that his decision to abdicate in 1086 was prompted by a desire to pass the succession to his own descendants instead of to his brother, for in the last month of 1085 Shirakawa was presented with an opportunity to amend Go-Sanjō's pattern of succession. In that month, Crown Prince Sanehito died of smallpox at the age of fifteen. Shirakawa and the court were now faced with the task of naming a new crown prince, a decision that was normally made with all due haste. The matter should have been quite simple: in accord with Go-Sanjō's instructions, Shirakawa should have named Sukehito crown prince immediately. Yet he made no decision for almost a year. It was clearly not an easy decision for him to make. He had not the slightest desire to effect the succession of Sukehito, but his father had instructed him to do so; furthermore, Go-Sanjō's mother, Yōmeimon'in, was still alive and was well disposed toward this prince. To break his promise to Go-Sanjō and name his own son crown prince was a move that required considerable deliberation on Shirakawa's part.

By the seventh month of 1086, however, Shirakawa appears to have reached a decision. Construction of a magnificent retirement palace was begun just south of the city along the banks of the Kamo River.[16] Land totaling over one hundred *chō* was required for the palace, and courtiers and commoners alike contributed land [17] for its many pavilions, storehouses, and extensive landscaped areas. According to the account in the *Fusō ryakki*, the new palace, called the Toba-dono from the name of the locale, was

---

[15] HRS, p. 38. Ōtoku 1/9/22.   [16] FSRK, pp. 326–27. Ōtoku 3/10/20.

[17] HRS, however, mentions only that the land for the villa was owned and contributed by Fujiwara no Suetsuna, governor of Bizen (p. 39, Kanji 1/2/5).

extraordinarily elaborate, with gardens and moats, and launching areas for small boats to cruise up and down the river (the Toba-dono could be reached by both land and water). This great undertaking required special tax levies from all the provinces. The building materials and furnishing were presented as "special contributions" (*bekkō*) by provincial governors [18] in anticipation of future favors. Shirakawa had obviously decided to abdicate and retire to the Toba-dono. The bustle of activity involved in the construction of the Toba-dono was described as resembling the removal of a capital.[19]

In the eleventh month of the year Shirakawa at length settled the succession issue. He named his own son Taruhito crown prince, and on the same day abdicated in his favor. Go-Sanjō's injunction had been ignored, and Prince Sukehito was cut off from imperial succession at least for the foreseeable future. Shirakawa had shifted imperial succession to his own descendants.

As abdicated sovereign, Shirakawa could expect to have considerable influence over his son the emperor and over the whole political scene at court. No longer the slave of the tedious ceremonies that emperors were required to perform, Shirakawa could devote more time and energy to protecting his son's position and to cultivating the fortunes of the imperial house. The motivation for Shirakawa's abdication thus appears to have been the very strong desire to transfer imperial succession to his own line and not some more elaborate plan to institute government by abdicated sovereigns. This is further suggested by Shirakawa's continuing concern with the matter of succession and the career of Prince Sukehito.

[18] From at least Michinaga's time most public and private buildings were built largely by such private contributions, normally by provincial governors. By such contributions, these persons hoped to gain appointment or reappointment to a lucrative post. While this practice, known as *jōgō*, is condemned by modern scholars as blatant corruption, it was openly accepted and quite common in the Heian period. Governors who obtained their appointments in this manner were designated "provincial governor by virtue of special contribution" (*bekkō zuryō*). For an account of this practice see Takeuchi Rizō, "Jōgō eishaku-kō," in his *Ritsuryōsei to kizoku seiken*, 1: 587–640.

[19] See n. 16, in this chapter.

This fourteen-year-old prince had obviously been passed over when Horikawa became emperor. His future became even less secure since the crown prince position was not immediately filled, despite the fact that it was customary to do so at the time of a new enthronement. Even though naming Sukehito crown prince might have been a conciliatory move, Shirakawa was apparently not prepared to risk the possibility that the prince might someday come to the throne. Following this second disappointment, Sukehito moved to the Hanazono Palace within the confines of the Ninna-ji, an imperial temple to the west of the city in Kadono district. There he seems to have devoted most of his time to poetry writing and other aesthetic pleasures. A number of the prince's discouraged supporters began to frequent the Ninna-ji, earning the epithet "courtiers of the third palace." [20] This became known to Shirakawa, and consequently he had to exercise caution to forestall any possible incident from that quarter.

No incident occurred for some time, but the succession issue was not entirely resolved. The position of crown prince continued to remain vacant for a period of eighteen years because no appropriate candidate—by Shirakawa's standards—was available. Shirakawa himself was partly to blame for this. In 1091, when the new emperor was only thirteen, Shirakawa made his thirty-four-year-old sister Atsuko consort of Horikawa.[21] Shirakawa was quite fond of his sister and honored her by the marriage (two years later she became empress [chūgū]), but it had mixed results, politically. If the marriage was designed, as is often suggested, to avoid a possible maternal connection with one of the other court families, it could not have been better conceived. Considering the great age difference between the spouses, however, it is not surprising that an heir was not forthcoming and in that sense it was ill-conceived. Ex-Emperor Shirakawa made offerings to the gods and prayed diligently for the birth of a child, but his efforts were to no avail.

[20] The Gempei seisuiki relates the story of Sukehito's life in the Hanazono. See Ryō Susumu, "San no miya to Murakami Genji," in his Heian jidai, pp. 102–3.
[21] CYK, 1: 56–57. Kanji 5/10/25.

Finally in 1098, when Horikawa was twenty, a more congenial marriage was concluded with Shishi, the daughter of Fujiwara no Sanesue. Sanesue was a Fujiwara but not a member of the regent's house. Furthermore, he was Shirakawa's uncle (Moshi's elder brother) and close associate, so the union was an expedient one politically. In the first month of 1103 Shishi gave birth to a son, to the great delight of Shirakawa, Horikawa, and the entire court. This was Prince Munehito, who was to become Emperor Toba.

Some idea of the anxiety posed by Horikawa's failure to produce an heir and the great relief that accompanied Toba's birth can be gleaned from Toba's own account of the event, as related to Fujiwara no Yorinaga.

Tonight the retired sovereign's tale touched upon the events at the time of his birth. "Before I was born, the late Horikawa was ill, and the entire court centered its attention on Prince Sukehito [as his successor]. The late retired sovereign Shirakawa once lamented: 'Although I had left my household [i.e., become a monk], I had neither taken the final vows nor accepted a priestly name. If anything should have befallen His Majesty, I could have reascended the throne. Furthermore, the empress [Atsuko] had no children, and since time was passing, the posthumously titled empress [Shishi] became consort. When she became pregnant, I offered prayers to the goddess of the Kamo Shrine for the birth of a son. In a dream she appeared to me in the sleeve of a garment, but she did not speak. Again in another dream she said that the child would be a boy, and she said that a certain item should be taken from the beams. Surprised in my dream, I searched along the beams and found a silver dragon. This dragon has been preserved and I still have it today. Furthermore, the garment in which it was dreamed she appeared was enshrined as her god body, and it is now in the priest's residence. Even now, I make offerings to it. Moreover, a woman entered the household of the empress and, meeting a lady in waiting, she said: "She will bear a boy. His nobility will be beyond description. He will have a blemish on his right buttock." Hearing this, the lady ran and told the late lord Kinzane, the crown prince's master. Wishing to meet the woman, Kinzane hurried out, but no one knew her whereabouts. People took her to be a goddess.' Very soon, I was born. I did have a blemish on my right buttock which I still bear today. Thus, there were several strange

occurrences. *My birth was not [completely the result] of human ef-*
fort." [22]

Shirakawa left no doubts as to his plans for this new prince. Five
months after his birth he was made an imperial prince (*shinnō*)
and given the name Munehito, and in his eighth month he was
named crown prince.[23] This hurried disposition of the position of
crown prince after eighteen years' vacancy is clear proof that
Shirakawa's intention had always been to transmit imperial succession in his own line and divert it from Go-Sanjō's. Finally the
purpose his abdication was designed to effect was accomplished.

The birth of Munehito created a rare situation in the history of
the Japanese imperial house. Within the house Shirakawa, Horikawa, and Munehito—grandfather, father, and son—served as abdicated sovereign, emperor, and crown prince. This was the first
instance of such imperial continuity since Uda, Daigo, and Suzaku
had held similar positions in the early tenth century, and it was
interpreted by at least one observer as a great sign, a matter for re-
joicing by both the court and the people.[24] More importantly, these
three positions within the imperial house were held by men un-
encumbered by sekkanke maternal relations. It was a time of imperial unity and independence rarely found in Japanese history.

Despite the settlement of the succession issue, however, there
was still a need for caution. Sukehito was still active, and in 1103
one of his consorts, a daughter of Minamoto no Morotada, gave
birth to a son. Toshifusa, the chieftain of the Genji, was well aware
of the potential benefit to his clan if this son should ever become
emperor. Although the boy's chances appeared slim after the designation of Munehito as crown prince, the Genji's hopes for family
success through marriage connections to a potential heir remained
strong.

[22] *Taiki*, 1: 67–68. Kōji 1/5/16.
[23] *HRS*, p. 47, Kōwa 5/8/17. To be named crown prince in one's first year was
extremely rare. *HRS* claims that Seiwa and Reizei were the only such instances.
[24] *CYK*, 2: 253. Kōwa 5/1/17.

Shirakawa's disposition of the succession issue was momentarily challenged when, in 1107, Emperor Horikawa died. Horikawa was a man of weak constitution prone to extended illness throughout his short life, and his death did not come as a shock.[25] Although only five years old at the time, Munehito succeeded him as Emperor Toba, and Shirakawa, as retired emperor and head of the imperial house, acted as guardian for his grandson. From this time his influence in court politics began to be significant. Shirakawa continued his dogged refusal to permit Prince Sukehito or his son a chance to capture the imperial succession. Since the new emperor Toba was only five years old and since Horikawa had no other heir, Shirakawa once again left the position of crown prince unfilled. Having expended this much energy to keep succession in his own line, he was not about to yield to his half-brother.

Then, in 1114 there occurred an event which ended the hopes that Sukehito or his son might someday become emperor.[26] In the tenth month of that year someone threw an anonymous note into the courtyard of the palace of Princess Reishi. The note exposed a plot against the life of Emperor Toba and identified the would-be assassin as a young man named Senjumaru. Senjumaru was under the tutlage of Shōkaku, head priest of the Daigo-ji and a son of Minamoto no Toshifusa, the chieftain of the Minamoto clan. The matter was brought before Shirakawa, who decided that it warranted further investigation. When Senjumaru was questioned, it was learned that the affair had been planned by another Daigo-ji priest named Ninkan. Ninkan, also a son of Toshifusa, had served as imperial exorcist for Prince Sukehito. Imperial gendarmes were dispatched to the Daigo-ji and Ninkan was seized.

Later that month the kugyō met in council to assign guilt in the matter. Ninkan was exiled to Izu and Senjumaru to Sado, and their unrecorded accomplices were also exiled. Besides frustrating any

---

[25] On the illness of Horikawa and his relationship with Shirakawa, see Akagi Shizuko, "Shirakawa-in to Horikawa tennō: Insei shoki no in to tennō."

[26] The incident is fully recorded in Fujiwara no Tadazane's diary, *Denryaku*, 4: 59–62, Eikyū 1/10/5–22. Also see Yoshimura Shigeki, "Eikyū gannen no Toba tennō in taisuru gigoku jiken ni tsuite," pp. 3–7.

possibility that Sukehito might become emperor, the incident had a decidedly poor effect upon the political fortunes of the Murakami Genji. Toshifusa was at the time the court elder; as minister of the left, he was technically of lower rank than the prime minister, Fujiwara no Tadazane, but he was twice the age of Tadazane and was respected by all the other courtiers. Yet two of the major figures involved in the plot on the emperor's life were his sons. There was discussion of punishment for all Murakami Genji courtiers, but according to the war chronicle *Gempei seisuiki*, Shirakawa's confidant, Fujiwara no Tamefusa, interceded on behalf of the Genji.[27] The upshot of the affair was that some members of the family were temporarily dismissed from their court positions: Toshifusa, Morotoki, Moroshige, and Moroyori. In the next year, however, they were allowed to return by an order from Shirakawa,[28] and in 1129 Ninkan too was pardoned and allowed to return to the capital.[29]

After the affair had been concluded, Shirakawa adopted a very conciliatory attitude toward Prince Sukehito and even adopted his son Arihito. According to Fujiwara no Yorinaga, Shirakawa was motivated to adopt Arihito because Toba as yet had no heir and the ex-sovereign was contemplating Arihito as a possible successor. There can be little doubt that Shirakawa had some misgivings about having broken his vow to Go-Sanjō and diverted succession to his own descendants. Perhaps he viewed this as a way to make some restitution.

In 1119, however, a son, Prince Akihito, was born to Toba, and Shirakawa no longer had to worry about succession. His long-standing attitude of caution toward Sukehito changed suddenly; now that there was no need to be concerned about an heir Arihito was given the surname Minamoto and made a subject. However, he was given the junior third rank, an honor unheard of since the days

27 Yoshimura, "Gigoku jiken," p. 7.
28 *Denryaku*, 4: 130. Eikyū 2/11/8.
29 CYK, 6: 61, Daiji 4/6/25. Ninkan was pardoned along with two other persons who had been exiled, Minamoto no Akikuni and Minamoto no Takayuki. Ninkan had been in exile seventeen years, Akikuni, nineteen, and Takayuki, fourteen.

of the Saga Genji; even Morofusa, founder of the Murakami Genji, had been given only the junior fourth rank.[30] This can be interpreted as further evidence of Shirakawa's misgivings over his disposition of the succession issue.

If Prince Akihito's birth was a relief to Shirakawa, to those—particularly the Murakami Genji—who had hoped for the eventual succession of Sukehito or his son the birth of Toba's heir was disastrous. While Morotoki could hint in his diary that Arihito might someday still become emperor, "since the affairs of men are decided in heaven," he realized that such would not in fact be the case.[31] He cited the example of Uda, who became emperor after having been made a subject, but he saw Arihito as being closer to Minamoto no Takaakira and Koichijō-in, both frustrated claimants for the throne, than to Uda.

Ex-Emperor Shirakawa: The Early Years, 1086–1100

The preceding examination of the politics of imperial succession during Shirakawa's lifetime demonstrates that it was his desire to divert imperial succession to his own line that led him to abdicate; Shirakawa's abdication itself and many of his postabdication activities were designed to put his own descendants in line for the succession and to protect them from other imperial family members, such as Sukehito and his line on the one hand and the sekkanke on the other. At the same time it is difficult to interpret Shirakawa's abdication as having been specifically designed to institute government by abdicated sovereigns, as has often been suggested; evidence to support such a view is lacking. An examination of some of the activities of Shirakawa after abdication will serve to clarify his role in court politics.

Many Japanese historians consider the building of the Toba-dono an event of major importance in Japanese history, heralding the advent of rule by abdicated sovereigns.[32] The construction of this

[30] Ryō, Heian jidai, pp. 11–12.

[31] Chōshūki, 1: 157. Gen'ei 2/8/7.

[32] See Murayama Shūichi, "Insei to Toba rikyū" pp. 56–79. See also the same author's Heian-kyō, pp. 146–76.

elaborate imperial villa is considered proof that Shirakawa intended to abdicate and rule from this palace. The construction of the Toba-dono was indeed a grand undertaking. Yet, considering the condition of imperial residences at the time, it is not surprising that a new palace was constructed.

The imperial palace—the emperor's residence and seat of imperial government—had by this time been frequently destroyed by fire or earthquake, and emperors commonly spent considerable periods of time at the residences of important court ministers, usually the Fujiwara regent. Retired sovereigns had most frequently resided in the Reizei-in or Suzaku-in, but these were older edifices which had themselves suffered the ravages of fire and earthquake, and neither seem to have been in use in the late Heian period. Go-Sanjō seems to have resided in several different places after his abdication, including the residence of Minamoto no Takafusa, the governor of Tajima. Therefore, it is hardly strange that Shirakawa should wish to build a new imperial villa for his postabdication use, particularly since the imperial house was enjoying a revival of its power and fortune. It seems unnecessary to read any further political implications than this into the construction of the Toba-dono.

Furthermore, if it had been Shirakawa's intention to abdicate and monopolize governmental powers from a retirement palace, it would have been more expedient to have remained in the center of things, as Saga had done after his abdication, rather than to move south of the city to Toba. Another indication that the Toba-dono did not represent to Shirakawa all that later historians have claimed is suggested by the selection of his name. Japanese emperors are known to history by their posthumous names, and from the early Heian period on these names were taken from the area or palace most closely associated with the emperor—Saga, Reizei, En'yū, and so on. Yet Emperor Shirakawa was named not for the Toba-dono but for another palace he frequented, the Shirakawa-in on the eastern fringes of the city. Moreover, Shirakawa himself seems to have decided on the name Shirakawa prior to his death.

Shirakawa had the Toba-dono constructed as a detached imperial palace, and he used it in that manner rather than as his main residence.[33] Most sources refer to Shirakawa as making a "visit" (gokō) to the Toba-dono and "returning" to the capital rather than the other way around. Actually, the Ōi-dono seems to have been his main residence while he was retired emperor. By contrast, Shirakawa's grandson spent a considerable amount of time at the Toba-dono and greatly added to the size of the villa. He actually seems to have spent more time there than Shirakawa, and it was from this palace that his name—Emperor Toba—was taken. Thus it is incorrect to picture the construction of the Toba-dono as a signal for the commencement of rule by abdicated sovereigns.

On the day that he abdicated in favor of his son Horikawa,[34] Shirakawa made the first appointments to his *in no chō*: these included five *bettō* (directors) and six *hōgandai* (scribes).[35] The five directors were Fujiwara no Sanesue, Fujiwara no Akisue, Ōe no Masafusa, Fujiwara no Nakazane, and Minamoto no Morotada. All five were longtime confidants of Shirakawa and had close connections with the imperial house, by association or marriage. They were all courtiers of middle rank, and none had close connections with the sekkanke. Furthermore, most had some degree of administrative talent and wealth gained from experience as provincial governors. The five men formed the nucleus of the group of close associates or confidants (*kinshin*) [36] of the ex-sovereign at the outset of his tenure as abdicated sovereign. The number was to increase considerably over the next forty years.

On the second day of the new year (1087) documents from the Grand Council of State granting land allotments (of an unknown amount) and imperial edict fields were handed over to Shirakawa.[37] His in no chō began to take shape over the next few months as he

[33] Shirakawa had numerous residences, both within the capital and on the outskirts, between which he was constantly moving. Among those were the Ōi-dono—which appears to have been his main palace within the city—Rokujō-dono, Takamatsu-in, Shirakawa-in, Muromachi-dono, Sanjō Karasuma-tei, and the Kasuga-dono.

[34] The details of the abdication and the appointment of various officials are recorded in general in FSRK, but for greater detail see the Yanagihara-ke kiroku, quoted in Tokyo Daigaku Shiryō Hensanjo, comp., Dai Nihon shiryō, ser. 3, 1: 3–10.

[35] Ibid., p. 7.

[36] See chapter 9 for a study of these kinshin.

[37] Dai Nihon shiryō, ser. 3, 1: 16.

appointed more personnel: Fujiwara no Kinzane became a director,[38] and Fujiwara no Akitaka was made a secretary (kurōdo).[39] There were also warriors in his service since there is a record of more than ten *mushadokoro* accompanying Shirakawa on a visit to the Byōdō-in at Uji.[40]

From the sources available to us today there does not seem to have been much of a change in the political complexion of the Heian court upon the abdication of Shirakawa. He did not, as is often suggested, suddenly become the sole master of the political scene, a supreme dictator who ruled from his retirement palace by issuing documents more authoritative than imperial edicts. Actually the sources show that the traditional decision-making apparatus, albeit somewhat modified during the course of the Heian period, did not wither away but continued to function as before.

The chancellor, Fujiwara no Morozane, was appointed regent for the young emperor Horikawa, and he remained the most influential courtier. The kugyō council did not change markedly in composition and remained the main source of political decisions. As retired sovereign, head of the imperial house, and father of the reigning emperor, Shirakawa naturally commanded a great deal of respect and political influence as well. Indeed, he could expect to have influence in the kugyō council since some of his close associates and members of the "imperial faction" belonged to this elite body. It is clear from diaries of the time that Shirakawa was visited quite frequently by many of the courtiers, including Morozane, at one or another of his palaces. But for at least the first fifteen years of his retirement Shirakawa does not appear to have been overly active in the public affairs of the Heian court. Certainly he was not an autocratic ruler. On the contrary, he seems to have devoted most of his time to entertaining at his various villas, making pleasure trips and religious pilgrimages,[41] conducting Buddhist and Shinto services, and supervising imperial family matters. He seems to have

---

[38] Ibid., p. 35. Ōtoku 3/12/28. The source is the *Saionji-ke kiroku*.
[39] *KGBN*, 1: 53. Hōan 1.
[40] *Dai Nihon shiryō*, ser. 3, 1: 119. The reference is from the *Tamefusakyō-ki*.
[41] Among the places he visited were Uji, Mount Hiei, Mount Kōya, and the Kumano shrines.

taken full advantage of the freedom of movement so long denied him as emperor.

Although historians have created the impression that retired sovereigns were fiercely anti-Fujiwara, Shirakawa does not appear to have been overly antagonistic toward the sekkanke, at least in the beginning. True, he did appoint mostly non-sekkanke courtiers to positions within his in no chō, in the manner of other retired sovereigns, but he was not nearly so anti-Fujiwara as, for example, Go-Sanjō had been. At one point he even appointed as director in his in no chō Tadazane, the young son of the regent Moromichi, who had succeeded his father Morozane. Perhaps Shirakawa felt that, once the imperial family had established itself as a free and independent entity, there was no reason to assume a hostile attitude toward the sekkanke. Normal precautionary measures were sufficient to avoid domination by the regent's house.

At any rate, the relationship between Shirakawa and Morozane —as well as his successor, Moromichi—does not appear to have been a hostile one. Besides consulting with the ex-emperor on many political matters, Morozane accompanied him on major festive outings and stayed with him in the Toba-dono on at least one occasion; [42] Shirakawa even resided with Morozane in his Ōmikado-tei for a while.[43] Morozane, not Shirakawa, appears to have been the final judge of all major political decisions. It was Morozane, for example, who decided the date for Horikawa's coming-of-age ceremony.[44]

The roles played by Shirakawa and Morozane shortly after the former's abdication are well illustrated in the affair of Minamoto no Yoshiie. Yoshiie and his warriors waged a prolonged struggle against the Kiyowara family in northern Japan. Almost a year after Shirakawa's abdication, the court received a report that Yoshiie had killed the leader of the rebels and won a victory.[45] Having already distinguished himself in the Former Nine Years' War,[46] Yoshiie

[42] Honchō seiki, p. 281. Kanji 1/8/28.   [43] GNJ, 1: 273. Kanji 3/5/7.
[44] Ibid., p. 214. Kanji 2/10/21.   [45] HRS, p. 39. Kanji 1/12/26.
[46] The Former Nine Years' War refers to the rebellion of the Abe family in the far northern province of Mutsu. The court dispatched Yoriyoshi and his son

became widely regarded as the foremost warrior in the land, and people in the eastern provinces began to commend their lands to him for protection. This was a matter of great concern for the court nobles who had heretofore monopolized the acquisition of *shōen*. In 1089 the kugyō met at Morozane's residence to discuss the matter,[47] and in 1091 an imperial edict was issued forbidding people to commend their lands to Yoshiie.[48] About ten days later Shirakawa met with the kugyō to discuss the problem of fighting between Yoshiie and his brother Yoshitsuna.[49] In 1092 still another imperial edict was issued prohibiting the commendation of shōen to Yoshiie,[50] demonstrating quite clearly the limited effect of the first edict.

This serious affair was decided through the normal decision-making process of the Heian court: discussion of the matter by the kugyō under the direction of the regent and prime minister; decision; and the issuance of an imperial edict. As retired sovereign and head of the imperial house, Shirakawa was involved in the discussions and must have had some influence on its ultimate outcome, but the matter was certainly not handled in an autocratic manner by the ex-sovereign. In fact the whole affair was handled according to quite normal procedures.

Moreover, on at least three occasions when courtiers were banished for improper actions as provincial governors, Shirakawa did not play any role, despite the fact that these courtiers were close associates of his. First, in 1088 the kugyō met several times to debate the guilt of Fujiwara no Sanemasa, Shirakawa's tutor and longtime confidant. Sanemasa was accused by the powerful Kyūshū shrine of Usa Hachiman-gū of firing arrows at its sacred shrine. The kugyō at length found him guilty and banished him and his accomplices to Izu.[51] In 1092 the kugyō met again to decide the

---

Yoshiie to chastise the Abe. The war covered the years 1051–1062 but is called the Nine Years' War because only the years of actual fighting were counted.

[47] *GNJ*, 1: 284. Kanji 3/10/10.

[48] *GNJ* 2: 133. Kanji 5/6/12. The edict also prohibited Yoshiie from entering the capital.

[49] *HRS*, p. 41. Kanji 5/6/21.   [50] *GNJ*, 2: 253. Kanji 6/5/5.

[51] *HRS*, p. 39. Kanji 2/11/30.

fate of Fujiwara no Tamefusa and Fujiwara no Nakazane, two of Shirakawa's kinshin. They had been accused of misdeeds by the Mount Hiei authorities, and they too were exiled.[52] Again, in 1093, another kinshin, Takashina no Tameie, was exiled for his involvement in a dispute with the Kōfuku-ji.[53] It seems unlikely that a man who was the "dictatorial ruler of the realm" would allow his close associates to be treated in this fashion by the other courtiers.[54]

In his early years of abdication Shirakawa demonstrated a good deal of concern with the continued growth of shōen throughout the country. On at least two occasions he discussed the matter of possible shōen regulations with Morozane's son, Moromichi. These discussions appear to have been in earnest and Shirakawa's opinion seems to have held some authority, since two months after his first discussion with Moromichi there were at least two cases of shōen confiscation.[55] At length, in 1099, a new shōen regulation ordinance was issued aimed at estates established since the 1087 ordinance.[56] Following the practice established in Go-Sanjō's reign, the Records Office (Kirokujo) was reopened in 1111, and the necessary officials —Nakamikado no Munetada among them—were appointed.[57] The effects of the ordinance and the reactivation of the Records Office are difficult to assess. The only known decision of the body appears to be the confirmation of Ōyama-shō in the province of Tamba, property of the powerful capital temple of Tō-ji.[58]

Until about 1100, then, ex-Emperor Shirakawa was by no means the supreme political figure at the Heian court. Aside from the matter of illegal shōen growth, Shirakawa does not appear to have been deeply involved in day-to-day political affairs. His main con-

[52] GNJ, 2: 290–91. Kanji 6/9/18, 20, and 28.

[53] GNJ, 3: 99–100. Kanji 7/8/26–27. In this case, at least, Morozane did explain the problem to Shirakawa after having been presented with the grievances by Kōfuku-ji monks.

[54] Takeuchi Rizō, Nihon no rekishi, vol. 6: Bushi no tōjō, p. 183, refers to Shirakawa as wan man jiten no kimi ("one-man ruler of the land").

[55] Besides the action taken in Yoshiie's case (see n. 50 in this chapter), a newly established manor in the province of Wakasa was also returned to public status. GNJ, 2: 248. Kanji 6/5/2.

[56] GNJ, 3: 282. Kōwa 1/5/12.   [57] CYK, 4: 84. Ten'ei 2/10/5.

[58] Heian ibun, 5: 1637–39, doc. 1811.

cern, as discussed earlier, was imperial succession, and he spent a good deal of time with his son, Emperor Horikawa. The emperor was a frail man to whom Shirakawa appears to have been devoted; he exerted considerable effort in the guardianship of his son. As for Horikawa himself, for the few years that he was emperor after attaining his majority, he seems to have had considerable power at court, working well with Morozane and Moromichi, the successive chancellors, and leading kugyō.[59]

Ex-Emperor Shirakawa: The Later Years, 1101–1129

In 1094 Fujiwara no Morozane became ill and resigned the *uji* chieftainship as well as the post of chancellor.[60] His son Moromichi succeeded him in both positions. Moromichi was by all accounts a very able and learned man,[61] perhaps potentially the greatest of all Fujiwara leaders. At thirty-three a long and prosperous future lay ahead of Moromichi. Unfortunately, he was never to have the chance to realize his potential as he died in 1099 at thirty-eight. The position of chancellor was not immediately filled, but Moromichi's son Tadazane was granted the right of document examination which was tantamount to holding the position.[62] About one month later Tadazane also succeeded to the uji chieftainship.[63]

Two years later, in 1101, Morozane died after an extended illness. Although he was still not technically appointed chancellor, Tadazane was the chieftain of the Fujiwara clan and the leading courtier among the Fujiwara. He was at last appointed chancellor in 1105. It was not that Tadazane was thought incapable, but his youth (he was twenty-eight in 1105) and lack of experience were severe handicaps in this aristocratic society which valued both age and experience. Even in 1106, by which time he was minister of the right as well as chancellor, Tadazane could not command the power that either Morozane or Moromichi had enjoyed. Minamoto no

[59] GKS, p. 204.   [60] GNJ, 3: 138–53. Gahō 1/3/9.
[61] See, for example, Honchō seiki, pp. 306–7. Kōwa 1/6/28. Moromichi's scholarly character is also apparent from reading his diary Gonijō Moromichiki.
[62] Denryaku, 1: 11. Kōwa 1/8/28.   [63] Ibid., p. 12. Kōwa 1/10/6.

Toshifusa, chieftain of the Minamoto, held the position of minister of the left and thus outranked Tadazane until the latter became chancellor. Even then, however, Toshifusa appears to have been much more influential in court circles. But it was Shirakawa, twice Tadazane's age, head of the imperial house, and father of the reigning emperor, who became the elder statesman of the Heian court.

Not surprisingly, it was during this period of misfortune within the sekkanke that Shirakawa's role in court politics began to expand. There is little doubt that for the next twenty years Shirakawa was the real power at court. Tadazane visited with the ex-sovereign on an almost regular basis to learn his views on governmental matters. According to his own diary, many of the actions that Tadazane took as chancellor and later as regent were at the "order of the ex-sovereign" (*in no ōse*). Tadazane appears to have handled most routine court affairs on his own initiative, in the manner of previous chancellors, but anything important required consultation with Shirakawa.

In particular, the ex-sovereign always expressed his opinion quite strongly on the matter of appointments; as Munetada remarked: "he carried out appointments unbound by law, yielding to his desires." [64] He was especially interested in the appointments to provincial governorships, and it was to these provincial posts that so many of his personal associates were appointed.[65] Shirakawa also decided everything that even remotely concerned the welfare of the imperial house, whose fortune and power he was determined to extend.

When Horikawa died in 1107, Munetada praised the virtues of the deceased emperor yet lamented the deteriorating conditions with the following observation. "Alas, it is a degenerate age, and the realm is in great confusion. But is it solely the fault of the emperor? No, it is because the priestly sovereign (Shirakawa) still lives, and the affairs of the land are split in two." [66] Tadazane was

[64] CYK, 6: 65. Daiji 4/7/7.   [65] See chapter 9.
[66] CYK, 3: 231. Kajō 2/7/19.

appointed regent for the new emperor, Toba, but he was unable to exercise any great influence over the boy because he lacked a close maternal connection.

As he had done for his son Horikawa, Shirakawa continued to act as guardian for his grandson Toba. Whatever action Tadazane took on the emperor's behalf appears to have been as a result of Shirakawa's advice. If Fujiwara regents had been able to exert considerable influence over emperors for most of the Heian period through their maternal connections, a paternal grandfather such as Shirakawa could do the same. Only a year later Munetada remarked that "the grandeur of the abdicated sovereign is equal to that of His Majesty, and at the present moment this abdicated sovereign is sole political master." [67]

Inevitably, there was hostility between the ex-sovereign and the regent, and the relatively amicable relationship that the two houses had enjoyed during Morozane's days came to an end. In 1122 an incident occurred which was to spell disaster for Tadazane. In accordance with long-standing custom, Shirakawa desired to make Tadazane's daughter Taishi one of Toba's consorts. Tadazane appears at first to have been delighted over the prospect, for it could only increase the welfare of his house. But for some unexplained reason he ultimately refused the offer. Furious, Shirakawa sent word to the kugyō council that Tadazane should be dismissed as chancellor.[68] His right of document examination was taken away, and Tadazane voluntarily secluded himself at Uji. He did not return to service at court until he was asked back by the ex-emperor Toba two years after Shirakawa's death.[69] So incensed was Shirakawa that he even left an injunction forbidding Tadazane's daughter from ever becoming an imperial consort.[70] After Tadazane's dismissal his eldest son, Tadamichi, was made chancellor, but he enjoyed no more power than his father.

For the last twenty years of his life, ex-Emperor Shirakawa was the most powerful and revered figure at the Heian court, living a

[67] CYK, 3: 410. Tennin 1/10/28.   [68] CYK, 5: 259. Hōan 1/11/12.
[69] CYK, 7: 301. Daiji 6/11/17.   [70] Chōshūki, 2: 155. Chōjō 2/6/2.

life of grandeur and power that few members of the imperial house in Japanese history ever enjoyed. Yet it is important to note that, despite his influential position in court politics, Shirakawa still operated through the established channels of the *ritsuryō* governmental system. He did not create a new form of political control which he ran as an absolute dictator. He did not disregard the emperor, the regent, and the kugyō council. On the contrary, he appears to have had all due respect for the imperial position as the ultimate sanctifier of political action, and he utilized the existing political apparatus rather than creating a new one.

Like all abdicated sovereigns, Shirakawa set up his own office which he staffed with close and reliable associates. There were, to be sure, certain differences between Shirakawa's in no chō and those of previous ex-emperors, which reflect the increased influence of the imperial house in Heian court life. First, Shirakawa's in no chō appears to have been larger. Exact figures are unavailable, and records for previous retired sovereigns are less complete, but the number of officials to serve in Shirakawa's office appears far greater than in any previous in no chō. At Shirakawa's death, Munetada recorded the names of 20 directors, 5 scribes, 4 secretaries, 5 assistants, and more than 80 warriors in the *in no hokumen*.[71]

Second, the position of in no hokumen (ex-sovereign's warriors of the northern quarter) was added during Shirakawa's tenure as abdicated sovereign. This was another body of armed guards to defend the ex-emperor's palace, and its establishment is a reflection of the growth of imperial house power and the unsettled conditions of the times.[72] A third and most significant difference between Shirakawa's in no chō and previous ones was the nature of the documents it issued. Kitabatake Chikafusa claimed in the *Jinnō shōtōki* that from Shirakawa's time onward documents from the abdicated sovereign's office became more important than imperial edicts.

An examination of the surviving in no chō documents does not corroborate this statement, however. It is true that, with the estab-

---

[71] CYK, 6: 76. Daiji 4/7/15.   [72] See appendix 1.

lishment of Shirakawa's in no chō, documents issued by this office increased tremendously. Prior to Shirakawa's time, the only extant inzen (ex-emperor's edict) was one issued by Uda in the early ninth century. There are only scattered references to other such documents. At least seven documents issued by Shirakawa's in no chō are extant today, and this does not appear to have been simply an accident of document preservation. An examination of these documents, however, shows that not one concerns matters of imperial government. They all deal with landholdings of some imperial family member or imperial temple.

Even those documents of the ex-sovereign's office mentioned in various source materials do not deal with public affairs. Public matters continued to be dealt with by imperial edict or edicts of the Grand Council of State. There is, for example, mention of an inzen issued in 1087 in Fujiwara no Tamefusa's diary.[73] This document is a pardon granted to Tachibana no Koretsuna, a courtier who had gotten in a fight with one of Shirakawa's messengers. Since I will deal with the matter of in no chō documents more extensively in chapter 8, I will not discuss them at length here. Suffice it to say that they did not, at least in Shirakawa's time, conflict with or overrule imperial edicts.

It is significant, however, that these documents deal mainly with landholdings of the imperial house. As noted earlier in this chapter, Shirakawa was quite concerned with the growth of illegal private lands throughout the country, and he attempted to curtail this growth. At the same time, he attempted to increase the landed wealth of the imperial house itself by the development of imperial edict fields. Compared with his successors Toba and Go-Shirakawa, however, Shirakawa seems to have been very hesitant to establish even legal shōen for the imperial house. None of his extant in no chō documents attempts to establish the rights to a new imperial holding, which suggests that shōen newly established by the imperial house during Shirakawa's lifetime were probably few.

The increased power and influence of the imperial house since

[73] *Dai Nihon shiryō*, ser. 3, 1: 132. The inzen is copied in *Tamefusakyōki*.

Go-Sanjō's time, however, made the abdicated sovereign an ideal object for the commendation of holdings by other landholders. While Shirakawa was abdicated sovereign, numerous palaces, villas, and temples were built for the imperial house by different courtiers as "special contributions," and shōen throughout the country were commended for the support of these various edifices. Thus the imperial house came to control an increasingly large number of estates, and as the head of the imperial house, Shirakawa became the ultimate protector and beneficiary of these estates.

Despite his own feelings on the matter, the shōen holdings of the imperial house increased during Shirakawa's lifetime. I will discuss this at length in chapter 10, but it is noteworthy that it was during Shirakawa's days that the imperial house began to develop a substantial private economic base of landholdings that enabled it to surpass the other great houses competing for political and economic power in Heian Japan.

Shirakawa was a truly remarkable figure in Japanese history. He carried the imperial house to a position of independence, power, and internal solidarity far beyond what Go-Sanjō could have imagined. For fifty-seven years—fourteen as emperor and forty-three as abdicated sovereign—Shirakawa was the principal figure at court, providing a continuity and direction to imperial efforts previously unknown in Japanese history. As Munetada has remarked, his long life as a political figure was unequaled.

Only the emperor Yōzei lived to be eighty-one, but he never reigned over the empire; he was even a deposed sovereign. Besides these two [Yōzei and Shirakawa], no other sovereign has lived to the age of seventy-seven. . . . His majesty filled the four seas and subdued the empire. . . . Since the time of Emperor Kammu there has been no such example. He should be termed a sage ruler, an eternal sovereign.[74]

Munetada also commented on Shirakawa's personal characteristics: "He was resolute. He showed clarity in meting out rewards and punishments. He displayed his love and hate, and he was conspicuous in his show of wealth." [75] Shirakawa was indeed the giant of his age. As both emperor and ex-emperor he participated ac-

[74] CYK, 6: 65. Daiji 4/7/7.   [75] Ibid.

tively in court politics as few before him. And yet to accept only a few quotes from Munetada and other courtiers—whose diaries are full of exaggerations—and conclude that he created a new form of rule in which the abdicated sovereign controlled the country in a dictatorial fashion would be a gross oversimplification and distortion of the actual situation.

During the time Shirakawa served as retired emperor, the kugyō council remained the major decision-making body at court. Shirakawa's method of exerting political influence was to cultivate the members of that body and win their allegiance by the granting of patronage. While previously the sekkanke had enjoyed a preeminent position—by virtue of its control over the emperor and the highest offices in the land—and had been able to attract numerous clients, Shirakawa's ability to reward such courtiers now surpassed that of the declining sekkanke. By attracting the clientage of many members of the kugyō and lower-ranking courtiers, including many who had once served as private house officials for the regent's house, Shirakawa was able to exert a considerable amount of influence in their council meetings.

Shirakawa's in no chō and the officials who served in it should not be regarded as constituting a new form of government replacing the old ritsuryō system. It was simply a reflection of the fact that the imperial house, under first Go-Sanjō and then Shirakawa, had completed its development as a private house. In the manner of other great families, it now had administrative offices and officials, as well as a growing number of private landholdings to finance it. The imperial family was no longer solely a public institution, but a well-organized house, much the same as the sekkanke, the Murakami Genji, or any other court family. The sanctity of the imperial lineage, however, gave the imperial house a singular advantage over the other houses. Once the Fujiwara had lost their control over the imperial institution, Shirakawa and his immediate successors made the imperial house a formidable entity, more than able to compete with other houses for real political power. With Shirakawa the imperial house entered a golden age in Japanese history.

❧ SIX ❧

The Insei *Period II: Toba*

SHIRAKAWA WAS succeeded as retired sovereign and head of the imperial house by Toba, the long-awaited heir of Horikawa. Although Shirakawa had "left his household" to become a monk, he was so uncertain of Horikawa's future that he had not taken the final vows or assumed a Buddhist name. If the frail Horikawa had died without an heir, Shirakawa would have been free to reascend the throne. All such fears were put to rest, however, with the birth of Toba in 1103. He was immediately made crown prince, and he ascended the throne upon the death of Horikawa in 1107.

During Toba's reign, Shirakawa continued to exercise his familial authority as head of the imperial house. He acted as guardian to Toba in the same manner as he had for Horikawa. In this advisory capacity he functioned much the same as the Fujiwara regents prior to the Go-Sanjō era. Shirakawa's relationship with his son Horikawa had been a close and loving one; it was, after all, Horikawa upon whom Shirakawa had pinned his hopes for the succession of his line. The relationship between the abdicated sovereign and his grandson Toba, however, was different.[1] Although Shirakawa took the role of father to Toba, the two never seem to have been close, especially after Toba reached his majority.

---

[1] The Shirakawa-Horikawa relationship is discussed in detail in Akagi Shizuko, "Shirakawa-in to Horikawa tennō: Inseī shoki no in to tennō," pp. 21–35.

Shirakawa was the major political figure at court throughout the reign of Toba and remained so even after Toba had been forced to abdicate. During the last twenty-odd years of his life Shirakawa totally dominated the court political scene. Many of his actions had repercussions only after Toba's abdication. Indeed, the most serious of these came immediately following Toba's death in 1156, with the outbreak of an armed revolt called the Hōgen disturbance. But before considering the complex set of relationships that led to the Hōgen conflict, let us first see how Toba came to be emperor and then abdicated sovereign.

The Accession and Reign of Emperor Toba

Toba became emperor at the age of five upon Horikawa's death in 1107. Whereas Horikawa had been an active participant in court politics, Toba was so young that Shirakawa and the regent Tadazane assumed the major roles at court. While there was some friction between these two powerful figures, Tadazane appears to have accepted the fact that Shirakawa would have his way in most matters, especially in the determination of appointments. For a while he avoided any serious trouble. It was the matter of selecting consorts for Toba that brought Shirakawa and Tadazane into open conflict and resulted in the latter's virtual retirement from court.

As discussed in chapter 5, Shirakawa wanted to make Tadazane's daughter Taishi an imperial consort for Toba, but Tadazane refused the honor and thereby incurred Shirakawa's wrath. No satisfactory reason has ever been given for Tadazane's action. The *Gukanshō* alleges that he refused because of some unspecified misdeeds in Toba's childhood that indicated he would be a tyrannical ruler.[2] While there may be some truth to this statement, certainly the earlier selection of Shirakawa's adopted daughter Shōshi as another imperial consort was a more important factor, as we shall see.

There had been further complications in the selection of Toba's

[2] *GKS*, pp. 207–8.

consort. Some years before, Shirakawa had adopted Shōshi, the daughter of his close retainer and a director of his in no chō, Fujiwara no Kinzane. Shirakawa was exceedingly fond of this girl. If accounts of their relationship are accurate, however, Shirakawa's love exceeded the limits of parental affection. At any rate, Shirakawa came to desire a match between Toba and Shōshi, and this proposed union may, as noted above, have been at the root of his trouble with Tadazane.

As Tadazane noted several times in his diary, Shōshi was indeed a "strange and unusual consort." [3] Before Shirakawa decided to make her a consort, Shōshi had been involved with Tadazane's son, Tadamichi. Arrangements for a marriage between Tadamichi and Shōshi had been made with Shirakawa, but the ceremony was postponed several times and was eventually called off. Subsequently, Shirakawa decided to make Shōshi an imperial consort, but widespread rumor about her conduct cast doubt upon her suitability for such an honor. It appears that, in addition to Tadamichi, Shōshi had also had an affair with Fujiwara no Suemichi, governor of Bingo province and son of Munemichi, an influential member of Shirakawa's in no chō.[4]

Throughout the last three months of 1117 there was discussion of Shōshi's entry into the women's quarters, but eventually Shirakawa prevailed. In the twelfth month of that year Shōshi was promoted to the third rank and then made an imperial concubine. Tadazane described the affair as "the strangest event in Japanese history." [5] A year later she was made empress (chūgū).

Shortly after she became empress, Shōshi gave birth to a son, Prince Akihito. This was the future emperor Sutoku, whose estrangement from Toba was a direct cause of the Hōgen disturbance of 1156. While the root of the discord between the two was imperial succession, it was complicated by a question of paternity. It is recounted in both the war chronicle Hōgen monogatari and the

[3] In Dai Nihon shiryō, ser. 4, 18: 421, Eikyū 5/10/10; p. 422, Eikyū 5/11/19; p. 428, Eikyū 5/12/20. The quotes are all from Tadazane's diary, Denryaku.
[4] Ibid., pp. 421–22, Eikyū 5/10/11; p. 422, Eikyū 5/10/15; p. 422, Eikyū 5/11/19.
[5] Ibid., p. 423. Eikyū 5/12/12.

Kojidan that Sutoku was not Toba's son at all but the offspring of a liaison between Shōshi and Shirakawa.

Whether the story is true or not, Sutoku was recognized as Toba's eldest son. Sutoku never actually served as crown prince, and in fact, there was no crown prince during Toba's reign. In 1123, when he was only twenty-one, Toba abdicated in favor of the five-year-old Sutoku, after first issuing an edict that formally named him crown prince.[6] The decision was not Toba's own but was made by his grandfather, Shirakawa. That Shirakawa forced Toba to abdicate is even more understandable if we accept the fact that the former was Sutoku's father. The ex-emperor's decision to make Toba abdicate in Sutoku's favor was no doubt designed to increase the honor and glory of the empress Shōshi. In 1124 she became a retired imperial lady (*nyoin*) with the issuance of an edict which granted her the palace name (*ingō*) Taikemmon'in. She gave birth to four more sons, one of whom became the emperor Go-Shirakawa.

Thus Shōshi became the mother of five princes and the most honored lady in the land. As nyoin she ranked just below the two abdicated sovereigns Shirakawa and Toba. The three, collectively referred to in the sources as "the three *in*" (*san'in*), were together frequently on outings, at festivals, and at Shinto and Buddhist ceremonies. Shōshi even went on a pilgrimage to Kumano with Shirakawa and Toba, the first time, it appears, that an imperial lady had made such a trip.[7] Shirakawa's fondness for Shōshi does not seem to have lessened after she became empress, and it is obvious that he wished the imperial succession to be transmitted through her sons. For his part, Toba does not seem to have held it against her that she had most likely been intimate with his grandfather. She remained his favorite consort and continued to bear him sons.

After his abdication, Toba enjoyed considerable freedom but little power as junior retired sovereign since Shirakawa continued to dominate court politics.[8] Like other abdicated sovereigns and

---

[6] *HRS*, p. 52. Hōan 4/1/28.   [7] Ibid., p. 56. Daiji 1/11/9.

[8] Shirakawa was variously referred to as *hon'in* or *ichi'in* (senior retired emperor), *dajō hōō* or *hōō* (priestly retired sovereign), and Toba as *shin'in* (newly abdicated emperor), *dajō tennō* or *jōkō* (abdicated emperor.)

imperial ladies,[9] Toba established an in no chō upon his abdication
to handle his personal affairs. Available sources yield little information about the composition and duties of Toba's in no chō during
Shirakawa's lifetime, but we can assume that it was considerably
smaller than his grandfather's. Furthermore, it appears that some
of the officials of Shirakawa's in no chō—such as Fujiwara no
Tsunetada and Fujiwara no Akimori—also served simultaneously
in Toba's private office, thus acting more broadly as retainers for
the entire imperial house.[10]

For a period of six and a half years Toba was junior retired emperor while Shirakawa continued to hold the dominant political
power at court. The three *in*—Shirakawa, Toba, and Shōshi—spent
much of their time enjoying the prestige and luxury of the imperial
revival, but Toba had little influence in politics despite the fact
that he was the (presumed) father of the reigning emperor. His actions following Shirakawa's death show that he had been displeased
with this state of affairs and jealous of the ex-emperor's influence.

As father of the reigning emperor and next in line for the headship of the imperial house, Toba was surely anxious for the power
and prestige that he would inherit upon Shirakawa's death. It could
not have pleased him that Shirakawa turned out to be one of the
most durable and vigorous emperors in Japanese history. Shirakawa
enjoyed continued good health and dominated the court year after
year. Toba was in the prime of his life yet had no significant political influence. Furthermore, if the story of Sutoku's paternity is
valid, it must have been equally unpleasant for Toba to be constantly reminded that the emperor was not his true son. With
several other sons of his own, he might have wished to alter the
succession scheme. In any event, there appears to have been a good
deal of anxiety and jealousy in Toba's relationship with his grandfather.

9 For a discussion of nyoin, see Ryō Susumu, "Nyoinsei no seiritsu," in his *Heian
jidai*, pp. 77–91.
[10] Many *kinshin* also served imperial ladies as well as abdicated sovereigns. This
aspect of retainers of the retired emperors will be further discussed in chapter 9.

Toba as Senior Retired Sovereign

Shirakawa finally died in 1129 and the twenty-seven-year-old ex-emperor Toba became senior, and until 1141 sole, retired sovereign. As head of the imperial house, he succeeded his grandfather as the most influential man at court. He inherited the personnel that had served in Shirakawa's in no chō, although he dismissed some of them. Fujiwara no Akimori, who had been in the service of both ex-sovereigns simultaneously, was dismissed along with his brothers for failing to serve Toba loyally while Shirakawa was still alive.[11] But for the most part Toba's closest associates were men or sons and grandsons of men who had served Shirakawa: Fujiwara no Munemichi's sons Koremichi, Narimichi, and Shigemichi; Fujiwara no Akisue's grandson Ienari; Kinzane's sons Saneyuki and Saneyoshi and his grandson Kinnori.[12] Besides these courtiers, the warriors in Shirakawa's service continued to serve Toba: Taira no Masamori's son and grandson, Tadamori and Kiyomori, are conspicuous examples.[13]

Although there was much continuity of personnel among those in the service of the ex-sovereigns Shirakawa and Toba, the passing of such a powerful political figure was bound to result in some changes at court. Indeed, the nature of court politics during the abdication years of Shirakawa and of Toba was entirely different. We have already seen that Shirakawa only gradually moved into the active arena of court politics, less because of his own desires than through the force of events: the early deaths of Morozane and Moromichi, and the ascendancy of Tadazane to the highest court circles at a young age. It was only after Tadazane became chancellor that Shirakawa came to participate actively and with great influence in court politics. From then on at least there was a severe

[11] *Chōshūki*, 2: 11, Daiji 5/4/26. Toba gave four reasons for the dismissal, but the gist of the problem appears to have been failure to serve faithfully. For the dismissal of Akimori's brothers, see ibid., p. 215, Chōjō 3/8/4.

[12] See chapter 9 and appendix 2.

[13] For a more detailed account of the relationship between the ex-sovereign Shirakawa and the Taira see chapter 8. Also see Ryō Susumu, "Rokujōin-ryō to Taira no Masamori," in *Heian jidai*, pp. 117–35.

struggle for power between the *sekkanke*, represented by Tadazane, and the imperial house, headed by Shirakawa. Eventually, as we have seen, Tadazane lost his position and left court. The family fortunes were at a low ebb while his son Tadamichi represented the sekkanke at court. The regent's house had not been less influential in hundreds of years.

With Shirakawa's death and Toba's inheritance of imperial family leadership, however, there was a great change in the court. This was marked first by Tadazane's return to service after more than ten years of isolation at Uji. It was a day of great happiness for the country, according to Munetada: ruler and subject were again united as one.[14] After his return to court, Tadazane reassumed the actual power and leadership of the Fujiwara regent's house, which had passed to Tadamichi during his absence. Tadamichi, however, maintained the positions of regent (later chancellor) and prime minister as well as clan chieftain. This had the effect of heightening the estrangement between father and son that had begun when Tadazane left court service.

With the return of Tadazane to court, however, both the sekkanke and the imperial house appear to have reversed their previous positions. Toba had been successful in persuading Tadazane to return to court service after his long absence,[15] and the two men remained on cordial terms. Furthermore, the ex-emperor decided to accept Tadazane's daughter as a consort. This was the girl Taishi, the very one whom Shirakawa had wished to make an empress years before; it had been Tadazane's refusal of this offer that had put him at odds with Shirakawa. Taishi must not have been undesirable to Toba, however, for now, in 1134, he made her empress. This was indeed a forceful move on Toba's part since there had "never been an example of making the wife of an abdicated sov-

---

[14] *CYK*, 7: 301. Tenjō 1/11/17. (Here Daiji 6/11/17).

[15] It was unprecedented for a former chancellor to return to service while another held the post, and the court was in a quandary over procedure. Toba eventually settled the matter by issuing an ex-emperor's edict (*inzen*) permitting Tadazane the right of document examination. *CYK*, 6: 275. Chōjō 1/1/14.

ereign an empress." [16] Yet despite criticism and talk at court,[17] Toba went ahead. Later, in 1139, she was given the palace name Kaya no in. Tadazane and Toba were now closely linked through this marriage.

Thus Toba's attitude toward Tadazane appears to have been the reverse of his grandfather's. Tadazane returned to court and drew close to Toba and the imperial house. Throughout the twenty-odd years between Shirakawa's death and Toba's there was cooperation between the imperial house and the sekkanke unseen in Shirakawa's time. Perhaps Tadazane had come to the conclusion that it was more beneficial for the sekkanke to cooperate with the newly invigorated imperial house than to struggle against it. He certainly had ample time to ponder the problem while at Uji. He was well aware that his own efforts to win the allegiance of courtiers had been largely undercut by Shirakawa. Furthermore, the Fujiwara owed their dominant position at court to cooperation with the imperial house through the positions of regent and chancellor. Why was it not possible to cooperate with an abdicated sovereign as well as a reigning emperor? Whatever thoughts ran through his mind, Tadazane's actions make clear his decision to cooperate with Toba for the enhancement of the sekkanke fortunes.[18]

It was not only in their attitude toward the sekkanke that Shirakawa and Toba differed. Their approach to the administration of imperial house affairs and their opinions on political matters also differed substantially. One conspicuous example was their respective attitudes toward the development of shōen holdings. As we have seen, Shirakawa was in firm opposition to the continued expansion of private landholdings, and he issued several regulation

<hr/>

[16] *Chōshūki*, 2: 187. Chōjō 3/3/2.   [17] Ibid.

[18] In 1150, for example, Tadazane commended some family *shōen* to Toba, who politely refused, then accepted them after Tadazane's insistence. See *Taiki*, 2: 44, Kyūan 6/10/12. In 1153 Tadazane gave 165 *ryō* of gold dust taken from Fujiwara holdings in Dewa and Mutsu to Toba to be used to cover expenses for prayers to hasten the recovery of his health. Ibid., p. 102, Nimpyō 3/9/17. Again in 1154 Tadazane had constructed a new palace and a small Buddhist hall in the Toba-dono in order to receive reappointment as (absentee) governor of Harima. Ibid., p. 129, Kyūju 1/7/29.

ordinances to this end. Even the one dating from Toba's reign (1107) appears to have been issued at Shirakawa's insistence. Shirakawa was frequently at odds with Tadazane over shōen holdings, and there are no documents issued by his in no chō related to shōen of the imperial house.

In contrast, Toba seems to have accepted the growth of private landholdings as the inevitable trend of the times. Not only is there no indication of any desire on his part to check such developments, but, on the contrary, he actively worked to increase the lands under imperial control. There are a number of extant in no chō documents from his period that concern imperial house rights to shōen holdings.[19] Shirakawa had not been completely inactive in accumulating private lands for the imperial house, but he seems to have been much less active than Toba.

During Toba's years as abdicated sovereign, imperial holdings—particularly those of the retired sovereign—grew tremendously. Even a cursory reading of the diaries and documents of the times reveals a great number of instances of commendation of shōen to the retired sovereign, from the highest-ranking members of the regent's house to the middle- and lower-ranking courtiers, and even members of the rising warrior class.

For the most part, these shōen were not in fact direct holdings of the retired emperor but, from Shirakawa's to Go-Shirakawa's day, were indirectly controlled. That is, the lands were almost always attached to an imperial temple (goganji), constructed at the wish of one member or another of the imperial house. During the years of Shirakawa, Toba, and Go-Shirakawa numerous goganji were constructed, almost all by "special contributions" from provincial governors, and then lands were commended to them for their sup-

---

[19] See documents 2145, 2208, 2243–45, 2253–56, etc., scattered throughout volumes 5 and 6 of *Heian ibun*. For documents issued by Taikemmon'in's in no chō concerning shōen rights, see ibid., 5: 1824, doc. 2122; p. 1842, doc. 2134; p. 1956, doc. 2310. For more extensive comments on the nature of shōen holdings of the imperial house see chapter 10. The in no chō documents of the retired emperor and retired imperial ladies are discussed in chapter 8.

port. Such holdings (ryō) were known by the name of the temple to which they were attached: Anrakujuin-ryō, Kongōshōin-ryō, Chōkōdō-ryō, and so on. These temple holdings formed the bulk of the imperial lands accumulated during the lives of these three sovereigns.[20]

The expansion of imperial lands and the increase in the number of retired imperial ladies during Toba's reign gave rise to a concern with the transmission of such holdings as well as the provision for the welfare of the various imperial family members. For both reasons, blocs of holdings began to be granted to different imperial ladies. During Toba's years the most famous bloc of holdings created was the Hachijōin-ryō. Hachijō-in was the palace name of Princess Shōshi, who was born in 1136 to Toba and his consort Bifukumon'in. In 1140 Toba gave her some twelve different holdings, and after her mother's death in 1160 she inherited all Bifukumon'in's lands. The total holdings of Hachijō-in reached some 230, thus making it one of the largest imperial blocs. In later years, when the imperial house split over the succession issue, the Hachijōin-ryō became the basic holdings of the Daikaku-ji branch.

If Toba's attitude toward estate holdings was somewhat more positive and in tune with the trend of the times than that of Shirakawa, his participation in the political process was little different. While he had the most influential voice at court, Toba did not by any means seek to abolish or circumvent the regular channels of imperial government but, like his grandfather, made full use of existing institutions. Whether or not court matters were previously discussed with him and his opinion learned, decisions were still reached by the discussions of the kugyō council. For the most part such discussions were held at the imperial palace, or, more correctly, at one of the provisional imperial palaces since the main palace had burned down in the mid-Heian period and was not rebuilt until after the Hōgen disturbance. On occasions, the kugyō met at the retired emperor's palace, as they had also done during Shirakawa's

[20] See chapter 10.

lifetime. Such times, however, were emergencies, and the conservative Toba appears to have been very concerned with following proper procedure and precedence in court matters.[21]

One incident during his years as abdicated sovereign demonstrates the infrequency with which Toba actively interfered with kugyō meetings and allowed his own associates to help make important decisions. This was at the time of an outbreak of violence in 1147 between warriors in the service of the ex-sovereign and some retainers of the Gion Shrine.[22] It occurred at a festival held at the Gion Shrine when Taira no Kiyomori—then only thirty, with a post in the important Ministry of Central Affairs (Nakatsukasa-shō), and in personal service to Toba—and some of his warriors quarreled with several of the retainers attached to the shine. Kiyomori's father Tadamori, a director in Toba's in no chō and governor of Bizen, accused seven of the temple retainers of starting the incident. But the Gion Shrine, with support from the monks at Enryaku-ji and the priests of the Hie Shrine, lodged a counter accusation against Tadamori and Kiyomori. Since Tadamori had protested to Toba, the ex-emperor called the kugyō together at his palace to discuss the issue. Besides the kugyō the former middle councillor Fujiwara no Akiyori, one of Toba's closest associates, also attended, at Toba's insistence. When the meeting was over, the written decision was presented to Toba, but Akiyori himself went to inform the ex-emperor of the decision. Punishment was a small fine to be paid by Kiyomori, but to avoid retaliation by the aroused monks and priests Minamoto no Tameyoshi and other warriors were ordered to guard Toba's palace.

Thus, in an incident which was regarded as a serious affair, and which could further be seen as a private matter involving the activities of Toba's retainers, the kugyō met at Toba's palace and were joined by a former kugyō, an associate of Toba's, by order of the abdicated sovereign. Such instances were not the norm; they oc-

[21] Hashimoto Yoshihiko, "Hōgen no ran zenshi shōkō," p. 35.

[22] The events ran from the fifteenth day of the sixth month to the fifth day of the eighth month of 1147 (Kyūan 3) and are recorded in Honchō seiki, pp. 548–62.

curred infrequently and only over serious matters. Furthermore, the forceful action taken against the armed monks was indeed a new approach during Toba's time, and it demonstrates a wide divergence from the conciliatory measures of Shirakawa who, it is said, could control everything but the flow of the Kamo River, the fall of the dice, and the armed monks.

Intrafamilial Rivalries in the Imperial House and Sekkanke

Thus the situation at court during the years Toba was senior abdicated sovereign was quite different from that during his grandfather's day. The change was partly due to the difference in the two personalities and their approaches to people and problems, but to a larger extent it was the result of the general revival of the imperial house as an active and forceful participant in the political process. The regent's house, long without serious opposition from other court families, had so dominated court life that when we speak of the Heian period we immediately think of the power and the glory of the Fujiwara: the "world of the shining prince." Due to the efforts of Go-Sanjō and Shirakawa and aided by a few timely misfortunes in the sekkanke, however, the imperial house had become revitalized and began to compete once again for actual power and wealth at court. By Shirakawa's death the sekkanke had been surpassed as the most powerful and influential of all houses, and even the chieftain of the Fujiwara began to seek favor from the abdicated sovereign who served as head of the imperial house. The emergence of the imperial house as a political force in the late Heian period had many repercussions at court, and the complex political maneuvers of certain members of both the imperial house and the sekkanke, leading to the conflict of 1156, are of the greatest importance.

While there was a reconciliation between the two great families at court during Toba's years as abdicated sovereign, the actions taken by his grandfather against certain persons, and now reversed

by himself, had their effect. Instead of fostering hostility and competition between families, the shifts in favoritism resulted in bitter
intrafamilial quarrels in both the imperial house and the sekkanke.
Within the sekkanke the relationship between Tadazane and Tadamichi continued to deteriorate, particularly after Tadazane supported his second son, Yorinaga, against Tadamichi. Eventually a
deep rift developed between Tadazane and Yorinaga on the one
hand and Tadamichi on the other. In the imperial house, Toba's
relationship with Sutoku, already strained, became openly hostile
in 1141, when the ex-emperor forced Sutoku's abdication in order
to bring to the throne Emperor Konoe, the son of his favorite empress Bifukumon'in. The complications of the split in the two
houses brought about alliances between the disaffected elements of
both and led directly to the Hōgen disturbance, one of the crucial
revolts in Japanese history (see below in this chapter).

In the regent's house relations between Tadazane and his eldest
son and original choice as heir, Tadamichi, had long been strained.
After Tadazane's return to court, their peculiar public and private
positions led to deeper conflict. The son was prime minister and
chancellor as well as uji chieftain, while the father was the former
chancellor, most commonly referred to as zenkō (short for zenjō
taikō, a term meaning "the chancellor's father who had become a
priest"). It was an unusual situation, to say the least, for a son to
hold offices superior to the father, unless of course the father had
gone into retirement. But Tadazane was quite active and, despite
Tadamichi's positions, directed most of the public and private
affairs of the family at court.

Tadazane's animosity toward Tadamichi led him to favor his
second son, Yorinaga, and he began to back this son at court with
the intention of undercutting Tadamichi's position. The house split
into two camps: Tadazane and Yorinaga on the one hand, and
Tadamichi on the other. Both sons saw their hopes for eventual
triumph in the formation of a close alliance with the imperial house.
There ensued a fierce struggle between the two men as both tried to
have their respective daughters made imperial consorts to Emperor

Konoe in the hope of producing an heir to the throne. Both Tadamichi and Yorinaga were reverting to the age-old custom of using
daughters to gain control of the imperial institution. The two
women in question were both adopted daughters: Teishi, Fujiwara
no Koremichi's daughter who had been adopted by Tadamichi; and
Tashi, the daughter of Fujiwara no Kin'yoshi, whom Yorinaga had
adopted.

Yorinaga obtained Tashi's appointment through his own efforts,
since both he and his father were on friendly terms—at least for the
moment—with Toba, but Tadamichi needed help from within the
imperial house. That help came from one of Toba's consorts,
Fujiwara no Tokushi, the daughter of Toba's kinshin Fujiwara no
Nagazane, referred to above by her palace name Bifukumon'in.
Toba had taken her as one of his wives after Shirakawa's·death, and
he was exceedingly fond of her. After Taikemmon'in's death in
1145, Bifukumon'in became Toba's favorite and her influence in
court politics was considerable.

Yorinaga first petitioned to have Tashi entered into the women's
quarters in 1142,[23] and, although Toba seemed agreeable at the
time, the step was not actually taken until 1150. In 1148 Bifukumon'in had taken Teishi as her adopted daughter, and it was
rumored that she was planning to make this girl the consort of
Prince Masahito (Emperor Go-Shirakawa), Toba's fourth son.[24]
Just after Tashi became Emperor Konoe's consort in the second
month of 1150, however, Tadamichi became the foster father of
Teishi and immediately got her named to the women's palace as
well. It appears that it was not actually Tadamichi but Bifukumon'in
who was behind this move; Toba had gone along with it and said
it was Tadamichi's idea.[25]

Perhaps the rumor that she was planning to have Teishi marry
Prince Masahito was just that. It was only a few days after Yorinaga
had succeeded in having Tashi made an imperial consort that
Bifukumon'in had adopted Teishi. While it took Yorinaga over a

[23] *Taiki*, 1: 71. Kōji 1/8/9.   [24] Ibid., p. 258. Kyūan 4/76.
[25] Hashimoto, "Hōgen no ran," p. 27.

year from the time Tashi was actually granted permission, to the
date the ceremony was concluded, Teishi's appointment was decided almost immediately and the ceremony was carried out within
two months. Judging from the fact that Bifukumon'in continued
to serve as the guardian and supporter of Teishi long after her marriage to Emperor Konoe, it is certainly possible that she had planned
all along to back Teishi against Tashi.[26]

This seems even more likely when one considers the relationship
between Yorinaga and Bifukumon'in. Yorinaga was upon several
occasions critical of Bifukumon'in's relatives, Ienari and Ieaki, her
close retainers Koremichi and Shigemichi, and even the lady herself.[27] Since there does not seem to be any specific incident that
accounts for Yorinaga's enmity toward her, it may well have been
his distaste for upstart courtiers who enjoyed powers once monopolized by his own house that led to his animosity. This and his keen
competition at court with people like Bifukumon'in's brothers for
increased honors were sufficient to engender Yorinaga's enmity for
a person with such powerful influence over Toba.

At any rate, both Yorinaga and Tadamichi, as well as Bifukumon'in, managed to have their respective daughters made imperial
consorts. Shortly thereafter, Tadazane began to exert his influence
actively on the side of Yorinaga, who was his second son, and this
brought about a final rift between the brothers. In 1150 Tadazane
took from Tadamichi the seal of the Fujiwara chieftainship, together with the lacquer utensils and tables that symbolized the
position, and bestowed them on Yorinaga.[28] On the tenth day of the

[26] Hashimoto also suggests this as a strong possibility, even stronger than the
rumor about her intentions for Teishi as Masahito's consort. Ibid.

[27] On two occasions Yorinaga refers to her brothers as *shodaibu*, a term for
middle-ranking courtiers used derogatorily by the kugyō. *Taiki*, 1: 117, Kōji 3/2/8.
On another occasion, Yorinaga was discussing the various visits of respect paid to
Toba, Sutoku, and other imperial family members on the first day of the new year.
He was uncertain whether Bifukumon'in was worthy of such a visit since, although
she was an empress and mother of Emperor Konoe, she was only the daughter of a
middle-ranking courtier. Ibid., p. 111, Kōji 3/1/1.

[28] *HRS*, p. 69, Kyūan 6/9/26. See also *Taiki*, 2: 40–41, same date. Tadazane
took the uji chieftainship away from Tadamichi because "the regency is granted
by the emperor, and I cannot take it away. The uji chieftainship I have abdicated,
and it does not require an imperial edict. If I seize the chieftainship and grant it to
you, what is there to fear?"

new year Yorinaga, until then minister of the left, was made Chancellor and given the right of document examination.[29] From that time on Tadamichi became completely estranged from his father and brother and, as we shall see, turned to Bifukumon'in for support at court.

The situation at court was now as follows. Toba, at age forty-nine, was senior retired emperor and had already taken the tonsure. Bifukumon'in was his principal consort, although Kaya no in was also frequently in his company. Toba's acknowledged son, but most likely his half-brother, Sutoku, was junior retired emperor and greatly at odds with Toba. Toba had made Bifukumon'in's son (Konoe) crown prince to Sutoku only three months after his birth and then had forced Sutoku to abdicate in his favor in 1141. Thus both Sutoku's and his son Prince Shigehito's chances for future power and glory seemed dim. The result of all this was a great animosity between the two retired emperors.

Within the sekkanke Tadazane, now sixty-three, was retired, having become a priest in 1140; and he devoted himself to the support of Yorinaga. Yorinaga, at age thirty, was chancellor and head of the Fujiwara uji, while Tadamichi was completely estranged from his father and brother. The imperial house and the sekkanke were both desperately split into opposing camps and little was required to touch off a major political crisis at court. The death of the young emperor Konoe in 1155, followed closely by Toba's death in 1156, brought about the eruption.

Before sketching further the outline of the shifting political alliances that led to the Hōgen disturbance, one more important character must be introduced: Fujiwara (Takashina) no Michinori, better known as the priest Shinzei. Michinori was born into a middle-ranking courtier family of the southern branch of the Fujiwara, long known for producing Confucian scholars. Unfortunately,

---

[29] HRS, p. 69. Nimpyō 1/1/10. See also Taiki, 2: 187, same date. Toba sent congratulations to Yorinaga on this auspicious occasion. Tadazane records a conversation in which he was informed that Yorinaga had not become regent because of Tadazane's request. Toba had decided it himself, as the regent's task was to instruct the emperor. Tadamichi had been instructing the emperor, but since he was lacking in filial respect Toba decided to make Yorinaga regent. (Yorinaga was widely known as a scholar.)

when Michinori was only seven his father died, and he grew up with
no family support at court, progressing very slowly in the bureaucracy for lack of any strong backing. Finally at the age of nineteen
Michinori became the adopted son of Takashina no Tsunetoshi
and married the daughter of Shigenaka. At this time he took the
Takashina name; and since he had entered a new house, he discontinued the traditional Confucian career of his original one.[30] Instead he embarked upon a political career in the regular court
bureaucracy.

With the backing of the Takashina, a family of increased influence since some of its members had become close associates of
both ex-emperor Shirakawa and Toba, Michinori made better
progress in his official career, mostly in the service of the imperial
house. He served Shōshi both when she was empress and after she
became the retired imperial lady Taikemmon'in. He also was a
secretary in Sutoku's office, and he held several positions in Toba's
in no chō.

In the fourth and fifth months of 1144, however, Michinori was
quite ill,[31] and in the seventh month he was at length permitted to
become a priest.[32] Although Yorinaga noted that he himself was
deeply pained at this decision, his new priestly status did not hinder
Michinori's activities at all. On the contrary, he enjoyed a good deal
more freedom, and now Michinori—under his religious name Shinzei—drew closer to Toba. After Toba's most trusted confidant
Fujiwara no Akiyori died in 1144, Shinzei seems to have become
the ex-sovereign's closest and most trusted adviser. For example, for
his loyal service he was placed in charge of the Kanzaki estate in
Hizen province, a manor that had been managed by Taira no Tadamori until his death. When Toba died it was Shinzei who handled
the entire burial and mourning procedure, most probably in accordance with Toba's prior instructions. He was also designated by
Toba as one of the eight casket bearers.[33] It was this same Shinzei
who was to be one of the major plotters as well as victors in the
Hōgen disturbance.

[30] SPBM, 2: 485.   [31] Taiki, 2: 121. Ten'yō 1/4/25, 1/5/9, 1/5/15.
[32] Ibid., p. 126. Ten'yō 1/7/22.   [33] HHK, 2: 111.

The Hōgen Disturbance

As noted above, Bifukumon'in was Toba's favorite consort. In 1139 she bore him a son, Prince Narihito, and within three months Toba had this boy named crown prince to succeed Sutoku, the position being unfilled at the time. When Narihito was only in his third year, Toba forced Sutoku to abdicate in the child's favor. Narihito thus became Emperor Konoe, whose favor Yorinaga and Tadamichi later attempted to win through their daughters. Toba apparently made Konoe emperor because of his love for Bifukumon'in, and it was his desire that the imperial succession should pass to Konoe and his descendants.[34] He was thus looking forward expectantly to the offspring of Konoe, hoping for a son born of Bifukumon'in's (and Tadamichi's) adopted daughter Teishi.

But Konoe was frail and sickly throughout his life and suffered from steadily worsening eyesight. Thus Bifukumon'in and Toba were forced to consider the possibility of choosing another imperial successor should Konoe fail to produce an heir. As far as Bifukumon'in was concerned, there were two likely successors, both young princes whom she had adopted and supported at court. One was Sutoku's son Shigehito. No doubt the junior retired sovereign had hopes for a revival of his own influence through this boy. Despite the friction between Toba and Sutoku, the fact that Shigehito had been adopted by Bifukumon'in [35] meant that the prince had a potential supporter able to influence the senior retired emperor.

The other possibility was Prince Morihito, son of Toba's fourth child, Prince Masahito. His mother had died giving birth to him, and Toba had immediately taken the infant and had him adopted by Bifukumon'in.[36] Since that time she had been a very strong supporter of Morihito's interests at court. At the age of nine Morihito was put under the tutelage of the priestly imperial prince Kakuhō

---

[34] This desire is referred to in numerous later sources as *Toba no gosoi*. For an interesting article on this see Tsuji Hikosaburō, "Toba-in no gosoi," pp. 42–51. For primary references to this plan see *Sankaiki*, 1: 157, Eiryaku 1/12/4, where Fujiwara no Koremichi states that Emperor Nijō's accession was in accord with the late exsovereign Toba's plan. Yoshida no Sadafusa also mentioned that Go-Shirakawa was protecting Toba's plan during the Hōgen disturbance. See Tsuji, p. 46.

[35] *Taiki*, 2: 47. Kyūan 6/12/1.   [36] Ibid., p. 169. Kyūjū 2/9/8.

at the Ninna-ji for the purpose of preparing him for the priesthood, but Bifukumon'in held up his initiation because of the possibility of his accession.[37]

The choice between these two princes—Shigehito and Morihito —was eventually made in the latter's favor, and this was largely the doing of Bifukumon'in. Although Toba too eventually supported Morihito, he was not at first enthusiastic.[38] As Konoe's eyesight grew worse, the chancellor, Tadamichi, repeatedly begged Toba to allow the emperor to abdicate in favor of Prince Morihito. Toba suspected that Konoe was not actually that ill and that this was in reality a plot concocted by Tadamichi to get a young boy on the throne and rule through him. Toba is said to have lamented once, "If this boy succeeds to the imperial rule, the realm will be in turmoil." [39]

But Konoe's illness was real enough. It grew worse, and in 1155 he died. Now the succession issue came to a head. As we have seen above, Bifukumon'in and Toba had originally wanted the throne to pass to Konoe's descendants, and Bifukumon'in had apparently settled on Morihito as a successor to Konoe. In fact it has been suggested that she too had been considering the possibility of having Emperor Konoe abdicate in Morihito's favor.[40] Toba had overcome his suspicions and was willing to honor Bifukumon'in's wishes. However, there was another problem: Morihito's father, Masahito, was still alive and had never been emperor.

The *Gukanshō* says that it was Tadamichi—author Jien's father —who convinced Toba that Morihito should not succeed because there had never been a case of a son passing over his father to be-

---

[37] Ibid.

[38] Ibid., p. 104. Nimpyō 3/9/23. The following is from an account in Yorinaga's diary of a conversation between Toba and Tadazane the previous day.

[39] After relating what Toba had said, Tadazane remarked (whether to Toba or Yorinaga is unclear) that Tadamichi must be crazy. Since Morihito's father Masahito was alive, he would probably try to control his son for his own purposes and would hardly allow Tadamichi to use his son to rule. Tadamichi's plan was the height of stupidity, Tadazane said. Ibid.

[40] A notation in Nakayama Sadachika's diary, *Sankaiki*, makes it quite clear that the accessions of both Go-Shirakawa (Masahito) and Nijō (Morihito) were the result of their support by Bifukumon'in. See n. 34 in this chapter.

come emperor.[41] But this does not seem likely, since we know that Tadamichi himself had petitioned three times to have the ailing Konoe abdicate in favor of Morihito.[42] Confronted with the need to make a decision, Toba, who was at the time of Konoe's death residing at the Toba-dono with Bifukumon'in, called together his associates among the courtiers to discuss the succession. Several times Toba sent messengers to Tadamichi seeking his opinion,[43] but when the decision was announced the next day it appeared to have been the retired sovereign and his associates who made it.

The choice was not an easy one. Sutoku's son Shigehito was the most appropriate successor. As for Morihito, however much Bifukumon'in may have desired his immediate accession, and despite her influence over Toba, he was almost out of the question because his own father, Prince Masahito, was still living. Toba was, however, willing to allow Bifukumon'in's favorite to become emperor eventually. Thus he settled on a compromise: Prince Masahito became emperor (Go-Shirakawa), and Prince Morihito, the future emperor Nijō, was made crown prince. That Go-Shirakawa was the choice not of his heart but of his respect for tradition is indicated by the fact that Toba is said to have considered him unqualified to become emperor.[44] In actuality, it was most probably Shinzei, Toba's close adviser and husband of Go-Shirakawa's wet nurse Kii no nii, who was most instrumental in convincing Toba to designate Go-Shirakawa as Konoe's successor.[45]

Thus imperial succession was decided to the satisfaction of Toba and Bifukumon'in. Shinzei, whose close relationship with Go-Shirakawa enabled him to control the court for a short period after Toba's death, had gained most by the decision, in which he had most likely played a significant role. Tadamichi was named chancel-

---

[41] GKS, pp. 216–17.

[42] Hashimoto also points this out, but many other scholars accept the Gukanshō story. As Hashimoto says, however, it appears to have been an effort on Jien's part to give his father the credit for deciding the succession issue. Hashimoto, "Hōgen no ran," pp. 32–33.

[43] HHK, 1: 327. Kyūjū 3/7/23.   [44] GKS, p. 216.

[45] Hashimoto, "Hōgen no ran," p. 33.

lor and could thus hope for a change of fortune. On the other hand, both Yorinaga and Tadazane fell out of favor after the accession. Sutoku, too, was displeased over the decision as he had pinned his hopes on Shigehito.[46]

Yorinaga had long enjoyed Toba's favor, but this was due more to his father's influence than his own merits. He was indeed a very learned man, but he appears to have been too scholarly and antiquarian for his time. As a Confucian scholar, he was fond of quoting from the *Spring and Autumn Annals* and of reading the old codes. Preaching frugality and condemning vulgar displays of wealth —particularly on the part of newly prosperous, middle-ranking courtiers—he went against the current of the times and appears to have made a number of enemies. But his ultimate downfall came from his supposed connection with Konoe's death.

Yorinaga's influence at court had come about as a result of the edict granting him the right of document examination, but at Go-Shirakawa's accession the anticipated edict of confirmation was not forthcoming. This was due to Toba's anger at Yorinaga. The anger sprang from a rumor to the effect that Konoe's death was the result of a curse cast upon him by Yorinaga and Tadazane.[47] Incredible as this may have seemed to Yorinaga, Toba and Bifukumon'in believed that he and Tadazane were actually implicated, and they were infuriated at the two.

While it is doubtful that there is any truth to the rumor that Tadazane and Yorinaga actually cast a spell on Konoe, it is not hard to understand Toba and Bifukumon'in's easy acceptance of it. Konoe had been close to Tadamichi, who, as was stated above, petitioned several times for permission to abdicate because of failing health; Konoe also hated Yorinaga.[48] Toba and Bifukumon'in

[46] Hashimoto, in discussing why Bifukumon'in chose Morihito over her other favorite, Shigehito, suggests that it was to ensure her own position at court. If Shigehito succeeded, it was possible that Sutoku might enjoy the kind of power as retired sovereign that Shirakawa and Toba had wielded and her own position would thus be undermined. With the young Morihito she anticipated no such problem. Hashimoto, "Hōgen no ran," pp. 33–34.

[47] *Taiki*, 2: 168–69. Kyūjū 2/8/27.

[48] Ibid., p. 52, Nimpyo 1/1/1; pp. 54–55, Nimpyo 1/1/6. Both these instances are mentioned in Hashimoto, "Hōgen no ran," p. 35.

had now lost their beloved son, to whose descendants they had wished to transmit the imperial succession, and in his grief the ex-emperor turned against Yorinaga and Tadazane, who were rumored to have caused his son's death. When Yorinaga petitioned to be appointed master for the new crown prince, Morihito, Toba denied his request because Yorinaga had not faithfully served Bifuku-mon'in or Morihito previously.[49]

Despite repeated prayers for a recovery of favor, Yorinaga and Tadazane became further estranged from the ex-sovereign and Bifukumon'in, while Tadamichi now enjoyed their trust. At the end of 1155 Kaya no in, Tadazane's daughter and another of Toba's consorts, died,[50] and her death eliminated Yorinaga and Tadazane's last possible link with the senior retired emperor. In the same year the seventy-eight-year-old Tadazane gave up his responsi-bilities for household affairs and retired to Uji. Yorinaga was shut off from almost all court activity in a situation reminiscent of his father Tadazane's when he lost his right of document examination over a dispute with Shirakawa. Surrounded solely by his lifelong household officials and retainers—all of whom were to be punished for their involvement in the Hōgen disturbance—and deserted by others with some social and political position to preserve, like his principal household official Chikataka, Yorinaga too retired to the seclusion of the Byōdō-in at Uji.

Likewise, the junior retired sovereign Sutoku had seen all hopes he had for his as well as his son's future brought to an abrupt end with the accession of Go-Shirakawa and the designation of Morihito as crown prince. Along with Yorinaga, Sutoku was isolated at court. The choice for both seems to have been whether to accept the situ-ation and live out their lives in frustration, or to take some precipi-tous action which might reverse the situation. The frustration of these two men was an invitation to revolt, and on the death of Toba they joined together in the armed revolt known from the calendrical era as the Hōgen disturbance.

---

[49] *Taiki*, 2: 169. Kyūjū 2/9/8.

[50] *HRS*, p. 71, Kyūjū 2/12/16. Four months prior to this she had taken the tonsure and become a nun. Ibid., Kyūjū 2/8/15.

On the second day of the seventh month of 1156 Toba died in
the Anrakuju-in palace at the Toba-dono at the age of fifty-four.[51]
Ill since the fifth month, Toba had sensed that Yorinaga and
Sutoku might rise in revolt. From the first day of the sixth month
he had ordered Minamoto no Yoshitomo and others to guard the
palace; and other warriors, both Minamoto and Taira, to guard the
Toba-dono. On the day after Toba's death Minamoto no Chikaharu
of Yamato province was seized and questioned, and he admitted
that Yorinaga, although in seclusion, had summoned him to the
capital.

On the eighth day important sutra readings for the deceased
ex-emperor were held at the Anrakuju-in, but Sutoku did not attend. On the same day an edict was issued ordering provincial governors to stop any mustering of troops in shōen owned by Tadazane
or Yorinaga. Also on that day Yoshitomo and others went to the
Higashi Sanjō Fujiwara residence looking for evidence of Yorinaga's
plotting. They questioned one of the Byōdō-in priests but discovered
nothing.

On the ninth day Sutoku secretly moved from the Toba Tanaka
palace to the palace at Kita-Shirakawa, and the next day he
gathered his troops there. The rumors of possible revolt had been
correct. A number of Taira and Minamoto warriors had gathered
there, including frustrated elements that had lost favor at court because of the late Toba's wrath, Minamoto no Tameyoshi, Yorikata,
and Tametomo among them. In the evening Yorinaga came up
from Uji, and other warriors came to join the two in the battle. At
Kita-Shirakawa, Sutoku and Yorinaga met in council, and a number
of followers were appointed officials of the ex-emperor.

Meanwhile, warriors were also gathered at the palace (the Takamatsu-dono) including Yoshitomo, Yoshiyasu, and Yorimasa of
the Genji, as well as Taira no Kiyomori. Kiyomori and Yoshitomo
were placed in command of the assembled warriors. After nightfall
they donned their armor, and on the morning of the eleventh

[51] *HHK*, 2: 111, Hōgen 1/7/15. The following account of the Hōgen disturbance
comes from the same source, through p. 126.

they set out for Shirakawa leading six-hundred-odd warriors along three different routes. The courtiers at the palace waited anxiously; Yorimasa and others returned shortly with the news that the battle had begun.

Soon smoke could be seen from the northeast quarter of the capital as the Kita-Shirakawa palace burned down. It appeared that victory belonged to the emperor's side as Sutoku and Yorinaga had fled. Neither one could be found immediately, but Yorinaga was apparently hit by an arrow while in flight. Tadazane, hearing the news, fled to Nara but later returned and threw himself on Tadamichi's mercy. While warriors searched for Yorinaga and Sutoku, rewards were bestowed and punishments meted out at the palace. An edict was issued declaring Tadamichi chieftain of the Fujiwara, while promotions in rank were given to those warriors who had routed the army of the retired sovereign.

The next day no one was able to learn the whereabouts of either Sutoku or Yorinaga, but on the thirteenth Sutoku was found hiding at the Ninna-ji. He was apprehended and exiled to Sanuki province on the island of Shikoku, where he remained until his death in 1167. On the fourteenth it was learned that Yorinaga had died from his arrow wound. All his official appointments were rescinded and his shōen holdings were declared confiscated.[52] The Hōgen disturbance had ended in disaster for Yorinaga and Tadazane and the ex-emperor Sutoku. The succession issue had been settled, and the decision made by the retired sovereign Toba and Bifukumon'in proved to be a lasting one. Go-Shirakawa remained emperor and his son Morihito, the real choice for succession, remained crown prince.

[52] Later these holdings were kept by the imperial house as edict fields. See ibid., pp. 156–58, Hōgen 3/3/29. The entire edict is reproduced there.

ᘑᘐ SEVEN ᘐᘑ

The Insei *Period III: Go-Shirakawa*

No ONE had ever seriously considered Prince Masahito (Go-Shirakawa) a candidate for imperial succession. The fourth son of the senior retired emperor Toba and Taikemmon'in, Masahito's single-minded indulgence in aesthetic pleasures, particularly the current poetic craze for *imayō*,[1] had led his father to remark that he was unqualified to be emperor. His days were spent in the enjoyment of cultural pursuits rather than in solemn preparation for imperial succession. Upon the death of Konoe in 1155 Masahito became emperor without ever having been crown prince. As we have seen, his accession was due largely to the support of Bifukumon'in and Tadamichi, both of whom were interested in his son rather than in him, and the advice of Shinzei, who stood to gain personally by Masahito's succession.

It was through this bit of good fortune that Go-Shirakawa became the seventy-seventh emperor in Japanese history and, later, the third abdicated sovereign to wield power in the so-called *insei* period. It was during this sovereign's lifetime that the political power of the courtiers was wrested away by the eastern warriors and actual rule by the military commenced. The political center of

---

[1] Imayō, a poetic form in four lines alternating seven and five syllables, enjoyed its greatest popularity in the late Heian period.

Japan, moreover, shifted from the capital at Heian to the strong-hold of the military government at Kamakura.

Since the rise of the warrior class and the titanic battles for su-premacy between the Minamoto and the Taira are well covered elsewhere,[2] I would like in this chapter to discuss the major de-velopments during Go-Shirakawa's reign, the events surrounding his abdication, and his conduct subsequent to abdication.

The Aftermath of the Hōgen Disturbance

The rifts in both the imperial house and the *sekkanke* were largely healed following the Hōgen disturbance, and the frustrated junior retired emperor Sutoku was exiled. Bifukumon'in, the ranking elder in the imperial house, had been entrusted by Toba with the guard-ianship of the family's political fortune and the matter of succes-sion. Go-Shirakawa was emperor and actual head of the imperial house, and his son Morihito, the favorite of Bifukumon'in and Tadamichi, was made crown prince. With the death of Yorinaga and the seclusion of Tadazane in his Chisoku-in residence, the re-gent's house was once again under the control of Tadamichi. In order to avert possible economic disaster, Tadamichi, again clan head as well as chancellor, exerted every effort to keep the sekkanke estates controlled by Yorinaga and Tadazane from confiscation as punishment for their participation in the Hōgen uprising.

We do not know exactly in what manner Tadazane had origi-nally transmitted his *shōen* to his children, but we do know that Tadamichi received some holdings which Tadazane later took back and commended to Toba.[3] Yorinaga and Kaya no in, Tadazane's daughter, also received some holdings but the numbers are un-known. Yorinaga on one occasion received eighteen holdings,[4] but there were probably more. The *Azuma kagami*, an official history of the Kamakura shogunate, records that Kaya no in received more

---

[2] The best-known work in English is Minoru Shinoda, *The Founding of the Kamakura Shogunate*, 1180–1185.

[3] *Taiki*, 2: 44. Kyūan 6/11/12.   [4] Ibid., 1: 259. Kyūan 4/7/17.

than fifty shōen holdings from her father.[5] Thus Tadazane had deeded over a considerable number of sekkanke holdings while maintaining control of the bulk of the lands until after the Hōgen affair. Besides his own personal holdings, Yorinaga had been given control over the shōen attached to the family temples (with the exception of the Byōdō-in, where Tadazane resided) in 1153.[6] Thus the two defeated Fujiwara leaders held a considerable amount of land between them that might possibly have been confiscated, but Tadamichi managed to avoid economic disaster by first having himself named uji no chōja in place of Yorinaga and then transferring ownership of most of the lands to himself and his son.[7] By these maneuvers Tadamichi salvaged most of the sekkanke holdings; only twenty-eight were confiscated and turned into *goin* lands.[8] As chieftain of the Fujiwara and chancellor for Go-Shirakawa, with whom he enjoyed a cordial relationship, Tadamichi's position had improved immeasurably as a result of the Hōgen insurrection, and the position of the sekkanke as a whole seemed more secure.

The Hōgen disturbance did, however, result in a crucial rupture between the warrior houses of Minamoto and Taira. Both had slowly risen to court positions of moderate importance during the reigns of Shirakawa and Toba as clients of the sekkanke and the imperial house. As a reward for loyal service as the "teeth and claws" of the Fujiwara, a number of Minamoto uji members of warrior origin had attained positions in central and provincial government. The Taira had risen at court as close retainers of the two preceding ex-sovereigns, Shirakawa and Toba; the first ties between the Taira and the imperial house came as the result of Masamori's commendation of certain lands to Shirakawa's eldest daughter, Rokujō-in.[9] Owing largely to the great prestige and influence of the

[5] *Azuma kagami*, 1: 219. Bunji 2/4/20.   [6] *HHK*, 1: 212. Nimpyō 3/10/18.

[7] Nobunori was shocked at this "unprecedented" manner in which the uji chieftainship was transferred. On the same day another edict was issued placing Tadazane's son, the priest Kakkei, in charge of Yorinaga's shōen which had previously been confiscated. *HHK*, 2: 118. Hōgen 1/7/11.

[8] Ibid., pp. 184–88. Hōgen 2/3/29.

[9] The original document is reproduced in *Heian ibun*, 4: 1346–47, doc. 1382. Also

two retired sovereigns, the Taira began to surpass the Minamoto warriors in the service of the court, but the old courtier families, failing to discern the importance of the rise of warrior houses, continued to consider both Minamoto and Taira warriors as new-comers and mercenaries for private hire.

Although Taira no Kiyomori and Minamoto no Yoshitomo had been in joint command of the troops that routed the adherents of Yorinaga and Sutoku, Kiyomori received a much greater reward for his service than did Yoshitomo, leaving the latter disgruntled and sowing the seeds for future conflict. Also the Minamoto suf-fered considerably as a result of the Hōgen disturbance. Capital punishment, long in disuse for aristocrats in Heian Japan, was re-vived, most probably at Shinzei's suggestion, and the leading Minamoto warriors from the losing side, the most prominent of whom was Tameyoshi, were executed.[10]

Several reasons can be adduced to explain why Kiyomori was so greatly rewarded and Yoshitomo neglected by the court for par-ticipation in the defeat of the rebels. First, the Taira chieftain had long been close to the retired sovereign Toba. Kiyomori and his father, Tadamori, were highly valued as private warriors in the ser-vice of the ex-emperor, although some scholars are suspicious of the Taira clan's claim to a glorious military heritage.[11] Both had in the past been rewarded far beyond the value of their actual martial ac-complishments, primarily because of the favor of the ex-sovereign. A second factor was the backing of Go-Shirakawa's most trusted ad-viser Shinzei, who seems to have realized sooner than most the po-tential of this rising warrior class. A final reason for Kiyomori's special treatment by the court in this affair was the long-held suspi-cion, first noted in the *Heike monogatari* but not substantiated in any reliable historical source, that Kiyomori might have been

---

see Ryō Susumu, "Rokujōin-ryō to Taira no Masamori," in Ryō, *Heian jidai*, pp. 119–35.

[10] Those judged guilty and sentenced to death were executed on the twenty-eighth and thirtieth days of the month. *HHK*, 2: 126. Hōgen 1/7/28–30.

[11] See Ryō, "Rokujōin-ryō to Taira no Masamori," pp. 125–28.

Shirakawa's son. The story alleges that, when Shirakawa gave the woman Gion no nyōgo to Tadamori, she was already pregnant by the retired emperor, and when Kiyomori was born Tadamori simply reared him as his own son. Another version claims that Kiyomori's mother was actually Gion no nyōgo's sister. Despite a lack of reliable proof, a good many Japanese historians are inclined to believe this story. Ishimoda Shō accepts it outright, and Takeuchi Rizō also finds it highly creditable. Certainly the existence of blood ties with the imperial house would help to explain the extraordinary favor in which Kiyomori was held by the court and the emperor. In any case, Kiyomori was rewarded beyond Yoshitomo for service in settling the Hōgen disturbance, and this fact led to increasing friction between the Taira and Minamoto houses. This friction eventually resulted in armed conflict which raged over the length and breadth of Japan.

The Reign of Emperor Go-Shirakawa, 1155–1158

Immediately after the death of Toba the political situation settled into a pattern reminiscent of earlier times. Since there was no abdicated sovereign, the emperor was both head of the imperial house and symbol of the imperial government. Tadamichi served as chancellor, advising the emperor on political affairs. But since he lacked the close maternal relationship with Go-Shirakawa that was the usual basis of power for either regent or chancellor, Tadamichi's influence was limited in comparison to many of his Fujiwara predecessors. It was actually the priest Shinzei, husband of Go-Shirakawa's wet nurse, Kii no nii, who enjoyed the greatest influence over the emperor.

Shinzei and Go-Shirakawa immediately set out to redress some of the "evil practices of the degenerate age" and revive older court procedures that had been dropped during the course of the Heian period. One of their first steps was to have another shōen regulation ordinance decreed and to revive the Kiroku Shōen Kenkeisho, or Records Office, in imitation of the action taken by Go-Sanjō in 1069.[12] Three months after the Hōgen affair an edict was issued appointing twelve scribes (yoriudo) to staff the new Records Office.[13] All of them were middle- or lower-ranking courtiers, either scholars or men with mathematical, economic, or other technical expertise. They were from the Nakahara, Otsuki, Miyoshi, Kiyowara, Sakanoue, and Koremune families, or from non-sekkanke Fujiwara houses. These scribes were to be under the direction of the three-member controlling board, which consisted of Fujiwara no Koretaka, Fujiwara no Toshinori, and Minamoto no Masayori. All three were close associates of Go-Shirakawa's, and Toshinori was Shinzei's son.

These officials were responsible for enforcing the two articles on shōen regulation that had been part of the seven-article addendum (shinsei) to the codes issued the previous month.[14] The last five articles concerned the illegal activities of the rebellious monks of the major Buddhist centers, while the first two dealt with general shōen problems. The first article ordered provincial governors to seize all shōen—regardless of ownership—which did not possess proper documentation but had been established subsequent to Go-Shirakawa's accession in 1155. This article laments the fact that numerous persons fail to go through proper legal channels to establish their rights of ownership of land; they either obtain provincial exemption or claim to possess inherited documents of tax exemption. The result was that, in places like Kyūshū where the whole area was controlled by a single individual, private influence exceeded imperial power.

The second article dealt with added lands (kanōden) that were illegally brought within the confines of shōen jurisdiction beyond the originally exempted area (hommen). Such added lands, whether they were taken away from a neighboring estate or taken out of the public domain, were to be prohibited; offenses were to be

---

[12] See chapter 4 for information on Go-Sanjō's Records Office.
[13] HHK, 2: 143. Hōgen 1/10/13.   [14] HHK, 2: 139. Hōgen 1/9*/18.

punished by confiscation of the entire shōen and arrest of the shōen officials. Those estates that had imperial edicts and documents from the offices of the retired sovereign Shirakawa or Toba exempting their added lands from taxation (that is, recognizing private ownership of the lands) were not to be confiscated immediately in accordance with this article, however. Holders of such shōen were to forward the imperial edict and the in no chō documents to the government, meaning here the Records Office, and await imperial decision regarding the status of their added fields.

This second article is important in understanding the legal authority and power of the abdicated sovereign and his office in the late Heian period. While a degree of dispensation was granted estates whose added fields had been confirmed by documents from the retired sovereign's office, still the central government required that the documents be examined and decisions rendered. These were lands that had been commended to the retired sovereign as a means of guaranteeing their tax-exempt status, but even such lands, nominally owned by the abdicated sovereign, required imperial approval to ensure absolute sanctity. Furthermore, this dispensation —legal status of the added lands to be determined by examination of the pertinent documents rather than outright confiscation—was permitted only for added lands. No such stipulation was made in regard to entire shōen established on the strength of in no chō documents. Thus it is clear that, contrary to Kitabatake Chikafusa's claim in the *Jinnō shōtōki*, in no chō documents, while they were of course quite influential, did not take precedence over imperial edicts. The possession of documents from the ex-sovereign's office alone was not sufficient to guarantee the ultimate legality of a shōen. An imperial edict possessed greater legal authority.

While the Records Office was revived in Go-Shirakawa's time to carry out the specific regulation ordinances of 1156, the office also appears to have had a new function that it did not have before. At least, there is no evidence that it had this function previously. It now arbitrated disputes between different landholders over the proper ownership of estates.[15] At least one document in the *Heian ibun,* a collection of extant Heian documents, points this out quite clearly.[16] Another mention of this arbitration function of the Records Office can be found in the diary of Taira no Nobunori, *Heihanki,* where Nobunori says that a document (*kanjō*) issued by the office decided a dispute between Fujiwara no Shigemichi and his brother Suemichi.[17]

The Hōgen shōen regulation ordinance was used as a model for later ordinances, and thus it was most likely an effective one. But it is important to understand that this ordinance was consistent with all previous attempts to check the growth of private estates: it made stringent stipulations for illegal landholdings but made no attempt to abolish or even to check the growth of estates that possessed proper documentation of ownership from the imperial government. Despite the frequent warnings about the dangers of continued shōen growth—Kujō Kanezane, for example, said that the imperial court "will be completely destroyed by shōen" [18]—the trend continued unabated, and successive regulation ordinances had the effect of aiding rather than checking such growth, since each legalized shōen established prior to the date of the new ordinance.

Another major project undertaken during Go-Shirakawa's reign at the urging of Shinzei was the reconstruction of the imperial palace, which had been burned frequently during the mid-Heian period. Since then successive emperors had spent most of their time in provisional imperial palaces, usually the residences of the regent or some other courtier. Tadamichi had earlier suggested reconstruction, but the ex-emperor Toba had claimed it was impossible in such a degenerate age.[19] Shinzei, however, was determined to carry out this massive project. Since it was "a matter of importance to the whole country," all estate holders, whether individual

[15] Kawakami Tasuke, *Nihon kodai shakaishi no kenkyū,* p. 406.
[16] *Heian ibun,* 6: 2418, doc. 2936.
[17] HHK, 2: 60. Hōgen 3/11/26. Also Kawakami, *Kodai shakaishi,* p. 408.
[18] *Gyokuyō,* 1: 329. Jōan 3/11/12.   [19] GKS, p. 225.

courtiers or Buddhist institutions, were required to contribute; levies were made on both taxable and nontaxable land to pay for the project.[20] Preparations were hastily made, and everyone, courtier and warrior alike, was involved in the undertaking. In the third month of the year the ceremony for the raising of the ridgepole was held, and the responsibilities for the various buildings were allotted to different offices or provinces.[21] By the tenth month construction was completed and the emperor moved into the new palace, where ceremonies and festivals could be held once again. The ceremonial poetry contest (*naien*) in the first month of the new year (1158) was said to be the first since the time of Emperor Go-Ichijō in 1034.[22]

Besides these two major undertakings—shōen regulation and reconstruction of the palace—Shinzei planned a revival of old ceremonies and court practices on a broad scale, and he seems to have had the emperor's complete confidence. His power and influence soared, and his sons advanced rapidly in positions of importance at court. As a man of learning—he was the compiler of the *Honchō seiki*, a national history designed to continue where the six national histories had ended, in the late ninth century—and of cultural interests as well, Shinzei was able to serve as more than political adviser to Go-Shirakawa. For example, he sought out men and women from all walks of life skilled in the composition of imayō and brought them to the emperor.[23] He made himself almost indispensible to Go-Shirakawa; and, since he was of comparatively humble origins, he naturally aroused feelings of jealousy and enmity on the part of other courtiers.

The Abdication of Go-Shirakawa

While it appears that Go-Shirakawa could have continued to control the court and imperial house as well as indulge in his poetry

---

[20] Ryō Susumu "Go-Shirakawa-in no jisei ni tsuite no ronsō," in Ryō, *Heian jidai*, p. 200.

[21] *HHK*, 2: 183–84. Hōgen 2/3/26.   [22] Ryō, "Go-Shirakawa-in," p. 200.

[23] Ibid., p. 200.

composition as emperor, he abdicated in 1158 after only three short years as sovereign.[24] His decision to abdicate appears to have been made rather suddenly, but the source materials yield no specific explanation for the action.

Several factors were, I believe, involved. First, it had always been assumed that Go-Shirakawa would abdicate in favor of his son Prince Morihito, who had been the choice of both Toba and Bifukumon'in for imperial succession. Go-Shirakawa's accession had been only a temporary expediency, a means of putting Morihito in the proper position for succession. The crown prince was now a young man of sixteen and by Japanese standards fully capable of performing the imperial duties. It is quite possible that Go-Shirakawa abdicated at the urging of Bifukumon'in, who, though a woman, was the elder in the imperial house and quite influential at court. As we know, she had long desired the accession of Morihito.

Japanese historians consider being emperor a Sisyphean task without adequate compensation and conclude that emperors were usually eager to retire to a life of luxury and pleasure. Surely, then, an emperor as addicted to the cultural life as Go-Shirakawa would have taken great delight in the freedom of movement permitted an abdicated sovereign, and perhaps a desire to flee the political problems at court may have played some part in his decision to abdicate. The *Hyakurenshō* does record that after his accession Prince Morihito (Emperor Nijō) conducted politics on the advice of the chancellor, without consulting his father.[25] But a careful study of the sources indicates that Go-Shirakawa was deeply involved in the political scene after his abdication and not solely devoted to the pursuit of the good life. Nijō's power was somewhat less arbitrary than the *Hyakurenshō* suggests.

It would appear that, while Go-Shirakawa's abdication was in accord with the order of imperial succession decided upon by Toba

---

[24] *Sankaiki*, 1: 74, Hōgen 3/8/6. See also HRS, p. 73, Hōgen 3/8/11, for the details of the abdication.

[25] HRS, p. 73.

and Bifukumon'in, he also planned to enjoy fully the political influence, prestige, and affluent life style that abdicated sovereigns had enjoyed since the time of Go-Sanjō. Immediately upon abdication, Go-Shirakawa began the organization of his in no chō with the appointment of Fujiwara no Tsunemune, Fujiwara no Nobuyori, and Fujiwara no Noriie as *inshi*.[26] Six days later he moved to the Takamatsu-dono, the reconstructed residence of Minamoto no Takaakira which Go-Shirakawa had used while the new imperial palace was being built; there he resided until it was destroyed by fire in 1159. On the same day he received the official title of *dajō tennō* and was allotted a number of bodyguards (*zuishin*).[27] Six directors and four scribes were also appointed to his in no chō on that day. The bettō, all Fujiwara uji members though not from the sekkanke, were Kinnori, Shigemichi, Akinaga, Korekata, and two of Shinzei's sons, Toshinori and Narinori.[28] All six men had long-standing personal connections with Go-Shirakawa. On the twenty-third day Go-Shirakawa was granted a number of *chokushiden* (imperial edict fields) for his support, and the preparations for the management of his in no chō appear to have been largely completed.

The *Hyakurenshō* statement that the new emperor Nijō and the chancellor together controlled political affairs is a description of an ideal political situation more than the actual one. There is evidence that, in the manner of the ex-emperors Shirakawa and Toba before him, Go-Shirakawa played an active role in the determination of major political matters. It appears in fact that Tadamichi also played an important role in the decision-making process, acting in concert with Go-Shirakawa. Upon Emperor Nijō's accession Tadamichi had turned over the positions of chancellor and clan chieftain to his son Motozane. Since both the emperor and the new chancellor were sixteen years of age, it is quite obvious that Go-Shirakawa and Tadamichi were acting in advisory capacities for their respective sons. Nijō and Motozane held the offices and pos-

26 HHK, 2: 330. Hōgen 3/8/11.   27 HHK, 2: 337. Hōgen 3/8/17.
28 HHK, 2: 336. Hōgen 3/8/17.

sessed the authority, but Go-Shirakawa and Tadamichi had by no means totally relinquished their political powers to their sons.

The Heiji Disturbance of 1159

After Go-Shirakawa's abdication, the influence of Shinzei, already quite strong while Go-Shirakawa had been emperor, continued to grow. His wife, Kii no nii, rose to the third and then the second rank, and his sons continued to enjoy favor and prestige at court. (Toshinori was by now a *kugyō*.) [29] Shinzei's influence bred jealousy among the other *kinshin* of the ex-sovereign, and his haughty attitude toward lower-ranking courtiers and warriors engendered further enmity. Among the kinshin of Go-Shirakawa at this time, the most bitterly opposed to Shinzei was Fujiwara no Nobuyori, whose appointment to a desired position had been blocked at Shinzei's suggestion. Another potentially dangerous foe had been made when Shinzei refused Minamoto no Yoshitomo's offer of his daughter in marriage to Shinzei's son Korenori. Yoshitomo, hoping for a revival of fortune after his mistreatment in the Hōgen affair, had been rebuffed as a rough and unworthy warrior. When Shinzei then decided to marry his son to one of Kiyomori's daughters, Yoshitomo became even more embittered against both Kiyomori and Shinzei. But these were not isolated cases; feelings against Shinzei ran high throughout court circles.

Eventually Nobuyori and Yoshitomo joined forces in an attempt to eliminate Shinzei permanently.[30] The two plotted to surround the Sanjō palace of Go-Shirakawa, where Shinzei and his family were staying, and to capture and kill them. They waited until Kiyomori, Shinzei's trusted ally and the most powerful warrior in the land, was away on a pilgrimage to Kumano before making their move. They finally acted in the last month of Heiji (1160); but the plan failed as Shinzei and his family, forewarned of the impending

[29] *KGBN*, 1: 446.

[30] The events of the Heiji disturbance are colorfully described in the *Heiji monogatari*, and the details are quite well known. See *HRS* pp. 74–5, Heiji 1/12/9–Eiryaku 1/6/14.

attack, escaped. A few days later, however, the plotters managed to capture and kill Shinzei. Nobuyori thereupon made a number of appointments of Minamoto warriors to court positions in a quickly arranged ceremony at the imperial palace. However, Nobuyori's arrogant and domineering attitude soon brought him into conflict with Korekata and Tsunemune, two of Go-Shirakawa's kinshin who had participated in the plot against Shinzei. These two now switched sides to join with Kiyomori, who rushed back to the capital with his warriors after hearing reports of the uprising. Receiving an imperial edict issued at the prompting of Tsunemune and Korekata, Kiyomori attacked the Genji warriors at the imperial palace and soon won the battle. Shinzei, Nobuyori, and Yoshitomo all lost their lives in this revolt, known from the era name as the Heiji disturbance.

Court Politics in the Reign of Emperor Nijō, 1160–1165

Even after the fighting ceased, the political situation at the capital remained tense. According to the Gempei seisuiki, it was from this time that the relationship between Go-Shirakawa and his son, Emperor Nijō, began to deteriorate. The emperor appeared to be acting on his own without consulting the ex-emperor at all. The Taira, under the leadership of Kiyomori, had chastised the Minamoto in his name, and Nijō had even made the Taira Rokuhara mansion his temporary palace. After a short stay with Bifukumon'in in the Hachijō-dono, Nijō returned to the imperial palace, where he accepted Yorinaga's adopted daughter Tashi into his women's quarters. This was a completely unprecedented action, since Tashi had been an empress of the former sovereign Konoe. For having thus been married to two different emperors Tashi had earned the historical epithet nidai no kisaki ("empress for two reigns").[31]

[31] For western-language material on Tashi, see Frederick Jouon des Longrais, Tashi: Le roman de celle qui espousa deux empereurs (nidai no kisaki). For a review of same, see William McCullough's comments in the Journal of the American Oriental Society, April–June 1970, pp. 267–77.

This strange action was taken by the emperor without consulting Go-Shirakawa. The *Gempei seisuiki* relates that Nijō was of the opinion that the emperor had neither father nor mother but, as sole guardian of the sovereignty, must make such decisions himself.[32] This is a borrowed piece of Confucian rhetoric with no applicability to the actual situation in Heian Japan. Throughout the entire period emperors paid yearly visits of respect to their parents, and the abdicated sovereign, as head of the imperial house and usually the father of the emperor, was as a rule consulted on major political matters, particularly matters involving the imperial kin group. Even the retired sovereign Go-Shirakawa was conscious of familial obligations to Bifukumon'in. Although she was not his mother, Go-Shirakawa paid visits of respect to Bifukumon'in, foster mother of the emperor and ranking elder in ·the imperial house. Emperor Nijō may have had little desire to share political power with his father, but the statement that the emperor has neither father nor mother—meaning, of course, that the emperor is not subject even to the authority of his parents—does not reflect the realities of Japanese political history.

If Emperor Nijō was indeed intent upon ruling directly with no interference from his father, Go-Shirakawa, then he was denying Japanese precedent. While Japanese court offices had largely been copied from Chinese models and Japanese practices described in Confucian language, the resemblance of Japanese political institutions to Confucian prototypes was external only; in substance they differed greatly. The Japanese emperor was almost never an ideal Chinese-style Son of Heaven, ruling over the entire land in an absolute fashion. Neither could the Japanese understand the concept of a public bureaucracy to serve the emperor based upon anything other than birth. In Japan a small circle of aristocrats ruled the masses of people, and one's lineage counted for everything. Kinship groups were the basis of political organization, and the imperial house was one such group. Even the emperor was af-

---

[32] *Gempei seisuiki*, p. 33.

forded few opportunities to act as a free individual rather than as a member of a larger kinship unit.

Within a house, the head of that house—normally the eldest male member—retained a good deal of control over the actions of the group, regardless of his current public position. Thus a Fujiwara minister like Tadazane could yield the position of regent to the emperor, and even give up his uji chieftainship, and still maintain control over the affairs of the house. The power and prestige of an office remained with the holder of the position long after his resignation or retirement. This was also true of the relative powers of the abdicated and reigning sovereigns. The emperor held the highest public position and possessed the authority of that office, yet the abdicated sovereign, as head of the house and father of the emperor, maintained a good measure of control over the emperor's actions. Nijō was certainly aware of this basic fact of Heian political life. And, as we shall see, although emperor, he was criticized as a disrespectful son for attempting to rule without Go-Shirakawa's advice.

Furthermore, the sources indicate that in actuality Nijō was not able to conduct politics without Go-Shirakawa's intervention, and the decision-making process during his reign appears to have been extremely complex. One example, taken from the *Sankaiki*, will suffice to demonstrate the complexity of the political situation at this time.[33]

In 1160 Taira no Kiyomori, then assistant governor-general of the Kyūshū headquarters as well as a captain in the palace guards, wished to yield his Kyūshū position to his son-in-law Narinori, a relatively minor arrangement which was quite common at the time. The author of the *Sankaiki*, Nakayama Tadachika, a close associate of the Taira clan as well as the imperial house (he served as a chief secretary for Nijō and a director in the offices of both the exemperor Go-Shirakawa and his adopted daughter Kenreimon'in), received a communication from Kiyomori requesting him to carry a message to Go-Shirakawa informing the ex-sovereign of his desire

33 *Sankaiki*, 1: 168. Eiryaku 1/12/29.

to resign the post. Tadachika went to one of Go-Shirakawa's palaces (probably the Hachijō Horikawa residence of Akinaga, to which he had moved after the destruction of the Sanjō-dono), where he informed the retired emperor of Kiyomori's desire through an attendant, Fujiwara no Yukitaka. Through Yukitaka Go-Shirakawa informed Tadachika that the information should be relayed to both the emperor and the former chancellor, Tadamichi. In a move indicative of where power actually lay, Tadachika reported the matter to Tadamichi, but Tadamichi sent him to the emperor. Tadachika went off to the residence of the chancellor, Motozane, and had the message related once more, and once again he was told to take it to the emperor for approval. He then had it reported to Nijō through the influential Tango no tsubone (the most familiar name for Takashina no Eishi, a favorite of Go-Shirakawa and mother of his daughter Sen'yōmon'in), and the emperor decided that the matter should be settled in accord with an edict (*inzen*) from Go-Shirakawa. Back at the ex-emperor's palace, where he had started the whole process, Tadachika received permission from Go-Shirakawa (through Motonaka, the governor of Mino, since all the close associates of the ex-emperor had retired), and he relayed the approval back through the same chain once again: first to Tadamichi, then to Motozane, and finally to the emperor for approval. Finally an imperial edict confirmed the matter, which was in reality a very simple one to have required such activity. The same sort of process involving the same actors appears to have been necessary to conclude a large number of court affairs,[34] though for most matters, of course, the kugyō met in council before the chancellor went to the emperor.

While this process was complex, we can discern fairly clearly the political roles of the four major court figures. The ex-sovereign and the former chancellor had considerable decision-making powers and "advised" their respective sons, the emperor and the chancellor. The final decision, however, whether actually made by the ex-emperor or not, required imperial promulgation to have legal force,

---

[34] Ryō, "Go-Shirakawa-in," in *Heian jidai*, pp. 210–11.

and thus Motozane and Nijō were the sources of legitimacy for political decisions. Much of the power may have lain in the hands of Go-Shirakawa, but legitimacy, or sovereignty, lay quite clearly with the constituted offices of the imperial government. Again we have evidence contradicting Chikafusa's claim that documents from the ex-sovereign had more authority than those of the emperor. However powerful such documents may have been, they did not enjoy the same degree of legal force as those of the imperial government.

The problem was, of course, that the four key persons in the system could rarely agree. Associates of all four were members of the kugyō council, so when the kugyō met to discuss matters a good deal of conflict was unavoidable. Bifukumon'in, too, was a strong influence at court until her death late in 1160, and this added another factor to the already complex picture. It was precisely that year, however, that can perhaps be singled out as marking a turning point in court affairs: from that time a deep rift began to open between those courtiers who served only the emperor and those who served as inshi of Go-Shirakawa.

In the sixth month of that year the former governor of Izumo, Minamoto no Mitsuyasu, and his followers were exiled to a remote province for having participated in a plot against the ex-emperor.[35] The exile of a few malcontents, however, was not enough to quell the bitter factionalism at court. In the middle of the year there was a seemingly slight change in the composition of the kugyō which was a sign of what was to come. For his service in killing the rebel Hyūga no Michiyoshi in Hizen province,[36] Taira no Kiyomori was granted the senior third rank, and shortly after that he was promoted to imperial adviser, making him a member of the elite kugyō group.[37]

Kiyomori managed to avoid the dangers of factionalism for a time by serving both the emperor and the ex-sovereign faithfully. Besides the possibility that he was actually a son of the late

---

[35] HRS, p. 74. Eiryaku 1/6/14. [36] Ibid. Eiryaku 1/5/15.
[37] KGBN, 1: 447–50. There were forty kugyō, including Kiyomori, at the time.

Shirakawa, Kiyomori also enjoyed favor with the imperial family through his sister-in-law Taira no Shigeko. Shigeko was in the service of Go-Shirakawa's sister Jōzaimon'in and lived together with the two retired imperial personages. She was especially favored by Go-Shirakawa, and in 1161 she gave birth to a son by him, thus raising the possibility that a prince of Taira blood might someday be in line for the imperial succession.

This boy was known as Takakura no miya before he was made an imperial prince and given a proper name, and it immediately became obvious that certain members of the Taira clan hoped to advance the fortunes of their house by supporting him as successor to the throne. Only two days after the birth of the infant, Shigeko's brother, Taira no Tokitada, and certain other Taira courtiers, including Kiyomori's son Atsumori, were dismissed from office for their involvement in a plot concerning this Taira child.[38] As we have seen, the line of imperial succession had long ago been determined by Toba and Bifukumon'in, and support for another line of succession, particularly coming from Taira courtiers, could hardly have been popular with most of the court at the time.

Despite the fact that succession was supposed to pass to the descendants of the reigning emperor, Nijō, there was as yet no heir. Thus Takakura no miya stood a very good chance of succeeding to the imperial position. Although the *Sankaiki* and other sources nowhere specifically mention it, it is more than likely that the plotters of Takakura no miya's succession had at least the tacit approval of Go-Shirakawa; and the possibility of transmitting imperial succession to this son was not at all unattractive to the ex-sovereign. The dismissal of the plotting courtiers, however, served only to widen the rift between the emperor and his court favorites, on the one hand, and Go-Shirakawa and his supporters on the other.

While a few Taira officials lost their court positions as a result of this incident, Kiyomori not only managed to come out unscathed, but he even improved his position when that year he was appointed provisional middle councillor.[39] He also managed to guard against

---

[38] *HRS*, p. 75. Eiryaku 2/9/5.   [39] *KGBN*, 1: 451.

any significant loss of Taira influence at court by securing the appointment of Taira no Tsunemori to Atsumori's position. While the *Gempei seisuiki* relates that from this time Kiyomori began to draw near to the emperor and deny the power of Go-Shirakawa, it is clear that he continued to serve both emperor and ex-sovereign skillfully, maintaining the trust of both.

Quite soon another incident occurred between the supporters of Go-Shirakawa and Nijō: several of the retired sovereign's associates were dismissed from their court positions in the eleventh month of 1161. The *Hyakurenshō* lists only Koretaka and Narichika,[40] but the *Sankaiki* mentions four others as well: Sane'ie, Motonaka, Tameyuki, and Noritada.[41] Neither source gives a reason for the dismissals, but the fact that the men were confidants of the ex-emperor suggests that it was an attempt on the part of Nijō and his associates to undercut Go-Shirakawa's influence. Perhaps it was in punishment for another plot of some sort.

On at least two occasions in 1162, associates of Go-Shirakawa were stripped of their court offices, and some were even exiled by the emperor. In the fifth month of that year Shige'ie, the governor of Noto, was dismissed because he had ordered the seizure of Minamoto no Masayori (a kurōdo no tō and thus a close confidant of Nijō) and Fujiwara no Kunitsuna, claiming that his action was in accord with an order from Go-Shirakawa.[42] In the sixth month more associates of the ex-sovereign lost their positions and were exiled: Minamoto no Sukekata and Fujiwara no Michiie as well as Taira no Tokitada and Noritada, both of whom had been dismissed the previous year for their involvement with the young Takakura no miya. This time they were accused of having cast a curse on the emperor at the Kamo shrine.[43] Quite obviously the emperor's anger at Tokitada had not yet cooled, and Tokitada in turn still harbored

---

[40] HRS, p. 75. The date given here is the ninth month, but this appears to be incorrect. The *Sankaiki* has the eleventh month and should be regarded as correct since the author was keeping a diary of the events.

[41] *Sankaiki*, 1: 220. Eiryaku 2/11/29.   [42] HRS, p. 76. Ōhō 2/5/8.

[43] HRS, pp. 76–77. Ōhō 2/6/23.

hopes for the succession of his young nephew. Both men were recalled to the capital in 1164.[44]

Thus, there were several occasions on which the emperor was able to dismiss and even exile associates of the retired sovereign Go-Shirakawa. While the ex-emperor did indeed enjoy a good deal of political influence, Nijō was a strong emperor, certainly the strongest to reign during the lifetimes of the three abdicated sovereigns at the end of the Heian period. No emperor had ever been so abrupt and forceful in his treatment of courtiers who were more devoted in their service to the retired emperor than to the sovereign himself. This type of action taken by a reigning sovereign against an abdicated emperor is further evidence that we must revise the concept of abdicated sovereigns during the so-called insei period as absolute dictators able to control court politics according to their will.

While there may be some justification for Nijō's actions against Go-Shirakawa (the emperor was after all supposedly the supreme ruler), he was criticized for his lack of filial piety toward his father, according to the Gempei seisuiki.[45] Some years later Kujō Kanezane recorded in his diary (the Gyokuyō) a conversation he had had with a court astrologer, Abe no Yasuchika. Yasuchika mentioned that in Nijō's reign one astrologer had been rewarded for his announcement of the appearance of a felicitous cloud in the realm. Yasuchika felt that this had to have been deceit on the part of the astrologer since such clouds appeared only in the reigns of sage emperors and filial sovereigns. While Nijō was certainly a wise ruler, Yasuchika said that he was lacking in the virtue of filial piety and thus no such cloud could have been sighted.[46] Thus it would appear that Nijō's attitude toward his father, Go-Shirakawa, was viewed by the court as disrespectful, despite his supposed claim that the emperor had no parents to answer to.

The discord between father and son did not last much longer,

---

[44] HRS, p. 78. Chōkan 2/6/27.
[45] Ryō, "Go-Shirakawa-in," in Heian jidai, p. 218.
[46] Gyokuyō, 1: 66. Kaō 1/4/10.

however. Besides the friction between them over the matter of political power, there was still the unsettled succession issue. As part of her overall plan for the disposition of the imperial succession, Bifukumon'in had married her own daughter Shushi to Nijō when he was made crown prince. After his accession, Shushi had become empress; but she fell ill soon after that and became a nun. As we have already seen, Nijō, to everyone's surprise, then took as his empress dowager Tashi, consort of the deceased Konoe. But she, too, soon absented herself from the emperor's company because of the death of her father in 1161. Finally, Nijō took Tadamichi's daughter Ikushi for empress, giving her the palace name Takamatsu no in. Yet none of these three women produced an heir for the emperor, and thus Go-Shirakawa's infant son by Shigeko was a strong contender for the position of crown prince. The only thing standing in his way was the fact that Toba and Bifukumon'in had already decided the proper order of succession, and although both were now dead there was a certain hesitancy to overturn their decision.

At length, in 1164, one of the palace women in the service of the emperor gave birth to a male imperial offspring. The lady was of comparatively low origin, and the infant was given to the empress Takamatsu no in to raise,[47] a sure sign that he was being considered as a potential candidate for succession. From at least the fifth month of that year the emperor was ill, and by the sixth month his illness had become quite serious. Thus preparations were hurriedly made for abdication in favor of the newborn prince.[48] On the seventeenth day of that month a discussion of the matter was held at the residence of the chancellor, Motozane, and it was decided that this infant, Prince Nobuhito (Emperor Rokujō), should be made crown prince. Only eight days later, however, before the ceremony installing the infant as crown prince could be held, Nijō suddenly abdicated in his favor. Nijō's situation was obviously critical, and he rushed to complete the abdication and accession ceremony before he died. His haste was most certainly aimed at preventing Go-

[47] HRS, p. 79. Eiman 1/6/7.   [48] Ibid. Eiman 1/6/17–7/28.

Shirakawa from removing the boy as crown prince after the emperor's death.

Nijō abdicated, set up his in no chō, and appointed inshi in the manner of all other abdicated sovereigns,[49] but about a month later he died at the age of twenty-three. The new emperor Rokujō was only seven months old, extraordinarily young even by Japanese standards. Motozane was made regent for the emperor, but he died the next year at only twenty-four. He had served Nijō faithfully as chancellor for seven years, and now he followed his sovereign closely in death.

The Brief Reign of Emperor Rokujō
1165–1168

Nijō may have died with a certain sense of relief at having secured the accession of his son, but his action was soon undone and the entire political situation altered by Go-Shirakawa and his associates. One scholar has suggested that Rokujō's accession was only a temporary expediency to ensure Takakura's accession—in the same manner that Go-Shirakawa became emperor only as a means of bringing about the accession of Nijō.[50] I cannot accept that interpretation at all. On the contrary, Nijō was quite sincere in his hopes for the infant Rokujō and obviously felt a responsibility to carry out the succession plan devised by the late ex-sovereign Toba. There was no reason for him to have desired the accession of any other person, least of all Takakura. The eventual accession of Takakura was due solely to the joint scheme of Go-Shirakawa and the Taira kinshin in his service, notably the leading member of the clan, Kiyomori. Less than three months after the accession of Rokujō and only a month and a half after Nijō's death, Taira no Tokitada was

[49] *Sankaiki*, 1: 285. Chōkan 3/6/29. (The era name was changed to Eiman during this month.) Besides various appointments to the positions of kurōdo, hōgandai, and *shutendai* (clerks), Taira no Shigemori was named to serve as one of two *shitsuji bettō*, or chief directors, of the in no chō.

[50] Kawanishi Sachiko, "Rokujō tennō no keibo mondai to dōtei sokui jiken ni kansuru jakkan no kōsatsu," pp. 40–42.

recalled to the capital.[51] As a supporter of the succession of Takakura no miya, he had run afoul of Nijō and lost his offices; a year
later he had been exiled for allegedly casting a curse upon the emperor. Now Tokitada was back at court, and there can be little
doubt that it was Go-Shirakawa and Kiyomori who were responsible
for his return.

Exactly six months after the new emperor's accession, Takakura
no miya was granted the status of imperial prince and given the
name Prince Norihito.[52] The first step toward the accession of this
son of Go-Shirakawa and Taira no Shigeko, long desired by
Tokitada, Atsumori, and others of the Taira clan, had been completed. Although the matter required an imperial edict to sanction
it, there can be no doubt that it was issued at Go-Shirakawa's instigation. That the situation at court was tense is indicated by the
strange events in the seventh month of the next year, as recorded
in the *Hyakurenshō*.[53]

On two occasions a girl in the vicinity of the Ninna-ji had a
similar dream: because the political situation at court was not in
accord with the law, the Kamo deity had left the country of Japan
and crossed the sea to another land. Worried, the officials of the
shrine had reported the matter to both the palace and the residence
of the regent Motozane. Also at that time the country was suffering
a severe drought, and prayers to the gods and deities had not been
efficacious. A certain Teikichi was brought to the palace to chant
sutras, and a great rainfall ensued, for which Go-Shirakawa rewarded him with the appointment as head of the Tō-ji. Yet all was
still not well. As though it were a portent, the Ōtemmon gate at
the palace suddenly collapsed on the twenty-fifth; and, predictably
enough, calamity followed when Motozane died the very next day.
A small temple was erected for him at the Kōryū-ji, where Nijō was
buried, as an indication of his service to the emperor. His younger
brother Motofusa was made regent and uji no chōja because his
son Motomichi was deemed too young.

[51] *HRS*, p. 79. Eiman 1/9/14.   [52] Ibid. Eiman 1/12/25.
[53] *HRS*, p. 80. Nin'an 1/7.

Shortly thereafter, in the tenth month, Prince Norihito was made crown prince in a ceremony held at the Sanjō-in detached palace.[54] The ex-emperor Go-Shirakawa had previously accompanied his son to the palace. Norihito stayed there until the twelfth month, when it was destroyed by fire, after which he moved to Tsuchimikado, the residence of Fujiwara no Kunitsuna,[55] a little known yet highly influential courtier who was close to the sekkanke as well as to the ex-sovereign.[56]

Go-Shirakawa was now clearly master of the political situation as well as unchallenged head of the imperial house. The next year both the emperor and the crown prince paid visits of familial respect at his palace. The *Hyakurenshō* records that the abdicated sovereign was grandfather of the emperor and father of the crown prince (an unusual arrangement), noting in particular that Go-Shirakawa had been responsible for the selection of the crown prince.[57] On the same day that Norihito visited the ex-emperor, his mother, Taira no Shigeko, was made an imperial consort. In the following month Shigeko's brother-in-law Kiyomori was named prime minister (*dajō daijin*), the highest position in the imperial bureaucracy.

The events following Nijō's death are thus quite clear. Nijō had followed Toba's succession plan, but Go-Shirakawa harbored other ideas. As crown prince for his grandson Rokujō, Go-Shirakawa chose his own son by a Taira woman, with the obvious collusion of his close associate and military backer Kiyomori. His desire was to force the abdication of the infant Rokujō and replace him with Prince Norihito. Rokujō's accession thus served, in effect, as a temporary measure until the accession of Prince Norihito (Takakura), but that was far from the intention of Nijō when he abdicated in favor of his own son. With the designation of Norihito as crown prince, Go-Shirakawa was assured of the accession of his own offspring,

---

[54] Ibid. Nin'an 1/10/10.   [55] Ibid. Nin'an 1/12/24.
[56] For information on the political career of Kunitsuna, see Yoshiba Hiroko, "Insei no seiji shutai ni kansuru ichikōsatsu: Gon-dainagon Fujiwara Kunitsuna-kyō kenkyū josetsu."
[57] *HRS*, p. 80. Nin'an 2/1/20.

quite an accomplishment for an emperor who had never even expected to become emperor himself. As relatives of the soon-to-be-emperor Norihito, Kiyomori and Shigeko achieved extraordinarily high court rank, owing chiefly to the favor of the retired sovereign.

The Rise of the Taira

Even before the accession of Prince Norihito as Emperor Takakura, the Taira clan had begun to surpass other families of long-standing importance at court. Since much of this was in accord with the plans of Go-Shirakawa, we can only accuse the ex-emperor of poor judgment. While it might appear that a court in which most of the kugyō were clients in his service would permit him to dominate the political scene, he seems to have completely misunderstood the possible threat posed by Kiyomori's advancement at court. As a maternal relative of the emperor, the Taira chieftain could be expected to attempt to use this connection to exercise control over the young emperor in the manner of a Fujiwara regent. As prime minister, thanks also to Go-Shirakawa's support, he would be doubly powerful. Go-Shirakawa appears to have misunderstood age-old Japanese political traditions. Maternal relationship to the emperor was one of the oldest means to political power for non-imperial court families. The ex-sovereign also seems to have over-estimated his own ability to control Kiyomori and the Taira clan after the accession of Takakura. It appears that, while Go-Shirakawa attempted to use the Taira to advance his own political ends against the sekkanke, and even against Emperor Nijō, he failed to consider the possibility that the Taira were also using him for similar purposes. That they could one day turn against their patron seems never to have occurred to him.

At any rate, Kiyomori soon resigned the post of prime minister due to illness and became a lay priest. This of course did not hinder his political effectiveness; it merely freed him from some of the more tedious and routine court functions required of the prime minister. In 1168 the emperor Rokujō "abdicated" in favor of

Prince Norihito [58] in accord with the plans of both Go-Shirakawa and Kiyomori. Upon his enthronement Takakura's mother Shigeko was promoted to empress dowager and she was later given the palace name Kenshummon'in.[59] Thus began the reign of the eight-year-old Takakura, and his enthronement was the signal for the commencement of a growing estrangement between Go-Shirakawa and Kiyomori.

As father of the emperor, head of the imperial house, and long-time patron of the Taira, Go-Shirakawa obviously expected to enjoy the greatest influence over the young emperor in the determination of court affairs. But he was not as powerful as he imagined. As gaiseki to the emperor, "head" of the Taira clan, and, perhaps most importantly, the most powerful warrior in the land, with adherents throughout Japan but particularly in the west and south,[60] Kiyomori was able to exercise much more actual power than Go-Shirakawa. The retired emperor had no one to blame but himself for Kiyomori's meteoric rise to dominance.

For several years the relationship between the two men remained somewhat cordial. In the third month of 1169 Go-Shirakawa made a trip to Mount Kōya accompanied by a retinue of courtiers which included the prime minister, Tadamasa. On his return to the capital he stopped for a visit at Kiyomori's Fukuhara residence in the province of Settsu.[61] In the sixth month the forty-three-year-old ex-emperor took priestly vows, becoming dajō hōō, or hōō (priestly abdicated sovereign). While this increased his influence among the priests of the Buddhist centers and while his religious activities proliferated from this time on, it was in no way a sign of failing interest in court politics. Go-Shirakawa continued to maintain strong influence in court affairs, and on several occasions the kugyō met at his palace to discuss and decide matters of state.

The feuds between the major Buddhist temples, in particular the three-sided struggle between the monasteries of Enryaku-ji, Mii-

[58] HRS, p. 81. Nin'an 3/2/19.   [59] Ibid. Nin'an 3/3/20.
[60] For the Taira position in Kyūshū, see Iida Hisao, "Heishi to Kyūshū," in Takeuchi Rizō Hakushi Kanreki Kinenkai, ed., Shōensei to buke shakai, pp. 33–68.
[61] HRS, p. 83. Kaō 1/3/23.

dera, and Kōfuku-ji, continued to be a major political problem; and Go-Shirakawa was as powerless to stop them as his great grandfather Shirakawa had been. The disputes involved material as well as ecclesiastical matters, and at one point the priest Gyōzen even committed suicide over the settlement of a shōen dispute that went against him.[62]

In the twelfth month of 1169 an enraged mass of Enryaku-ji monks stormed into the capital bearing the sacred *mikoshi* (portable shrine) of the Hie shrine and gathered at the palace.[63] They charged that Masatomo, the local representative of the governor of Owari (Fujiwara no Narichika), had engaged in a fight with some persons working for the Hie shrine in that province. Go-Shirakawa quickly called the kugyō together for a meeting, and they decided to imprison Masatomo; but the monks were not satisfied until Narichika was dismissed from office and exiled to Bitchū as well. Only three days later, however, Narichika was absolved and two Taira courtiers—Tokitada again and Nobunori—were dismissed and exiled. The monks were so outraged at this that in the first month of 1170 Go-Shirakawa was again forced to call the kugyō to council, and the original decision was upheld. Tokitada and Nobunori were recalled from exile, and Narichika was sent off again. We should note that, while Go-Shirakawa appears to have played a leading role in all these decisions, on each occasion an imperial edict was issued to initiate the exile or recall of an official. It was not within the ex-emperor's authority to take such actions.

Kiyomori and Go-Shirakawa continued on fairly cordial terms for the next five or six years. The ex-sovereign visited Kiyomori at his Fukuhara residence on numerous occasions, and once he even went to the Taira clan shrine at Itsukushima in the province of Aki. He was always in the company of Shigeko, now known at Kenshummon'in, having received that palace name in 1169. In 1171 the relationship between the two major political figures of the day was further solidified when Go-Shirakawa took Kiyomori's daughter Tokuko as his adopted daughter and made her Takakura's consort.[64]

---

[62] HRS, p. 84. Kaō 1/10/13.   [63] HRS, pp. 84–85. Kaō 1/12/28–2/1/27.
[64] HRS, p. 86. Jōan 1/12/2.

The birth of a son would then make Kiyomori the grandfather of an imperial prince, possible successor to the imperial line. Nonetheless, Go-Shirakawa still seems not to have feared anything from the Taira.

But despite his warrior background Kiyomori was following the pattern of the Fujiwara in his effort to enhance the position of his own house at court. Once having reached the kugyō council through the patronage of Go-Shirakawa, he set out to forge strong marriage ties with the imperial family, hoping for the eventual accession of a grandson. At the same time he used his own influence to get other Taira family members appointed to leading court positions and won the clientage of many lesser courtiers by advancing their interests. The *Heike monogatari* claims that the influence of the Taira was so great that there were sixteen kugyō and thirty *denjō-bito* (courtiers in attendance upon the emperor) from the house. While the influence of the Taira was great and its rise to power meteoric, however, there were never sixteen Taira kugyō at any one time. In 1183, during the reign of Kiyomori's grandson Antoku, there were twelve Taira kugyō out of a total of fifty-seven, or little more than a fifth of the entire group. Certainly this is not enough to warrant the *Heike monogatari*'s claim that anyone who was not a Taira was not a person. In comparison with what Taira influence had been before, there was indeed a great upsurge in the period between 1165 and 1180; but aside from Kiyomori as prime minister the only Taira courtiers to hold major posts were Munemori and Shigemori, both of whom held the post of *naidaijin* (great minister of the center).

The Rift between Go-Shirakawa and Kiyomori, 1175–1180

During the next decade the Taira enjoyed great political and economic good fortune. There was little but envy and jealousy in the hearts of the sekkanke and other houses that had long enjoyed power and prestige at court. It was bad enough to be of warrior origin and a newcomer—and a successful one at that—but Kiyomori's proud and haughty attitude seems to have created widespread animosity among the courtiers. At last even Go-Shirakawa began to fear the extent of Kiyomori's power, and a rift developed between the two men.

Now once again courtiers in the service of the retired sovereign were seized and exiled for misdeeds. In 1175 Nobuhiro, one of Go-Shirakawa's supervisors was arrested by a Taira captain of the guards.[65] The next year, Go-Shirakawa's fiftieth, was a decidedly poor one for the fortunes of the imperial house. Go-Shirakawa's favorite consort, Kenshummon'in, died, as did the thirteen-year-old junior retired sovereign Rokujō. Go-Shirakawa was particularly grieved over the death of Kenshummon'in. Two other retired imperial women also died that year: Takamatsu no in and Kujō-in, empresses of Nijō and Konoe respectively. Taira no Morikata, a kurōdo in the service of Jōzaimon'in (Toba's second daughter), was exiled to the island of Sado for having killed the courtier Tametsuna in the previous year.[66]

Finally, in the sixth month of 1177, the friction between Go-Shirakawa and Kiyomori broke out into the open with the discovery of the Shishigatani affair, a plot by the ex-sovereign's associates against Kiyomori and the Taira. Kiyomori learned of the plot from Minamoto no Yukitsuna, who leaked the information to the Taira chieftain.[67] Kiyomori had Narichika, Naritsune, and Moromitsu arrested. Moromitsu, better known by his priestly name Saikō, was executed and the others were exiled. Two days later a number of other associates of the ex-emperor were similarly arrested and exiled, among them the priest Shunkan, bettō of the Hosshō-ji, most famous of the family temples belonging to the imperial house. No

[65] HRS, p. 91. Angen 1/7/15.

[66] HRS, p. 92. Angen 2/3/19. Tametsuna was murdered on Angen 1/9*/29. The affair was investigated during the first two months of the next year, and it turned out to be a complicated love triangle involving the daughter of the late Fujiwara no Akiyoshi.

[67] HRS, p. 95. Jijō 1/6/1–18.

action was taken against Go-Shirakawa himself, but the ex-sovereign had been appropriately warned of the dangers of plotting against Kiyomori.

The political situation now became extremely tense; the power of the retired emperor had been challenged, and courtiers were divided in their loyalties between Go-Shirakawa and Kiyomori, both of whom enjoyed a measure of control over Emperor Takakura. The court was greatly unsettled, and because of fear that the unrest might somehow be the work of the angry spirits of the defeated parties in the Hōgen disturbance—Yorinaga and Sutoku—an edict was issued posthumously appointing Yorinaga prime minister and giving the deceased junior retired sovereign, then known as Sanuki no in, the name Sutoku-in ("virtue-worshiping retired sovereign").[68] As in the case of all unsettled political situations in traditional Japan, the chronicles record an unusual number of natural calamities and portents for the period: fires, comets, pestilence, and the like. The physical violence that had come to characterize life in the capital continued unabated. In 1178 a retainer of Kiyomori, Nakazane, was murdered in the Gojō Ōmiya area of the city, and in 1179 one of Go-Shirakawa's supervisors, Minamoto no Arimasa, was killed at Ichijō Imadegawa.

In the eleventh month of 1178 Kiyomori's daughter Tokuko gave birth to a prince of the emperor Takakura, and the possibility of enhanced political prospects appeared to the Taira. If this boy could be made emperor, Go-Shirakawa would be almost completely cut off from influence over the reigning sovereign, and the Taira would have less of a problem dealing with the intransigent ex-emperor. The future must indeed have looked bright to Kiyomori when, only one month after his birth, he succeeded in having this infant (future Emperor Antoku) made crown prince.

The year 1179 proved to be the crucial one in the struggle between Go-Shirakawa and Kiyomori. Still free to move about after the abortive Shishigatani incident, Go-Shirakawa and his kinshin, joined by other anti-Taira courtiers, continued to plot the destruc-

[68] *HRS*, pp. 95–96. Jijō 1/7/29.

tion of the Taira. In the eleventh month of the year the capital was filled with apprehension, and warriors clogged the city streets. On the fifteenth day Kiyomori, reportedly angry at the courtiers, was rumored to have left the city for Kyūshū, leading his entire clan.[69] On that same day an edict was issued at Kiyomori's instigation dismissing Motofusa as chancellor and naming Motomichi to replace him, not only as chancellor, but as Fujiwara clan chieftain as well. The suspected reason was that Motofusa was plotting the overthrow of the Taira and their adherents in collusion with Go-Shirakawa. On the seventeenth day a rash of dismissals and new appointments to court positions was carried out at Kiyomori's command—Kanezane recorded that in this turbulent age the imperial position and those of regent and chancellor were meaningless.[70] Thirty-nine persons, from the prime minister on down, lost their court positions; most of these were kinshin of the retired sovereign. The massive attack on these officials thus confirmed the rumor that Kiyomori was planning to seize and dismiss the ex-emperor's kinshin. Some were simply dismissed from office, and others were exiled. Tameyuki and Tameyasu, special favorites of Go-Shirakawa, were executed, and Ōe no Tonari committed suicide. Not content with this, Kiyomori now moved against the ex-sovereign himself.[71]

Mune'ie, one of Go-Shirakawa's bettō, was seized, and the documents listing the landholdings of the retired emperor were taken for examination. On the twentieth Kiyomori had Go-Shirakawa taken to the Toba-dono in the south of the city and held in seclusion. Warriors were placed on guard, and only a few associates—the priest Seiken, and two or three women—were allowed access to the ex-sovereign. On the fourteenth day of the next month, apparently in order to eliminate some of Go-Shirakawa's influence in the imperial house, a goin no chō was established for the new emperor, Takakura. The goin, it will be remembered, was an office in charge

[69] HRS, p. 99. The following information comes from the entries between Jijō 3/11/15 and 3/12/16.

[70] Gyokuyō, 2: 310. Jijō 3/11/17. The same source, pp. 310–11, lists all the dismissals and appointments, as does Sankaiki, 2: 313–14.

[71] HRS, pp. 99–103. Jijō 3/11/21–4/12/28.

of management of financial matters for a sovereign in anticipation of his abdication. After abdication, the goin and its officials became the basis for the in no chō. This was the first time that a goin no chō had been established while there was an abdicated sovereign, according to the *Hyakurenshō*. It is possible that Kiyomori had seized some lands held by Go-Shirakawa and had them transferred to the new emperor's (and thus to Kiyomori's) control, but there is no proof that such was the case. Neither the *Sankaiki* nor the *Gyokuyō* mentions the matter of the goin no chō. However, it was at least an indication that Kiyomori was preparing to have this infant grandson succeed the emperor Takakura. In the second month of 1180 Takakura did abdicate in favor of the young prince and grandson of the Taira chieftain, who became Emperor Antoku.

Go-Shirakawa was not without support, however, and anti-Taira activities continued. In the fifth month Go-Shirakawa was transferred from the Toba-dono to the Hachijō Karasuma residence of Toshimori, where the Taira forces could better guard him. On the very next day Prince Mochihito, a son of Go-Shirakawa who was passed over for succession because of his mother's rather low origins, was exiled to Tosa for plotting against the Taira; but he escaped to the Onjō-ji, where the monks were in sympathy with him. On the twenty-sixth day Mochihito, along with Minamoto no Yorimasa and other Genji warriors, clashed with Taira forces. Both the prince and Yorimasa were killed in this encounter.

To avoid further trouble Kiyomori in the sixth month moved the capital to his own bailiwick at Fukuhara. Both of the abdicated sovereigns and the infant emperor were escorted to the new capital. But it was already too late to avoid calamity. Prince Mochihito had issued a princely edict (*ryōji*) calling for the chastisement of the Taira, and by the ninth month rumors of the revolt of Minamoto no Yoritomo in the east had reached the capital region. An edict was issued demanding Yoritomo's seizure, and Taira no Koremori marched eastward after the rebels. He returned in the eleventh month with the report of a huge concentration of enemy warriors. The rush of events forced Kiyomori to return the capital to Heian

—to everyone's delight—in order to be closer to the center of activity. Upon the return to Heian Go-Shirakawa was kept at the Taira stronghold in Rokuhara and later moved to the residence of the junior abdicated sovereign, where most of the kugyō council meetings appear to have been held during this hectic period.

After Takakura and Kiyomori died in 1181, Go-Shirakawa was once again permitted to participate in governmental affairs,[72] and for the four years during which the war between the Taira and the Minamoto raged, he appears to have been the major political figure. The meetings of the kugyō were generally called by him and held at his palace. But his fate is well known. He backed the Minamoto against the Taira in hopes of regaining his own dwindling power but soon learned that the Minamoto had no intention of allowing him to reassume his former position. Next he turned to plotting dissension among the various Minamoto generals and was for a time successful. But the conclusion of the war between the two great warrior houses hastened the end of courtier power in Japan. Not until the Shōkyū War in 1221 did the eastern warriors gain total mastery over the country, but with the demise of the Taira and the establishment of the Kamakura shogunate by 1185, the power of the courtier class, and along with it that of the ex-sovereign, waned. Go-Shirakawa remained abdicated sovereign, head of the imperial house, and the focus of the Heian court until his death in 1192. But he was hardly able to force political decisions in the direction he wished since the country was still in a chaotic state and Yoritomo controlled the military power. Go-Shirakawa's most forceful action during this time was a defensive one: he refused to allow the issuance of an edict naming Yoritomo shogun.

Go-Shirakawa's In no Chō

Go-Shirakawa thus came to leadership of the imperial house and the position of abdicated sovereign in a tremendously unsettled

[72] HRS, p. 105. Yōwa 1/1/17.

period in Japanese history. Although the ex-emperor Go-Toba enjoyed a degree of power prior to the Shōkyū War, Go-Shirakawa
was really the last of the ex-sovereigns to enjoy the new fortunes
of the independent imperial house carved out by Go-Sanjō and
Shirakawa. He had control over a large body of private officials in
his house office, but how large this body was is difficult to judge.
An 1159 kudashibumi was signed by twenty-four bettō,[73] which we
can safely assume included all of them at that time. Another document of 1160 lists twenty bettō and eight hōgandai [74] while still
another in 1161 has twenty-seven bettō and nine hōgandai.[75] In
1179, as we have seen, thirty-nine officilas were dismissed from
office, and most of these were Go-Shirakawa's associates. Unfortunately, we have no record of what, if any, positions they held in
his in no chō. It is clear, however, that after his original appointment of six bettō Go-Shirakawa's in no chō grew rapidly and became quite large.

Like Toba before him, Go-Shirakawa also amassed a great number
of shōen for the imperial house. He constructed numerous palaces
and temples by soliciting (or receiving without solicitation) "special contributions" from provincial governors and other courtiers,
and he received numerous commendations of landholdings for their
support. He lumped together a number of these holdings for the
support of one particular temple, the Chōkōdō, and these were
passed down within the imperial house as the Chōkōdō-ryō, a huge
portfolio of shōen that became the major financial basis of the
Jimyōin branch of the imperial house during the dynastic split in
the fourteenth century.

Although he was as vigorous as Toba in the acquisition of shōen,
Go-Shirakawa appears to have been somewhat in agreement with
Shirakawa concerning the general evils of extensive privatization of
land. As we have seen, he and Shinzei did issue a fairly effective
shōen regulation ordinance while he was emperor. Later, in 1173,
when the disputes among the armed monks of the great Buddhist

---

[73] *Heian ibun*, 6: 2450–51, doc. 2979.   [74] Ibid., 7: 2498–2500, doc. 3093.
[75] Ibid., pp. 2521–22, doc. 3138.

institutions were at their height, Go-Shirakawa had an edict issued ordering the confiscation of landholdings belonging to the temples.[76] He apparently discussed the matter with no one but made the decision entirely on his own. Kanezane criticized this action, not for its harshness, but rather for its laxity. Shōen were destroying the country, he said, and all of them, whether they belonged to temple, shrine, or courtier, ought to be abolished. The court ought to emulate the actions of Go-Sanjō and try to return to the practice of the Engi era. The abolition of shōen holdings of just a few Nara temples would accomplish nothing, in Kanezane's view.[77]

Even though this was only a partial attack on the problem, and the holdings were soon restored to their owners, it does indicate that Go-Shirakawa was aware of the problem posed by increasing control over the land by private persons and institutions. That he did not feel such dangers applied to the imperial house, which was in effect the imperial government, is clear from the growth of imperial holdings during his lifetime.

With the death of Go-Shirakawa the insei period proper comes to an end, although some scholars include Go-Toba in the period. At the end of the Heian era three successive abdicated sovereigns —Shirakawa, Toba, and Go-Shirakawa—enjoyed extensive political influence at court and made the imperial house the focus of court politics once again. Truly these years were a golden age of the imperial house in recorded Japanese history. In the remote past the house may have been the omnipotent entity of which Japanese historians have always dreamily written, but this is extremely doubtful. The Engi and Tenryaku periods in the tenth century may have been models for later statesmen to emulate, but in actuality imperial power was not particularly marked in this period. It was during the so-called insei period, criticized by historians of both Confucian and Marxist leanings, that the imperial house as a whole— abdicated sovereigns, retired imperial ladies, emperors, princes, and princesses—enjoyed more glory and prestige as well as actual po-

[76] HRS, p. 89. Jōan 3/11/11.   [77] Gyokuyō, 1: 329. Jōan 3/11/12.

litical power and wealth than at any other time in Japanese history. Confucians rankle at the fact that the emperor was less powerful than the ex-sovereign, a perversion of Confucian governmental ideals. Marxists see the "despotic" ex-sovereigns as the last reactionary stage of a corrupt aristocratic rule which was soon to be replaced by the new and dynamic feudal warrior class. But in terms of actual power and wealth, the imperial house enjoyed its real golden age during the insei period, 1086–1185.

✌ TWO ❧

The In no Chō

✺᠄ EIGHT ᠈✺

The Structure and Function of the In no Chō

PART ONE was a discussion of the role of abdicated sovereigns in the politics of the Heian period. Particular attention was focused upon the so-called *insei* period, 1086–1185, when the three ex-sovereigns Shirakawa, Toba, and Go-Shirakawa successively dominated the court. I attempted to show that these abdicated sovereigns were not absolute dictators who enjoyed total mastery of court politics. All three were quite powerful in their day, but their power was always circumscribed by the emperor and the constituted offices of the imperial government, whose authority they never questioned. I suggested that the *in no chō* (ex-sovereign's office) was not a body of officials serving the retired emperor in the same manner that the court officials served the reigning emperor, but a private office for the management of the affairs of the ex-sovereign and other members of the imperial house. I also presented evidence contradicting the assumption that documents issued by the ex-sovereign's office possessed greater authority than those of the imperial government. In sum, I tried to show that, while the abdicated sovereigns Shirakawa, Toba, and Go-Shirakawa had considerable political *power*, this power was not the same as the authority possessed by the emperor and his government.[1]

---

[1] The terms authority, power, and influence are extremely broad ones and have been the focus of great discussion among political scientists for generations. The

In this second part, I would like to examine in greater detail the nature of the in no chō: the types of documents it issued, the kinds of persons who served the ex-sovereign closely, and the landholdings of the imperial household which the in no chō seems to have managed. Let us first look at the structure and function of the in no chō.

The Organization of the In no Chō

The in no chō developed over the course of the early Heian period to serve the needs of the abdicated sovereign. It was not an office established during the insei period as a device by which the abdicated emperor could control politics. With very few exceptions, all the bureaus and administrative positions within the in no chō had been in existence long before the latter part of the Heian period. As far back as the earliest instances of abdication in Japan, it is

---

sense in which I use the terms is that expressed in Harold Lasswell and Abraham Kaplan, *Power and Society* (New Haven: Yale University Press, 1950):

"To exercise influence is to affect the policies of others as to weight, scope, and domain" (p. 83). Power is a type of influence; "a form of influence is a form of power wherever the effect on policy is enforced by relatively severe sanctions" (p. 84). "Power is a special case of the exercise of influence: it is the process of affecting the policies of others with the help of (actual or threatened) severe deprivations for the nonconformity with the policies intended" (p. 76). "Authority is formal power" and is "thus the expected and legitimate possession of power. We say 'expected' because the actual power structure does not necessarily coincide with that described in the political formula; and 'legitimate' because the formula is the source and basis of legitimacy" (p. 133). "Every power group seeks to acquire authority or to exercise effective power over authorities" (p. 137).

For the most part, the Heian power structure can be described as formalistic since authority was most frequently divorced from effective power. Yet "authority is never completely powerless" (p. 134); and even during the latter part of the Heian period, when the ex-sovereign exercised influence over the decision-making process and held effective power, the emperor and the organs of imperial government remained the source of legitimacy. The emperor's authority was never challenged, and if he chose to assert himself the emperor could wield considerable power. The Japanese imperial institution enjoys authority on religious and ceremonial, rather than political, grounds. Thus, holders of effective power throughout Japanese history have attempted to exercise power over, or to control, this authority rather than to usurp it. In this respect, the abdicated sovereign was no different from a regent, shogun, or prime minister.

evident that there were offices and officials, either informally or formally constituted, to manage the affairs of retired sovereigns.

By at least the abdication of Saga in 823, the term *inshi* was used to designate officials of the ex-sovereign. Chief among these officials was the director (bettō). During the mid-Heian period, the number of bureaus and officials in the service of successive abdicated sovereigns seems to have increased. In the *Saikyūki*, for example, there is mention of *hōgandai* (supervisors) and *shutendai* (clerks) in the retinue of the abdicated sovereign; bureaus such as the *kurōdo-dokoro* (private household bureau), *mushadokoro-chō* (warrior's bureau), and other lesser ones are also mentioned.[2]

Although these various officials and bureaus were associated with the abdicated sovereign, there does not appear to have been a general term for the collective body until the abdication of En'yū in 964. In that year the sovereign abdicated and held a ceremony for the opening of his office (*in no chō no kotohajime*).[3] As far as can be determined, this is the first mention of the term in no chō in the sources for this period. Although Japanese scholars usually regard this as the founding of the in no chō, it is important to point out that this office was no different from previous ones. En'yū appointed the same types of officials and maintained the same kinds of bureaus as previous ex-sovereigns. We simply know that from at least this time the entire arrangement was referred to as the in no chō. And even though this is the first appearance of the term in the sources available to us today, we cannot be sure that it had not been in use previously. There is no indication in the sources that a new office was being instituted or even a new word being coined.[4]

The in no chō, then, took shape long before the latter part of the Heian period. Our documentary evidence for this latter period is fuller, but even so it is evident that, with the increase of power on the part of abdicated sovereigns in the eleventh and twelfth

---

[2] *Saikyūki*, in Kondō Heijō, ed., *Shiseki shūran*, pp. 380–81.

[3] *Shōyūki*, 1: 49–50.

[4] The major source for this period is Ononomiya Sanesuke's diary, *Shōyūki*. Since Sanesuke was a close associate of En'yū, his diary contains considerable information about the ex-emperor's activities. The *Nihon kiryaku* is another important source.

centuries, the size and scope of authority of the in no chō increased significantly. Within this context, let us first consider the bureaus that constituted the in no chō and the officials that staffed it in the late Heian period. Table 3 indicates the bureaus within the in no

TABLE 3

The structure of the In no Chō

Kurōdo-dokoro	Mizuishin-dokoro
(private household bureau)	(bureau of official bodyguards)
Fudono	Mushadokoro-chō
(secretariat)	(warriors' bureau)
Tsukae-dokoro	In no hokumen
(attendants' bureau)	(bureau of ex-sovereign's warriors
	of the northern quarter)
Meshitsugi-dokoro	
(servants' bureau)	

Shimmotsu-sho
(ex-sovereign's kitchen)
Gofuku-dokoro
(bureau of ceremonial dress)
Saiku-sho
(ex-sovereign's workshop)
Mimaya
(ex-sovereign's stable)
Bechinō-sho
(special warehouse)

chō.[5] (For a more detailed description of their functions, see appendix 1.) There were most likely a few other bureaus not shown in the table such as a custodial bureau and some kind of women's quarters for those ladies who were in frequent attendance upon the ex-emperor, but I have found no specific mention of them. Besides

[5] Besides the afore-mentioned *Saikyūki,* information about the officials and bureaus within the ex-sovereign's office can be found in several encyclopedic compilations: *Shūgaishō,* in *Kojitsu sōsho,* 22: 366; *Gōke shidai,* in ibid., 2: 507, Koji Ruien Kankōkai, ed., *Koji ruien,* 15: 44–93. The best secondary work discussing these officials and bureaus is Yoshimura Shigeki, *Insei.* Yoshimura is one of the leading scholars of the insei, and much of information on the structure of the in no chō, both in the text and appendix 1, is based upon Yoshimura's volume.

the relatively low-ranking officials such as the kurōdo (stewards) and *shoshū* (miscellaneous attendants), there were three major officials in the in no chō who were not attached to any of the specific bureaus. These were the bettō, hōgandai, and shutendai.

BETTŌ (DIRECTOR)

Directors had been the senior officials in the in no chō since the early Heian period, when there were only a few. By the insei period, however, the number of directors had risen with the expansion of the power and prestige of the ex-sovereign. Frequently there were more than twenty. Furthermore, the rank of in no chō directors underwent a change over the course of the Heian period. Earlier directors were usually courtiers of the fourth or fifth rank, but in the latter part of the period most were kugyō.

It is unlikely that the duties of the directors were too numerous, and it appears obvious that on many occasions appointments were merely honorary, as when Shirakawa appointed the twelve-year-old Tadazane to serve as bettō in his in no chō. While the ex-sovereign was in frequent consultation with these directors concerning both public and private matters, their specific duties were evidently not time consuming, since all were simultaneously fulfilling some official government function which was of primary importance.

Certain of these directors, however, were charged with handling the majority of administrative tasks of the in no chō. A few were designated *shitsuji*, or *shitsuji bettō* (chief directors), and they seem to have spent considerable time in the performance of duties on behalf of the retired sovereign. Right below the chief directors in terms of importance was another director who served as *nen'yo*, or *azukari* (director for the current year). The name apparently derives from the fact that in the early years of the insei period the position seems to have been rotated annually among the different directors. Later it came to be regarded as a separate office to which two persons were normally appointed each year. These were usually kugyō or at least *denjōbito*. Another position, *chō no kanjin*, or *chōkan* (steward of the ex-sovereign's office), appears in various diaries, and while the function of this official is not known it is suspected that it was similar to the nen'yo position. Perhaps it was even an alternate term.

HŌGANDAI (SUPERVISORS)

Next in importance to the directors were the supervisors, who were in charge of the everyday business of the in no chō. In general, it appears that men of promise who were not yet within the ranks of the kugyō were appointed to this position. Originally most were of the fifth and sixth rank with experience as secretaries to the sovereign, but by Shirakawa's time men of the fourth rank were frequently appointed. Many supervisors later became directors, either for the same ex-emperor or for the subsequent one.

SHUTENDAI (CLERKS)

The clerks were scribes in the employ of the ex-emperor, and their chief duty appears to have been the drafting of documents. This was an extremely important task, and thus persons with considerable experience in documentation and with outstanding calligraphy were appointed as shutendai. During the insei period there were generally two or three clerks. The character *dai* (meaning "instead of," or "in place of") in the terms hōgandai and shutendai was added to distinguish them from similar positions in various governmental bureaus.

Structurally, the in no chō was quite similar to the *mandokoro* (administrative office) of the regent's house and other courtier houses discussed in chapter 2. In fact, in the *Shūgaishō* the list of officials in the sekkanke mandokoro is included in the section devoted to a discussion of the officials of the ex-sovereign's office.[6] Likewise, the *Koji ruien*, an encyclopedia of Japanese history and

[6] *Shūgaishō*, p. 366.

society completed in 1914, treats both officials of the ex-sovereign and household officials of courtier families under the same category.[7] In its structure, then, the ex-sovereign's office was essentially a house administrative office similar to those of other leading figures at the Heian court. Retired imperial ladies also had in no chō on a slightly smaller scale, but with similarly titled officials and issuing identical documents.

The in no chō differed from the offices within the imperial government in the same manner that other house offices did: officials who served in the office were selected by the head of the house (in the case of the in no chō, the ex-sovereign) rather than appointed through court procedures. Their personal relationship with the retired sovereign was normally their most important qualification for appointment to the in no chō. Furthermore, they did not serve exclusively as inshi but simultaneously held positions in the imperial bureaucracy. Often their bureaucratic post was attained through the patron–client relationship formed with the ex-sovereign whom they served. In this respect, the officials of the retired sovereign were no different from household officials of leading courtiers, except that their ultimate social and political influence was often greater because of the position of their patron.

The Documents of the In no Chō

The ex-sovereign in the late Heian period thus possessed a rather imposing private office to serve his various needs. Two questions about this office, however, must be answered before one can make any final conclusions about its position in Heian political society. First, what was its major function? Second, what was the scope of its authority? Fortunately, a number of documents issued by the in no chō of Shirakawa, Toba, and Go-Shirakawa survive today.[8] An

[7] *Koji ruien*, 15: 94, sec. 20, entitled "inshi."

[8] While working on in no chō documents, I became aware of the existence of an unpublished thesis on the subject by Suzuki Shigeo: "Inseiki in no chō no kinō ni tsuite," University of Tokyo, 1961. Mr. Suzuki, currently on the staff of the Historiographical Institute at the University of Tokyo, provided me with a copy of his

examination of these documents provides the answer to these questions.

With very few exceptions, the documents deal in one way or another with estate holdings.[9] More specifically, they can be broken down into (1) those dealing with estate holdings of the ex-emperor

thesis and kindly discussed many different aspects concerning in no chō documents with me. In particular, he provided me with considerable information on document transmission and preservation in the late Heian period. My discussion of the in no chō owes much to his help.

For the sake of convenience, the period to be considered in the examination of these documents is 1086 to 1183, when Yoritomo began to issue documents as the leader of the eastern warriors and the authority structure became extremely complex.

Eighty-one extant in no chō documents and *inzen* are collected in *Heian ibun*. The following is a list of those documents, broken down according to ex-sovereign and type of document. The volume and document numbers of the individual documents appear under each heading.

Shirakawa

Inzen	Kudashibumi	Chō (communiqués)
4.1759	5.1814	4.1714
5.1844		10.4975
5.1845		

Toba

Inzen		Kudashibumi		Chō	
5.2253	6.2505	5.2208	6.2558	5.2145	5.2339
5.2268	10.5016	10.5001	6.2575	5.2243	6.2536
10.4994	6.2599	10.5004	6.2577	5.2244	
9.4708	6.2622	5.2411	6.2582	5.2245	
5.2402	6.2669	5.2412	6.2774	5.2254	
6.2462	6.2765	6.2491	6.2834	5.2255	
6.2484	10.5028	6.2541		5.2256	

Go-Shirakawa

Inzen		Kudashibumi	
6.2952	7.3721	6.2979	7.3765
6.2957	7.3722	7.3093	8.3833
7.3113	8.4007	7.3138	8.3836
9.4859	8.4035	9.4811	8.3881
9.4861	8.4043	7.3375	8.3884
7.3557	8.4093	7.3386	8.4012
7.3703	8.4097	7.3521	8.4013
7.3630	8.4095	7.3593	8.4107
7.3714	8.4100	9.4876	10.5084
7.3715		7.3666	

Takakura
Kudashibumi
8.3946

[9] The exceptions are all documents from the post-Hōgen period, while Go-Shirakawa was abdicated sovereign and the court situation was complicated by the

himself, (2) those concerning estates of retired imperial ladies, and (3) those pertaining to holdings of confidants (*kinshin*) of the ex-emperor. From this it seems safe to conclude that one of the primary functions of the in no chō was to serve as an administrative agency for the estate holdings not only of the abdicated sovereign but of the entire imperial house, including retired imperial ladies and even confidants of the ex-sovereign. This supports my earlier assertion that the in no chō should be regarded as the private familial administrative office of the abdicated sovereign who acted as head of the imperial house.

As an office the in no chō issued two types of documents: communiqués (*chō*) and orders (*kudashibumi*). The communiqué was one of the original types of documents established under the *ritsuryō* system of government in the Nara period. It was a document issued by one office to another office or person not under its jurisdiction; there was no legal superior-subordinate relationship between the issuer and recipient of the communiqué. The document was thus one of transmission (*dentatsu monjo*) rather than order (*meirei monjo*). In the Heian period the communiqué was widely adopted by new offices that developed outside the ritsuryō state structure, as well as by household administrative offices, temples, and shrines. The in no chō also employed the chō in the conduct of its business with other, nonsubordinate offices and individuals. Communiqués of the in no chō were drafted by one of the clerks, who affixed his seal at the end of each document. This was followed by the seals of some or all of the bettō and hōgandai, with their official posts and ranks duly listed.[10] The overwhelming majority of the extant communiqués from the period in question are addressed to provincial government offices; a few are addressed to temples.

---

rise of a new warrior segment and the struggle between Go-Shirakawa and Emperor Nijō. For a discussion of these, see Jeffrey P. Mass, "The Emergence of the Kamakura Bakufu," esp. pp. 128–29.

[10] Since there is no "official" list of the ex-sovereign's officials, there is no way of knowing exactly how many there were at any one time. It seems safe to assume, however, that all bettō and hōgandai affixed their seals to the document.

To understand the function of the communiqué and the relationship between the in no chō and provincial government offices requires a brief discussion of the process of document transmission.[11]

During the latter part of the Heian period provincial governors normally resided in the capital; they were represented in the province by a deputy and absentee headquarters staffed by local officials. When a communiqué of the ex-sovereign's office was addressed to the government of a particular province in regard to an estate within its borders, it was first sent to the governor in Heian. The governor would then have a provincial governor's order (*kokushi no chōzen*) drafted ordering a certain course of action in regard to the estate in question. The order normally contained some phrase like "a communiqué of the ex-sovereign's office is attached." The governor then sent the communiqué along with his own order back to the in no chō. The in no chō, acting as agent for the ex-sovereign, who was the ultimate protector (*honjo*) of the estate, then sent the documents to the proprietor (*ryōke*) of the estate in the province. The proprietor in turn forwarded the documents to the absentee headquarters in care of a messenger of the ex-emperor. Together the ex-sovereign's messenger and the provincial governor's messenger then proceeded to the estate in question, checked its boundaries, and drove boundary stakes (*bōji*) into the ground to mark the borders (*shiishi*). Thus the estate was recognized by the provincial authorities as exempt from taxation. There were occasions when the provincial governor's order was forwarded directly to the absentee headquarters, but the ultimate effect was the same.

The governor was, of course, in no legal sense subordinate to the ex-sovereign or his office, and thus he was under no obligation to order his deputy to grant the request in the in no chō communiqué. Provincial governors were quite frequently confidants of the ex-sovereign,[12] however, who depended upon his favor for their position, or who hoped in the future to gain such favor. The abdicated

[11] I am indebted to Mr. Suzuki for his assistance on this subject.
[12] See chapter 9 for a discussion of this phenomenon.

sovereign's power and prestige were sufficient to secure the issuance of a provincial governor's order commanding that local officials comply with the in no chō communiqué.

From an examination of the communiqués issued by the in no chō during the insei period, it must be concluded that their function was to secure the issuance of provincial governors' orders to local officials at the absentee headquarters. The ultimate aim was to secure provincial exemption for certain estate holdings in which the ex-sovereign, a retired imperial lady, or a confidant of the ex-emperor held interests. The document that would guarantee the sanctity of these interests from provincial government interference was the order of the provincial governor, not the communiqué of the in no chō. At least in the case of the communiqué, documents of the ex-emperor were not of greater authority than those of the imperial government's legally constituted offices. They possessed sufficient weight, however, to secure the issuance of such government documents.

The second kind of document issued by the in no chō was the *kudashibumi* (order). This was a type of document that came into use during the Heian period after the spread of offices not called for in the ritsuryō system. Its function was to transmit orders from a superior office to a subordinate one, and it came to be used by government bureaus, temple and shrine offices, and the private offices of high-ranking courtiers and imperial personages. Thus the administrative offices of the sekkanke and of major temples, the in no chō of both ex-sovereigns and retired imperial ladies, and the sovereign's private office all issued similar documents transmitting their orders to subordinate offices or persons.

Like the communiqué, the kudashibumi of the in no chō was drafted by one of the clerks. Besides his own seal the document also bore the seals of numerous bettō and hōgandai, giving it a very prestigious and important appearance. According to the standard interpretation of Japanese scholars,[13] kudashibumi were "sent

---

[13] Aida Nirō, *Nihon no komonjo*, 1: 258–300. See also Satō Shin'ichi, *Komonjo-gaku*, pp. 109–20.

down" (*kudasu*) from superior to subordinate offices. In the case of the kudashibumi of the in no chō, well over half are addressed to the official of an estate under the jurisdiction of the ex-sovereign or to the officials of an estate belonging to an imperial temple (*goganji*). This is logical because, as holder of the highest level of proprietary rights to such lands, the ex-sovereign was certainly superior to the officials of those estates.

But a considerable percentage of the kudashibumi are addressed to local officials in various provinces. According to the standard interpretation, then, it would appear at first glance that such local officials were under the jurisdiction of the ex-sovereign. This cannot be the case, however, since the private offices of retired imperial ladies, high-ranking courtiers, and temples all issued kudashibumi to local officials. The local officials were certainly not under the jurisdiction of all these private offices. We must look beyond the address on the document to the procedures involved in documentation to discover the real function of these kudashibumi.

In actuality, the kudashibumi frequently played a role quite similar to the communiqué in securing the issuance of provincial governors' orders. The local officials serving in the absentee headquarters considered themselves solely under the jurisdiction of the provincial governor they represented. Sometimes kudashibumi from the in no chō were sent to an estate official, and, since it was a matter internal to the estate, no cooperation or even acknowledgment from the local officials was necessary. On other occasions, however, where disputes with the local officials or neighboring estates were involved or an estate was to be established, the cooperation of the local officials was necessary. In those cases, the kudashibumi from the in no chō seem to have been addressed to the local officials. There are even kudashibumi addressed to both estate officials and the local officials.

In cases where the local officials were recipients of an in no chō kudashibumi, however, the matter was not decided by the kudashibumi itself. A provincial governor's order sent by the governor himself was required along with it. This is clear from the body of many of the kudashibumi. They usually direct the officials to take a certain action "in accord with the provincial governor's order." There are also several extant examples of provincial governor's orders issued in conjunction with in no chō kudashibumi on the same day. These orders all tell the local officials to carry out the action "in accord with the orders of the ex-sovereign's office." Many times kudashibumi were sent to the absentee headquarters with the orders of the provincial governor attached, in the same manner as the chō.

The same procedure was followed by other imperial house members and high-ranking courtiers as well. They, too, issued kudashibumi to local officials, but these local officials were certainly not under their legal jurisdiction. When such kudashibumi were sent to local officials, it was not the kudashibumi that directed their actions but the provincial governor's order that was attached to or forwarded separately but in conjunction with the kudashibumi.

Thus the kudashibumi of the in no chō appear to have had at least two functions. First, when addressed to an estate official, they were direct orders from a superior to a subordinate official. Second, when addressed to local government officials, they functioned in the same manner as the communiqué in securing the issuance of a provincial governor's order to the absentee headquarters. At least insofar as extant documents are a fair indicator of trends in documentation, in the late Heian period kudashibumi of the in no chō and other private administrative bodies increasingly outnumbered communiqués, and thus it is possible that the former were beginning to take over the function of the latter. Indeed, there are no extant communiqués from Go-Shirakawa's period.[14]

A third kind of document must also be discussed here. As I have mentioned several times, the abdicated sovereign issued personal edicts (*inzen*). These were not official documents issued by the in no chō but rather totally private ones similar in form and nature to the private documents issued by other imperial house members and high-ranking courtiers: the *rinji* of the emperor, *ryōji* of other im-

[14] Actually, there are two communiqués contained in *Heian ibun*, but both of them are dated after 1183.

perial house members, and *migyōsho* of court nobles.[15] They were
quite simple in form, drafted and issued on the instructions of the
ex-sovereign by one of his officials. Unlike the in no chō documents,
the inzen were not always drafted by a shutendai, but always a very
close associate, whether bettō, hōgandai, or shutendai.

There are about as many extant inzen as there are kudashibumi,
and both far outnumber the chō; but the diaries of the time mention inzen much more frequently than the other two documents.[16]
The contents of the inzen are more diverse than either the chō
or the kudashibumi, but in one respect they are similar. They deal
with the private affairs of the imperial house, and most are concerned with estate holdings. They function similarly to the kudashibumi as both direct orders to subordinates and a means of securing
the issuance of public government documents.

Thus all three types of documents associated with the ex-emperor
could be used to secure the issuance of orders by the provincial
governor to the local officials, who would confirm the legality of an
estate. But earlier I pointed out that such provincially exempted
estates were not sufficiently secure from official reprisals. The governor of a province served for four years, and if he were reappointed,
which was a relatively frequent occurrence, his term could extend
to eight years. However, the holder of a provincially exempted estate
could not assume that the next governor would automatically adopt
a similar policy toward his estate. Frequently new governors disallowed provincially exempted estates upon the assumption of their
office, even though later they might once again permit such estates
to exist. Because of this uncertainty, holders of estates looked for

[15] For an excellent discussion of these documents, see Satō, *Komonjogaku*. For a
more detailed examination of the origins of the migyōsho, see Hayashiya Tatsusaburō, "Migyōsho no hassei," in Hayashiya, *Kodai kokka no kaitai*, pp. 351–78.

[16] A number of actions are recorded as having been taken in accord with the
edict of the ex-sovereign—the granting of the right of document examination to
Tadazane by Toba, for example. I suspect, however, that courtiers sometimes attributed actions to an edict of the ex-sovereign rather than to a mere order or
request; extant inzen deal almost exclusively with private rather than public matters. Nakamura Naokatsu also concurs with this in his recent work *Nihon komonjogaku*, 1: 433.

something more permanent than the provincial governor's order to guarantee the tax-exempt status of their holding.

Thus some estate holders looked toward more powerful court figures, such as the regent, for a more secure status. Many turned for aid to the person of the ex-sovereign, the most revered and powerful figure at the time, and sought the issuance of a document from his in no chō. Because of his position in court society—extralegal or extra-institutional to be sure, but nonetheless powerful—the ex-sovereign's documents were of relatively high authority. As we have seen, they carried enough weight to get provincial governors to issue orders to their subordinates to confirm the legality of estate holdings. But just how much ultimate effect did such a document from the ex-sovereign have?

In the late Heian period Japan was a battleground where the institutions of imperial government clashed with the interests of the rising feudal society. The struggle between public and private institutions for control over land was particularly fierce. In most cases the issue was decided by litigation rather than force of arms, and the whole case of ownership rested upon the nature of the documents in the possession of the persons claiming estate ownership. In such disputes, the person with the most authoritative, or orthodox, documents would be recognized as the legal owner; less authoritative documents were liable to result in the confiscation of the estate in question.

In this battle of documentation it is quite clear what relationship documents from the ex-sovereign or his office bore to documents issued by the Grand Council of State and the provincial governments. The most obvious fact that emerges from a study of estate documentation is that, to be considered a completely legal, tax-exempt entity, permanently in the possession of the immediate holder and his descendants, an estate had to have an official charter from the Grand Council of State, the highest organ of the imperial government. Only a document from this body could guarantee the security of the estate over a long period of time. For this purpose, the documents of the in no chō were insufficient.

A few examples should suffice to demonstrate the fact that imperial government documents were more authoritative than those
of the in no chō. An edict dated Chōjō 1/9/23 (1132) was issued
to the Daigo-ji Enkō-in concerning the status of its Ushihara estate
in the province of Echizen.[17] It seems that in 1086, during the
governorship of Minamoto no Takazane, two hundred *chō* of
empty land had been claimed by the temple, cleared and cultivated,
and recognized as tax free by Takazane. Successive governors, however, alternately disallowed portions of the estate and then reestablished the original boundaries. Finally the matter was referred to
Shirakawa's in no chō. The temple was an imperial temple, having
been founded for Kenshi, Shirakawa's beloved consort. Thus it
looked to the ex-sovereign for protection. In this edict, the court,
after reviewing the case, acknowledged the claim of the temple to
be correct, recognized the legitimacy of the boundaries established
by Takazane, and informed the temple that the provincial officials
had been so notified. Thus no more provincial or district interference in the estate was to be permitted. Only a document of this
sort could make such a guarantee, even when the chief consort of
the abdicated sovereign was the ultimate protector of the holding.

Again, in 1162, a request for the issuance of an edict was forwarded to the court by the priests of the Daidembō-in in Ōhō
2/11.[18] It is a rather long document pleading their case and point-
ing out the evil practices perpetrated against Yamahigashi-shō, one
of their estates in the province of Kii. This was one of five estates
designated for the support of the temple when Toba established it
in 1132. It received an inzen from Toba to this effect and then subsequently a charter from the Grand Council of State confirming
the legality of the estate sometime in the Chōjō era (1132–34).
Later, however, local temple and shrine officials, disregarding the
charter, claimed that the estate and its residents owed them certain
services which they were not fulfilling. The temple forwarded the
charter to the in no chō, where it was reviewed. An inzen was sent
to the governor about the matter, and he in turn ordered that, "in
accord with the ex-sovereign's edict," the temple and shrine officials

[17] *Heian ibun*, 5: 1909–10, doc. 2241.   [18] Ibid., 7: 3580–82, doc. 3234.

must desist from their claim. Yet the temple and shrine officials still refused to cease their activities. The Daidembō-in priests sought an imperial decision on the previously issued charter, one that would clearly establish the validity of their claim and thus the exempt status of the Yamahigashi estate. While they seem to be somewhat confused about the relative authority of the charter and the documents from the ex-sovereign, there is a statement in the document that is enlightening: "While the charter of the Grand Council of State and the ex-sovereign's edict similarly derive from the imperial pleasure, eternal and unperishable documentary certification is limited to the charter of the Grand Council of State." Thus the priests asked that another document be issued to them, reiterating the contents of the earlier charter and guaranteeing their legal rights for all time.

In both these cases, then, even though the estates in question already possessed documents from the ex-sovereign, the temples sought documents from the Grand Council of State as a higher guarantee of the rights to the land. These are not isolated examples. The Daidembō-in's Shibuta estate, also in Kii, similarly received such a document from the Grand Council of State about one year after obtaining a kudashibumi from Toba's in no chō. Other examples abound. Another slightly different case, involving the replacement of lost documents, also points up the same fact. The information is contained in an edict dated Jijō 3/8/22 (1179).[19] The intent of the document is to confirm forever the rights of Fujiwara no Tsunako and her descendants to the Yugeshima estate in the province of Iyo, but it is the procedure that is of interest.

The estate had long been held by Tsunako's mother-in-law, but in 1171 the mother-in-law transferred the holding to Tsunako along with the requisite documents. Tsunako also received a kudashibumi from the in no chō recognizing her claim to the estate.[20] It seems

[19] Ibid., 8: 2983, doc. 3885.
[20] The document does not make it clear why Tsunako should have had any connection with Go-Shirakawa, but an examination of the lady's background suggests the answer. She was the daughter of Kunitsuna, an official of the ex-emperor, as well as wet nurse for Kenreimon'in, so she was quite probably a very close associate of Go-Shirakawa's.

that in 1177 her father's mansion had burned down, and with it all the documents pertaining to Tsunako's Yugeshima estate. Fortunately, however, the in no chō had preserved a copy of the kudashibumi, so she sent that to the proper offices requesting that, in accord with the principles of hereditary transmission and this kudashibumi, her estate be recognized, and an edict issued to her to serve as documentary proof for the future. The edict grants her request.

In this case Tsunako had lost her most important documents demonstrating legal rights to her estate; presumably these were either a provincial government exemption or a charter, or perhaps both. All that remained was a copy of the kudashibumi from Go-Shirakawa's in no chō, an important document, but obviously not authoritative enough to stand as solid legal grounds for the future. Thus she did not petition the in no chō for the issuance of another document but sought the issuance of a document from the Grand Council of State to give her claim the highest possible authority. Her procedure is indicative of the limits of the in no chō's authority.

A final example demonstrating the relationship between the documents of the in no chō, provincial government, and Grand Council of State is provided in a series of three documents contained in the Kōya-san collection.[21] A kudashibumi from Go-Shirakawa's in no chō addressed to the local officials of Bingo province calls for allotment of the rice from an estate in the province controlled by the Kongōbu-ji for use in certain Buddhist ceremonies. At the end of the document the order is given to both local government and estate officials. Five days after this was issued two documents were issued by the Grand Council of State. One is an edict ordering the provincial governor of Bingo to comply "in accord with the orders of the ex-sovereign's office." The other is a communiqué to the Kongōbu-ji informing the priests of the action taken. Although the document is no longer in existence, there was probably also a provincial governor's order to the absentee headquarters telling the local officials to comply with the kudashibumi.

[21] Tokyo Daigaku Shiryō Hensanjo, comp., *Dai Nihon komonjo, Iewake I, Kōya-san monjo I*, pp. 4–12, docs. 3–5.

Thus the relationships between the documents are clear. The in no chō document secured the issuance of governmental orders which made the matter legal: the edict to the provincial governor was a confirmation by the highest legal authority, and the communiqué issued to the temple described the nature of the action taken.

On the basis of this evidence we can say that the documents issued by the ex-sovereign and his office were not more authoritative than documents of the imperial government. It was desirable for the holder of an estate to possess them, but they did not guarantee the sanctity of the holding to the extent that documents from the Grand Council of State did. They could be of use in securing the issuance of provincial documents recognizing the estate, and they were extremely influential when requesting imperial recognition of holdings; but, in themselves, they did not possess the public, legal authority to guarantee the permanent establishment of an estate. Like the documents issued by other heads of houses and administrative offices, inzen, in no chō kudashibumi, and chō were private documents which possessed the highest authority when issued to estate officials and others under the jurisdiction of the abdicated sovereign. But when they were employed on a broader societal scale, they were less authoritative than imperial government documents.[22]

In its structure and in the documents it issued, then, the in no chō was little different from other house administrative offices. It was larger, more influential, and in control of greater landholdings, all of which was a reflection of the great prestige and power of the abdicated sovereigns at the end of the Heian period. But from an examination of the type of documents issued by the in no chō it is

---

[22] At least one legal authority of the twelfth century felt otherwise. In a decision over the confiscation of an estate belonging to the Kumano shrine, in the province of Kai, Nakahara no Naritomo noted that the estate possessed a kudashibumi from Toba's in no chō. He declared that, since there was no distinction between abdicated and titular sovereign, a document from the ex-sovereign's office was the same as an imperial edict. See Takeuchi Rizō, *Nihon no rekishi*, vol. 6, *Bushi no tōjō*, pp. 188–89. This reference is frequently used by Japanese scholars to support the *Jinnō shōtōki* claim that documents of the ex-emperor were more authoritative than imperial documents, but this is only one instance. All other indications are that imperial documents remained more authoritative than those issued by the in no chō.

clear that its most important function was the management of the considerable estate holdings of the imperial house—ex-sovereign, retired imperial ladies, and confidants. An indication that estate management was the major function not only of the ex-sovereign's in no chō but also of the in no chō of retired imperial ladies is found in the body of a complaint lodged by the priests of the Tō-ji in 1162.[23] Among other items the document mentions that, "when the retired sovereign Toba fell ill, the various estates were passed to the in no chō of Bifukumon'in." Prior to that time Toba's in no chō officials had managed the estates, but as he sensed death approaching, he transferred control to Bifukumon'in's in no chō.[24]

The ex-sovereign's office was an administrative office for the management of imperial family affairs, primarily the estate holdings under its proprietorship. It was not an alternate court in competition with the regular offices of the imperial government. Its documents did not supersede those of the imperial government in authority. Despite the power and influence of the abdicated sovereign, the emperor and his imperial government remained the source of authority in the latter part of the Heian period. The abdicated sovereign and his office were aware of that fact and made full use of it to advance the political and economic interests of the imperial house.

[23] *Heian ibun*, 8: 2583, doc. 3235.
[24] This is consistent with Toba's general policy of entrusting all imperial house affairs to Bifukumon'in after his death.

⊰§ NINE §⊱

A *Study of the* In no Kinshin

AMONG THE courtiers who served in the *in no chō* was a group of close associates or confidants of the ex-sovereign, variously referred to in the literature as *in no kinshin, in no kinjū,* or *in no kōsuru tomogara.* While these *kinshin* (as I will call them) may have first received appointments in lesser positions in the in no chō, they all eventually became directors. Furthermore, all chief directors seem to have been kinshin. This group has been the focus of criticism by historians since the Kamakura period—both by traditional writers such as Jien, who saw them as usurping much of the power and wealth long enjoyed by the *sekkanke,* and by modern scholars, who generally see them as an emergent class of wealthy provincial governors of middle rank parasitically using the ex-sovereign to further their own interests. However, few concrete studies of the kinshin have been done.[1]

This chapter analyzes the significance of these kinshin on the basis of available information by identifying the individuals known

[1] The best general article on the subject is Hashimoto Yoshihiko, "Insei seiken no ichikōsatsu." For more specific studies of aspects of the kinshin group, see these four articles by Kōno Fusao: "Shirakawa-in no kinshindan no ichikōsatsu: Ninzuryō o chūshin toshite"; "Shirakawa-in no kinshindan no ichikōsatsu (1): Fujiwara Nagazane o chūshin toshite"; "Shirakawa-in no kinshindan no ichikōsatsu (2): Fujiwara Nagazane no chichi Akisue ni tsuite"; and "Shirakawa-Toba ryōinseika no nin-kura no kami ni tsuite."

to be kinshin, looking at their genealogy, marriage ties, and political careers, and discussing their role in the period under examination.

For organizational purposes, I have relegated the bulk of data on individual kinshin to appendix 2. One significant fact about these kinshin is that they seem to have come from a small number of families which I shall call kinshin families. The genealogical charts comprising figures 2–8, which illustrate the marriage relationships between these kinshin families and the imperial house, include all the kinshin who appear in the appendix.

All of these individuals are ones I have found mentioned in some source as confidants of the abdicated sovereigns Shirakawa, Toba, and Go-Shirakawa. It is certainly possible that there were more, but I am confident that the group specified above constitutes the majority.[2] Certainly the names of many more who served as officials in the in no chō are known, but I am here concerned only with the kinshin, that is, those officials of the in no chō who were especially close to the ex-sovereigns and enjoyed considerable social and political influence because of this association. It was these kinshin who were attacked by Jien in the Gukanshō as being unduly influential in court politics, coming between the sovereign and his "proper" advisors (i.e., the sekkanke). And it was some of these same kinshin—those persons exercising power in government due to their close personal relationship with Go-Shirakawa—against whom Kiyomori (himself once a kinshin) turned in his coup of 1179.

What generalizations can we make about these kinshin from the above available information? The information can be divided into two categories: data concerning personal relationships and genealogy, and data on career patterns. Let us examine these in order.

The first and most obvious fact to emerge from the information is that mentioned above: the tendency of these kinshin to come from a certain limited number of families. Once a person established a close relationship and became a kinshin of Shirakawa, his

[2] A few kinshin who do not belong to one of the major kinshin families do not appear in the charts, but information concerning them is included in appendix 2.

FIGURE 2

The Kanjūji-Hamuro Fujiwara

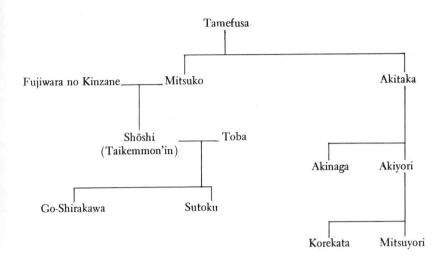

FIGURE 3

The Takashina family

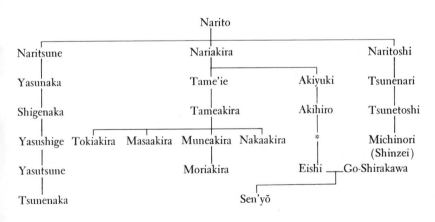

* Name unknown.

FIGURE 4

Descendants of Fujiwara no Yoshikado

```
        Takatoki
           |
        Kiyotaka
     ┌─────┴─────┐
  Sadataka    Mitsutaka
```

FIGURE 5

Descendants of Fujiwara no Matsushige

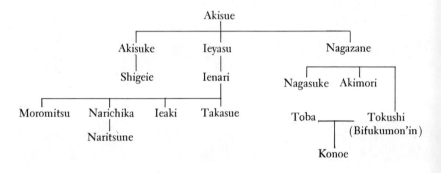

```
                              Akisue
          ┌───────────────────┼────────────────────────┐
        Akisuke             Ieyasu                   Nagazane
           |                   |                ┌───────┼────────┐
        Shigeie             Ienari          Nagasuke  Akimori    |
  ┌─────────┬──────────┬────────┐             Toba ──────── Tokushi
Moromitsu Narichika  Ieaki   Takasue              |      (Bifukumon'in)
              |                                  Konoe
          Naritsune
```

FIGURE 6

Descendants of Fujiwara no Michitaka

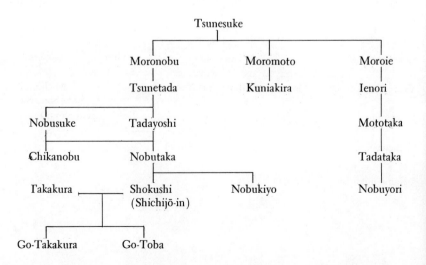

```
                          Tsunesuke
          ┌──────────────────┼──────────────────┐
       Moronobu          Moromoto            Moroie
          |                  |                  |
       Tsunetada         Kuniakira           Ienori
   ┌──────┴─────┐                               |
Nobusuke    Tadayoshi                        Mototaka
   |            |                               |
Chikanobu   Nobutaka                         Tadataka
   |      ┌─────┴──────┐                        |
Takakura ─── Shokushi   Nobukiyo             Nobuyori
       |    (Shichijō-in)
  ┌────┴─────┐
Go-Takakura  Go-Toba
```

FIGURE 7

The Kan'in Fujiwara

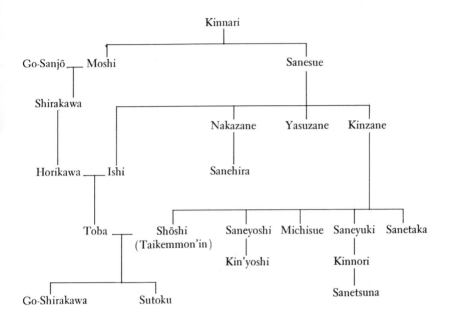

FIGURE 8

The Ise Taira

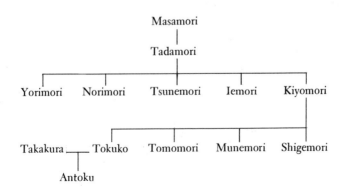

descendants normally became kinshin of Shirakawa's successors, Toba and Go-Shirakawa. His sons were appointed to lesser positions within the in no chō, usually *hōgandai* but often *kurōdo* or *hikurōdo*, and later rose to be *bettō* and trusted confidants of the same ex-sovereign or his successor. Often the first appointment of the son of a kinshin to the in no chō was made when he was very young and depended solely upon his father's close relationship with the ex-sovereign. The majority of kinshin, then, came from a small number of court families who hereditarily served the ex-sovereigns as his most trusted officials in the in no chō. It is in this context that I speak of the existence of kinshin families.

The analogy between these kinshin families and the families that served as hereditary household officials (*keishi*) for the sekkanke and other high-ranking courtier houses is immediately apparent. The intensely personal nature of the patron–client (i.e., house head–house official) relationship is similar in both instances. Both keishi and kinshin served the regent or ex-sovereign in this private capacity as a means of social, economic, and political advancement, while their primary job was a concurrent post held in the imperial bureaucratic structure. It is interesting to note that many of those courtiers who became hereditary confidants of the ex-sovereigns in the late eleventh century—Tamefusa is an excellent example—had traditionally been house officials of the sekkanke. It appears that such families simply transferred their loyalties from the regent's house to the ex-sovereign as the latter's political fortunes rose at the expense of the former's. The nature of the client's dependent relationship upon the patron was similar; only the focus of the clientage had changed.

Although the establishment of the initial relationship between a kinshin family and an ex-sovereign might depend upon a number of factors, such as close service at court during the reign of the emperor, or the commendation of landholdings, one common factor was a marriage relationship with the imperial house. The politics of marriage was an important aspect of Heian court life. To marry into a court family of higher rank was a common means of social and political mobility within the courtier class. For a provincial governor, for example, nothing was more desirable than to marry one's daughter to a Fujiwara lord. Marriage to imperial offspring, however, was another matter. During the period of Fujiwara supremacy, women entering the palace as imperial concubines or empresses came almost entirely from the Fujiwara regent's house, thus making it all but impossible for other families to make marital connections on that level.

In the late Heian period, however, after the imperial house had broken the restraints placed upon it by the sekkanke, women from other houses entered the women's quarters with increasing frequency. Practically all kinshin families, certainly the most influential among them, enjoyed such marital connections with the imperial house, and the mothers of Shirakawa, Horikawa, Toba, Sutoku, Konoe, Go-Shirakawa, Antoku, and Go-Toba were all from one or another of these kinshin families. Such maternal relationships with the imperial house were a major factor in determining the power and influence exercised by these kinshin during the insei period.

Besides this common pattern of providing empresses and consorts, the kinshin families tended to intermarry among themselves with high frequency, indicating that they were a relatively closely knit group of courtiers.[3] Sons and daughters other than those entering the imperial family most frequently married into other high-ranking houses rather than low-ranking ones. It seems clear that these kinshin families were able, by the contraction of advantageous marriages, to play the game of marital alliance with considerable success, advancing their social, political, and economic positions.

Besides marriage bonds, many kinshin families enjoyed yet another strong tie with the imperial house and the ex-sovereign. These were the emotional bonds forged between the wet nurse and her ward. It was common practice in the aristocratic households of Heian Japan to leave the early feeding—and even the rearing—

---

[3] The "Shirakawa-in no kinshindan" articles by Kōno illustrate well the interlocking marriage relationship of kinshin families; the first one cited in n. 1, above, is particularly valuable.

of children to a wet nurse; [4] this was particularly true in the case of the imperial house. Many of the women from these kinshin families served as wet nurses for the successive sovereigns in the eleventh and twelfth centuries. Some kinshin were thus "breast brothers" (chi-kyōdai) of emperors during this period, and they and their families benefited enormously from such a close relationship.

One final fact about these kinshin families is revealing: many kinshin not only served the ex-sovereigns but also performed administrative duties in the offices of other imperial house members, such as the crown prince, empress, or retired imperial lady. In this respect, then, the kinshin can be seen as confidants of the entire imperial house rather than simply of the ex-emperor.

The information about these kinshin also provides a good deal of data on their bureaucratic careers, and here a number of significant points can be made. (1) The kinshin were largely of middle rank but tended to advance during the period of their association with the ex-sovereigns. (2) They held governorships of one or more provinces. (3) They held similar posts in the capital.

With the exception of the Kan'in Fujiwara, all the kinshin families at the beginning of the insei period were of middle rank and traditionally served as provincial governors and house officials in the service of kugyō families. In many instances there had been kugyō members from their house a century or so before, but in more recent times they had not known such success. In other words, all were from families of only minor political success—in comparison with some other Fujiwara lineages, the Kan'in Fujiwara were politically unsuccessful—who found in the person of the abdicated sovereign as head of the imperial house a patron who offered the potential for improving their position in society.

Over the last hundred years of the Heian period, the court rank of these kinshin families tended to rise. While a member of the family who became a confidant of Shirakawa—for example, Tame-fusa, Akisue, or Masamori—might become a kugyō only shortly be-

4 Wada Hidematsu, "Rekishijō ni okeru menoto no seiryoku," in Wada, Kokushi kokubun no kenkyū, pp. 182–201.

fore death, by virtue of appointment to the junior third rank, his descendants—Ienari, Akiyori, or Kiyomori—invariably became third-ranking courtiers earlier in their lives and advanced beyond their father or grandfather's position. By virtue of their association with the imperial house and the ex-sovereigns in particular, the kinshin families attained significant political, social, and economic mobility during the insei period. Certainly, the loyalty of these clients to their patron, the ex-sovereign, was amply rewarded.

The bureaucratic career patterns of these kinshin also show important similarities. The most obvious is that almost all held provincial governorships at one time or another, a high percentage being career provincial governors who served in that capacity for several decades. In fact, the status of provincial governor was so common among the associates of the ex-sovereign that the expression "ex-emperor's confidant and provincial governor" (kinshin zuryō) became common usage. Other officials in the in no chō, not quite so close to the retired emperor, seem also to have shared this background since the term inshi zuryō ("ex-emperor's official and provincial governor") also appears frequently in the literature of the period.

Many kinshin families—the Ise Taira, the Takashina, and the Kanjūji Fujiwara—were traditionally provincial governor houses whereas the Kan'in Fujiwara, as a kugyō house, did not come to hold such provincial appointments until the insei period, and even then they were normally provisional governors. This is representative of the trend during the entire twelfth century: kugyō houses, which had previously looked askance at the socially unimportant provincial posts, began actively to seek such positions for their family members.[5] Why was it that the kugyō sought these provincial ap-

---

[5] Munetada comments on the fact that "recently the offspring of kugyō are becoming provincial governors. All are persons who ought to be so rewarded. This is truly a deep court favor" (CYK, 4: 63, Ten'ei 2/7/29). Tadazane said that it was the strangest thing imaginable for the chancellor and prime minister to also hold a provincial governorship. While it was understandable in the current situation, "in a normal reign it would be an unacceptable situation" (Denryaku, 4: 266. Eikyū 4/11/16).

pointments? Why should the ex-sovereign have sought association
with provincial governors, and why should he have had his associates repeatedly appointed to such offices? A number of reasons can
be suggested.

First, the provincial governor was in the best possible position to
accumulate private wealth. The process of private encroachment on
public lands during the Heian period, particularly by Buddhist institutions, had the effect of decreasing public revenues. Due to this decrease in revenue, official salaries became difficult to pay.[6] Provincial
governors, however, were in the most advantageous positions as tax
assessor and collector, and, having a considerable degree of local
autonomy, they could enrich themselves from the produce of their
province.

Provincial governors notoriously misused their power to extract
wealth from the peasants, as the numerous extant complaints from
local officials attest.[7] Poor government, characterized by frequent
and harsh exactions from the peasants, appears to have been the
rule rather than the exception at the provincial level. Upon completion of a tour of service in a province the governor frequently
returned to the capital accompanied by his household officials and
retainers in a retinue laden with the riches of the province. This
wealth was used to support an ostentatious life style in the capital
and became a source of considerable criticism (and envy) by kugyō
courtiers. So notorious was the provincial governor's greed that one
story holds that even "when a provincial governor falls, he comes
up with a handful of dirt." [8]

[6] The best discussion of Heian official salaries, and the problems involved in
their payment, is found in Murai Yasuhiko, *Kodai kokka kaitai katei no kenkyū*,
pp. 119–74.
[7] The most famous, of course, is the series of thirty-one complaints made by the
peasants and district officials of Owari against Governor Fujiwara no Motonaga in
988. See *Heian ibun*, 2: 473–85, doc. 339.
[8] *Konjaku monogatari*, 5: 118. This saying, which was a commentary on the
general situation at the time, appears in the story of Fujiwara no Nobutada, the
governor of Shinano. While en route to the capital, his horse fell off a cliff, send-
ing Nobutada over the precipice. Fortunately, he caught himself on some tree limbs
growing out of the cliffside. His retainers lowered a basket for Nobutada and were
commanded to pull it up. When they pulled it up, they found it contained mush-

The potential for wealth was the major reason courtiers, even some from the highest ranks, sought provincial appointments in late Heian times. An alliance between the ex-sovereign and provincial governors was mutually advantageous. The latter could provide economic support for the increasingly lavish life style of the ex-emperor and the entire imperial house. Conversely, the ex-sovereign, by virtue of his headship of the imperial house and exalted position at court, could guarantee their continued appointment to lucrative provincial posts, or to important positions in the capital.

The wealth of such provincial governors served as an important means for advancement at court. Wealthy provincial governors lavished contributions on their court patrons. Most contributions were made to construction projects, such as the building of a temple or a mansion. Fujiwara no Michinaga, for example, had the Hōjō-ji built in 1019,[9] and provincial governors outdid one another in their contributions of labor and supplies for this magnificent temple to which Michinaga soon moved. For such contributions provincial governors were frequently appointed or reappointed to governorships; the *Kugyō bunin*, a record of kugyō appointments, lists a considerable number of persons who were "governor by virtue of special contribution" (*bekkō zuryō*). This practice became rampant during the insei period, and all the palaces and temples constructed for Shirakawa, Toba, and Go-Shirakawa were built by the "special contributions" of kinshin zuryō or others wishing to acquire the patronage of the abdicated sovereigns.

Another possible explanation of the tendency for ex-emperors to seek associates among the provincial governors was the authority the latter enjoyed over their provinces. We have seen that one of the primary function of the in no chō was the management of the estate holdings of the ex-sovereign and other imperial household

---

rooms! On the second attempt, Nobutada himself came up, clutching more mushrooms. Despite his misfortune and personal danger, he could not resist the opportunity to acquire something as valuable as mushrooms when he found them growing on the cliffside.

[9] Construction of the temple began in 1019 and it was called the Muryōju-in when dedicated in 1020. Eventually, in 1022, the name was changed to Hōjō-ji.

members. In no chō documents were frequently used to obtain provincial or central government recognition of holdings belonging to the ex-sovereign,[10] but the cooperation of the provincial governor was normally the key to the establishment of shōen.[11] Since the abdicated sovereigns—Toba and Go-Shirakawa in particular—were interested in the expansion of imperial holdings, there was no better group of persons than the provincial governors to whom the ex-emperors could have extended their patronage.

One scholar has postulated what could be yet another reason for the alliance between governors and ex-emperors.[12] Provincial governors acted as go-betweens in the process of estate commendation during the tenth, eleventh, and twelfth centuries. A proprietor of a holding in a province might wish to guarantee the sanctity of his land by commendation to a higher-ranking person. Frequently, he commended the holding to the governor. But governors usually found it necessary to seek still higher protection and thus made a second-level commendation to the ex-sovereign, a Buddhist institution, or the sekkanke. Even in cases where the provincial governor was not the recipient of the first level of commendation, he could serve as go-between for the provincial proprietor of an estate and a high-ranking courtier with whom the proprietor had no channel of communication.

During late Heian times the kinshin zuryō thus provided important economic support for the abdicated emperors, and in a larger sense for the entire imperial house. It is not difficult to see why they were sought as clients by the ex-emperors. As a reward for their support, the ex-sovereigns were able to advance the interests of these clients at court; specifically, they helped the kinshin to obtain appointment or reappointment to governorships and posts in the capital.

[10] See chapter 8.

[11] Moromichi, for example, commented that it was actually the provincial governors who were responsible for the secret establishment of shōen, and that such activities continued for eight years (one term, and reappointment for another) of their governorship. GNJ, 3: 23. Kanji 7/3/3.

[12] Murai, Kodai kokka, p. 388.

The abdicated emperor was able to obtain appointments for his kinshin in several ways. First, by virtue of the fact that he was head of the imperial house and father or grandfather of the emperor, the ex-emperor commanded a good deal of influence at court; his suggestions—or perhaps orders—regarding official appointments were not easily disregarded by the kugyō, among whom were, of course, some of his own associates. Second, the retired sovereign was granted the right to appoint persons of his choice to certain offices and ranks. Under the yearly rank and office allotment (nenkyū) system he could make a certain number of specific appointments, and he normally appointed kinshin or their offspring.[13] Under the provincial allotment (bunkoku) system, the ex-emperor could appoint provincial governors to a small number of specified provinces.[14] These never numbered more than two or three at any one time, but over the course of the insei period a number of kinshin were appointed to provincial governorships by "allotment of the retired sovereign (inbun)."[15]

There was thus a very close interdependence between the ex-emperors and a number of provincial governors during the insei period, and the actions of these governors received a substantial amount of attention in the literature of the time. Munetada, for example, listed seven developments of Shirakawa's reign and tenure as abdicated sovereign; five of these concern the activities of provincial governors: the extent of their wealth, the fact that four or five persons in one family held governorships concurrently, the young age at which one could receive such appointments, the fact that thirty-odd provinces had become hereditarily controlled by the same house, and the fact that provincial officials were not paying

[13] The nenkyū system is discussed in Tokinoya Shigeru, "Nenkyū seido no kisoteki kōsatsu."

[14] The newest and best discussion of the provincial allotment system is in Hashimoto Yoshihiko, "Ingū bunkoku to chigyōkoku."

[15] During Shirakawa and Toba's years the allotment provinces were not fixed. Of the provinces whose governorships were empty, one or two were assigned to the ex-sovereign, who could then appoint a governor of his choice. By Go-Shirakawa's time, however, these provinces came to be fixed as Harima, Bizen, and Mino. See Murata Masashi, "Ingū gobunkoku no kenkyū."

taxes, rents, and services owed to Shinto shrines and Buddhist temples.[16] Thus, by the time of Shirakawa's death, a number of middle-ranking courtiers who held provincial governorships had raised their political, social, and economic positions considerably through their association with the ex-sovereign. During the years of Toba and Go-Shirakawa, the association was to continue with even greater benefits for the sons and grandsons of these courtiers.

The governorships, and provisional governorships, to which kin-shin tended to be appointed were overwhelmingly in the central and western areas.[17] The ten provinces to which kinshin were most frequently appointed were as follows (numbers indicate rank order):

1.	Harima	6.	Bizen
2.	Iyo	6.	Sanuki
3.	Tamba	8.	Tajima
3.	Mimasaka	9.	Owari
5.	Bitchū	9.	Ōmi

[16] CYK, 6: 79. Taiji 4/7/18.

[17] The provinces in which in no kinshin served as governors can be broken down as follows (an apostrophe indicates provisional governors):

Hokurikudō

Kaga	5
Noto	2
Echigo	6
Etchū	3, 2'
Echizen	3, 1'
Wakasa	4
Total	23 + 3'

Tōkaidō

Kai	1
Musashi	2
Tōtomi	4
Mikawa	2
Owari	7
Ise	1
Hitachi	2
Total	19

Tōsandō

Ōmi	5, 2'
Kōzuke	1
Total	6 + 2'

San'indō

Tamba	11
Tango	4
Tajima	8
Inaba	3
Hōki	2
Izumo	3
Iwami	1
Oki	2
Total	34

San'yōdō

Harima	15, 4'
Bizen	5, 4'
Bitchū	7, 3'
Bingo	2, 2'
Aki	3
Mimasaka	7, 4'
Suo	3
Total	42 + 17'

Nankaidō

Awaji	2
Awa	1'
Sanuki	7, 2'
Iyo	13, 4'
Tosa	2, 1'
Total	24 + 8'

Saikaidō

Chikuzen	1
Higo	1
Total	2

Kinai

Yamato	1
Settsu	2
Kawachi	1
Total	4

In terms of the traditional Japanese geographic divisions—five capital provinces and seven circuits—the provinces in the San'yōdō were most likely to have associates of the retired sovereign as governor. The provinces comprising the San'yōdō lay along the Inland Sea, stretching from about present-day Ōsaka in the east to the tip of Honshū in the west. Close behind these provinces were those of the San'indō (the backside of the San'yōdō, or the area along the Sea of Japan), the Nankaidō (present-day Shikoku), and the Hokurikudō (the area along the Sea of Japan to the north and east of the capital). Few kinshin were appointed to governorships in the northern, eastern, or southern provinces. The provinces in which kinshin served tended to be centrally located large or relatively large provinces—both in terms of size and population—with high or reasonably high rates of productivity. They were thus the type of province well suited to absentee governors who wished to amass considerable private wealth which could be used to further their political careers. It was also in these larger, wealthy, western and southwestern provinces that the bulk of the estate holdings of the retired sovereign were located.

Besides experience as provincial governors the kinshin families all tended to hold similar posts at court: *kurōdo* and *kurōdo no tō*, *kura no kami* and *ōkura no kyō*, and *shuri no daibu*. In fact, these offices, which I will discuss in detail below, appear to have been monopolized by associates of the ex-sovereign. What effect did this have upon their influence? What was the significance of these positions?

The kurōdo-dokoro was the governmental organ closest to the person of the emperor and thus of great importance in Heian times. In particular, this office was responsible for the drafting and issuance of edicts. While there was a director in charge of the office, he was appointed only sporadically, and the daily affairs of the sovereign's private office were controlled by the two chief secretaries, or kurōdo no tō. Many kinshin served as both kurōdo and kurōdo no tō during the reign of an emperor and then continued to serve him in the in no chō after his abdication. Other kinshin were

named to the positions of secretary and chief secretary during the
reign of the ex-sovereign's son. Thus, this important position close
to the emperor was a means for courtiers to establish a close personal relationship with a reigning sovereign as well as a means by
which an ex-sovereign could exercise a measure of control over the
direction of court affairs.

The positions of kura no kami and ōkura no kyō were similar
and related positions. The kura no kami headed the imperial
treasury (kura-ryō), a subordinate bureau within the Ministry of
Central Affairs. The bureau was in charge of what was considered
the private wealth of the imperial house: gold, silver, gems, and
other items contributed by the provinces; robes belonging to the
emperor and empresses; and materials to be offered to shrines during imperial ceremonies. This office was traditionally held by chief
secretaries of the sovereign's private office, controllers, and imperial
guards. But Munetada records that during Shirakawa's time the
kura no kami was usually a provincial governor,[18] and more importantly that these governors tended to be kinshin of the ex-sovereign. This was true throughout the insei period. The rich kinshin
zuryō, then, frequently managed the imperial treasury and most
probably contributed portions of their own wealth to its upkeep.

The ōkurashō, or Ministry of the Treasury, on the other hand,
was one of eight ministries of the ritsuryō imperial system. It was
the public treasury in charge of the contributions in kind (chō)
and currency from the provinces, and responsible for the establishment of prices, and weights and measures. Prior to the adoption of
the Taihō and Yōrō codes there seems to have been no distinction
between the private treasury of the imperial house and the public
treasury, but the two had eventually become separated and the
codes reflected this. During the insei period, associates of the ex-
sovereign quite frequently headed both of these economically important offices.

The post of shuri no daibu (head of the Office of Palace Repairs)
was another for which wealthy provincial governors were aptly

18 CYK, 2: 49. Jōtoku 1/4/30.

suited. Since large sums of money were needed to repair the great palace enclosure, which was frequently damaged (particularly by fire), it was logical to appoint persons with control over large sums of private wealth in a time when public revenues were continually on the decrease. Expenditure of personal wealth on such public projects was certain to win even greater favor from the imperial house and serve as a significant "special contribution" for which a kinshin could expect to be amply rewarded.

The kinshin families studied here, then, all forged close relationships with the ex-sovereign and came to serve as hereditary officials not only for the ex-emperor but for the imperial house as a whole. They tended to be middle-ranking provincial governors who had amassed considerable wealth and sought an alliance with the imperial house as a means of social, political, and economic advancement for their families, in the same manner that such families had earlier sought the patronage of the sekkanke. The relationship proved a beneficial one for both parties. The kinshin served in the in no chō of the ex-sovereign as well as in offices of other imperial family members and provided a significant source of economic support for the household. In turn, the ex-sovereign utilized his influence to advance their interests at court. All the kinshin families showed significant improvement of their status at court during the latter Heian period, and one of these families, the Ise Taira, rose to be the most powerful house in the land.

~§ TEN §~

Imperial Estates in the Late Heian Period

AN EXAMINATION of *in no chō* documents indicated that a primary
function of this office was the management of imperial *shōen*, including those nominally controlled by imperial temples, retired imperial ladies, and even close associates of the imperial house. In this
chapter I want to examine in greater detail those imperial estates
over which the ex-emperors and their office exercised control, in
order to determine the extent of such holdings, the manner in
which they were acquired, and the nature of imperial control and
transmission of these lands.

The process of estate development in Japan, covering almost
eight hundred years, from the mid-eighth century to the late sixteenth century, was a struggle between the forces of imperial or
public ownership of the land and those who desired to exercise
private control over it. In the fourteenth and fifteenth centuries the
forces of private control won a complete victory, and by the late
sixteenth century essentially no public land remained in Japan. The
major period of shōen development, however, came during the
Nara and Heian periods, when there came into existence a manorial
system characterized by a complex set of legal arrangements governing both lands and peoples.

There are many different ways of looking at this process of estate development, but one can identify three distinct periods in the formation of a fully developed manorial system.[1] The first period began in the mid-eighth century with the edicts allowing permanent private possession of lands developed by cultivators and was characterized by large-scale development of virgin lands by the major Buddhist institutions. These lands were cleared and managed by the Buddhist temples and the persons working the lands under their jurisdiction. This was the origin of the classic Japanese estate holding.

This development of virgin lands began to slow down, however, by the end of the ninth century; and a second period of estate development, initiated by the shōen prohibitions of the Engi era, was ushered in. This period, covering the tenth century, saw both temples and courtiers begin to receive in increasing frequency the commendation of landholdings from provincial proprietors who sought the protection of these institutions or courtiers.[2] The third

[1] Scholars have traditionally divided the process of estate development into two major periods, separated by the Engi prohibitions of the very early tenth century. The first period was characterized by temple holdings created by clearing and cultivating new lands. The second period saw the growth of estates commended to court nobles and Buddhist temples for protection. There are other ways of dividing the development of estates into periods, and the three-fold division I have followed here is essentially that proposed by Murai Yasuhiko in his *Kodai kokka kaitai katei no kenkyū*, p. 372.

[2] The act of commendation (*kishin*) has long been a problem for scholars. What was commended? What were the relative powers of the person commending the estate and the recipient of the commendation? The general interpretation has been that the cultivator of a certain landed area, desirous of avoiding taxation and other forms of interference from the local officials, "commended" his land to a more influential person who could guarantee its tax-exempt status. Under this commendation, the cultivator seems to have given up legal ownership to a higher-ranking protector (*ryōke* or *honjo*); the cultivator maintained the managerial rights to the estate and simply forwarded a percentage of the estate yield to the protector.

Several scholars have recently criticized this interpretation. Nagahara Keiji, in his book *Nihon hōkensei seiritsu katei no kenkyū* pp. 57–62, showed that commendation agreements differed widely but concluded that the rights of the protector were more extensive than a percentage of the income. Murai (*Kodai kokka*, p. 394) feels that Nagahara overemphasized the rights of the protector.

One can only say that the rights enjoyed by the recipient of the commendation differed widely. Some merely held legal ownership and received a percentage of the yield but had no managerial authority. Other protectors enjoyed fairly extensive managerial rights, including appointment of officials and so forth.

stage came during the eleventh and twelfth centuries, when the process of commendation became widespread, and the commended estate (*kishinchi-kei* shōen), characterized by several levels of commendation, each level possessing certain rights (*shiki*) to the estate, developed throughout the land. Whereas the first two periods were largely dominated by temple holdings, the third and final period was one in which the shōen of courtiers constituted the greater portion of the total estates in the land.

It was during this third period, in the eleventh and twelfth centuries, that the imperial house under the leadership of the abdicated sovereign began to participate actively in the acquisition of estate holdings and eventually became the largest private landholder in the country. To understand both why and how the imperial house became such a large private landholder requires a brief discussion of the nature of imperial finances prior to the late Heian period.

The traditional equation of the imperial house with the Japanese nation has made it extremely difficult to separate the private and public aspects of imperial politics and economics. Under the *ritsuryō* system of government, control of the land legally rested with the emperor as head of state. The tax revenues from public lands provided for the maintenance of the emperor and the members of his family. Besides these public revenues, however, the imperial house retained some control over lands that could be considered private. These included the edict fields (*chokushiden*) and edict pastures (*chokushimaki*), official lands (*kanden*), gift lands (*shiden*), and lands for the support of retirement and temporary palaces (*goinden*). The public and private aspects of these various types of imperial lands, however, are not well understood. The income from the edict fields, for example, was allotted to the support of the imperial house, even though public labor and water were utilized for reclamation and cultivation of the fields.

That these edict fields were fairly extensive and a drain on the public revenue is indicated by the fact that the Engi shōen prohibitions first enumerated these fields as primary offenders in the alienation of public lands. From that time on, such lands established for imperial support by special edicts were prohibited, and the imperial house became even more dependent upon revenue from public lands. For at least two reasons, however, this created serious economic problems for the house. The first was the increase of imperial progeny during the early Heian period (Kammu, Heizei, and Saga were particularly prolific), and the other was the increasingly luxurious life style of the Heian court. Some alleviation of the imperial financial problem was provided by the practice of dynastic shedding and the creation of offshoot clans—the Taira and Minamoto—to cut down the number of family members provided for by public revenues. The basic problem, however, was that, while the population and consumption of the Heian court, including the imperial house, increased, there was no equivalent increase in the amount of land under cultivation and available for taxation to provide effectively for this rising cost of living.

In fact, as public revenue became insufficient for the maintenance of adequate salaries for courtier officials, the amount of land under public control began to decrease because both courtiers and Buddhist institutions continually extended their private control over the public domain. The problem, while worse in some areas than others, soon grew to crisis proportions. An edict in 1107, for example, bemoaned the fact that in the province of Kii "eight- or nine-tenths of every district is [held as] private estates, and there is scarcely any public land." [3] Almost a century earlier, in 1025, Ononomiya Sanesuke had lamented the growth of private estates: "All the land in the realm belongs to one family [i.e., the sekkanke], and there is not even a small plot of public land." [4]

While the entire court suffered from the declining public revenue, the imperial house was more adversely affected than other families. The emperor was the head of the governmental structure and thus it was inappropriate for him to participate in the alienation of land in the public domain. Besides this institutional restraint, he was hardly a free agent able to seek commendations

[3] Heian ibun, 5: 1525, doc. 1670. [4] Quoted in Murai, Kodai kokka, p. 213.

from provincial landholders. Because they were completely dominated by the sekkanke, the emperor and the entire imperial house
were considerably different from nonroyal noble families. In short,
the imperial house did not possess the private familial organization necessary for successful political and economic competition.
It had no well-organized *mandokoro* staffed by private house officials and other clients; instead, persons serving the imperial house
were public officials in the imperial bureaucracy not essentially
dedicated to the advancement of the fortunes of the imperial family. Unable to receive the commendation of provincial estate holdings, the imperial house did not possess a private familial land base,
as did the regent's house, the Takashina, Ōe, and other courtier
families. True, a pattern of imperial family organization—the headship of the abdicated sovereign, and the in no chō—was developing, but the hold of the sekkanke over successive emperors greatly
retarded development of the apparatus needed to compete for effective power.

Then, the accession of Emperor Go-Sanjō over the strong objections of Yorimichi brought about a change in imperial fortunes.
The domination of the regent's house was broken, and Go-Sanjō
embarked upon a course intended to revive imperial political and
economic power. As emperor he played a stronger personal role in
the determination of court politics than any emperor since at least
Saga, attacking the shōen holdings of both powerful religious institutions and important court families. At the same time he built
up the landholdings of the imperial house by establishing new edict
fields throughout the country. Many of these were lands confiscated
from temples and courtiers. Although euphemistically termed edict
fields, they were essentially indistinguishable from the estate holdings of other nobles at the time. The accumulation of such private
landholdings marked the beginning of active participation by the
imperial house in the struggle for land.

Under the successive ex-emperors Shirakawa, Toba, and Go-
Shirakawa, the imperial house accumulated a vast number of shōen
holdings of diverse origin and ultimately surpassed both the

sekkanke and the major religious institutions as a landholder.[5] Later sources refer to lands that came into imperial ownership at this time as "lands accumulated during the three reigns (*sandai gokishō no chi*)." Since land control has always been one of the major determinants of political power in Japan, the imperial house, with this powerful economic base that had been established by the ex-sovereigns, was able to exercise once again the political power it had enjoyed in earlier centuries.

Among the families at court the sekkanke and the imperial house were the two most powerful and prestigious, and thus it was natural that they became the focus of the ever-increasing commendation of estates from middle- and lower-ranking courtiers. While the shōen holdings of the two houses were similar in many respects, there were significant differences as well.

If the greatest period of shōen accumulation by the imperial house came after the time of Go-Sanjō, for the regent's house it was after the passing of Michinaga, and particularly in the days of Yorimichi.[6] The vast majority of shōen of the two houses were of the *honjo*, or *honke*, type, that is, the house held the ultimate proprietorship of the shōen in question. The rights of the ultimate proprietor of an estate could be of two kinds: a portion of the produce of the estate without any administrative control, or both a percentage of the produce and administrative control.[7] Where both income and administrative rights were enjoyed by the ultimate protector (be it either the imperial house or the sekkanke), house officials, other family members or close associates were appointed to serve as shōen officials.[8]

Where the ultimate proprietor received only certain income

---

[5] Nagahara, *Hōkensei*, p. 37. Nagahara notes that the Tōdai-ji had 92 shōen at the end of the tenth century but had only 73 at the beginning of the thirteenth. In the mid-thirteenth century the Konoe and Kujō branches of the regent's house of the Fujiwara had about 250 estates. The imperial house had far more, the holdings of the Chōkō-dō alone numbering over 100.

[6] Takeuchi Rizō, "Fujiwara seiken to shōen," in Takeuchi, *Ritsuryōsei to kizoku seiken*, 2: 371. See also Murai Yasuhiko, *Heian kizoku no sekai*, pp. 428–29, and the chart on sekkanke estate transmission in his appendix.

[7] Nagahara, *Hōkensei*, pp. 69–70, 72.   [8] Ibid., pp. 72–73.

rights to the shōen but did not enjoy administrative control, the person who had commended these rights was invariably another courtier. There seem to have been few such arrangements made directly between the actual cultivator or local proprietor of an estate and the sekkanke or imperial house. Instead, middle-ranking courtiers serving as provincial governors acted as go-betweens. In such cases the administrative control of the estate remained with the courtier who initiated the commendation.

While there were some imperial estates in which the ex-sovereign did enjoy direct administrative control,[9] the overwhelming majority were ones in which the imperial house possessed only income rights. Administrative control remained in the hands of the proprietor, who was, as we have seen, most frequently a courtier of middle rank. Most of these men were *kinshin zuryō*, or soon attained that status. The sekkanke, on the other hand, controlled many shōen in which they enjoyed both income and administrative rights. Certainly, they had a number of holdings to which they enjoyed only certain income rights, but these were far fewer proportionately than those held by the imperial house.

Furthermore, there were very few shōen the regent's house commended one step further, that is, to the imperial house, for even greater protection. Later records of the Kujō branch of the sekkanke yield only three such cases, while the Konoe branch appears to have had none.[10] This indicates that the regent's house adopted a position of competitive equality with the imperial house in the commendation of estates by lower-ranking courtiers. Since the two houses were the most powerful at court, both could effect legal recognition of estate holdings and thus were the focus of commendation. But even when the actual power of the imperial house had eclipsed that of the Fujiwara, the regent's house did not engage in further commendation of its estates to the ex-sovereign.

The holdings of the sekkanke also included many more estates that had been directly commended by local landholders than did those of the imperial house. This indicates that the regent's house

9 Ibid., p. 68.   10 Ibid., p. 71.

was closely connected with the provincial areas and suggests a greater interest in the organization of provincial military potential.[11]

Perhaps the most significant difference between imperial and sekkanke shōen is that few imperial estates remained under the nominal control of either the abdicated or titular sovereign. Instead, the vast majority were under the nominal control of an imperial temple or a retired imperial lady. However, even though these imperial estates were commended to a temple—or to an imperial lady—general management of the rights of the imperial house to the estate was the prerogative of the ex-sovereign. While the temple's mandokoro or the lady's in no chō administered these matters to a certain degree, the ex-sovereign's office seems to have exercised ultimate authority over the imperial lands.

Why should a majority of imperial holdings have been under the nominal control of temples? The most common explanation of this phenomenon is that it was a reflection of the deep Buddhist faith of the imperial house during this period. It was indeed the "latter day of the law" when the construction of temples and bestowal of gifts upon such temples was considered a path toward salvation. Moreover, the ex-emperors all eventually took the tonsure and, as hōō (priestly retired sovereign), ranked high in the Buddhist world. However, this explanation is not entirely satisfactory, for the imperial house could not claim to have a monopoly upon faith. It was not uncommon in Heian society to become a priest or to take up residence in a temple. And the regent's house did not commend all of its shōen to family temples, although most sekkanke courtiers were devout Buddhists.

A more convincing explanation can be found in the fact that the imperial house was still the symbol of the bureaucratic state and thus was perhaps not reconciled to the acquisition of public lands for private purposes by the emperor or ex-emperor. One of the reasons cited for the development of the insei was that it allowed the ex-emperor, unhampered by the institutional bonds of public office, to acquire shōen for the house.[12] Even though the ex-sovereigns did

[11] Ibid., p. 72.   [12] Ishimoda Shō, *Kodai makki seijishi josetsu*, p. 366.

in actuality acquire extensive estate holdings, perhaps the tradition of the imperial house as a public body symbolizing imperial government caused emperors and ex-emperors to be circumspect in the manner in which they controlled such holdings. Go-Sanjō, for example, established a number of edict fields that were administered like shōen yet did not bear that name. I have already noted that Shirakawa was extremely unsure of the propriety of imperial shōen. And even though both Toba and Go-Shirakawa were quite active in estate acquisition, most of their estate holdings were under the nominal control of temples or imperial ladies. Perhaps even abdicated emperors were influenced by the public position of the imperial house in Japanese society.

During the latter part of the Heian period, then, the imperial house came to exercise control over an extensive land area. Besides the public income they received from the sustenance lands granted to emperors, ex-emperors, empresses, and imperial ladies, and the income from their allotment provinces, the ex-emperors Shirakawa, Toba, and Go-Shirakawa managed a large number of imperial shōen. These included estates under the nominal control of temples and imperial ladies as well as goin lands which supported retirement palaces of the house.

The information that follows is a synthesis of Japanese scholarship on the extent of imperial shōen.[13] These figures represent only a portion of the total imperial holdings, and new information is continually being discovered which will more clearly determine the number of imperial shōen in the late Heian period.

Goin Holdings

Certain lands were set aside for the support of the retirement palaces (goin) of the imperial house. A reigning emperor selected one goin as his future retirement palace, and the goin-chō managed the lands. After he had abdicated and moved to the palace, the sov-

[13] See, for example, Okuno Takahiro, Kōshitsu gokeizaishi no kenkyū, esp. pp. 1–52; Teishitsu Rinyakyoku, comp., Goryōchi shikō, esp. pp. 87–170; Watanabe Sumio, "Kōbu kenryoku to shōensei," in Iwanami kōza Nihon rekishi, vol. 5: 183–89; and Okuno Takahiro, "Kōshitsu goryō shōen," in Nihon rekishi.

ereign's in no chō was organized at the palace and came to control the goin lands. Both the palaces and the lands were transmitted by an emperor to his descendants as private property. While our records are not detailed, prior to the insei period there appear to have been at least 2,000 *chō* of land allotted for the support of the Reizei-in, the Suzaku-in, and the Junna-in.[14] A few of these holdings were in the eastern provinces, but the majority were in the provinces close to the capital. A document of transmission drawn up on the occasion of the death of Go-Ichijō in 1036 mentioned Reizei-in and Suzaku-in plus the Ishihara-in and the Gojō-in. Also included were four estates, but presumably the lands previously allotted for the support of the Reizei-in and Suzaku-in were still connected with these two palaces.

Goin holdings increased tremendously during the reign of Go-Shirakawa. As a result of their participation in the abortive Hōgen insurrection, Fujiwara no Yorinaga and two of his adherents, Taira no Tadasada and Taira no Masahiro, had their estates confiscated by the emperor. In all, Go-Shirakawa confiscated 43 estates in 21 provinces; 28 of these were Yorinaga's.[15] The estates were all made goin holdings and turned over to officials of the goin-chō. The estates remained under imperial jurisdiction and were controlled after Go-Shirakawa's abdication by the in no chō.

Imperial Temple Holdings (Goganji-ryō)

SHIRAKAWA

Rikushōji

Among the imperial temples constructed by the sovereigns of the insei period were six temples collectively referred to as the *rikushōji* ("six *shō* temples"). The term arose from the fact that each con-

---

[14] Teishitsu Rinyakyoku, comp., *Goryōchi shikō*, pp. 93–95. Figures for the different holdings presented hereafter should be considered composites of four different sources. The *Goryōchi shikō* first listed a large number of imperial shōen. In the *Nihon rekishi daijiten*, Okuno Takahiro added to this number in his entries for individual blocs of imperial estates. Watanabe Sumio added several more in "Kōbu kenryoku to shōensei," and Okuno then contributed even more in his article "Kōshitsu goryō shōen."

[15] *HHK*, 2: 184–89. Hōgen 2/3/29.

tained the character *shō* (excellent, superior) in its name. The first
and most well-known of these was the Hosshō-ji, founded in 1077
by Emperor Shirakawa.[16]

The Hosshō-ji was located slightly to the east of the capital
proper in the Shirakawa area of Yamashiro province, an area of
which the emperor was particularly fond. The location corresponds
to the present Okazaki Park in Kyoto, but all that remains to suggest the presence of the temple is the name of a bus stop, Hosshōji-
chō. It was apparently a magnificent temple, consisting originally
of an Amida hall, a lecture hall, a lotus hall, and an enormous
pagoda; and later additions by Shirakawa and other imperial family
members greatly increased its size.[17] Shirakawa made frequent trips
to the temple for various religious services, often spending the
night there. After its establishment, the Hosshō-ji came into control
of a number of shōen commended by Shirakawa and other courtiers. Today at least 33 holdings in 15 provinces, mostly near the
capital, can be accounted for. The Hosshō-ji holdings were far more
extensive than those of any of the other five shō temples.

The next of the rikushōji was the Sonshō-ji, constructed by order
of the emperor Horikawa in 1102.[18] It was also located in the
Shirakawa region, just to the west and north of the Hosshō-ji. We
have little knowledge of the temple or its holdings, although 19
holdings in 9 provinces have been identified by scholars. Almost
half of these shōen were in the neighboring province of Ōmi.

In 1119 Toba constructed the Saishō-ji in the Shirakawa area.[19]
The temple was located between the Hosshō-ji and the Sonshō-ji,
and it had at least 5 shōen in 4 provinces commended for its support. Toba's consort Taikemmon'in had yet another temple constructed in the same general vicinity in 1128,[20] the Enshō-ji, which
had 5 holdings in as many different provinces.

[16] *HRS*, p. 35. Jōryaku 1/12/18.

[17] Hayashiya Tatsusaburō, "Hosshō-ji no sōken," in *Koten bunka no sōzō*, pp. 157–
80, is the fullest account of the construction of the Hosshō-ji. See also Takeuchi
Rizō, "Rikushōji no igi," in *Ritsuryōsei to kizoku seiken*, 2: 561–62. Takeuchi
stresses the private, familial nature of all these imperial temples constructed during
the insei period, comparing them to similar temples of the sekkanke.

[18] *HRS*, p. 45. Kōwa 4/7/21.   [19] *Teiō hennenki*, p. 308. Gen'ei 1/12/17.

[20] Ibid., p. 314. Taiji 3/3/13.

With the construction of Sutoku's Seishō-ji in 1139[21] and Konoe's Enshō-ji in 1149[22] in Shirakawa, the complex of six imperial temples in the same region was completed. These last two temples appear to have had 10 shōen holdings each, distributed over 6 and 8 provinces respectively. Later all these temples were grouped together to form one bloc of estates which was transmitted from one imperial house member to another. Besides the shōen enumerated here, there were at least 5 others, bringing the total of known rikushōji holdings to 89. We have no idea, of course, what percentage of the total holdings of the temples this figure represents, but there is no question that it was an important portion of the imperial estates during the late Heian period.

Kongōju-in, Shōraku-in, Shōkongō-in, Rengezō-in, and Shin midō

Besides initiating the construction of the rikushōji, Shirakawa was also responsible for the building of several other temples. In 1076 he built the Kongōju-in for his father, Go-Sanjō, in the Eastern Pagoda area of the enormous Enryaku-ji complex on Mount Hiei.[23] In 1085 he built the Shōraku-in. He also constructed the Shōkongō-in (1101), the Rengezō-in (1114), and the Shirakawa Shin midō (1123). Except for one shōen of the Shōkongō-in, however, we have no record of holdings for these temples, although they must have existed.

HORIKAWA

Shōbodai-in

Emperor Horikawa died at a relatively young age, but he did reign for twenty years under the watchful eye of his father Shirakawa. Besides the aforementioned Sonshō-ji, Horikawa also built the Shōbodai-in in accord with the vow of his consort Atsuko (a daughter of Go-Sanjō). The temple was dedicated in 1109, about

---

[21] Ibid., p. 315. Hōen 5/10/26.
[22] Ibid., p. 320. Kyūan 5/3/20. The characters for *en* in the two Enshō-jis described above are different.
[23] HRS, p. 35. Jōhō 3/6/13.

a year after Horikawa's death.[24] Located in the Kyōgoku section of the capital, it was first called the Kyōgoku-dō and only later renamed the Shōbodai-in. At least three holdings in Shinano, Tajima, and Ōmi are known to have been controlled by this imperial temple.

TOBA

Toba and his two consorts Taikemmon'in and Bifukumon'in were extremely active in the area of temple construction during the first half of the twelfth century. Besides the Saishō-ji, which was built while he was still emperor, Toba's imperial temples include the Tokuchōju-in, Hōshōgon-in, Shōkōmyō-in, and Anrakuju-in, all of which were constructed after the death of Shirakawa in 1129, when Toba was senior retired sovereign.

Tokuchōju-in

The Tokuchōju-in was located east of the Kamo River and south of Shichijō in Rokuhara, an area that was to become the stronghold of the Ise Taira. It was also in this vicinity that Go-Shirakawa was to build the Rengeō-in and his Hōjū-ji palace. The temple was built for Toba in 1132 by Taira no Tadamori, one of his most trusted kinshin and governor of Bizen.[25] The temple had at least 5 shōen in 4 provinces for its support.

Hōshōgon-in

The Hōshōgon-in was constructed in the same year by the kinshin zuryō Fujiwara no Ienari, the governor of Harima.[26] It was another imperial temple located in the Shirakawa area, and it appears to have been quite an impressive complex of buildings. Besides Toba, Emperor Sutoku also attended the dedication ceremony. There were at least 15 estate holdings in 10 provinces under the nominal control of this imperial temple.

[24] HRS, p. 48. Ten'in 2/6/29.   [25] HRS, p. 59. Chōjō 1/3/13.
[26] Ibid. Chōjō 1/10/7.

Shōkōmyō-in

In 1136 Toba dedicated the Shōkōmyō-in south of the capital near his Toba palace, but there is no record of the shōen that were commended for the temple's maintenance.

Anrakuju-in

Toba had his associate Ienari build another temple in 1137, the Anrakuju-in, located within the confines of the Toba palace, where the ex-sovereign spent so much time.[27] The pagoda of the Anrakuju-in and one other small building are all that remain today of this important temple. It is at present maintained by the imperial household agency because the pagoda contains the remains of the emperors Toba and Konoe. The shōen holdings of the Anrakuju-in were quite extensive and later became the core of the Hachijōin-ryō, one of the two largest blocs of imperial estates in the medieval period. At least 71 estates in 31 provinces have been identified, but not all of these date from the Heian period. A more accurate estimate of the Heian period holdings is about 43 in 28 provinces.[28]

TAIKEMMON'IN

Hōkongō-in

Taikemmon'in was responsible for the construction of at least one other temple besides the Enshō-ji. In 1130 she had Fujiwara no Mototaka, governor of Harima and a powerful kinshin of both Toba and Taikemmon'in, build the Hōkongō-in on the western fringes of the capital in the Kadono district of Yamashiro province. It was actually a reconstruction of the Ten'an-ji, a temple constructed during the time of the Emperor Montoku in 858.[29] The

27 *HRS*, p. 60. Hōen 3/10/15.
28 Nagahara, *Hōkensei*, pp. 66–67. His information is based upon the *Anrakuju-in komonjo* collected in the Historiographical Institute at the University of Tokyo.
29 Mōri Hisashi, *Hōkongō-in*, p. 2. I am indebted to the staff of the temple for providing me with this small volume and showing me the remains of the temple. The buildings of the Hōkongō-in that remain are located in the western part of Kyoto, just a few hundred yards from the Hanazono railroad station. When I

temple was small in comparison with many others erected by the imperial house, but it was famous for its beautiful architecture and landscaping. The Hōkongō-in appears to have had some 40 estates in 18 provinces.

Kankikō-in

After the death of Taikemmon'in, Bifukumon'in became Toba's favorite and exercised a considerable degree of influence both within the imperial house and among the court nobles. In 1141 she had the Kankikō-in built in the Shirakawa region; Toba attended the dedication ceremony with her.[30] The temple had at least 41 shōen holdings in 19 provinces.

Kongōshō-in

In 1142 Bifukumon'in held the dedication ceremony for this temple which was also located in Shirakawa. Thus far 23 estates in 7 provinces have been identified as Kongōshō-in holdings; 14 of these were in nearby Ōmi.

Rengeshin-in

In 1174, long after the death of Toba, his daughter Hachijō-in erected the Rengeshin-in within the walls of the Ninna-ji, another imperial temple in the Omuro area.[31] When the temple was dedicated, Go-Shirakawa attended the ceremony along with Hachijō-in. The known holdings of the temple number 16 in 13 provinces.

Kongōshin-in

Besides the Enshō-ji, Konoe built at least one other temple, the

---

visited the temple in the spring of 1969, it was in the process of being moved to allow for the widening of the road that runs in front of it.

[30] HRS, p. 62. Eiji 1/21/21.   [31] HRS, p. 89. Jōan 4/2/23.

Kongōshin-in in 1154; but, being ill, he was unable to attend the dedication ceremony.[32] Located in the Toba area south of the capital, the Kongōshin-in was erected for the emperor by Fujiwara no Ieaki, governor of Bingo, and the governor of Harima, Fujiwara no Akichika. It had 5 holdings in 5 different provinces.

GO-SHIRAKAWA

Rengeō-in

The Rengeō-in, better known as the Sanjūsangen-dō, is the most famous of the imperial temples built during Go-Shirakawa's life; it was constructed for the ex-sovereign by Kiyomori in 1164.[33] It contains 1,001 thousand-armed Kannon statues and is today one of the major tourist attractions in Kyoto. There are numerous important cultural treasures preserved in its buildings. It had at least 33 estate holdings in 25 provinces.

Chōkō-dō

If the Sanjūsangen-dō is today the most famous temple associated with Go-Shirakawa, in the Heian and Kamakura periods the Chōkō-dō was perhaps better known and certainly more important with respect to its shōen holdings. The temple was erected within the confines of the ex-sovereign's Rokujō palace when he moved there in 1183. It consisted at first of only one Buddhist hall, but later other buildings were added to make it a large and impressive temple complex. Little remains today as a reminder of its former glory. Only a few small buildings rebuilt in the Tokugawa period still stand amidst small, crowded shops in the Gojō area west of Kawaramachi, and few people have ever heard of the temple.[34] It is open only on the anniversary of Go-Shirakawa's death. The Chōkō-dō received shōen commendations from both Go-Shirakawa and other court nobles.

[32] HRS, p. 70. Kyūju 1/8/9.
[33] HRS, p. 78, Chōkan 2/12/17. Teiō hennenki, p. 332.
[34] Yashiro Kuniji, writing in the mid-1920s, mentioned that the temple was still standing but lamented that even the people living in the area had little knowledge of its existence, let alone its history. See "Chōkōdō-ryō no kenkyū," in Yashiro, Kokushi sōsetsu, p. 2.

The fourteenth-century chronicle *Baishōron* recorded that the Chōkō-dō imperial bloc of holdings numbered 180, but these are not all verifiable today. Okuno Takahiro has uncovered some 130 and concedes the possibility that the *Baishōron* account is true. This is not a figure for the Heian period, however. A list of contributions by various shōen to the temple in 1191 totaled 93 holdings, which is probably closer to the Heian period figure.

Saishōkō-in

The Saishōkō-in was an imperial temple that Go-Shirakawa had constructed for his Taira consort Kenshummon'in in 1173.[35] It served as one of his palaces and is thought to have been located in the vicinity of the Rengeō-in in the southeastern portion of the capital. There seem to have been about 33 holdings of the temple in 20 provinces.

Shin Kumano-sha and Shin Hie-sha

As well as being a devout Buddhist, Go-Shirakawa was also a firm believer in the native (Shinto) gods, particularly those of the Kumano and Hie shrines, both of which he visited frequently. In 1160 he established the Shin Kumano-sha to stand guard over his Hōjū-ji residence in the area of the Rengeō-in. At the same time and in the same area he constructed the Shin Hie-sha. Shōen were commended to both shrines: 31 in 15 provinces to Shin Kumano, and 9 in 7 provinces to Shin Hie.

Holdings of Retired Imperial Ladies (Nyoin-ryō)

With the exception of the Rokujō-in holdings established during Shirakawa's time, the portfolios of estates under nominal control of retired imperial ladies date from the period during which Toba and Go-Shirakawa were abdicated sovereigns. The imperial house appears to have followed the principle of divided inheritance, as did other court families. When the house came into the possession

[35] *HRS*, p. 88. Jōan 3/10/21.

of extensive estate holdings in the insei period, transmission of this private property among members of the dynastic group became more crucial than it had been.

Both as a means of providing for the support of imperial ladies and in order to avoid the disaster that could befall one huge bloc of holdings in the event of confiscation, Toba divided the imperial temple holdings among his consorts Taikemmon'in and Bifuku-mon'in and his daughters Jōzaimon'in and Hachijō-in. The hold-ings of Hachijō-in, for example, included estates belonging to the Anrakuju-in, the Kankikō-in, and the Rengeshin-in as well as ones commended directly to the lady herself. Nyoin-ryō were thus com-binations of imperial temple holdings plus other holdings of the ladies.

ROKUJŌ-IN

The holdings of Rokujō-in were unlike other nyoin-ryō. The Rokujō-in was a palace Shirakawa had Fujiwara no Akisue con-struct for his (Shirakawa's) daughter Ikuhōmon'in in 1075. When she died the same year, Shirakawa had the palace converted into a temple for the repose of her soul. The temple continued to enjoy the sustenance households she had controlled, and the emperor himself commended certain holdings for its support; other courtiers, like Fujiwara no Kuniakira, also made commendations to it. We have already seen how Taira no Masamori's commendation of some lands in Iga had been the first link between the Taira and the imperial house. In total the Rokujō-in had 17 holdings in 11 provinces.

TAIKEMMON'IN

The Taikemmon'in holdings consist of the estates of the Enshō-ji and Hōkongō-in. She ordered construction of both and maintained some measure of control over them. Upon her death, the Enshō-ji

estates were combined with the other rikushōji holdings, while
her daughter Jōzaimon'in inherited the Hōkongō-in and its shōen.

BIFUKUMON'IN

Bifukumon'in's holdings included her own temples Kankikō-in and
Kongōshō-in as well as at least 9 estates transmitted to her by Toba
on his death.

JŌZAIMON'IN

Besides inheriting the Hōkongō-in estates from her mother, Jōzaimon'in also received the commendation of other shōen. In the
Kamakura period there were at least 25 other estates within the
Jōzaimon'in bloc, but we do not know how many of them date
from the late Heian period.

HACHIJŌ-IN

Hachijō-in is the palace name of Princess Shōshi, daughter of Toba
and Bifukumon'in. Toba left her the Anrakuju-in estates and 21
others, and Bifukumon'in left her the Kankikō-in holdings when
she died. The holdings of Hachijō-in also included the estates of
her own Rengeshin-in. She thus was in nominal control of a large
group of estates, although ultimate management rested with Go-
Shirakawa and his in no chō. In later years the Hachijō-in holdings
numbered more than 220.

SHICHIJŌ-IN

Shichijō-in was Fujiwara no Nobutaka's daughter Shokushi. She
was Takakura's consort and the mother of both Go-Toba and Go-
Takakura. Besides the 5 estates of her own Kankiju-in, Shichijō-in
came into possession of a large block of imperial holdings. These
included goin lands confiscated from Yorinaga, holdings confis-

cated from the Taira, estates held by the imperial house since Shirakawa's time, and shōen commended directly to the lady herself. There were at least 59 holdings, but of course most of these were the estates of imperial temples previously enumerated.

KENSHUMON'IN

Takakura's mother was Taira no Shigeko, daughter of the influential courtier Tokinobu. She was granted the palace name Kenshummon'in. She constructed the Saishōkō-in, and her holdings, which Go-Shirakawa took upon her death, included at least the 33 estates from this temple.

IMPUMON'IN

Impumon'in was Go-Shirakawa's eldest daughter. She inherited from him the Kongōshō-in holdings—once Bifukumon'in's—as well as his Oshi no kōji palace.

At the present moment this seems to be all the imperial estates that can be identified, but it is certainly only a fraction of the actual lands controlled by the imperial house in the late Heian period. The Meiji-Taishō scholar Yashiro Kuniji claimed that there were over 1,000 imperial shōen in 59 provinces.[36] This estimate seems quite low, however; Shimizu Masatake has catalogued over 5,600 estates in his Shōen shiryō,[37] and scholars today agree that imperial estates must have comprised at least half that figure.

Thus, during the last hundred years of the Heian period the Japanese imperial house came into the possession of extensive private estate holdings spread throughout the country. The successive

[36] Ibid. Ishimoda quotes this figure in Kodai makki, p. 360. John Hall also claims 1,000 estates in 59 provinces (Hall, Government and Local Power in Japan, 500–1700, p. 20). I am able to account for at least 60 provinces. Only Shima, Hida, Sado, Buzen, Ōsumi, Satsuma, Iki, and Tsushima seem to have been without imperial shōen.

[37] Shimizu Masatake, Shōen shiryō.

ex-sovereigns Shirakawa, Toba, and Go-Shirakawa held ultimate administrative control over the family's rights in these estates, although most were nominally under the control of imperial temples or retired imperial ladies. The income from these estate holdings, along with that received from the sustenance fields and allotment provinces of the various members of the family, constituted an extremely important economic base for the political power of the imperial house during the insei period.

~~§ ELEVEN ɛ~

Insei: A Redefinition

IN THE latter part of the eleventh century the abdicated sovereign
emerged as an important figure in Japanese political society. Japanese historians have explained this phenomenon by the concept of
insei, usually translated as "cloister government." They see the abdicated emperors, beginning with Go-Sanjō, as having established a
new system of government and wrested power and authority away
from the emperor and the existing imperial state structure. Western
historians, in turn, have adopted this approach to the politics of
the late Heian period with little modification. Minoru Shinoda
speaks of the existence of "two courts," referring to the emperor
and his court and cloister government.[1] Likewise, John Brownlee
states that during this period sovereignty normally resided with the
ex-emperor.[2]

My research, however, has led me to take a different view of the
political position of abdicated sovereigns, and to conclude that the
accepted definition of insei is based upon certain assumptions that
do not stand up under a close examination of primary source materials. By way of summary, let me reiterate those areas of weakness
I see in the concept of insei.

[1] Minoru Shinoda, *The Founding of the Kamakura Shogunate, 1180–1185*, p. 46.
[2] John S. Brownlee, "The Shōkyū War and the Political Rise of the Warriors,"
p. 64.

First, there is no evidence suggesting that the emperor Go-Sanjō had any intention of creating a new form of government to be controlled by the ex-sovereign. Neither did his son Shirakawa have any such intentions. Both were deeply concerned with reviving the fortunes of the imperial house and avoiding domination by the regent's house, but they did not create a new political system which superseded the traditional organs of imperial government.

Second, the *in no chō* should not be regarded as a government created by ex-sovereigns in order to control the country. It was a private familial office for the imperial house which developed over the course of the Heian period as a means of building a private base of power for that house. It was controlled by the abdicated sovereign, who, as senior member of the imperial house, unhampered by the burdensome duties of the emperor, acted as head of the house. The function of the in no chō was to handle the private affairs, primarily the management of estate holdings, of the imperial house; and it was staffed in a manner similar to other house offices.[3]

Third, the abdicated sovereign did not possess greater authority than the emperor in the late Heian period. Sovereignty continued to reside with the emperor. An analysis of the documents issued by ex-sovereigns and their office demonstrated clearly that supreme authority lay with the emperor and the constituted offices of imperial government. While the ex-sovereigns Shirakawa, Toba, and Go-Shirakawa indeed exercised considerable political power and influence, they appear to have maintained the greatest respect for imperial sovereignty. Like all other holders of actual power in premodern Japan, abdicated emperors sought to utilize rather than supplant the imperial position.

Finally, the abdicated sovereigns of late Heian times were not the absolute despots that Japanese historians have made them out to be. They were powerful to be sure, frequently the most powerful figures of their times, but it is simply not correct to characterize

---

[3] It will be remembered that retired imperial ladies also had in no chō which performed similar private functions for them.

them as ruling the country in a high-handed, dictatorial fashion. Japanese decision making has always been a group process, and in Heian times decisions were made in the *kugyō* council meetings. The abdicated sovereigns by no means sought to eliminate or circumvent this decision-making body. On the contrary, it was through close associates in this body that ex-sovereigns exercised political influence.

Essentially, the concept of insei is based upon several assumptions that appear to be false. Like feudalism, insei is a term that was created by later historians attempting to explain certain historical phenomena. Early writers like Jien and Chikafusa held definite biases against the political influence of the ex-sovereigns in the late Heian period, and these biases are evident in their analysis of the period. Unfortunately, later historians relied heavily upon Jien and Chikafusa as well as upon pseudo-historical literary works. Even in the use of primary materials scholars have failed to exercise proper caution. Several courtier diaries from the late Heian times provide our most important source of information about the period. But, despite the fact that these are clearly full of exaggerations, historians have tended to accept uncritically the statements they contain about the power of the ex-sovereign and the authority of his documents.

The concept of insei appears to be a very neat way of explaining the political events of the last hundred years of the Heian period, but a careful examination of primary materials demonstrates that many of the assumptions upon which the concept is based are false. Because this concept has oversimplified and thus distorted our view of the period, we might do better to avoid using it altogether; at the very least, we must redefine it.

In the last hundred years of the Heian period the imperial house, under the active headship of successive ex-sovereigns, reemerged as a major force in Japanese political society. After a long period of domination by the Fujiwara regent's house during which it had been unorganized and an unsuccessful contestant for the rewards of political power, the imperial house secured a measure of independence and set out to compete with other kinship blocs for actual power at court. Competition with other kinship blocs required a well-organized house administrative body, private landholdings, and a group of clients in the service of the house. The satisfaction of all these requirements came during the period from 1086 to 1185, and it provided the base that allowed the imperial house to surpass other kinship blocs in terms of power and wealth. It is this reemergence of the imperial house in late Heian times that Japanese historians have tried to characterize by the concept of insei.

Organization of the In no Chō

Kurōdo-dokoro (Private Household Bureau)

The kurōdo-dokoro was obviously modeled upon the similar office that served the needs of the emperor, but, whereas the emperor's *kurōdo-dokoro* was an important office staffed by high-ranking members of the court aristocracy, those courtiers who served in the kurōdo-dokoro of the ex-emperor were lower-ranking individuals. There were three types of officials in this bureau: *in no kurōdo, in no hikurōdo,* and *shoshū.* The kurōdo (stewards) were generally men of the fifth and sixth rank, and usually there seem to have been four of them, also in imitation of the emperor's office. These men headed the bureau and, together with the lower-ranking hikurōdo (assistants) and shoshū (miscellaneous attendants) under their direction, carried out the miscellaneous business of the in no chō, in the same manner that the emperor's kurōdo waited upon his every need. They do not appear, however, to have performed secretarial duties as did their counterparts in the emperor's service.

Meshitsugi-dokoro (Servants' Bureau)

The *meshitsugi-dokoro* was a bureau of servants (*meshitsugi*) who performed ceremonial service tasks for the ex-sovereign. For example, at poetry contests they were responsible for the preparation of the ink used by the courtiers. In some instances they acted as messengers for the abdicated sovereign. The chief of servants (*meshitsugi no kami*) was in charge of this bureau.

Fudono (Secretariat)

The *fudono* was originally the place where documents were kept, but it gradually came to function as the bureau in which most of the important business of the ex-emperor was conducted, such as the hearing of complaints or the discussion of political matters with associates.

Mizuishin-dokoro (Bureau of Official Bodyguards)

The *mizuishin-dokoro* was one of three semimilitary subordinate offices of the in no chō. Official bodyguards (mizuishin) were appointed by the new emperor to serve an abdicated sovereign, and the appointment of these bodyguards was usually made in conjunction with the bestowal of the title *dajō tennō*. The offer of the bodyguards was frequently refused several times by the abdicated sovereign before being accepted, in accord with Heian custom. The official bodyguards were selected from among the middle- and lower-ranking members of the inner palace guards (*konoefu*), but in fact these bodyguards seem to have been more ceremonial than military. Originally there appear to have been ten guards, five each from the left and the right division, but later the number increased to a total of twelve or fourteen.

Formally, the main function of these official bodyguards apparently was to accompany the ex-emperor on outings and trips. Another function was to act as guards, armed with bow and arrows, for the ex-sovereign's palace. However, there are very few records of actual martial acts attributed to these bodyguards, and most references are to their serving as messengers, taking care of horses at gatherings of courtiers at the ex-emperor's palace, or presenting gifts of food to victorious wrestlers. Their most "militant" action seems to have been participation in the horse races held at the Toba-dono.

Mushadokoro-chō (Warriors' Bureau)

The *mushadokoro-chō* was a second office of guards serving the ex-sovereign. The warrior guards (*musha-dokoro*) in this office performed duties similar to those of the mizuishin: they guarded the palace, accompanied the ex-emperor on his outings (generally following the procession), and served as messengers. The major differences between the two types of guards appear to lie in their respective qualifications and numbers. Whereas the official body-guards were members of the inner palace guards, the ex-emperor's warrior guards were usually selected from the *takiguchi* (imperial guards of the sovereign's private office) after abdication and were consequently closer to the ex-sovereign personally and of higher rank. Furthermore, there were anywhere from ten to thirty musha-dokoro as opposed to about twelve mizuishin.

In no Hokumen (Warriors of the Northern Quarter)

In addition to the two abovementioned bodies charged with the protection of the ex-emperor and his palace, Shirakawa established a third such body, the *in no hokumen*, shortly after his abdication.[1] The guards who served in this body were called in no hokumen, or *hokumen bushi* ("the ex-sovereign's warriors of the northern quarter"), a name derived from the fact that they served in the northern quarter of the retired sovereign's palace, the most crucial area of the palace for the discussion of political matters.[2]

The hokumen were divided into an upper and a lower division,

[1] GKS, p. 105.

[2] Robert K. Reischauer has rendered in no hokumen or hokumen bushi as "north-facing warriors," which is misleading. The term hokumen does literally mean "north facing" but it refers to a specific area within the palace where business was conducted, and thus I have chosen to translate it as "northern quarter."

assignment to which reflected their respective court ranks.[3] Their duties do not seem to have been too different from those of the other two bodies of guards, but only the lower division—those not yet admitted to the status of attendants to the ex-sovereign (*in no denjōbito*)—were required to accompany him on his outings. Primary sources tell of many more martial activities on the part of the hokumen than the other two bodies, and their guard duty was extended to include the apprehension of offenders against the ex-emperor. The greatest difference between the hokumen, the mizuishin, and the mushadokoro was again a matter of qualifications. The warriors of the northern quarter clearly were more important and bore a closer relationship to the ex-sovereign than the other two. In fact the most important qualification for the position seems to have been a close relationship to the abdicated emperor. There are a number of references to the fact that mushadokoro frequently later become hokumen in the service of the retired emperor.

I could find no support for the *Gukanshō* claim that Shirakawa originally set up this office in conjunction with his plan for ruling the country as ex-emperor and also as a means to guard against any possible untoward action by Prince Sukehito (from whom he had wrested the succession). Close associates of nonmilitary background were appointed to this bureau in its early years, and the name itself was probably coined after the body was in existence. Shirakawa simply met with some of his associates in the northern quarter of his palace. Later the number expanded, specific duties arose (chief among them being protection of the palace), and the term in no hokumen came into use. In the beginning the word warrior was not included; that was added only later when the bureau had developed into a more powerful and important one. Thus it is highly misleading to suggest that Shirakawa had the kind of specific goals claimed by Jien when he "founded" the in no hokumen.

[3] This information on the ex-sovereign's warriors of the northern quarter is derived largely from Yoshimura Shigeki, "In no hokumen-kō."

Shimmotsu-dokoro (Ex-sovereign's Kitchen)

The bureau that handled the kitchen duties for the palace of the retired sovereign was called the *shimmotsu-dokoro*. It not only provided him with his daily meals but also took charge of the preparation of dishes for ceremonial occasions. Little is known about the internal operation of this kitchen bureau, but like the *mizushi-dokoro* (sovereign's kitchen) it most likely had a director (*bettō*) in charge of a staff of assistants (*azukari*), cooks, and the like.

Gofuku-dokoro (Bureau of Ceremonial Dress)

The *gofuku-dokoro* was in charge of the various ceremonial robes belonging to the ex-sovereign. The director and assistant, plus the various menials attached to the bureau, were responsible for the storage, cleaning, and repair of the numerous robes required for proper social attire in Heian court society. Since the requirements of dress during this period were incredibly complex and the number of garments required quite large, this was no simple wardrobe department but an important bureau in the ex-sovereign's palace.

Saiku-sho (Ex-sovereign's Workshop)

The ex-sovereign's workshop was responsible for the general maintenance of articles belonging to the retired sovereign. Similar workshops were part of the household organization of most high-ranking court nobles, as well as temples and provincial government offices. The workmen would construct or repair ceremonial carriages and palanquins, do blacksmith work, and so forth.

Bechinō-sho, or Betsunō-sho (Warehouse)

The *bechinō-sho* was a warehouse for the storage of rice and vegetables for the ex-sovereign's table. A certain portion of the land rent (*jishi*) of the ex-sovereign's property was kept here for this purpose.

The provisions were then used for the retired sovereign's table or for ceremonial purposes.

Tsukae-dokoro (Attendants' Office)

The attendants' office seems to have handled all the articles and utensils needed for the ex-emperor's various ceremonial functions and was engaged in all manner of miscellaneous tasks. The original term seems to have come from the fact that the *meshitsukae*, attendants or servants, served there, but the persons associated with the bureau later were relatively high-ranking supervisors and clerks, so the name is somewhat misleading.

⇜ APPENDIX TWO ⇝

In no Kinshin

The Kanjūji and Hamuro Fujiwara

The Kanjūji and Hamuro branches of the Fujiwara clan, descendants of Tamefusa and Akitaka, trace their lineage to the late ninth-century courtier Takafuji. The family was only of middle rank at court, with many of the members serving as household officials of the *sekkanke*.[1] Tamefusa was responsible for a revival in the fortunes of the family during the reigns of Go-Sanjō and Shirakawa, and his second son, Akitaka, whose descendants were known as the Hamuro Fujiwara, expanded the familial influence through his connection with Shirakawa.

TAMEFUSA (1049–1115)

Tamefusa was one of the outstanding courtiers of his day, equally praised as a scholar and official during the reigns of Go-Sanjō and Shirakawa. His reputation was such that he was included with two other courtiers, Ōe no Masafusa and Fujiwara no Korefusa, as one of the "former three fusas" (*saki no sambō*).[2] Although he has been praised by later historians, Tamefusa did not rise to the pin-

---

[1] *Gyokuyō*, 3: 147, Bunji 2/1/27. Unless otherwise indicated, information about the kinshin comes from *Sompi bummyaku* and *Kugyō bunin*.

[2] Sometimes Minamoto no Toshifusa is included in place of Korefusa.

nacle of court officialdom. He entered the ranks of the *kugyō* only at the age of sixty-three, and at the time of his death he was no more than an imperial adviser of the senior third rank. However, since there had been no kugyō in the family since the time of Tamesuke in the late tenth century, this was still a significant achievement.[3]

The majority of Tamefusa's appointments were in the capital: he held the posts of sovereign's private secretary (kurōdo), head of the Office of Palace Repairs (*shuri no daibu*), right controller (*udaiben*), and head of the Ministry of the Treasury (*ōkura no kyō*). He did, however, hold provincial governorships in Tōtomi, Kaga, and Owari. When Go-Sanjō established his in no chō, Tamefusa was appointed supervisor (hōgandai),[4] and later he served as a director (bettō) in Shirakawa's in no chō. At the same time Tamefusa served as a household official for both Morozane and Moromichi, continuing the family tradition of service to the sekkanke.

Tamefusa had seven sons, all of whom were relatively successful in the imperial bureaucracy. His daughter Mitsuko was also instrumental in furthering the family fortunes. She was married to the powerful courtier and in no kinshin Fujiwara no Kinzane and was also the wet nurse to Horikawa and Toba. Her own daughter Shōshi (Taikemmon'in) was adopted by Shirakawa and later made consort of his son Toba. Shōshi was the mother of both Sutoku and Go-Shirakawa.

AKITAKA (1071–1129)

While his elder brother Tametaka continued the Kanjūji branch of the family and served as a household official for the sekkanke, Akitaka became a powerful political figure under the patronage of Shirakawa, and his descendants came to be known as the Hamuro Fujiwara. Rising quite rapidly in the bureaucracy, Akitaka became a kurōdo at age seventeen and later was made kurōdo no tō. He

---

[3] CYK, 4: 15. Ten'ei 2/1/24.   [4] "Tamefusakyōki." Ōtoku 2/12/29.

served as head of the imperial treasury (*kura no kami*) and governor in Wakasa, Harima, and Ōmi. He was a provisional middle councillor of the senior third rank at the time of his death.

Akitaka enjoyed considerable political influence as a confidant of Shirakawa. He was appointed in no kurōdo shortly after Shirakawa's abdication and later rose to be supervisor and finally chief director of the ex-sovereign's private office. He was also chief director of Taikemmon'in's in no chō. Nakamikado Munetada, himself a supervisor in the service of Shirakawa, recorded that after the decline of Tadazane's power Akitaka controlled all political affairs in the land. His authority and wealth were tremendous, and everyone yielded to his desires. Munetada also said the country deeply mourned the loss of such a noble minister when he died in 1129.[5] During the latter years of Shirakawa's life Akitaka is said to have visited him nightly to discuss politics, earning him the epithet "nocturnal chancellor" (*yoru no kampaku*).[6] Among his eight daughters, one was married to the prime minister Koremichi and was mother of Konoe's consort Kujō-in, another was the wife of the minister of the left Saneyoshi, a third was married to the middle councillor Toshitada, and still another was the wife of Tadataka, another in no kinshin.

AKIYORI (1094–1148)

Akitaka's eldest son, Akiyori, was appointed as a secretary to Toba at age fourteen and later held a similar position during the reign of Sutoku. He served as governor in Izumo, Tango, and Tamba as well as provisional governor (*gon no kami*) of Harima. He was at one time minister of popular affairs (*minbu no kyō*), and ultimately he became a provisional middle councillor. Like his father, Akiyori was an influential kinshin of Shirakawa during the ex-sovereign's last years,[7] but it was as a director in Toba's in no chō

[5] CYK, 6: 14–15. Taiji 4/1/15.   [6] *Ima kagami*, p. 37.   [7] GKS, p. 334.

that he was called the most powerful courtier in the land.[8] One of his daughters married Taira no Tokinobu and became the mother of Kenreimon'in, who in turn was the mother of Emperor Antoku.

AKINAGA (1117–1167)

Akinaga was the third son of Akitaka. His mother was a daughter of the courtier Minamoto no Akifusa. He served as governor in Kii, Etchū, Mikawa, and Tōtomi, and also held the capital posts of kurōdo and kurōdo no tō. He was provisional middle councillor and junior second rank at the time of his death. Akinaga became an influential confidant of Go-Shirakawa, having been named a director in 1159.

MITSUYORI (1124–1173)

Akiyori's eldest son, Mitsuyori, became a kurōdo at the age of nine and later served as kurōdo no tō, head of the imperial treasury, assistant in the Office of Palace Repairs, governor of Bitchū and Hōki, imperial adviser, and major councillor. In 1160 he was appointed director in Go-Shirakawa's in no chō,[9] but four years later he resigned both his court and in no chō positions to become a priest.

KOREKATA (1125–?)

Korekata was Akiyori's second son, and his mother (as well as Mitsuyori's) was Nijō's wet nurse. He was also kurōdo no tō, a controller, and governor of Echizen, Tamba, Tōtomi, and Owari, rising ultimately to be an imperial adviser of the junior third rank. He was a supervisor for Toba in his eleventh year, and in 1160 he became a director in Go-Shirakawa's in no chō. In the same year, however, he was dismissed from his offices and exiled for his in-

---

[8] Hashimoto Yoshihiko, "Insei seiken no ichikōsatsu," p. 38. Hashimoto quotes from the *Honchō shinshū ōjōden.*

[9] *Gyokuyō*, 3: 147. Bunji 2/1/27.

volvement in a plot against the ex-emperor in conjunction with Fujiwara no Tsunemune.[10]

The Takashina Clan

The Takashina clan was a middle-ranking courtier family which traced its lineage back to Prince Takaichi, a son of Temmu. Family members served in the various ministries of the imperial bureaucracy, as provincial governors, and as household officials of higher-ranking courtiers. Their influence increased immeasurably in the latter part of the Heian period through the family's association with the three successive abdicated sovereigns.

TAME'IE (1038–1106)

When Tame'ie died in 1106 Munetada recorded that he had been a kurōdo and later enjoyed a forty-year career as a provincial governor in the provinces of Suo, Mimasaka, Harima, Iyo, Ōmi, Echizen, Tango, and Bitchū.[11] He had considerable influence as a confidant of the retired emperor Shirakawa, whom he served as in no bettō. He also held the same position in the household offices of Shirakawa's daughter, Ikuhōmon'in. In 1093 Tame'ie was exiled and relieved of his post as governor of Ōmi over a dispute with the Kōfuku-ji, but after a few years he was recalled and appointed governor of Echizen, doubtless owing to the influence of Shirakawa.

TAMEAKIRA (1057–1103)

Tame'ie's eldest son, Tameakira, also enjoyed a long career as a provincial governor, never rising above the fourth rank. Munetada said that, after he was made a kurōdo by the retired emperor Shirakawa, Tameakira was especially favored and served repeatedly

10 HRS, p. 74, Eiryaku 1/2/20, 3/11. As noted already Korekata's mother was wet nurse to Nijō, and Tsunemune's daughter was the emperor's mother. Together they tried to support the emperor against Go-Shirakawa.
11 CYK, 3: 150. Kajō 1/11/16.

as governor of large provinces—Echigo, Tajima, Kaga, and Tamba.[12] Along with Fujiwara no Takatoki, Tameakira was considered the most favored of Shirakawa's kinshin.[13] Besides being a director for Shirakawa, Tameakira, like his father, was also a director in the household of Ikuhōmon'in.

The special treatment Shirakawa bestowed upon the Takashina family in general and Tameakira in particular is clearly indicated in the abovementioned exile of Tame'ie. As the eldest son, Tameakira should have been implicated, lost his position, and suffered exile, but the fourth son of Tame'ie, Tametō, was punished in his place, losing his post as the governor of Awa. Yet Tametō, too, was restored to his post after only a very short period of time, causing Munetada to question the rationale behind this action.[14]

YASUNAKA (DATES UNKNOWN)

Yasunaka was a cousin of Tame'ie who was never a man of importance at court and seems to have had no particular connection with the retired emperor. He did, however, have two daughters who had important relations with other inshi. One daughter was the concubine of Minamoto no Kuninobu, who served as nen'yo and bettō in Shirakawa's in no chō. The other was a concubine of Fujiwara no Suenaka, a provisional middle councillor as well as an official in the in no chō.

NAKAAKIRA (1087–1107)

Nakaakira was the eldest son of Tameakira. Because of his early death, he really had no opportunity to gain any degree of influence as a kinshin of Shirakawa. Nevertheless, it is quite obvious that he was high in the retired emperor's favor. He had been appointed in no kurōdo at the age of twelve and shortly thereafter was made kurōdo for Horikawa; he was governor of Tajima and a denjōbito

---

[12] CYK, 2: 311. Kōwa 5/12/21.   [13] Honchō seiki, p. 348, Kōwa 5/12/20.
[14] CYK, 1: 92. Kanji 7/10/18.

of both the emperor and the retired sovereign. Munetada recorded that an appointment as kurōdo at age twelve was unheard of, surpassing even the appointment of Fujiwara no Ieyasu to the same post at age thirteen.[15]

The *Sompi bummyaku*, a genealogy of court families, does not list Nakaakira as a son of Tameakira; only Muneakira is so recorded. However, Munetada recorded in his diary on the death of Tameakira that his sons Nakaakira, Muneakira, Masaakira, and Tokiakira all served as kurōdo and were appointed to the governorships of large provinces.[16] At the death of Shirakawa, three other members of the Takashina family—Tamechika, Tamemoto, and Tameyori—served as hikurōdo in the in no chō.[17] These three are not listed in the *Sompi bummyaku* either, but judging from their names, the office they held, and the time at which they held it, would appear that they were sons, or possibly grandsons, of either Tametō or Tameakira. All of these men may well have been kinshin.

MICHINORI (SHINZEI) (?–1159)

Shinzei was actually the son of Fujiwara no Sanekane, and he is commonly referred to as a Fujiwara. He did, however, become a member of the Takashina clan, taking the name when he was adopted into the family of Shigenaka and married his daughter. Although all fourteen of Shinzei's sons are listed under the Fujiwara name in the *Sompi bummyaku*, he himself remained a member of the Takashina family; he even refers to himself as Takashina no Michinori in the *Honchō seiki*, an official history he compiled.[18]

One of Shinzei's wives was a wet nurse to Go-Shirakawa, and another also served at his court. He was quite close to both Go-Shirakawa and Toba.

Emerging victorious in the Hōgen insurrection of 1156, Shinzei reinstituted the Kirokujo (Records Office) and revived ancient court ceremonies. He was widely disliked at court for his influence,

---

[15] *CYK*, 2: 101–2. Shōtoku 2/8/24.   [16] See n. 11 in this appendix.
[17] *CYK* 6: 76. Taiji 4/7/15.   [18] *Honchō seiki*, p. 371.

and, when Nobunori and Minamoto no Yoshitomo raised the Heiji
insurrection in 1159, he was forced to commit suicide. Because of
the nature of his relationship with Go-Shirakawa, Shinzei might
have become the most powerful of all the retired emperor's kinshin
had he lived. As it was, twelve of his fourteen sons were exiled after
the Heiji affair, including seven who were priests. Only his fourth
son, Narinori, returned to serve Go-Shirakawa as in no bettō.

MORIAKIRA (DATES UNKNOWN)

Moriakira was the son of Muneakira and the governor of Tōtomi
who served as bettō in Toba's in no chō.

YASUTSUNE (DATES UNKNOWN)

Yasutsune was a son of Yasushige who served as governor of
Kawachi, Izumo, Settsu, and Iyo, head of the Ministry of the
Treasury, and chief of the Right Division of the Capital Office
(ukyō no daibu). As a confidant of Go-Shirakawa, he held the positions of hikurōdo and kurōdo before becoming a bettō. In the
coup of 1179 he lost his court position and was exiled.[19]

EISHI (?–1216)

Eishi, the great granddaughter of Tame'ie's brother Akiyuki, was
of the same generation of the Takashina family as Yasutsune and
Muneakira. Once married to one of Go-Shirakawa's kinshin, she
later became the favorite of the retired emperor himself, giving
birth to Sen'yōmon'in and receiving the title of Tango no tsubone.
Quite influential politically, she met with Ōe no Hiromoto when
he came to the capital in 1186 and even waited upon Yoritomo on
his first visit the following year. Kanezane once remarked that all
court affairs passed through her lips.[20]

[19] Gyokuyō, 2: 301. Jijō 3/11/17.   [20] Ibid., 3: 129. Bunji 1/12/28.

TSUNENAKA (DATES UNKNOWN)

Tsunenaka was a son of Yasutsune who lost his posts at court and in the in no chō in 1179, along with his father, because of his association with Go-Shirakawa. He had been kurōdo, kura no kami, and governor of Harima and Iwami earlier, and he was governor of Hitachi in 1179.

Descendants of Fujiwara no Yoshikado

Yoshikado was the sixth son of Fujiwara no Fuyutsugu, and his descendants were courtiers of middle or low rank throughout the Heian period. During the reigns of Daigo and Suzaku in the late ninth and early tenth centuries, Kanesuke had risen to middle councillor, but he was the last kugyō until the insei period, when the family prospered through connections with the retired sovereigns.

TAKATOKI (DATES UNKNOWN)

Takatoki was governor in the large provinces of Inaba, Tajima, and Ōmi and served also as kurōdo. He was appointed hōgandai soon after Shirakawa established his in no chō, but he later advanced to bettō and became one of the most powerful of the retired emperor's kinshin. Takatoki and Takashina no Tameakira were considered to be the two most favored kinshin in Shirakawa's time.[21]

KIYOTAKA (?–1162)

Takatoki's eldest son, Kiyotaka, was at one time kurōdo, kura no kami, and governor of Kii, Tamba, Sanuki, Echigo, and Iyo, as well as provisional governor of Harima. He surpassed his father, rising as far as middle councillor of the second rank. Like his father, however, Kiyotaka was a kinshin of Shirakawa. After Shirakawa's death,

[21] See n. 13, above.

Kiyotaka served as bettō in the household of Taikemmon'in and Bifukumon'in as well as in Toba's in no chō. Kiyotaka's wife was a daughter of Takashina no Tameyuki and was wet nurse to Toba's son Konoe. Three of Kiyotaka's five daughters were married to other in no kinshin: Fujiwara no Kinnori, Fujiwara no Nagasuke, and Fujiwara no Tsunemune. His second son, Takamori, was married to the daughter of Taira no Masamori.

MITSUTAKA (1127-?)

Mitsutaka was the eldest son of Kiyotaka. His mother was the wet nurse of Konoe. Besides serving as governor of Awaji, Aki, Izumo, Tajima, and Bitchū, Mitsutaka was a kurōdo kura no kami, and finally middle councillor. He was appointed hōgandai in the private office of the retired sovereign Toba and was also a bettō in the in no chō of Bifukumon'in.[22] Mitsutaka was dismissed from office after the Heiji insurrection because of his relationship with Nobuyori, but he was later restored to his former position and became a confidant of the retired emperor Go-Shirakawa.

SADATAKA (1134-1170)

Sadataka was another son of Kiyotaka and kinshin in Go-Shirakawa's in no chō. Although only thirty-seven at his death, Sadataka had been governor of Bitchū (twice), Kaga, Tajima, Tamba, Mikawa, Etchū, and Iyo, and chief of the Left Division of the Capital Office (sakyō no daibu). He also served in Bifukumon'in's in no chō.

Descendants of Fujiwara no Matsushige

Still another branch of the Fujiwara traced its ancestry to Matsushige, third son of Uona, the great minister of the left. Matsushige was governor of Mimasaka although he never rose

[22] HHK, 1: 290. Nimpyō 4/12/8.

above the fifth rank. His descendants were, with few exceptions, middle-ranking provincial governors. It was Akisue who brought the family to a position of influence at court through his relationship with Shirakawa.

AKISUE (1054–1123)

Despite the fact that his father, Takatsune, was only a middle-ranking courtier, Akisue's family relations were extremely favorable for a successful political career. He was the adopted son of Fujiwara no Sanesue, an influential member of Go-Sanjō's court and a bettō in Shirakawa's in no chō. Sanesue's sister Moshi was Go-Sanjō's empress and the mother of Shirakawa. One of his daughters was the empress of Horikawa and the mother of Toba. Akisue's own mother, Shinshi, was the favorite wet nurse of Shirakawa,[23] and he accorded her son Akisue special treatment. Akisue was also the son-in-law of Fujiwara no Tsunehira, a confidant of Go-Sanjō during the short duration of his in no chō.

Akisue was appointed kurōdo and head of palace repairs, and he served as the governor of the provinces of Sanuki, Tamba, Owari, Iyo, Harima, and Mimasaka, his career as a provincial official spanning over twenty years.

Akisue had six daughters, all of whom married high-ranking courtiers with close connections to the abdicated sovereigns Shirakawa and Toba. His eldest daughter was the wife of Fujiwara no Munemichi, the second daughter married Fujiwara no Nakazane, the third daughter was married to Fujiwara no Tsunezane, his fourth daughter was married to Fujiwara no Atsukane (whose mother was Horikawa's wet nurse), his fifth daughter was the wife of Fujiwara no Saneyuki, and his last daughter married Minamoto no Masasada. Akisue himself became a kugyō only shortly before his death, but all his daughters married men of higher rank and position.

[23] CYK, 1: 92–93. Kanji 7/10/1.

NAGAZANE (1075–1133)

Nagazane was the eldest son of Akisue, and his rapid advancement at court seems to have been due largely to his father's relationship with Shirakawa. He first served as provisional governor of Mimasaka at the age of eleven, and at sixteen he became a hōgandai in Shirakawa's in no chō. He became shuri no daibu in 1122 when his father resigned the position, and served as governor in the provinces of Inaba, Owari, Iyo, and Harima. At one time he also held the position of kura no kami. Nagazane surpassed his father in office and was a provisional middle councillor of senior third rank at the time of his death.

Nagazane served as an in no bettō after having first been hōgandai, and he seems to have been quite close to Shirakawa. Munetada said of him that he advanced rapidly at court although he was without intelligence, distinction, the proper years of service, or marriage relations with the imperial family, suggesting that his success was due solely to the sponsorship of Shirakawa.[24] The same author repeatedly criticized Nagazane, at one point saying that never before had a man of so little ability been able to advance as far as councillor.[25] Perhaps because of these faults, Nagazane seems to have been somewhat in disgrace during his last years. After his death, however, his daughter Tokushi became the favorite of the abdicated emperor Toba, and in 1139 she gave birth to the future emperor Konoe. She was subsequently given the palace name Bifukumon'in, and Nagazane was posthumously appointed prime minister, junior first rank.

IEYASU (1080–1136)

The second son of Akisue, Ieyasu also rose rapidly in official rank. At the age of fourteen he was a kurōdo in the service of Yōmeimon'in and then a kurōdo at court. He served as governor to the provinces of Echizen, Tango, Tajima, Tamba, Harima, and Iyo. Ieyasu also held the positions of kura no kami and shuri no daibu,

---

[24] CYK, 6: 234. Taiji 5/10/5.   [25] CYK, 3: 62. Chōjō 2/8/19.

and at his death had attained the position of imperial adviser. As an official in the in no chō, Ieyasu was a bettō said to be without peer among the kinshin of Shirakawa.[26] His wife was the wet nurse to Toba's son, Sutoku.

AKISUKE (1089–1155)

Akisuke was Akisue's third son. At the age of only eleven he became a kurōdo and in the same year was made a hōgandai in Shirakawa's in no chō. Akisuke served as governor or provisional governor in the provinces of Mimasaka, Ōmi, Echigo, Kaga, and Bingo. In 1147 he was made a bettō in Toba's in no chō as a reward for having built an Amida hall for the ex-emperor.

AKIMORI (DATES UNKNOWN)

The eldest son of Nagazane, Akimori was governor of Owari, Bizen, and Hōki, and at one point he also held the position of shuri no daibu, as had his father and grandfather before him. Like his father Nagazane, Akimori was also an influential kinshin in Shirakawa's time. Toba, however, upon becoming senior retired emperor, dismissed Akimori from the ranks of his kinshin, apparently because he did not serve Toba as faithfully as was expected.[27]

NAGASUKE (1111–1155)

Nagasuke was the second son of Nagazane, and he was married to a daughter of Fujiwara no Kiyotaka, a powerful kinshin during the time of both Shirakawa and Toba. He held the position of kura no kami and was governor of Kai and Tamba. Nagasuke was a denjōbito in Toba's in no chō, but he lost his position in the in no chō, and other brothers also became the objects of the wrath of the ex-emperor. Although the reasons are not clear, it would appear that Nagasuke, Akiyori, and other brothers suffered because of

[26] *Eishōki*, p. 210. Taiji 4/7/15.   [27] *Chōshūki*, 2: 11. Taiji 5/4/20.

Akimori's actions or were guilty of the same unfaithful service themselves. In either instance, from this time the descendants of Nagazane ceased to serve as kinshin of the abdicated sovereign.

IENARI (1106–1154)

Ienari was the second son of Ieyasu, and he became the most influential member of the family during his service in Toba's in no chō. As a provincial governor he served in Wakasa, Sanuki, Kaga, and Harima; he also held the post of kurōdo. Ienari surpassed both his father and grandfather at court, rising as far as middle councillor. Shirakawa seems to have trusted Ienari greatly as he was placed in charge of the management of the Toba Palace upon the death of the ex-emperor, from which time on it was said that all the affairs of the land had fallen into Ienari's hand.[28] He continued to serve the abdicated sovereign Toba until his death in 1154.

SHIGEIE (1128–?)

Shigeie was a son of Akisuke. He received an appointment as a hōgandai in the service of Taikemmon'in at the age of seven. The same year he was made kurōdo and then went to serve as governor of Owari, Suo, Chikuzen, Settsu, Kōzuke, Wakasa, and Noto. In 1170 Shigeie was appointed bettō in Go-Shirakawa's in no chō.

TAKASUE (1126–?)

Ienari's eldest son, Takasue, was appointed kurōdo and in the same year made a hōgandai in Toba's in no chō. He was governor in Tajima, Echigo, and Tosa, and provisional governor in Sanuki. In 1165 he was appointed to serve the ex-emperor Go-Shirakawa as in no bettō. When Kenreimon'in was empress, Takasue held the position of chief of the empress's household (*chūgū no daibu*), and he served also as bettō in Takakura's in no chō.

[28] Ibid.

IEAKI (1127–1172)

Ienari's second son, Ieaki, was appointed kurōdo and made a hōgandai in Toba's in no chō at the age of eight. He also held the position of head of the imperial treasury and served as governor of Bingo and Harima.

NARICHIKA (1137–1177)

Ienari's third son, Narichika, was appointed governor of Echigo at age seven and later held the governorship of Sanuki. Narichika was one of the most noted and powerful of Go-Shirakawa's kinshin. Defeated in the Heiji insurrection along with Fujiwara no Nobuyori, Narichika was exiled to Bizen but was able to return to his court post through the intercession of Taira no Shigemori, his son-in-law. In 1177 Narichika was involved in the Shishigatani plot against the Taira and was captured along with the priests Shunkan, Saikō, and others.[29] Again he was exiled to Bizen, but Kiyomori ordered him put to death. His son Naritsune was also exiled for his father's crime.

MOROMITSU (?–1177)

Moromitsu's actual parents are unknown, but he is listed in the *Sompi bummyaku* as the sixth son of Ienari. There is a notation that he was made Ienari's son by imperial edict. He first seems to have served as a household official in the service of Fujiwara no Michinori (Shinzei). After the defeat in the Heiji insurrection, Moromitsu fled with Shinzei and subsequently became a Buddhist priest, taking the name Saikō. He later returned to the capital and entered the service of the ex-emperor Go-Shirakawa, becoming his number one kinshin, according to Fujiwara no Kanezane.[30] Moromitsu was also captured at Shishigatani and was executed the next day.

---

[29] *Gyokuyō*, 2: 51. Jijō 1/6/1.   [30] Ibid.

Descendants of Fujiwara no Michitaka

Michitaka was regent and then kampaku for the emperor Ichijō at the end of the tenth century. After his death his younger brother Michinaga took control of the fortunes of the sekkanke, and it was his descendants who brought the Fujiwara to the peak of their power. Michitaka's descendants were by contrast only moderately successful at court, usually rising to the fourth and sometimes even the third rank. During the insei period, however, many members of the family became clients in the service of the ex-emperors Shirakawa, Toba, and Go-Shirakawa, and the family improved its position at court immeasurably.

MORONOBU (1041–1094)

Moronobu was provisional head of palace repairs, senior fourth rank, and governor of Harima at his death. He also was at one time kura no kami. While we have no other information regarding his official career, we know that he served Shirakawa, Horikawa, and Ikuhōmon'in. In particular he was an important kinshin of the ex-sovereign Shirakawa, serving as chief director of his in no chō.[31]

KUNIAKIRA (1064–1105)

Moronobu's cousin Kuniakira was also a kinshin and chief director in the service of Shirakawa. At his death, Munetada reports, Shirakawa was so distressed that he called off a festival scheduled for that day.[32] Since he never rose above the fourth rank, Kuniakira is not listed in the *Kugyō bunin*, and the *Sompi bummyaku* simply says that he was governor of Iyo and kura no kami. Munetada lists the governorships of Bizen and Echigo among the posts he held. When his father died, Kuniakira was in his early teens, and he was adopted by Minamoto no Toshiakira, who was most probably his

[31] *CYK*, 1: 116. Kanji 8/1/10.   [32] *CYK*, 3: 38. Chōji 2/4/17.

brother-in-law. His mother was also a wet nurse for Shirakawa, so Kuniakira was a "breast brother" of the retired sovereign.[33]

TSUNETADA (1075–1138)

Moronobu's eldest son surpassed his father at court, becoming a middle councillor of senior third rank. He also held the positions of *Dazai no daini*, head of the imperial treasury, chief of the left division of the Capital Office, provisional governor of Echizen and Bizen, and governor of Suo, Aki, and Ōmi. Tsunetada was also master of the empress's household when Taikemmon'in was empress, director of the in no chō for both Shirakawa and Toba, and an important confidant. His wife, a daughter of Kinzane, was wet nurse to Toba.

MOTOTAKA (1075–1132)

Mototaka was the eldest son of Ienori (who is not recorded as having served the ex-sovereign but may have had some connection with Toba and Shirakawa since his daughter served Bifukumon'in). He was a provincial governor with a career spanning thirty-six years in Mimasaka, Harima (three times), Iyo (twice), Sanuki, Tamba, and Bizen. His mother was a wet nurse for the emperor Horikawa. He served as shuri no daibu and kura no kami before becoming an imperial adviser. He was chief director of Shirakawa's in no chō.

TADAYOSHI (1094–1158)

Tsunetada's eldest son, Tadayoshi, held the posts of kurōdo no tō, shuri no daibu, kura no kami, sakyō no daibu, and Dazai no daini before he became an imperial adviser. He was a kinshin of Toba, serving as director in his in no chō, but he had earlier been close to Shirakawa and even attended the ex-sovereign's visit to Kumano as one of his warriors of the northern quarter.

---

[33] See Oboruya Hisashi, "Fujiwara Kuniakira-ron."

NOBUSUKE (?–1184)

Nobusuke was the third son of Tsunetada, and his mother was the same as Tadayoshi's. He was also a bettō in the service of Toba [34] and he served at least as head of the right division of the Capital Office.

TADATAKA (1102–1150)

Mototaka's son Tadataka was appointed governor of Tamba at the unprecedented age of ten,[35] and from that time on he served in many provincial posts where he amassed considerable wealth. Among the provinces in which he was governor were Harima and Iyo. He also served as hōgandai for Shirakawa who was responsible for his early and rapid advancement. Tadataka had two daughters, one married to the regent Motozane, and one the wife of Takasue. He was an extremely influential kinshin during Toba's time, serving as chief director of the in no chō.[36] He was himself married to a daughter of Akitaka.

NOBUTAKA (1126–1179)

Nobutaka was the eldest son of Nobusuke, and he rose to the position of provisional imperial adviser (*hisangi*) of the senior third rank. He was also shuri no daibu, Dazai no daini, and governor of Inaba and Iyo. He served in the in no chō of Go-Shirakawa, and one of his daughters even became a consort of the ex-emperor's son, Takakura. This was Shokushi, better known by her palace name Shichijō-in, mother of both Go-Toba and Go-Takakura. One of his wives was a daughter of Taira no Kiyomori.

CHIKANOBU (1138–1197)

Another son of Nobusuke, Chikanobu also was a kinshin of Go-Shirakawa who had held the posts of shuri no daibu, Dazai no daini,

---

[34] *Honchō seiki*, p. 653. Kyūan 5/5/13.   [35] *CYK*, 4: 94. Ten'ei 2/10/25.
[36] *Honchō seiki*, p. 724. Kyūan 6/8/3.

and kura no kami, as well as governorships in Bitchū and Iyo. As a youth he had also served the ex-emperor Toba, but he became a powerful kinshin in Go-Shirakawa's time. He was dismissed from office in the coup of 1179 but later returned to court and eventually became a middle councillor.

NOBUYORI (1133–1159)

Nobuyori early became a favorite of Go-Shirakawa. His father was Tadataka and his mother a daughter of the powerful kinshin Akiyori. He was a kurōdo no tō for Go-Shirakawa and also served the empress Fujiwara no Shōshi (Jōzaimon'in). He was governor of Tosa and twice governor of Musashi. Shortly after the abdication of Go-Shirakawa, Nobuyori became involved in a feud with another kinshin of the ex-emperor, Shinzei, which developed into the Heiji insurrection. For his participation in this revolt Nobuyori was executed at the young age of twenty-seven. He had already reached the position of middle councillor by that time and, under the patronage of Go-Shirakawa, would most likely have been one of the most influential men at court.

NOBUKIYO (1159–1216)

Nobutaka's eldest son, Nobukiyo, passed through all the councillor positions and finally rose to be great minister of the center. He was a courtier in the attendance of the ex-emperor Go-Shirakawa as a young man, doubtless as a result of the influence of his father and his sister Shichijō-in.

The Kan'in Fujiwara

The Kan'in branch of the Fujiwara traces its lineage to Kinsue, the Kan'in prime minister during the reign of Go-Ichijō in the early eleventh century. Thereafter the family was always of moderate influence at court, producing major and middle councillors of the second rank. In contrast with most other kinshin families, the

Kan'in Fujiwara were thus already kugyō before the establishment of any connection with the ex-sovereigns. After Sanesue became a confidant of the retired sovereign Shirakawa, however, the fortunes of the family improved considerably.

SANESUE (1035–1091)

Sanesue was an extremely influential courtier in Go-Sanjō's and Shirakawa's time, rising ultimately to be a major councillor of the second rank. He held provisional governorships in Bizen, Mimasaka, and Ōmi, but most of his appointments were to capital posts: kurōdo no tō, chief of the Left Division of the Capital Office, master of the crown prince's household, and master of the empress's household. He served in the in no chō of both Go-Sanjō and Shirakawa, and much of his influence upon these successive sovereigns stemmed from his marital connections with the imperial house. His sister Moshi was a consort of Go-Sanjō's and mother of Shirakawa, and his own daughter Ishi was one of Horikawa's consorts and the mother of Toba. Sanesue was posthumously appointed prime minister, a custom commonly followed for courtiers whose daughters gave birth to an emperor.

KINZANE (1053–1107)

Sanesue's eldest son, Kinzane, followed a career pattern similar to that of his father. He also served as provisional governor of Mimasaka, and Bizen, kurōdo no tō, master of the crown prince's household, and in the household of the empress. He was a valuable kinshin of Shirakawa as well, having been appointed a director in the in no chō in 1088. At his death he was a provisional major councillor of the junior second rank.

YASUZANE (1061–1102)

Yasuzane was Sanesue's second son, and he too reached the second court rank. Since he died at the relatively young age of forty-three, he had advanced only to provisional middle councillor, however. He was provisional governor in Harima, Mimasaka, and Iyo, and kurōdo no tō. He was appointed to serve in Shirakawa's in no chō in the same year as his elder brother and performed a similar function in the in no chō of Yōmeimon'in, mother of the late Go-Sanjō.

NAKAZANE (?–1121)

Sanesue's third son, Nakazane, also rose to the position of provisional major councillor of the second rank and held the same type of official posts as had his father and elder brothers: provisional governor of Harima, Bitchū, and Bingo, governor of Tango and Bitchū, kurōdo no tō, and in the empress's household. One of his wives was the daughter of Akisue, another powerful kinshin and the adopted son of Nakazane's father Sanesue.

SANETAKA (1079–1127)

Sanetaka, Kinzane's second son, served as kurōdo, kurōdo no tō, provisional governor of Iyo, vice governor of Mimasaka, Bizen, and Sanuki, and in the crown prince's household, and he ultimately rose to middle councillor of the senior third rank. Like his father, uncles, and brothers Sanetaka was also a director of Shirakawa's in no chō and a close associate of the ex-emperor.

SANEYUKI (1093–1162)

Kinzane's third son, Saneyuki, enjoyed a long bureaucratic career spanning more than eighty years, and reached the highest position within the Grand Council of State: prime minister, junior first rank. Besides holding all the requisite councillor positions along the way, Saneyuki also served as kurōdo no tō, governor of Mimasaka, and provisional governor of Etchū, Bizen, and Iyo. He was first appointed bettō in Shirakawa's in no chō in 1108 and became a close confidant.

MICHISUE (1029–1128)

Kinzane's fourth son, Michisue, was another middle councillor of the third rank to come from the Kan'in Fujiwara. He was a "breast brother" of the emperor Horikawa, since his mother served as the emperor's wet nurse. Like so many others of the family, he was also kurōdo no tō, as well as governor of Mimasaka, and provisional governor of Etchū and Ōmi. He became a director in Shirakawa's in no chō at the age of twenty-one.

KINNORI (1103–1160)

Kinnori was the eldest son of Saneyuki and a daughter of Akisue. He served as kurōdo and kurōdo no tō, as well as holding all the councillor positions as he rose to be a great minister of the center of the second rank. He held provisional governorships in Sanuki, Bizen, Bitchū, and Iyo as well as the vice-governorship of Mimasaka. He was bettō and close confidant of the retired sovereign Toba.

KIN'YOSHI (1114–1161)

Kin'yoshi was the eldest son of Saneyoshi, the great minister of the left in 1156–1157. His mother was a daughter of the courtier and kinshin Akitaka. On his way to becoming great minister of the right and second rank, Kin'yoshi served as kurōdo, kurōdo no tō, and governor of several provinces. In 1145 he became a bettō of the ex-emperor Toba.

SANETSUNA (1127–1180)

Kinnori's son Sanetsuna served the retired sovereign Go-Shirakawa as bettō, and it was his status as a kinshin that lost him his court positions in Kiyomori's coup of 1179. At the time he was a provisional middle councillor of the senior third rank, but previously he had held the posts of kurōdo no tō, controller, and provisional governor of Tosa, Bitchū, and Awa.

The Ise Branch of the Kammu Taira

The Taira clan was an offshoot of the imperial house, composed of different lineages descended from the emperors Kammu, Nimmyō, Kōkō, and Montoku. Some members of the clan remained in the capital as middle-ranking officials during the Heian period, while others settled down in the provinces and became powerful local leaders. Among the latter, the most famous was the Ise branch, usually taken to mean the members of the clan related to Masamori. From his time, the Ise branch of the clan drew close to the three successive ex-emperors in the latter part of the Heian period and the family prospered greatly, reaching its zenith under the headship of Kiyomori. Although the Taira never seem to have developed the tradition of the clan headship typical of other clans, Kiyomori exercised a good deal of control over and influence on behalf of the other branches of the family. Thus when we speak of the Taira influence and power we can also include non-Ise Taira such as Tokinobu and his descendants.

MASAMORI (DATES UNKNOWN)

Masamori was responsible for building the base from which the Ise Taira made considerable political and economic progress in court society in late Heian Japan. The son of Masahira, the governor of Dewa, Masamori controlled certain lands in the provinces of Ise and Iga. As a powerful regional figure he was first appointed to serve in the office of the imperial police (kebiishi-chō) and then made governor of the island province of Oki. In 1099 Masamori commended some of his lands from estates in Iga to the Rokujō-in, a Buddhist hall dedicated to the soul of Shirakawa's favorite daughter, Ikuhōmon'in (she had died in 1096). This was the beginning of a long and profitable association between the Taira and the ex-sovereigns. Masamori first served in Shirakawa's *in no hokumen* and later rose to be a director and a close confidant of the ex-emperor.

After his commendation of the Iga lands, Masamori's career advanced considerably. He was appointed governor of Inaba and then in 1107 was appointed by the court to chastise the rebel Minamoto no Yoshichika, who had revolted in the Izumo area. The next year Masamori defeated and beheaded the rebels. When the news reached the capital, he was rewarded by appointment to the governorship of the "superior" province (*jōkoku*) Tajima.[37] There was widespread disapproval of this action, not only because it seemed inappropriate to appoint one of such low origins to this important post, but also because of doubts as to Masamori's actual military accomplishments.

He seems to have had no distinguished background that might have justified his appointment to chastise Yoshichika, son of Yoshiie ("the greatest warrior in the land") and a renowned warrior himself. Indeed, no reason other than his personal relationship with Shirakawa can explain his appointment. Although Masamori claimed to have killed Yoshichika, there were several rumors that Yoshichika subsequently appeared in the capital region.[38] These rumors seriously undercut Masamori's credibility as a warrior.

Despite such doubts, however, it was from this time that the military reputation of the Taira began to develop. In 1113 Masamori was designated to stop the armed Enryaku-ji monks, and in 1119 he was responsible for the capture of robbers in the capital. He rose to the junior fourth rank and held governorships—frequently due to the support of Shirakawa—in Wakasa, Tamba, and Sanuki. He is thought to have died sometime between 1145 and 1150.

[37] Provinces were divided by size into four categories: superior, large, medium, and small.

[38] For a discussion of the Yoshichika affair, see Ryō Susumu, *Heian jidai*, pp. 126–28.

TADAMORI (1095–1153)

Tadamori was Masamori's eldest son and heir, and he followed a course similar to his father's. He was in the office of the imperial police and the left division of the outer palace guards (saemon-fu), as well as governor in Harima, Ise, and Bizen. In 1129, while he was governor of Bizen, he captured a group of pirates who were terrorizing the Inland Sea region. In 1138 he again subdued Inland Sea pirates, but his actions were criticized by a number of people. In his diary Chōshūki, Minamoto no Morotoki claims that those whom he brought back as prisoners were not pirates at all but simply local persons who were not his vassals. The next year he and his warriors kept armed Kōfuku-ji monks from entering the capital.

Masamori and Tadamori, then, had established a reputation for martial accomplishments which enabled the Taira to rival the Minamoto as warriors. Both men had advanced at court through the patronage of the ex-sovereign. Tadamori was hikurōdo and bettō for Shirakawa as well as chief director in Toba's in no chō. Surpassing his father, Tadamori rose as far as the senior fourth rank.

KIYOMORI (1118–1181)

Tadamori's eldest son, Kiyomori, brought the Ise Taira to the peak of its power at court, ultimately becoming prime minister and seeing his own grandson Antoku become emperor. Much of Kiyomori's story has already been told in chapter 7, and there is no need to repeat it here. Kiyomori enjoyed a very close relationship with the three successive ex-sovereigns in late Heian times through the influence of his father and grandfather. Before Shirakawa died in 1127 Kiyomori had already been made hikurōdo. Later he served both Toba and Go-Shirakawa and through their patronage was appointed to governorships in Higo, Aki, and Harima, and also to the post of dazai no daini. During his tenure in these offices he built up strong local followings in the western provinces. It was his strength in this area that formed the base of power which was to serve him well in later years.

Besides the help given to him by these ex-sovereigns, Kiyomori owed a great deal of his political success to the advantageous marriages of his daughters. Tokuko was Takakura's empress and the mother of Antoku, while Moriko was married to the chancellor Motozane. Other daughters were married to Motozane's son Motomichi, Fujiwara no Kanemasa, and Fujiwara no Nobutaka, while his youngest daughter was in the service of Go-Shirakawa as an imperial concubine. Thus Kiyomori utilized quite skillfully the techniques of patronage and marriage alliances to advance the position of his house at court.

YORIMORI (1133–1186)

Yorimori was Tadamori's fifth son and the younger brother of Kiyomori. He served in the outer palace guards, as Dazai no daini, and as governor of Oki and Owari. Unlike his father and grandfather, however, he advanced to kugyō status and held mostly capital posts; kurōdo, kura no kami, and shuri no daibu. He was captain of the left division of outer palace guards in 1179, at the time of his dismissal from office as a result of Kiyomori's coup against the kinshin of Go-Shirakawa. He was later restored to his position and rose to be a major councillor of the second rank.

Although there is no actual record of it, it is certainly possible that Tadamori's other sons—Iemori, Tsunemori,—also may have been confidants of Toba or Go-Shirakawa. They all held posts as provincial governors, kurōdo no tō, kura no kami, or master of the empress's household, which were positions most frequently staffed by kinshin.

NORIMORI (1128–1185)

Tadamori's third son, Norimori, was also a kinshin of the ex-sovereigns Toba and Go-Shirakawa. He was governor of Awaji,

Yamato, Etchū, Hitachi, and Nōtō, and kura no kami, rising to be a second-ranking middle councillor. He was a hōgandai in Toba's in no chō, and later hōgandai and bettō for Go-Shirakawa. He drowned in the sea at the battle of Dannoura in 1185.

❧ APPENDIX THREE ❧

Japanese Sovereigns, 645–1185

Reign number	Sovereign	Reign dates	Preaccession name	Crown prince
35	Kōgyoku *	642–45	Takara	Naka no Ōe
36	Kōtoku	645–54	Karu	Naka no Ōe
37	Saimei *	655–61	Kōgyoku	Naka no Ōe
38	Tenji	668–71	Naka no Ōe	Ōama
39	Kōbun	671–72	Ōtomo	
40	Temmu	673–86	Ōama	Kusakabe
41	Jitō *	690–97	Uno no sarara	
42	Mommu	697–707	Karu	
43	Gemmei *	707–15	Ahe	Obito
44	Genshō *	715–24	Hidaka	Obito
45	Shōmu	724–49	Obito	Abe
46	Kōken *	749–58	Abe	Funado; Ōi
47	Junnin	758–64	Ōi	
48	Shōtoku *	764–70	Kōken	
49	Kōnin	770–81	Shirakabe	Osabe; Yamabe
50	Kammu	781–806	Yamabe	Sawara; Ate
51	Heizei	806–09	Ate	Kamino
52	Saga	809–23	Kamino	Ōtomo
53	Junna	823–33	Ōtomo	Masara
54	Nimmyō	833–50	Masara	Tsunesada Michiyasu

Reign number	Sovereign	Reign dates	Preaccession name	Crown prince
55	Montoku	850–58	Michiyasu	Korehito
56	Seiwa	858–76	Korehito	Sadaakira
57	Yōzei	877–84	Sadaakira	
58	Kōkō	884–87	Tokiyasu	Sadami
59	Uda	887–97	Sadami	Atsuhito
60	Daigo	897–930	Atsuhito	Yasuakira
				Yoshiyori
				Yutaakira
61	Suzaku	930–46	Yutaakira	Nariakira
62	Murakami	946–67	Nariakira	Norihira
63	Reizei	967–69	Norihira	Morihira
64	En'yū	969–84	Morihira	Morosada
65	Kazan	984–86	Morosada	Kanehito
66	Ichijō	986–1011	Kanehito	Iyasada
67	Sanjō	1011–16	Iyasada	Atsuhira
68	Go-Ichijō	1016–36	Atsuhira	Atsuakira
				Atsuyoshi
69	Go-Suzaku	1036–45	Atsuyoshi	Chikahito
70	Go-Reizei	1045–68	Chikahito	Takahito
71	Go-Sanjō	1068–72	Takahito	Sadahito
72	Shirakawa	1072–86	Sadahito	Sanehito
				Taruhito
73	Horikawa	1086–1107	Taruhito	Munehito
74	Toba	1107–23	Munehito	Akihito
75	Sutoku	1123–41	Akihito	Narihito
76	Konoe	1141–55	Narihito	
77	Go-Shirakawa	1155–58	Masahito	Morihito
78	Nijō	1158–65	Morihito	
79	Rokujō	1165–68	Nobuhito	Norihito
80	Takakura	1168–80	Norihito	Tokihito
81	Antoku	1180–85	Tokihito	
82	Go-Toba	1184–98	Takahira	Tamehito

* Female sovereign.

✌§ APPENDIX FOUR ɞ☙

Abdicated Sovereigns and Their Major Consorts

Abdicated sovereigns	Major consorts	
	Family name	*Palace name*
Go-Sanjō	Fujiwara no Moshi	
	Minamoto no Motoko	
Shirakawa	Fujiwara no Kenshi	
Toba	Fujiwara no Shōshi	Taikemmon'in
	Fujiwara no Tokushi	Bifukumon'in
	Fujiwara no Taishi	Kaya no in
Go-Shirakawa	Taira no Shigeko	Kenshummon'in

Bibliographic Note

FOR THE scholar engaged in research on the Heian period of Japanese history, several types of basic materials are essential: chronological histories (*hennenshi*), courtier diaries (*kuge nikki*), documents (*komonjo*), war tales (*gunki monogatari*) and other literary works, and encyclopedias of ancient court practices (*yūsoku kojitsusho*).

There are a number of chronological histories for the Heian period, and they are of two types. First, there are the official compilations, histories compiled at the command of the emperor. These include the six national histories (*rikkokushi*)—*Nihon shoki, Shoku Nihongi, Nihon Kōki, Shoku Nihon Kōki, Nihon Montoku Tennō jitsuroku*, and *Nihon sandai jitsuroku*—which cover Japanese history through 887, and the *Honchō seiki* which covers the period 935 to 1153. Second, there are also unofficial chronological histories of Japan for the period compiled privately by courtiers or Buddhist prelates. The most important of these for a study of the late Heian period are the *Fusō ryakki* and the *Hyakurenshō*. While all of these histories contain useful information about court politics, the treatment is uneven, and many days, months, and even years have no entries at all.

There are a number of diaries of Heian courtiers which are extant, and these are particularly valuable sources of information on Heian social and political life. Unfortunately, they have been little used by Western historians. For the late Heian period, at least six of these diaries are indispensable: *Chūyūki* (Nakamikado Munetada), *Gonijō Moromichiki* (Fujiwara no Moromichi), *Denryaku* (Fujiwara no Tadazane), *Taiki* (Fujiwara no Yorinaga), *Chōshūki* (Minamoto no Morotoki), and *Heihanki* (Taira no Nobunori).

Yet a third basic type of materials essential for a study of Heian history is the documents of the period. It is fortunate that extant documents of the Heian period,—public as well as private orders, communiqués, deeds, and so on—have almost all been collected and edited by Takeuchi Rizō, former head of the Historiographical Institute at the University of Tokyo. His collection of extant documents of the Heian period, *Heian ibun*, has probably had more effect upon the study of early Japanese history than any other work. Unfortunately, until quite recently these documents were not used by Western scholars in the study of Heian Japan.

Besides these three types of basic materials for the study of Heian Japan, certain literary works, pseudo-historical chronicles, and collections of tales dating from medieval times are also quite valuable if used with care. In particular, the war chronicles *Hōgen monogatari*, *Heiji monogatari*, and *Heike monogatari* provide important information for late Heian politics. Likewise, many of the tales in the *Konjaku monogatari* and the *Kojidan* provide background material for aspects of Heian life often neglected in the primary sources.

The encyclopedic works *Gōke shidai*, *Hokuzanshō*, *Saikyūki*, and *Shūgaishō* also contain a wealth of information concerning much of the ceremonial life of the Heian court. The first three were compiled by Heian courtiers well versed in court ceremony—Ōe no Masafusa, Fujiwara no Kintō, and Minamoto no Takaakira, respectively—while the last is a mid-Kamakura work usually attributed to Tōin Kinkata.

Finally, there are two interpretive histories dating from medieval times that are absolutely essential in a study of Heian political history. These are Jien's *Gukanshō* and Kitabatake Chikafusa's *Jinnō shōtōki*. Both of these works were written with specific political motives in mind, but the influence they have had upon the work of later historians is extensive. As I pointed out in chapter 1, these works have not only provided Japanese historians with many facts of ancient history but have also been largely responsible for the formulation of many of the terms, concepts, and definitions employed by contemporary Japanese historians. Indeed, the whole problem of the insei which I have investigated in the preceding pages really has its beginnings in these two works.

Bibliography

Chronicles, Diaries, and Documents

Azuma kagami. 吾妻鏡。2 vols. In *Kokushi taikei* 國史大系。(vols. 32–33). Rev. ed. Tokyo: Yoshikawa Kōbunkan, 1968.

Chōshūki. 長秋記。2 vols. In *Zōho shiryō taisei* 增補史料大成。(vols. 16–17). Kyoto: Rinsen Shoten, 1965.

Chōya gunsai. 朝野羣載。In *Kokushi taikei* 國史大系。(vol. 29A). Rev. ed. Tokyo: Yoshikawa Kōbunkan, 1964.

Chūyūki. 中右記。7 vols. In *Zōho shiryō taisei* 增補史料大成。(vols. 9–15). Kyoto: Rinsen Shoten, 1965.

Dai Nihon komonjo. 大日本古文書。Compiled by Tokyo Daigaku Shiryō Hensanjo. 東京大學史料編纂所。Tokyo, 1901–.

Dai Nihon shiryō. 大日本史料。Compiled by Tokyo Daigaku Shiryō Hensanjo. 東京大學史料編纂所。Tokyo, 1901–.

Denryaku. 殿暦。5 vols. In *Dai Nihon kokiroku*. 大日本古記錄。Tokyo: Iwanami Shoten, 1960–70.

Eishōki. 永昌記。In *Zōho shiryō taisei* 增補史料大成。(vol. 8). Kyoto: Rinsen Shoten, 1965.

Fusō ryakki. 扶桑略記。In *Kokushi taikei* 國史大系。(vol. 12). Rev. ed. Tokyo: Yoshikawa Kōbunkan, 1965.

Gempei seisuiki. 源平成衰記。Edited by Hakubunkan Henshūkyoku. 博文館編集局。Tokyo: Hakubunkan, 1902.

Gōke shidai. 江家次第。In *Kojitsu sōsho* (vol. 2). 古實叢書。Tokyo: Yoshikawa Kōbunkan, 1953.

Gonijō Moromichiki. 後二條師通記。3 vols. In *Dai Nihon kokiroku*. 大日本古記錄。Tokyo: Iwanami Shoten, 1956–58.

Gonki. 權記。2 vols. In *Zōho shiryō taisei* 增補史料大成。(vols. 4–5). Kyoto: Rinsen Shoten, 1965.

Gukanshō. 愚管抄。In *Nihon koten bungaku taikei* 日本古典文學大系。(vol. 86). Tokyo: Iwanami Shoten, 1967.

Gyokuyō. 玉葉。Compiled by Kokusho Kankōkai. 國書刊行會。3 vols. Tokyo, 1906-7.

Heian ibun. 平安遺文 Compiled by Takeuchi Rizō. 竹內理三。13 vols. Tokyo: Tōkyōdō, 1965.

Heihanki. 平範記。5 vols. In *Zōho shiryō taisei* 增補史料大成。(vols. 18-22). Kyoto: Rinsen Shoten, 1965.

Heike monogatari. 平家物語。2 vols. In *Nihon koten bungaku taikei* 日本古典文學大系。(vols. 32-33). Tokyo: Iwanami Shoten, 1959-60.

Hōgen monogatari. Heiji monogatari. 保元物語・平治物語 In *Nihon koten bungaku taikei* 日本古典文學大系 (vol. 31). Tokyo: Iwanami Shoten, 1961.

Hokuzanshō. 北山抄。In *Kojitsu sōsho* 古實叢書。(vol. 31). Tokyo: Yoshikawa Kōbunkan, 1954.

Honchō seiki. 本朝世紀。In *Kokushi taikei* 國史大系。(vol. 9). Rev. ed. Tokyo: Yoshikawa Kōbunkan, 1964.

Hyakurenshō. 百鍊抄。In *Kokushi taikei* 國史大系。(vol. 11). Rev. ed. Tokyo: Yōshikawa Kōbunkan, 1965.

Ima kagami. 今鏡。In *Kokushi taikei* 國史大系。(vol. 21B). Rev. ed. Tokyo: Yoshikawa Kōbunkan, 1965.

Jinnō shōtōki. 神皇正統紀。In *Nihon koten bungaku taikei* 日本古典文學大系。(vol. 87). Tokyo: Iwanami Shoten, 1965.

Kojidan. 古事談。In *Kokushi taikei* 國史大系。(vol. 18). Rev. ed. Tokyo: Yoshikawa Kōbunkan, 1965.

Konjaku monogatari. 今昔物語。5 vols. In *Nihon koten bungaku taikei* 日本古典文學大系 (vols. 22-26). Tokyo: Iwanami Shoten, 1959-63.

Kugyō bunin. 公卿補任。5 vols. and index in *Kokushi taikei* 國史大系。(vols. 53-57 and index 1). Rev. ed. Tokyo: Yoshikawa Kōbunkan, 1964-66.

Nihon Montoku jitsuroku. 日本紀略。In *Kokushi taikei* 國史大系。(vol. 3). Rev. ed. Tokyo: Yoshikawa Kōbunkan, 1966.

Nihon kiryaku. 日本後紀。2 vols. In *Kokushi taikei* 國史大系。(vols. 10-11). Rev. ed. Tokyo: Yoshikawa Kōbunkan, 1965.

Nihon kōki. 文德實錄。In *Kokushi taikei* 國史大系。(vol. 3). Rev. ed. Tokyo: Yoshikawa Kōbunkan, 1966.

Nihon Sandai jitsuroku. 日本三代實錄。In *Kokushi taikei* 國史大系。(vol. 4). Rev. ed. Tokyo: Yoshikawa Kōbunkan, 1966.

Nihon shoki. 日本書紀。2 vols. In *Nihon koten bungaku taikei* 日本古典文學大系。(vols. 67-68). Tokyo: Iwanami Shoten, 1965.

Ōkagami. 大鏡。In *Nihon koten bungaku taikei* 日本古典文學大系。(vol. 21). Tokyo: Iwanami Shoten, 1960.

Ruijū kokushi. 類聚國史。2 vols. In *Kokushi taikei* 國史大系。(vols. 5-6). Rev. ed. Tokyo: Yoshikawa Kōbunkan, 1965.

Ruijū sandaikyaku. 類聚三代格。In *Kokushi taikei* 國史大系。(vol. 25). Rev. ed. Tokyo: Yoshikawa Kōbunkan, 1965.

Ryō no gige. 令義解。*Kokushi taikei* 國史大系。(vol. 22). Rev. ed. Tokyo: Yoshikawa Kōbunkan, 1966.

Saikyūki. 西宮記。Suppl. vol. in Kondō Heijō 近藤瓶城。, ed., *Shiseki shūran.* 史籍宗覽。Tokyo: Kondō Kappansho, 1902.

Sankaiki. 山槐記。3 vols. In *Zōho shiryō taisei* 增補史料大成。(vols. 26-28). Kyoto: Rinsen Shoten, 1965.

Shoku Nihongi. 續日本紀。In *Kokushi taikei* 國史大系。(vol. 2). Rev. ed. Tokyo: Yoshikawa Kōbunkan, 1966.

Shoku Nihon kōki. 續日本後紀。In *Kokushi taikei* 國史大系。(vol. 3). Rev. ed. Tokyo: Yoshikawa Kōbunkan, 1966.

Shōyūki. 小右記。7 vols. In *Dai Nihon kokiroku.* 增補史料大成。Tokyo: Iwanami Shoten, 1959-.

Shūgaishō. 拾芥抄。In *Kojitsu sōsho* 古實叢書。(vol. 22). Tokyo: Yoshikawa Kōbunkan, 1952.

Shunki. 春記。In *Zōho shiryō taisei* 增補史料大成。(vol. 7). Kyoto: Rinsen Shoten, 1965.

Sompi bummyaku. 尊卑分脈。4 vols. and index in *Kokushi taikei* 國史大系。(vols. 58–60B and index 2). Rev. ed. Tokyo, 1965–67.

Taiki. 台記。3 vols. In *Zōho shiryō taisei* 增補史料大成。(vols. 23–25). Kyoto: Rinsen Shoten, 1965.

"Tamefusakyōki." 爲房公記。Manuscript owned by Tokyo Daigaku Shiryō Hensanjo. 10 vols.

Teiō hennenki. 帝王編年記。In *Kōkushi taikei* 國史大系。(vol. 12). Rev. ed. Tokyo: Yoshikawa Kōbunkan, 1965.

Teishinkōki. 貞信公記。In *Dai Nihon kokiroku.* 大日本古記錄。Tokyo: Iwanami Shoten, 1956.

Tōdai-ji yōroku. 東大寺要錄。In *Zoku zoku gunsho ruijū* 續々羣書類徒。(vol. 11). Tokyo: Takeki Insatsusho, 1909.

Books and Articles in Japanese

Aida Nirō. 相田二郎。*Nihon no komonjo.* 日本の古文書。2 vols. Tokyo: Iwanami Shoten, 1962.

Akagi Shizuko. 赤木志津子。"*Kugyō buin yori mita ōchō no seisui.*" 公卿補任より見た王朝の盛衰。*Ochanomizu shigaku* 御茶の水史學。no. 6 (June 1963): 51–58.

———. "*Sekkan jidai no tennō.*" 攝關時代の大皇。In *Kodaigaku Kyōkai,* 古代學協會。ed. *Sekkan jidaishi no kenkyū.* 攝關時代史の研究。Tokyo: Yoshikawa Kōbunkan, 1965.

———. "*Shirakawa-in to Horikawa tennō: Insei shoki no in to tennō*" 白河院と堀川天皇—院政初期の院と天皇。*Shintōgaku* 神道學。no. 53 (May 1967): 21–34.

Akamatsu Toshihide. 赤松俊秀。*Kamakura bukkyō no kenkyū.* 鎌倉佛教の研究。Kyoto: Heiryaku-ji Shoten, 1957.

———. "*Kamakura bunka.*" 鎌倉文化。In *Iwanami kōza Nihon rekishi* 岩波講座日本歷史。vol. 5. Tokyo: Iwanami Shoten, 1962.

———. *Zoku Kamakura bukkyō no kenkyū.* 續鎌倉佛教の研究。Kyoto: Hieryaku-ji Shoten, 1966.

Arimoto Minoru. 有本實。"*Inseishi no dōkō.*" 院政史の動向。*Nihon rekishi* 日本歷史。no. 87 (September 1955): 17–22.

Fujiki Kunihiko. 藤木邦彦。*Heian jidai no kizoku no seikatsu.* 平安時代の貴族の生活。Tokyo: Shibundō 1960.

———. "*Nara-Heianchō ni okeru kenseika no kasei ni tsuite.*" 奈良・平安朝に於ける權勢家の家政について。In *Jimbun kagaku-ka kiyō.* 東京大學教育學部，人文科學紀要。(Tokyo Daigaku Kyōikugaku-bu), no. 1 (April 1952): 1–20.

———, and Inoue Mitsusada, ed. 井上光貞。*Taikei Nihon sōsho,* 大系日本叢書。vol. 1: *Seiji I.* 政治 I 。Tokyo: Yamakawa Shoten, 1967.

Fujimoto Kō'ichi. 藤本孝一。"Enkyū shōen seiriryō ni kansuru gakusetsu no hihan." 延久莊園整理令に關する學說批判 Nihon rekishi 日本歷史。no. 313 (June 1974): 34-47.

Gotō Yōichi. 後藤陽一。"Sōsōki no insei ni tsuite." 創始期の院政について。 Shigaku kenkyu 史學研究。12, no. 4 (1942): 33-37.

Hashimoto Yoshihiko. 橋本義彥。Fujiwara Yorinaga. 藤原賴長。Tokyo: Yoshikawa Kōbunkan, 1964.

――――. "Goin ni tsuite." 後院について。Nihon rekishi, 日本歷史。no. 217 (June 1966): 11-25.

――――. "Hōgen no ran zenshi shōkō." 保元の亂前史小考。Nihon rekishi 日本歷史。no. 174 (November 1962): 24-36.

――――. "Ingū bunkoku to chigyōkoku." 院宮分國と知行國。In Takeuchi Rizō Hakushi Kenreki Kinenkai, 竹內理三博士還曆記念會, ed., Ritsuryō kokka to kizoku shakai, 律令國家と貴族社會。pp. 575-91. Tokyo: Yoshikawa Kōbunkan, 1969.

――――. "Insei seiken no ichikōsatsu." 院政政權の一考察。Shoryōbu kiyō (Kunaichō) 宮內廳, 書陵部紀要。no. 4 (March 1955): 36-53.

――――. 攝關政治論。"Sekkan seiji-ron." Nihon rekishi 日本歷史。no. 246 (October 1968): 60-66.

Hayashiya Tatsusaburō. 林屋辰三郎。Chūsei bunka no kichō. Tokyo: Tokyo Diagaku Shuppankai, 1953. 中世文化の基調。

――――. Kodai kokka no kaitai. 古代國家の解體。Tokyo: Tokyo Daigaku Shuppankai, 1955.

――――. Koten bunka no sōzō. 古典文化の創造。Tokyo: Tokyo Daigaku Shuppankai, 1964.

――――. Zusetsu Nihon bunkashi taikei 圖說日本文化史大系。vol. 5: Heian jidai II. 平安時代ト。Tokyo: Shōgakkan, 1957.

Hirano Kunio. 平野邦雄。"Taika zendai no shakai kōzō." 大改前代の社會構造。In Iwanami kōza Nihon rekishi 岩波講座日本歷史。vol. 2. Tokyo: Iwanami Shoten, 1962.

Hirata Toshiharu. 平田俊春。Heian jidai no kenkyū. 平安時代の研究。Tokyo: Yamaichi Shobō, 1943.

――――. Sōhei to bushi. 僧兵と武士。Tokyo: Nihon Kyōbunsha, 1965.

Hōgetsu Kiego. 寶月圭吾。Chūsei ryōseishi no kenkyū. 中世量制史の研究。Tokyo: Yoshikawa Kōbunkan, 1961.

Ienaga Saburō. 家永三郎。"Asukachō ni okeru sesshō seiji no honshitsu: Shōtoku taishi no sesshō no shiteki chi'i." 飛鳥朝に於る攝政政治の本質—聖德太子の攝政の史的地位。Shakai keizai shigaku 社會經濟史學 8, no. 6 (June 1938): 33-54.

――――. "Kodai no tennō seiji." 古代の天皇政治。Nihon rekishi 日本歷史。no. 49 (June 1952): 2-5.

Iida Hisao. 飯田久雄。"Heishi to Kyūshū." 平氏と九州。In Takeuchi Rizō Hakushi Kanreki Kinenkai, 竹內理三博士還曆記念會, ed., Shōensei to buke shakai. 莊園制と武家社會。Tokyo: Yoshikawa Kōbunkan, 1969.

Inoue Mitsusada. 井上光貞。Nihon kodai kokka no kenkyū. 日本古代國家の研究。Tokyo: Iwanami Shoten, 1965.

――――. Nihon no rekishi, vol. 1: 日本の歷史1, Shinwa kara rekishi e. 神話から歷史へ。Tokyo: Chūō Kōronsha, 1965.

――――. "Ritsuryō taisei no seiritsu." 律令體制の成立。In Iwanami kōza Nihon rekishi 岩波講座日本歷史。vol. 3. Tokyo: Iwanami Shoten, 1962.

Ishii Ryōsuke. 石井良助。 *Nihon hōsei shiyō.* 日本法制史要。Tokyo: Kōbundō, 1949·
———. *Tennō.* 天皇。Tokyo: Kōbundō, 1950.
———. Tennō no fushinsei no dentō ni tsuite." 天皇の不親政の伝統について。
Nihon rekishi 日本歴史。no. 49 (June 1952): 10-13.
Ishii Susumu. 石井進。"Insei jidai." 院政時代 In *Kōza Nihonshi* 講座日本史。
vol. 2. Tokyo: Tokyo Daigaku Shuppankai, 1970.
———. "Kamakura bakufu-ron." 鎌倉幕府論。In *Iwanami kōza Nihon rekishi*
岩波講座日本歴史。 vol. 5. Tokyo: Iwanami Shoten, 1962.
———. "Kamakura bakufu to ritsuryō seido chihō gyōsei kikan to no kankei:
Shokoku ōtabumi sakusei to chūshin to shite." 鎌倉幕府と律令制度地方行政機關
との關係―諸國大田文作成を中心として。*Shigaku zasshi* 史學雑誌。66, no. 11 (No-
vember 1957): 956-94.
Ishimoda Shō. 石母田正。*Chūseiteki sekai no keisei.* 中世的世界の形成。Tokyo:
Tokyo Daigaku Shuppankai, 1950.
———. "Kodai-hō." 古代法。In *Iwanami kōza Nihon rekishi* 岩波講座日本歴
史。vol. 4. Tokyo: Iwanami Shoten, 1962.
———. *Kodai makki seijishi josetsu.* 古代末期政治史序說。 Tokyo: Iwanami
Shoten, 1964.
Iwama Takeo. 岩間武雄。"Insei seiin ni kansuru ichikaishaku." 院政成因に關す
る一解釋。*Shigaku kenkyū* 史學研究。5, no. 1 January (1933): 76-83.
Kamei Katsuichirō. 龜井勝一郎。*Chūsei no seishi to shūkyōkan.* 中世の生死と
宗教觀。Tokyo: Bungei Shunjūsha, 1964.
Katsuno Ryūshin. 勝野隆信。*Sōhei.* 僧兵。Tokyo: Shibundō, 1958.
Kawaguchi Hisao. 川口久雄。*Ōe no Masafusa.* 大江匡房。Tokyo: Yoshikawa
Kōbunkan, 1968.
Kawakami Tasuke. 川上多助。*Nihon kodai shakaishi no kenkyū.* 日本古代社會
史の研究。Tokyo: Kawade Shobō, 1947.
Kawanishi Sachiko 河西佐知子。 "Ōhō gannen ni okeru Hachijō nyoin ingō
senge no shiryō haikei: *Hyakurenshō* o sozai to shite." 應保元年に於ける八條院女
院院號宣下の史料背景一百錬抄を素材として。 *Seiji keizai shigaku* 政治經濟史
學。 no. 47 (December 1966): 1-3.
———. "Rokujō tennō no keibo mondai to dōtei sokui jiken ni kansuru jakkan
no kōsatsu." 六條天皇の繼母問題と同帝即位事件に關する若干の考察。*Seiji keizai*
shigaku 政治經濟史學。no. 50 (March 1967): 40-42.
Kawasaki Tsuneyuki, ed. 川崎庸之。*Jimbutsu Nihon no rekishi* 人物日本の歴史
vol. 3: *Ōchō no rakujitsu.* 王朝の落日。Tokyo: Yomiuri Shimbunsha, 1966.
Kitayama Shigeo. 北山茂夫。*Nihon no rekishi* 日本の歴史 vol. 4: *Heian-kyō.*
平安京。Tokyo: Chūō Kōronsha, 1965.
———. *Ōchō seijishiron.* 王朝政治史論。Tokyo: Iwanami Shoten, 1970.
———. "Sekkan seiji." 攝關政治。In *Iwanami kōza Nihon rekishi* 岩波講座
日本歴史。vol. 4. Tokyo: Iwanami Shoten, 1962.
Koji Ruien Kankōkai, ed. 古事類苑刊行會。*Koji ruien.* 古事類苑。 60 vols.
Tokyo: Koji Ruien Kankōkai, 1931-36.
Kōno Fusao. 河野房男。"Shirakawa-in no kinshindan no ichikōsatsu." 白河院の
近臣團の一考察。 *Nihon rekishi* 日本歴史。 no. 152 (February 1961): 20-38;
no. 155 (May 1961): 72-91.
———. "Shirakawa-in no kinshindan no ichikōsatsu: Ninzuryō o chūshin toshite."
白河院の近臣團の一考察―任受領を中心として。*Nihon rekishi,* 日本歴史。no. 145
(July 1960): 36-51.

———. "Shirakawa-Toba ryōinseika no nin-kura no kami ni tsuite." 白河鳥羽兩院政下の任内藏頭について。 *Nihon rekishi* 日本歴史。 no. 204 (May 1965): 47–62.

Kuroda Toshio. 黒田俊雄。 "Chūsei no kokka to tennō." 中世の國家と天皇。 In *Inwanami kōza Nihon rekishi*, 岩波講座。 vol. 6. Tokyo: Iwanami Shoten, 1962.

———. *Taikei Nihon rekishi*, vol. 2: 體系日本歴史 II, *Shōensei shakai*. 莊園制。 Tokyo: Nihon Hyōronsha, 1967.

Kuroita Katsumi. 黒板勝美。 *Kokushi no kenkyū*. 國史の研究。 3 vols. Tokyo: Iwanami Shoten, 1936.

Matsumoto Shimpachirō. 松本新八郎。 *Chūsei no shakai no kenkyū*. 中世の社會の研究。 Tokyo: Tokyo Daigaku Shuppankai, 1956.

Mezaki Tokue. 目崎徳衞。 "Seijishijō no Saga jōkō." 政治上の嵯峨上皇。 *Nihon rekishi* 日本歴史。 no. 248 (January 1969): 13–27.

Mitobe Masao. 水戸部正男。 "Denka no watari-ryō no seikaku." 殿下渡領の性格。 *Hōseishi kenkyū* 法制史研究。 no. 4 (1953): 238–47.

———. *Kuge shinsei no kenkyū*. 公家新制の研究。 Tokyo: Sōbunsha, 1961.

Mizuno Yū. 水野祐。 *Nihon kokka no seiritsu*. 日本國家の成立。 Tokyo: Kōdansha, 1968.

Mōri Hisashi. 毛利久。 *Hōkongō-in*. 法金剛院。 Kyoto, 1960.

Murai Yasuhiko. 村井康彦。 *Heian kizoku no sekai*. 平安貴族の世界。 Tokyo: Tokuma Shoten, 1965.

———. *Kodai kokka kaitai katei no kenkyū*. 古代國家解體過程の研究。 Tokyo: Iwanami Shoten, 1965.

———. "Shōensei no hatten to kōzō." 莊園制の發展と構造。 In *Iwanami kōza Nihon rekishi* 岩波講座日本歴史。 vol. 4. Tokyo, 1962.

Murata Masashi. 村田正志。 "Ingū gobunkoku no kenkyū." 院宮御分國の研究。 *Kokushigaku* 國史學。 no. 32 (October 1937): 1–15.

Murata Masatoki. 村田正言。 "Insei ni kōsō shitaru Fujiwara no Tadamichi." 院政に抗争したる藤原忠通。 *Kokushigaku* 國史學。 no. 17 (November 1933): 26–47.

Murayama Shūichi. 村山修一。 "Fujiwara no Tadazane ni tsuite." 藤原忠實について。 *Kyōto Joshi Daigaku kiyō* 京都女子大學紀要。 no. 6 (Feburary 1953): 23–34.

———. *Fujiwara Teika*. 藤原定家。 Tokyo: Yoshikawa Kōbunkan, 1962.

———. *Heian-kyō*. 平安京。 Tokyo: Shibundō, 1957.

———. "Insei to Toba rikyū." 院政と鳥羽離宮。 *Shirin* 史林。 15 (1953): 56–79.

———. et al., comp. *Jōnan*. 城南。 Kyoto, 1967.

Nagahara Keiji. 永原慶二。 *Nihon hōkensei seiritsu katei no kenkyū*. 日本封建制成立過程の研究。 Tokyo: Iwanami Shoten, 1961.

———. *Nihon no chūsei shakai*. 日本の中世社會。 Tokyo: Iwanami Shoten, 1968.

Nakamura Naokatsu. 中村直勝。 "Goin to goinryō." 後院と後院領。 *Rekishi to chiri* 歴史と地理。 10, no. 3 (July 1923): 25–30.

———. *Nakamura Naokatsu Nihonshi*. 中村直勝日本史。 4 vols. Kyoto: Shirakawa Shoin, 1965–71.

———. Nihon komonjagaku. 日本古文書學。 3 vols. Tokyo: Kadokawa Shoten, 1971–.

Naoki Kōjirō. 直木孝次郎。 *Jito tennō*. 持統天皇。 Tokyo: Yoshikawa Kōbunkan, 1960.

————. *Nihon kodai no shizoku to tennō*. 日本古代の氏族と天皇。 Tokyo: Hanawa Shobō, 1964.

————. *Nihon no rekishi*, 日本の歴史 vol. 2: *Kodai kokka no seiritsu*.古代國家 の成立。 Tokyo: Chūō Kōronsha, 1965.

Nihon gaishi. 日本外史。 Tokyo: Iwanami Shoten, 1929.

Nihon rekishi daijiten. 日本歴史大辭典。22 vols. Tokyo: Kawade Shobō, 1956–61.

Ōae Akira. 大饗亮。 "Heian jidai no keishi seido." 平安時代の家司制度。 *Hōkei gakkai zasshi* (Okayama Daigaku) 岡山大學, 法經學會雜誌。 10, no. 3 (December 1960): 23–37.

————. "Heian jidai no rōdōsei to keninsei." 平安時代の郎等制と家人制。 *Hōkei gakkai zasshi* (Okayama Daigaku) 岡山大學, 法經學會雜誌。 11, no. 2 (September 1961): 133–64.

————. "Heian jidai no shiteki hogo seido." 平安時代の私的保護制。 *Hōkei gakkai zasshi* (Okayama Daigaku) 岡山大學, 法經學會雜誌。 11, no. 1 (June 1961): 1–33.

Oboruya Hisashi. 朧谷壽。 "Fujiwara Kuniakira-ron." 藤原國明論。 *Kodai bunka* 古代文化。25, no. 2/3 (March 1973): 66–77.

Ōkubo Toshikane 大久保利謙。et al., ed. *Shiryō ni yoru Nihon no ayumi*. 史料に よる日本の步み。 4 vols. Tokyo: Yoshikawa Kōbunkan, 1960.

Okuno Takahiro 奥野高廣。 *Kōshitsu gokeizaishi no kenkyū*. 皇室御經濟史の 研究。Tokyo: Unebi Shobō, 1942.

————. "Kōshitsu goryō shōen." 皇室御領莊園。 *Nihon rekishi* 日本歴史。 no. 184 (September 1964): 79–86.

————. "Kōshitsu goryō to jinja." 皇室御領と神社。 *Kokushigaku* 國史學。 no. 55 (July 1951): 1–15.

Ryō Susumu. 龍肅。 *Heian jidai*. 平安時代。 Tokyo: Shunjūsha, 1962.

————. *Kamakura jidai*. 鎌倉時代。 2 vols. Tokyo: Shunjūsha, 1957.

————. *Kamakura jidai no kenkyū*. 鎌倉時代の研究。 Tokyo: Shunjūsha Shōhakkan, 1944.

Sakamaki Shōzaburō. 酒卷正三郎。 "Insei seiken shiron." 院政政權史論。 *Hōsei shigaku* 法政史學。9 (1957): 81–95.

Satō Ken'ichi. 佐藤堅一。 "Hōkenteki shujūsei no genryū ni kansuru ichishiron: Sekkanke keishi ni tsuite." 封建的主徒制の源流に關する一試論—攝關家家司につ いて。 In Yasuda Motohisa, 安田元久, ed., *Shoki hōkensei no kenkyū*. Tokyo: Yoshikawa Kōbunkan, 1964. 始期封建制の研究。

Satō Shin-ichi. 佐藤進 。 *Komonjogaku*. 古文書學。 Tokyo: Hōsei Diagaku Shuppankyoku, 1968.

Shimizu Masatake. 清水正健。 *Shōen shiryō*. 莊園志料。2 vols. (and index by Takeuchi Rizō). Tokyo: Kadokawa Shoten, 1965.

Shinjō Tsunezō. 新城常三。 "In no Kumano mōde: Insei no ichikōsatsu." 院の 熊野詣—院政の一考察。 *Rekishi chiri* 歴史地理。88, no. 2 (July 1957): 25–49.

Suzuki Shigeo. 鈴木茂男。 "Inseiki in no chō no kinō in tsuite: In no chō hakkyū monjo o tsūjite mitaru." 院政期院廳の機能について—院廳發給文書を通じて見たる。 Unpublished graduation thesis. University of Tokyo, 1961.

Taga Munehaya. 多賀宗隼。 *Jien*. 慈円。 Tokyo: Yoshikawa Kōbunkan, 1959.

Takeda Sachiko. 武田佐知子。 "'Fukai jōten' ni tsuite." 不改常典について。 *Nihon rekishi* 日本歴史。309 (February 1974): 54–66.

Takeuchi Rizō. 竹內理三。 "Heike oyobi insei seiken to shōensei." 平家及び院政政權と莊園制。 *Rekishigaku kenkyū* 歷史學研究。no. 225 (November 1958): 28-33.

———. "Heishi seiken no shojōken." 平氏政權の諸條件。 *Nihon rekishi* 日本歷史。no. 163 (January 1962): 2-12.

———. "Insei no seiritsu." 院政の成立。In *Iwanami kōza Nihon rekishi* 岩波講座日本歷史。vol. 4. Tokyo: Iwanami Shoten, 1962.

———. *Jiryō shōen no kenkyū.* 寺領莊園の研究。Tokyo: Unebi Shobō, 1942.

———. "Kodai kara chūsei e: Heishi seiken no shiteki i'chi." 古代から中世へ—平氏政權の史的地位。*Nihon rekishi* 日本歷史。no. 176 (January 1963): 16-27.

———. *Nihon hōkensei seiritsu no kenkyū.* 日本封建制成立の研究。Tokyo: Yoshikawa Kōbunkan, 1955.

———. *Nihon no rekishi,* 日本の歷史 vol. 4: *Bushi no tōjō* 武士の登場。Tokyo: Chūō Kōronsha, 1965.

———. *Ritsuryōsei to kizoku seiken.* 律令制と貴族政權。2 vols. Tokyo: Ochanomizu Shobō, 1957-8.

Takikawa Masajirō. 滝川政次郎。Nihon hoseishi 日本法制史。Tokyo: Kangensha, 1959.

Tanaka Shigehisa. 田中繁久。"Kugyō Heishi to Iga Heishi no bunseki." 公卿平氏と伊賀平氏。 *Kodaigaku* 古代學。15, no. 2 (December 1968): 101-32.

Teishitsu Rinyakyoku, 帝室林野局。comp. *Goryōchi shikō.* 御料地史稿。Tokyo: Teishitsu Rinyakyoku, 1937.

Toda Yoshimi. 戶田芳美。*Nihon ryōshusei seiritsu no kenkyū.* 日本領主制成立の研究。Tokyo: Iwanami Shoten, 1967.

Tokinoya Shigeru. 時野谷滋。"Nenkyū seido no kisoteki kōsatsu." 年給制度の基礎的考察。*Shigaku zasshi* 史學雜誌。59, no. 3 (March 1950): 20-59.

Tokushi yoron. 讀史余論。Tokyo: Iwanami Bunko, 1967.

Toyoda Takeshi. 豐田武。"Chūsei no tennōsei." 中世の天皇制。*Nihon rekishi* 日本歷史。no. 49 (June 1952): 5-10.

Tsuchida Naoshige. 土田直鎭。*Nihon no rekishi,* 日本の歷史 vol. 5: *Ōchō no kizoku.* 王朝の貴族。Tokyo: Chūō Kōronsha, 1965.

Tsuda Sōkichi. 津田左右吉。*Nihon jōdaishi kenkyū.* 日本上代史研究。Tokyo: Iwanami Shoten, 1947.

Tsuji Hikosaburō. 辻彦三郎。"Toba-in no gosoi." 鳥羽院の御素意。*Kokushigaku* 國史學。no. 52 (May 1950): 42-51.

Tsuji Zennosuke. 辻善之助。*Jimbutsu ronsō.* 人物論叢。Tokyo: Yūzankaku, 1925.

———, Kuroita Katsumi, 黑板勝美。et al. *Kōshitsushi no kenkyū.* 皇室史の研究。Tokyo: Higashi Fushimi no Miyazō-han, 1932.

Wada Hidematsu. 和田英松。*Kanshoku yōkai.* 官職要解。Tokoy: Meiji Shoin, 1943.

———. *Kokushi kokubun no kenkyū.* 國史國文の研究。Tokyo: Yūzankaku, 1926.

———. *Kokushi setsuen.* 國史說苑。Tokyo: Meiji Shoin, 1939.

———. *Kōhsitsu gosen no kenkyū.* 皇室御撰の研究。Tokyo: Meiji Shoin, 1933.

Watanabe Naohiko. 渡邊直彦。"Saga ınshi no kenkyū." 嵯峨院司の研究。*Nihon rekishi* 日本歷史。no. 210 (November 1965): 44-59.

Watanabe Sumio. 渡邊澄夫。"Kōbu kenryoku to shōensei." 公武權力と莊園制。

In *Iwanami kōza Nihon rekishi* 岩波講座日本歷史。vol. 5. Tokyo: Iwanami Shoten, 1962.

Watanabe Tamotsu. 渡邊保。*Genji to Heishi.* 源氏と平氏。Tokyo: Shibundō, 1955.

―――. *Heike ichimon.* 平家一門。Tokyo: Jimbutsu Ōraisha, 1964.

Yashiro Kuniji. 八代國治。"Goin no kō 後院の考。*Shigaku zasshi* 史學雜誌。15, no. 9 (September 1904): 35-55.

―――. *Kokushi sōsetsu.* 國史叢說。Tokyo: Yoshikawa Kōbunkan, 1925.

Yasuda Motohisa. 安田元久。*Bushidan.* 武士團。Tokyo: Hanawa Shobō, 1954.

―――. *Minamoto Yoshiie.* 源義家。Tokyo: Yoshikawa Kōbunkan, 1966.

―――. *Nihon hōkensei seiritsu no shozentei.* 日本封建制成立の諸前提。Tokyo: Yoshikawa Kōbunkan, 1960.

―――. *Nihon no rekishi* 日本の歷史 vol. 7: *Insei to Hesihi.* 院政と平氏。Tokyo: Shōgakkan, 1974.

―――. *Shoki hōkensei no kōsei.* 初期封建制の構成。Tokyo: Kokudosha, 1950.

Yoshiba Hiroko. 吉葉汎子。"Insei no seiji shutai ni kansuru ichikōsatsu: Gondainagon Fujiwara Kunitsuna-kyō kenkyū josetsu." 院政の政治主體に關する一考察。*Seiji keizai shigaku* 政治經濟史學。nos. 48–52. (January–May 1967).

Yoshimura Shigeki. 吉村茂樹。"Eikyū gannen no Toba tennō ni taisuru gigoku jiken ni tsuite." 永久元年の鳥羽天皇に對する疑獄事件について。*Jōchi shigaku* 上智史學。no. 8 (October 1963): 3-7.

―――. "In no hokumen-kō." 院北面考。*Hōseishi kenkyū* 法制史研究。no. 2 (1951): 45-71.

―――. *Insei.* 院政。Tokyo: Shibundō, 1958.

―――. "Insei hassei ni kansuru ichikōsatsu." 院政發生に關する一考察。*Kokushigaku,* 國史學。no. 61 (March 1953): 1-14.

―――. *Kokushi seido.* 國司制度。Tokyo: Hanawa Shobō, 1962

―――. *Kokushi seido hōkai ni kansuru kenkyū.* 國司制度崩壞に關する研究。Tokyo: Tokyo Daigaku Shuppankai, 1957.

―――. *Komonjogaku.* 古文書學。5th ed. Tokyo: Iwanami Shoten, 1967.

―――. "Ryō Susumu-cho 'Heian jidai.'" 龍肅著「平安時代」。*Nihon rekishi* 日本歷史。no. 176 (January 1963): 96-99.

Books and Articles in Western Languages

Asakawa Kanichi. *Land and Society in Medieval Japan.* Tokyo: Japan Society for the Promotion of Science, 1965.

Buxton, Jean. " 'Clientship' among the Mandari of the Southern Sudan." In Ronald Cohen and John Middleton, eds., *Comparative Political Systems.* Garden City, N.Y.: Natural History Press, 1967.

Brownlee, John S. "The Shōkyū War and the Political Rise of the Warriors." *Monumenta Nipponica* 24, no. 12 (1969): 55-77.

Fox, Robin. *Kinship and Marriage.* Middlesex, England: Penguin Books: 1967.

Goody, Jack. "Introduction" to Goody, ed., *Succession to High Office.* Cambridge: Cambridge University Press, 1966.

Hall, John W. *Government and Local Power in Japan, 500–1700: A Study Based on Bizen Province.* Princeton: Princeton University Press, 1966.

————. "A Monarch for Modern Japan." In Robert E. Ward, ed,. *Political Development in Modern Japan*. Princeton: Princeton University Press, 1968.

Jouon des Longrais, Frederick. *Tashi: Le roman de celle qui espousa deux empereurs (nidai no kisaki)* (1140–1202). Tokyo: Maison Franco-Japonaise, 1965.

Kiley, Cornelius J. "State and Dynasty in Archaic Yamato." *Journal of Asian Studies* 33, no. 1 (November 1973): 25–49.

Krader, Lawrence. *Formation of the State*. Englewood Cliffs, N. J.: Prentice-Hall, 1968.

Lasswell, Harold and Abraham Kaplan. *Power and Society*. New Haven: Yale University Press, 1950.

McCullough, William. "Japanese Marriage Institutions in the Heian Period." *Harvard Journal of Asiatic Studies* 27 (1967): 103–67.

Mair, Lucy. *Primitive Government*. Rev. ed. Middlesex, England: Penguin Books, 1964.

Mass, Jeffrey P. "The Emergence of the Kamakura Bakufu." In John W. Hall and Jeffrey P. Mass, eds., *Medieval Japan: Essays in Institutional History*, pp. 127–56. New Haven: Yale University Press, 1974.

Morris, Ivan. *The World of the Shining Prince*. New York: Alfred A. Knopf, 1964.

Passin, Herbert. "Japanese Society." In *Encyclopedia of the Social Sciences*, 8: 236–42. New York: Macmillan, 1968.

Ponsonby-Fane, R. A. B. *The Imperial House of Japan*. Kyoto: Ponsonby Memorial Society, 1959.

Sansom, George B. *A History of Japan to 1334*. Stanford: Stanford University Press, 1958.

Shinoda, Minoru. *The Founding of the Kamakura Shogunate, 1180–1185*. New York: Columbia University Press, 1960.

Varley, H. Paul. *Imperial Restoration in Medieval Japan*. New York: Columbia University Press, 1971.

————. *The Ōnin War*. New York: Columbia University Press, 1966.

Webb, Herschel. *The Japanese Imperial Institution in the Tokugawa Period*. New York: Columbia University Press, 1968.

Glossary

bettō 別當
  director of a household or religious administrative office

chō 牒
  communiqué issued by both government and household offices

Dajō Tennō 太上天皇
  honorific title for abdicated sovereign

goin 後院
  retirement palace

hōgandai 判官代
  supervisor in the ex-sovereign's private office

honjo 本所
  central proprietor of a shōen

honke 本家
  protector or patron of a shōen at the highest level

ie 家
  household

in no chō 院廳
  ex-sovereign's private office

in no kinshin 院の近親
  confidants or close associates of the retired sovereign

insei 院政
  Japanese term used to describe political system in which ex-sovereign was final authority; "cloister government"

inshi 院司
  general term for officials serving the ex-emperor

inzen 院宣
  edict or directive of an abdicated sovereign

jin no sadame 陣の定
  formal meeting of Heian nobles to decide matters of state

jōi 讓位
  abdication

kampaku 關白
  chancellor

keishi 家司
  household official

kudashibumi 下文
  order; document issued from a higher authority to a lower one

kugyō 公卿
  highest level of noble class

mandokoro 政所
  family administrative headquarters

ryō 領
  landholdings, often a large portfolio of shōen

sekkanke 攝關家
  sublineage of Fujiwara clan which traditionally held positions of regent (sesshō) or chancellor (kampaku)

sesshō 攝政
　regent
shōen 莊園
　landed private estate; manor
uji 氏
　largest kinship unit; clan

uji no chōja 氏の長者
　clan chieftain
zuryō 受領
　general term for provincial governor
　class in mid- and late Heian times

INDEX

Entries are taken from the text only; material from the appendices is not included.

michi, 93, 101–2, conflict with Go-Sanjō, 103–6, 108–9, 115–17, 121, 126, 132, 258–59; Fujiwara no Yorinaga, 16, 136, 139, estrangement with Tadamichi, 166–69, and Hōgen Disturbance, 170–81, 207, 263; Fujiwara no Yoritada, 84, 89; Fujiwara no Yoshifusa, 67–69, 74; Fujiwara no Yoshinaga, 115, 122; Fujiwara no Yoshinobu, animosity with Yorimichi, 103, 115, 121, 122, 131; Fujiwara no Yukinari (Kōzei), 107

Fuko (sustenance households), 64–65, 70–71, 73, 78, 99

Funya no Watamaro, 52–53

Furuhito, Prince, 38–39

Fusō ryakki, 120

Gemmei, Empress, 42–44

Gempei seisuiki, 139, 190–91, 195

Genshō, Empress, 43–44, 50

Gion no nyōgo, 182

Gion Shrine, 129, 164

Go-Daigo, Emperor, 107n, 110

Goganji (imperial temple), 90, 162, 228, 262; holdings of, 262–70

Go-Ichijō, Emperor, 91–93, 95, 98, 101–2, 108, 121, 186, 263

Goin (retirement palace), origins, 64–66; 99, 117, 208–9, 262; holdings of, 262–63

Go-Reizei, Emperor, 92–93, 95, 98, 101–2, 104–5, 109–10, 113

Go-Sanjō, Emperor, 3, 5, 6, 36–37, 82, 93; as crown prince, 100–5; and political factions, 106–9; economic policies of, 110–19; abdication of, 119–24; 125–34, 137, 144, 146, 151–52, 165, 183, 188, 211–12, 258–59, 262, 265, 275–76; see also Takahito, Prince

Go-Shirakawa, Emperor, 127, 151, 162, 167; and Hōgen Disturbance, 173, 175, 177; as emperor, 178–86; abdication of, 186–89; and Heiji Disturbance, 189–90; relations with Emperor Nijō, 190–99; in reign of Emperor Rokujō, 199–20; and rift with Taira, 202–10; organization of *in no chō*, 210–13, 217, 223, 229, 233n,

238, 242–43, 247, 250, 258, 262–63, 266, 268–70, 272, 274, 276; see also Masahito, Prince

Go-Suzaku, Emperor, 92–93, 101–2, 104, 108, 113

Go-Toba, Emperor, 4n, 212, 243, 272

Grand Council of State (*Dajōkan*), 28–29, 60, 111, 114, 142, 151, 231; documents of, 231–35

Gukanshō, 5, 62, 115, 118–20, 155, 172, 238

Gyokuyō, 197

Hachijōin (Princess Shōshi), 163, 268, 271; holdings of, 163, 267, 272

Hall, John W., 8, 10, 15, 34, 273n

Heian ibun, 185

Heihanki, 185

Heiji Disturbance, 189–90

Heike monogatari, 181, 205

Heizei, Emperor, 51–58, 62, 66, 257

Hie Shrine, 164, 204; holdings of, 270

Hōgandai (supervisor) 78, 85–86, 142, 150, 188, 211, 219, 221; definition, 222, 225, 227, 242

Hōgen Disturbance, 155–56, 163, 165–66, 169–77; aftermath of, 179–82, 183, 189, 207, 263

Hōgen monogatari, 156

Honchō seiki, 186

Honjo (central proprietor), 226, 259

Honke (patron of estate), 259

Horikawa, Emperor, 127, 132, 135–38, 142–43, 146, 149, 154, 243, 264–66

Hosshō-ji, 206, 264

Household officials, system of, Nara, 19–21; system of, Heian, 21–26, 223, 242, 245–46, 258

Hyakurenshō, 120, 187–88, 196, 200–1, 209

Ichijō, Emperor, 87, 89–90

Ie (household), 11, 18, 192

Ima kagami, 105

Imayō, 178, 186

Immutable law, 43–44

Imperial house, place of in political scheme, 31–34, 50, 54, 56, 58–62, 65–67, 70–75, 80–81, 84, 86–87, 92–

Studies of the East Asian Institute

The Ladder of Success in Imperial China, by Ping-ti Ho. New York: Columbia University Press, 1962.
The Chinese Inflation, 1937–1949, by Shun-hsin Chou. New York: Columbia University Press, 1963.
Reformer in Modern China: Chang Chien, 1853–1926, by Samuel Chu. New York: Columbia University Press, 1965.
Research in Japanese Sources: A Guide, by Herschel Webb with the assistance of Marleigh Ryan. New York: Columbia University Press, 1965.
Society and Education in Japan, by Herbert Passin. New York: Bureau of Publications, Teachers College, Columbia University, 1965.
Agricultural Production and Economic Development in Japan, 1873–1922, by James I. Nakamura. Princeton: Princeton University Press, 1966.
Japan's First Modern Novel: Ukigumo of Futabatei Shimei, by Marleigh Ryan. New York: Columbia University Press, 1967.
The Korean Communist Movement, 1918–1948, by Dae-Sook Suh. Princeton: Princeton University Press, 1967.
The First Vietnam Crisis, by Melvin Gurtov. New York: Columbia University Press, 1967.
Cadres, Bureaucracy, and Political Power in Communist China, by A. Doak Barnett. New York: Columbia University Press, 1967.
The Japanese Imperial Institution in the Tokugawa Period, by Herschel Webb. New York: Columbia University Press, 1968.
Higher Education and Business Recruitment in Japan, by Koya Azumi. New York: Teachers College Press, Columbia University, 1969.
The Communists and Chinese Peasant Rebellions: A Study in the Rewriting of Chinese History, by Jamse P. Harrison, Jr. New York: Atheneum, 1969.
How the Conservatives Rule Japan, by Nathaniel B. Thayer. Princeton: Princeton University Press, 1969.
Aspects of Chinese Education, edited by C. T. Hu. New York: Teachers College Press, Columbia University, 1970.
Documents of Korean Communism, 1918–1948, by Dae-sook Suh. Princeton: Princeton University Press, 1970.

Japanese Education: A Bibliography of Materials in the English Language, by Herbert Passin. New York: Teachers College Press, Columbia University, 1970.
Economic Development and the Labor Market in Japan, by Koji Taira. New York: Columbia University Press, 1970.
The Japanese Oligarchy and the Russo-Japanese War, by Shumpei Okamoto. New York: Columbia University Press, 1970.
Imperial Restoration in Medieval Japan, by H. Paul Varley. New York: Columbia University Press, 1971.
Japan's Postwar Defense Policy, 1947–1968, by Martin E. Weinstein. New York: Columbia University Press, 1971.
Election Campaigning Japanese Style, by Gerald L. Curtis. New York: Columbia University Press, 1971.
China and Russia: The "Great Game," by O. Edmund Clubb. New York: Columbia University Press, 1971.
Money and Monetary Policy in Communist China, by Katharine Huang Hsiao. New York: Columbia University Press, 1971.
The District Magistrate in Late Imperial China, by John R. Watt. New York: Columbia University Press, 1972.
Law and Policy in China's Foreign Relations: A Study of Attitudes and Practice, by James C. Hsiung. New York: Columbia University Press, 1972.
Pearl Harbor as History: Japanese-American Relations, 1931–1941, edited by Dorothy Borg and Shumpei Okamoto, with the assistance of Dale K. A. Finlayson. New York: Columbia University Press, 1973.
Japanese Culture: A Short History, by H. Paul Varley. New York: Praeger, 1973.
Doctors in Politics: The Political Life of the Japan Medical Association, by William E. Steslicke. New York: Praeger, 1973.
The Japan Teachers Union: A Radical Interest Group in Japanese Politics, by Donald Ray Thurston. Princeton: Princeton University Press, 1973.
Japan's Foreign Policy, 1868–1941: A Research Guide, edited by James William Morley. New York: Columbia University Press, 1974.
Palace and Politics in Prewar Japan, by David Anson Titus. New York: Columbia University Press, 1974.
The Idea of China: Essays in Geographic Myth and Theory, by Andrew March. Devon, England: David and Charles, 1974.
Origins of the Cultural Revolution, by Roderick MacFarquhar, New York: Columbia University Press, 1974.
Shiba Kōkan: Artist, Innovator, and Pioneer in the Westernization of Japan, by Calvin L. French. Tokyo: Weatherhill, 1974.
Insei: Abdicated Sovereigns in the Politics of Late Heian Japan, by G. Cameron Hurst. New York: Columbia University Press, 1975.
Embassy at War, by Harold Joyce Noble. Edited with an introduction by Frank Baldwin, Jr. Seattle: University of Washington Press, 1975.
Rebels and Bureaucrats: China's December 9ers, by John Israel and Donald W. Klein. Berkeley, University of California Press, 1975.
Deterrent Diplomacy, edited by James William Morley. New York: Columbia University Press, 1976.
Neo-Confucianism and the Political Culture of Late Imperial China, by Thomas A. Metzger. New York: Columbia University Press, 1976.
House United, House Divided: The Chinese Family in Taiwan, by Myron L. Cohen. New York: Columbia University Press, 1976.